Second

LAW AND ETHICS IN EDUCATIONAL LEADERSHIP

DAVID L. STADER
Southeast Missouri State University

PEARSON

Boston   Columbus   Indianapolis   New York   San Francisco   Upper Saddle River
Amsterdam   Cape Town   Dubai   London   Madrid   Milan   Munich   Paris   Montreal   Toronto
Delhi   Mexico City   São Paulo   Sydney   Hong Kong   Seoul   Singapore   Taipei   Tokyo

Vice President and Editorial Director: Jeffery W. Johnston
Senior Acquisitions Editor: Meredith D. Fossel
Editorial Assistant: Andrea Hall
Vice President, Director of Marketing: Margaret Waples
Marketing Manager: Christopher Barry
Senior Managing Editor: Pamela D. Bennett
Project Manager: Kerry Rubadue
Production Manager: Laura Messerly
Senior Art Director: Jayne Conte
Cover Designer: Karen Noferi
Cover Art: Fotolia
Full-Service Project Management: Munesh Kumar/Aptara®, Inc.
Composition: Aptara®, Inc.
Printer/Binder: R.R. Donnelley/Harrisonburg
Cover Printer: R.R. Donnelley/Harrisonburg
Text Font: ITC Garamond Std

Credits and acknowledgments for material borrowed from other sources and reproduced, with permission, in this textbook appear on the appropriate page within the text.

Every effort has been made to provide accurate and current Internet information in this book. However, the Internet and information posted on it are constantly changing, so it is inevitable that some of the Internet addresses listed in this textbook will change.

Library of Congress Cataloging-in-Publication Data

Stader, David L.
  Law and ethics in educational leadership / David L. Stader. — 2nd ed.
    p. cm.
  ISBN-13: 978-0-13-268587-0
  ISBN-10: 0-13-268587-6
  1. Teachers—Legal status, laws, etc.—United States.   2. Teachers—Professional ethics—United States.
3. Educational law and legislation—United States.   I. Title.
  KF4175.S673 2013
  371.200973—dc23

                                          2011047687

10

ISBN 10:   0-13-268587-6
ISBN 13: 978-0-13-268587-0

PREFACE

Law and Ethics in Educational Leadership, Second Edition, takes a real-world, problem-based approach that emphasizes the knowledge, skills, and dispositions necessary for successful PK–12 leadership. The textbook presents educator candidates and instructors with a user-friendly approach to the study of legal issues, including how changes in law and society affect school leadership and how to apply ethical frameworks to future decision making. Case studies are designed to expose PK–12 leadership candidates to the ambiguity presented by many of the problems they will face as school leaders. Rather than rote memorization, this textbook encourages candidates to analyze, evaluate, and synthesize legal knowledge and ethical frameworks and present their views in a logical and coherent manner. The textbook provides instructors and candidates with an overview of several new U.S. Supreme Court decisions affecting PK–12 education, an emphasis on school safety issues, student and employee use of social media, and an overview of student-on-student victimization such as sexual harassment, bullying, cyberbullying, and dating violence. Instructors also have access to PowerPoints and a test bank that includes decision sets similar to the School Leaders Licensure Assessment (SLLA) and Interstate School Leaders Licensure Consortium (ISLLC) certification examination.

NEW TO THIS EDITION

Several new objectives provide the new framework for the second edition, including: (1) the integration of content about computers and the Internet into other more applicable chapters, (2) the clarification of legal issues surrounding religion in public schools, (3) improvement to the scope and sequence of chapters, and (4) a reorganization of the chapters to maximize the readability and coherence of the material for better candidate learning.

In addition to these objectives, updated discussions of new and emerging legal trends are included across the board. For example, discussions of the legal issues surrounding student Internet or electronic speech are expanded, clarifications of the legal issues regarding teacher use of electronic communication such as Facebook are explored, and an examination of the legal rights and school district responsibility for the education of legal and illegal aliens are incorporated into this edition. The following bulleted points summarize the major changes to the text:

- The chapter entitled *Computers and the Internet* in the first edition has been eliminated. The important legal issues surrounding computers and student and teacher Internet speech in the eliminated chapter now are integrated into the other, more appropriate chapters. For example, legal issues surrounding student off-campus speech have been added to Chapter 4, *Student Privacy and First Amendment Rights,* and the guidelines governing the search of employee computers owned by the district have been moved to Chapter 12, *Teacher Constitutional Law.* This change is designed to improve readability and improve candidate understanding of the complexity presented by electronic speech.
- Legal issues regarding school safety are consolidated into a single Chapter 7, *School Safety.* The chapter consolidates safety issues such as weapons in school,

zero tolerance, teacher-on-student victimization, student-on-student sexual harassment, and student-on-student sexual harassment based on real or perceived sexual orientation. This change was in response to several reviewer suggestions to improve logic and readability and promote student understanding.
- New material on school safety issues such as bullying, cyberbullying, date violence, and legal issues surrounding surveillance cameras was also added to Chapter 7, *School Safety*.
- The discussion of student off-campus speech including Internet speech has been increased to reflect new challenges and court decisions.
- The vast majority of the introductory case studies that provide the framework for discussion and most of the *Connecting Standards to Practice* case studies are new to this edition. These new case studies and performance assessments reflect the evolving challenges school leaders face, such as student cell phones, student off-campus speech, and employee speech related to their job descriptions.
- A section on teacher use and misuse of social networking sites has been added to Chapter 12, *Teacher Constitutional Law*. This material is new to this edition.
- A section on the legal rights of legal and illegal alien school children was added to Chapter 8, now entitled *Equal Protection, English Language Learners, and Desegregation*. English language learners make up the fastest-growing population in many states, including Texas, California, and Arizona. In fact, many schools and districts have become "majority minority" since the publication of the first edition. Understanding the rights of these children and the legal responsibilities of school districts will remain important for the foreseeable future.
- This second edition contains new research including several recent U.S. Supreme Court, circuit court, and district court cases germane to educational law that have been decided since the publication of the first edition.
- Chapter 1 is more appropriately entitled *Introduction: Law, Ethics, and Educational Leadership*. The change in name reflects the substantial content changes made to this chapter. The conceptual framework changed from the ELCC (2002) standards to the 2009 Interstate Leadership Licensure Consortium (ISLLC) standards, new to this edition. This change is made for several reasons including the following: (1) the 2009 ISLLC standards reflect new research on the role of campus and district leaders in the improvement of outcomes for all students, (2) the ISLLC standards are designed to guide schools of education and departments of educational leadership specifically to determine what educational leaders need to know, and (3) the ISLLC standards are designed to help colleges of education effectively convey this knowledge to future leaders.

ACKNOWLEDGMENTS

I acknowledge the contributions of many friends and colleagues. I especially thank my friend and colleague Tom Graca for writing the chapter on tort liability and risk management. I also thank the reviewers of this second edition, including Sidney L. Brown, Alabama State University; Steven M. Brown, Northeastern Illinois University; and Earnest Walker, Carson-Newman College. Last, but certainly not least, I thank my wife, Cathy, for her encouragement and patience.

BRIEF CONTENTS

CONTENTS

CHAPTER 1

Introduction
Law, Ethics, and Educational Leadership

INTRODUCTION

The study of school law is a well-accepted practice in school leader preparation programs. However, future school leaders need more than knowledge of law. They need a conceptual framework to aid in the analysis, synthesis, and evaluation of this knowledge and to apply these skills to various ill-defined situations. Ethical frameworks have also been shown to be essential in the development of competent school leaders. In addition, standards are essential tools in the preparation of these leaders. This chapter introduces school leadership candidates to the importance of ethical frameworks and the Interstate School Leadership Licensure Consortium (ISLLC) standards (Council of Chief State School Officers [CCSSO], 2008). It introduces future campus and district leaders to the link between the ISLLC standards, the concept of ethical frameworks, and the importance of knowledge of law.

FOCUS QUESTIONS

1. What are the ISLLC standards for school leaders?
2. How may the ISLLC standards be used to guide educational leadership preparation?
3. What is ethics, and why are ethical frameworks important to school leadership?
4. How are legal and ethical decision making interwoven?

KEY TERMS

Ethics	ISLLC standards
Ill-structured problems	Useful strategic knowledge

CASE STUDY

Tough Times Continue at Riverboat School District

After 5 years as principal of Riverboat High School, Sharon Grey settled into her new role as Assistant Superintendent for Curriculum and Instruction for Riverboat School District (RSD). RSD was set adjacent to the southern boundaries of Capital City, a city of approximately 75,000 individuals. Capital City hosted the state capitol and was home to several businesses and industries, as well as a small land-grant university. The city also provided employment for most of the families of current RSD students. Over the past 5 years, total district enrollment had increased from approximately 4,000 students in grades PK–12 to almost 5,000 students. As a result of the enrollment increases, the district had added a new middle school and two elementary schools. The additional facilities had resulted in a total of one 9–12 high school, two 6–8 middle schools, and five PK–5 elementary schools. District enrollment data indicated that approximately 60% of the students were White, 20% were African American, and 20% were Latino. Latino families and students were by far the fastest growing population in the district.

Data collected by the Bureau of Economic Development indicated that the northern part of the district would continue to grow for at least the next 5 to 10 years. Most current residents were well educated and employed by state government, by one of several companies in the area, or in one of many personal service occupations. Consequently, the current unemployment rate for Riverboat School District was around 5.2%. Cohort projection data, gathered from the elementary and middle schools, indicated a steady increase in students. In 5 years RSD would grow from the current 5,000 students to approximately 6,000 students. These data, combined with projections from the Bureau of Economic Development, indicated that at the end of the 5-year projection period, more than 60% of RSD enrollment would be African American, Latino, or Asian/Pacific Islander. Free and reduced-price lunches would be needed for approximately 40% of the student population during this period, in contrast to the current figure of 20%.

In addition to the new facilities and changing demographics, the district had seen an almost complete change in campus leadership. Sharon had noted that for many of the principals and assistant principals, this was their first administrative experience in their particular roles. Therefore, a significant part of Sharon's responsibilities was to serve as mentor, confidant, and advisor to district principals, assistant principals, and athletic directors. Because of several recent lawsuits, the superintendent had made it clear to her new campus school leaders that they should seek Sharon's counsel when faced with difficult decisions. It did not take long for this part of Sharon's job description to be put to use.

Flyers at Pocono

During the first week of the new school year, Pocono Elementary School principal Lana Aldridge called Sharon, "Hi, Sharon, sorry to bother you the first week of school, but I have a potential problem I would like to discuss." Lana went on to explain that

Pocono Elementary School traditionally allowed community groups such as the YMCA, Boy Scouts, Girl Scouts, and sports leagues to distribute informational and advertisement flyers at school. Occasionally, these flyers were brought to school by students. All was well at Pocono until fifth-grader Allison brought a colorful flyer inviting fellow fourth- and fifth-grade students to a "back-to-school" party at her church. The party featured "snacks, Ping-Pong, foosball, and Christian fellowship." Allison had been given the flyers by the youth minister of the church. Apparently, Allison's plan was to give a stack of the flyers to a representative of each of the fourth- and fifth-grade classes and for the students to hand out the flyers to their classmates during the school day. Lana followed this explanation by stating, "I think if we allow Allison and her friends to distribute the flyer here at school, it will appear as if Pocono Elementary is endorsing the party. We should not allow the distribution of the flyer, right?"

LEADERSHIP PERSPECTIVE

Future school leaders will be required to understand, address, and solve problems they will encounter (Copland, 2000). The types of problems future leaders will face can be viewed in a variety of ways. Most useful to this textbook is the classification of problems into routine, structured problems and nonroutine, ill-structured problems (Leithwood & Steinbach, 1995). Structured problems present familiar issues that experienced leaders have solved before. In contrast, ill-structured problems are more complex. Such problems are often characterized by a lack of clarity, present a number of potential obstacles, and are "messy" in that the values and potential conflicts embedded in the problem are not readily apparent. Also, a number of options for solutions are available for consideration (Leithwood & Steinbach, 1995).

One of the real-life challenges of problem solving is the social context inherent in many ill-structured problems (Leithwood & Steinbach, 1995). A significant part of the social context of problem solving is that the way problems are presented to school leaders frequently reflects a preconceived solution generated from the frame of reference of the problem presenter (Copland, 2000). The framing of the problem by the presenter may be absolutely correct. However, rejecting or embracing the preconceived solution before the problem has been clearly defined may be a fatal mistake. Excellent campus and district leaders have the ability to recognize the inherent challenges of ill-structured problems and reframe the problem, at least temporarily, in solution-free terms. "Flyers at Pocono" may serve as an example. Lana Aldridge has presented Sharon with a predefined solution: to not allow Allison to distribute the flyers at school. If Sharon Grey embraces this solution, the decision may result in charges that the school district is against religion. If, however, Lana Aldridge allows Allison to distribute the flyer, it is possible that at least some elementary students and parents will believe that the church event is endorsed or at least supported by the school. Either way, controversy may follow. In short, ill-structured problems present school leaders with *dilemmas*, with no easy or clear-cut solutions.

THE ISLLC CONCEPTUAL FRAMEWORK

A conceptual framework provides a foundation for thinking about the dilemmas presented by ill-structured problems. This conceptual framework has been provided by six standards for school leadership developed by the ISLLC (CCSSO, 2008). The 2008 ISLLC standards build on the 1996 standards (ISLLC, 1996) and reflect new information, research, and lessons learned since the original ISLLC standards were published. The 2-year process of updating the ISLLC standards to reflect this new research and knowledge was led by the National Policy Board for Educational Administration (NPBEA) Interstate School Leaders Licensure Consortium Steering Committee. The steering committee worked with several member organizations, practitioner-based organizations, researchers, and higher education officials in the revision process. Once the draft revisions were developed, the NPBEA/ISLLC Steering Committee distributed copies and gathered feedback from member organizations, researchers, and other groups. Based on their research and feedback from various organizations and individuals, the final 2008 ISLLC standards were published by the CCSSO. These six *ISLLC standards*, and the comprehensive descriptors that accompany them, are designed to provide "high-level guidance and insight about the traits, functions of work, and responsibilities expected of school and district leaders" (CCSSO, 2008, p. 5). Standards have been shown to be essential tools in developing pre-service programs for principals. The 2008 ISLLC standards in particular provide guidance and insight into the heart of educational leadership preparation by beginning to answer the following questions:

- How do schools of education determine what education leaders need to know to ensure that every child meets academic achievement standards?
- How can schools of education effectively convey that knowledge in a coherent fashion (CCSSO, 2008, p. 5)?

These six revised standards are:

Standard 1: An education leader promotes the success of every student by facilitating the development, articulation, implementation, and stewardship of a vision of learning that is shared and supported by all stakeholders.

Standard 2: An education leader promotes the success of every student by advocating, nurturing, and sustaining a school culture and instructional program conducive to student learning and staff professional growth.

Standard 3: An education leader promotes the success of every student by ensuring management of the organization, operations, and resources for a safe, efficient, and effective learning environment.

Standard 4: An education leader promotes the success of every student by collaborating with faculty and community members, responding to diverse community interests and needs, and mobilizing community resources.

Standard 5: An education leader promotes the success of every student by acting with integrity, fairness, and in an ethical manner.

Standard 6: An education leader promotes the success of every student by understanding, responding to, and influencing the political, social, economic, legal, and cultural context.

[*Note.* The ISLLC standards were developed by the CCSSO and member states. Copies may be downloaded from the Council's website at www.ccsso.org.]

For example, the case study "Flyers at Pocono" requires Sharon and Lana to expand their toolbox of knowledge and skills to include an understanding of the legal consequences of decision making, model self-awareness and ethical behavior, and build and sustain positive relationships with community partners. As this case study and the ISLLC standards illustrate, school leadership candidates and practicing leaders need knowledge of the law. But knowledge of law is not enough. Future leaders need ethical frameworks to guide how they use this knowledge. In other words, both knowledge and applicability (when, how, and why) are important. As Leithwood and Steinbach (1992) point out, in the absence of knowledge, one has nothing to think about. In the absence of reasonably well-developed thinking skills, one may or may not apply any acquired knowledge in appropriate circumstances. Leithwood and Steinbach (1992) use the phrase *useful strategic knowledge* to more comprehensively portray the idea of combining knowledge acquisition with general thinking skills. Useful strategic knowledge can be viewed as the ability to analyze, synthesize, and evaluate knowledge in a coherent and useful manner.

ISLLC Standard 5D

ISLLC Standard 5B

ISLLC Standard 4D

RELATING LAW AND ETHICS TO EDUCATIONAL LEADERSHIP

The study of law in educational leadership preparation curricula is for the most part well-accepted practice. Make no mistake: Public schools operate under a comprehensive and sometimes confusing set of local, state, and federal laws and policies, and certain legal requirements do exist. There is no excuse for not understanding or choosing to ignore certain laws or policies because of personal biases, because of personal beliefs, or for expediency. Laws, regulations, and policies are in place for a reason, and the general public and boards of education in particular take a dim view of school leaders who make decisions outside established law or written school board policy.

School leaders are expected to make rational decisions in an irrational environment and defend these decisions based on established legal and ethical principles. Of the countless decisions made each year by thousands of school administrators nationwide, only a few make headlines, and even fewer are confronted with a legal challenge. An impartial judge and jury do not magically appear to adjudicate disputes among teachers, students, and school authorities. In addition, federal and state judges are hesitant to second-guess the decisions of school administrators or boards of education, and legal challenges to administrative decisions are often difficult. For all practical purposes, therefore, school administrators are "the law" and generally serve as chief investigator, prosecutor, judge, jury, and executioner (Sperry, 1999). These circumstances often create an environment where protecting the fundamental rights of teachers, parents, and students often falls to the very persons with the most power to violate these rights.

There is no question that legal principles do provide guidance. Contrary to conventional wisdom, however, the vast majority of decisions school leaders face cannot be addressed with an exact or fixed legal response (Sperry, 1999). Consequently, as Rebore (2001) implies, the addition of ethical principles to knowledge of law provides a deeper understanding of the implications of decision making on the lives of the affected individuals.

Defining Ethical Leadership

The view that an understanding of ethics is crucial to the proper stewardship of the nation's schools has emerged as a widely accepted part of the knowledge base necessary for effective school leadership (Cranston, Ehrich, & Kimber, 2003; Fullan, 2003; Furman, 2003; Greenfield, 2004; Sergiovanni, 1992). The ISLLC standards embrace both an understanding of law and the value of ethics in the preparation of educational leaders. Specifically, **ISLLC Standard 5.0** calls for school leaders who "promote the success of every student by acting with integrity, fairness, and in *an ethical manner*" [italics added] (CCSSO, 2008). Ethical leadership is choosing to do the right thing based on sound reasoning, rather than simply reacting with little foresight to every challenge. First and foremost, ethical decision making requires considerations of how people should be treated and always involves the terms *right, fair,* or *just* (Strike, Haller, & Soltis, 1998). Perceptions of *right, fair,* and *just,* however, are much like perceptions of beauty—always in the eye of the beholder. Thus, ethical leadership requires consideration of why some action should, or should not, be taken (Rebore, 2001). In short, an ethical decision always involves choosing among alternatives, and choosing among alternatives is essentially concerned with two different questions: (1) What is right, or what is wrong? (2) What is good, or what is bad? Inherent in considering these questions is the understanding that some types of actions are right and others wrong. Rebore (2001) emphasizes that any decision carries a personal consequence for the decision maker. *He or she personally changes with every decision.* In other words, school leaders are defined by the decisions they make, not by their position of authority, the academic degrees they hold, or their personality.

As Normore (2004) points out, however, developing morally competent leaders requires more than the inclusion of ethical behavior into a set of standards. Indeed, incorporating ethics into educational leadership preparation curriculum and instruction is required. However, this incorporation may be easier to prescribe than to accomplish (Begley, 2001). Part of the problem is that the meaning of the term *ethics* is somewhat ambiguous (Begley, 2006; Cranston et al., 2003). In some instances ethics is defined in terms of what is right and wrong. For example, Colgan (2004) uses the term *ethics* (or lack thereof) in the context of fraud, malfeasance, and corruption involving school district officials. The term *ethics* is also commonly used to describe a code of conduct. For example, the American Educational Research Association publishes a code of ethics for educational researchers (American Educational Research Association, 2011). In other contexts, the terms *ethics, values,* and *morality* are used interchangeably (Begley, 2006). For example, Sergiovanni (1992), Fullan (2003), and Greenfield (2004) use the term *moral leadership* in the context of leadership fairness and integrity, and Rebore (2001) uses the term *ethics* in a similar context. However, there is a difference among these connotations. Ethics is the study of conduct and considers how individuals ought to act (Johnson, 1999). As Paul Begley (2006) states,

> The study of ethics should be as much about the life-long personal struggle to be ethical, about failures to be ethical, the inconsistencies of ethical postures,

the masquerading of self-interest and personal preference as ethical action, and the dilemmas which occur in everyday and professional life when one ethic trumps another. (p. 571)

Ronald Rebore (2001) defines ethics as follows: "What does it mean to be a human being, how should human beings treat one another, and how should the institutions of society be organized?" (p. 5). This book will follow Rebore's premise, defining *ethics* by considering the following questions:

- What does it mean to be a school leader?
- How should the human beings in schools treat one another?
- How should the educational institutions that we call "school" be organized?

Ethical Frameworks

Future school leaders need more than just a definition of ethics. As Begley (2006) contends, future leaders require frameworks and ways of thinking about problems that encompass the full range of leadership requirements. However, these ethical frameworks should be viewed as an initial organizer and as a way of thinking about a problem, not as a recipe or prescription. School leadership situations are much too complex for that. Rather than a model or procedural guides, this textbook includes several ethical frameworks designed to encourage reflection on the consequences decisions have for others as well as for the school leader personally.

It should be noted that not all problems facing school leaders present ethical dilemmas. Structured problems rarely do so. *Ill-structured problems*, on the other hand, are much more complicated and often involve choosing between alternatives that at least some members of the school community are not going to like. At the same time, future school leaders should be aware that the application of ISLLC standards and an ethical framework may be inappropriate in some situations. For example, **ISLLC Standard 2A** calls for school leaders to nurture and sustain a culture of collaboration. One well-accepted way to meet this standard is participatory decision making and seeking consensus from faculty. As Begley (2006) suggests, however, faculty consensus may reflect what is best for the faculty but may not necessarily serve the best interest of students. In these cases, a school leader could point to consensus and the use of an ethical framework to justify what may on the surface look like a rational and defensible decision. In addition, Begley (2006) reminds us that some ethical postures may be unethical when:

- A cultural ethic is imposed on others;
- An ethic is used to justify otherwise reprehensible action;
- An ethical posture veils a less defensible value; and
- An ethic is used to trump a basic human right (p. 581).

LAW, ETHICS, AND DECISION MAKING

The ISLLC standards require that school leaders use legal and ethical considerations in the decisions they make. This combination is embedded throughout the standards but is particularly addressed in **ISLLC Standard 5**. But how can school leaders accomplish this—for example, how can Sharon Grey in the opening case study, "Flyers at

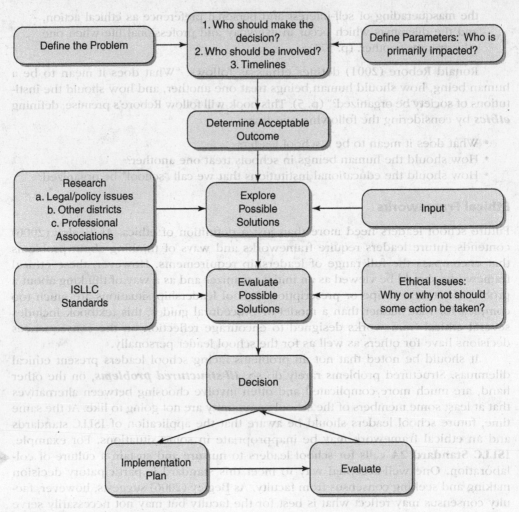

FIGURE 1-1 Decision-making model.

Pocono," apply knowledge of law and ethical frameworks to help Lana Aldridge consider why some action should or should not be taken?

Combining Ethical and Legal Principles with Decision Making

Figure 1-1 presents a decision-making model that considers the balance of ethical and legal principles as reflected in ISLLC Standard 5.

Stage One would include the following steps:

1. *Defining the problem:* It can be argued that the most important step is clearly defining the problem. Without a clear understanding of the problem, it is very difficult to develop a reasonable solution. In this illustration, the problem can be

expressed as: "Students would like to distribute flyers inviting fellow fourth- and fifth-graders to a church-sponsored event."

2. ***Defining the parameters:*** At this point, only students at Pocono Elementary and their parents are involved. However, the problem could be more widespread and could significantly affect the culture of the school and community perceptions of the school.

3. ***Primary decision maker:*** This is a leadership concern, and Sharon should be involved. However, she would most certainly wish to involve other groups, including teachers, students, parents, and possibly the superintendent or other central office personnel, in the decision-making process.

4. ***Acceptable outcome:*** The only acceptable outcome as defined by **ISLLC Stand-** **◀ ISLLC Standard 5** **ard 5** is a solution that is legally and ethically defensible.

Stage Two would include researching the problem, obtaining input from various groups and individuals, and exploring possible solutions. These steps can be further defined as follows:

1. ***Research:*** In this case Sharon needs to determine several facts, including legal guidelines for the distribution of religious materials at a public elementary school, and to develop her understanding of past policy and practice at Pocono and other elementary schools in the district. Sharon also needs to know district policy regarding the distribution of community nonprofit flyers and how these policies are applied to students at RSD.

2. ***Input:*** Armed with this information, Sharon may wish to present the problem to various groups, including teachers, counselors, students, and parents, and solicit possible solutions to the problem.

3. ***Evaluation of possible solutions:*** This step symbolizes the legal and ethical dilemmas that consider the terms *right, fair,* and *just*. However, what is "right" to some students and their parents (the opportunity to participate in a church-sponsored event) is not "fair" to another group of students and their parents (those who believe that public schools should remain neutral regarding religion). It is possible that the practice of distributing community information has become entrenched in the culture of the school district. If this is the case, courage will be required to make a meaningful change in practice.

Stage Three includes making, implementing, and evaluating the decision.

1. ***Decision:*** As in most cases like this one, several options will be open to Sharon. Choosing the best course—that is, what is best for all—may be contrary to established traditions at Pocono. However, effective leaders understand their obligations and accept the consequences of their decisions.

2. ***Implementation plan:*** Implementing the decision involves effectively communicating the problem and how it is contrary to social justice, and communicating and implementing policy and practice to address the problem.

3. ***Evaluation:*** The evaluation of any decision relates directly to Step 4 in Stage One and considers whether the decision results in the predetermined acceptable outcome. If so, it is a valid and good decision. If not, Sharon would need to backtrack to Stage Two.

Linking to PRACTICE

Do:
- Understand that management skills and legal knowledge are necessary for successful school leadership.
- Understand that effective school leaders move beyond management and legal knowledge by integrating ethical considerations into their approach to solving problems, challenges, and conflict.

Do Not:
- Ignore law or policy because of personal biases or expediency.
- Disregard or underestimate the naturally occurring imbalance of power among administrators, teachers, students, and parents inherent in school leadership.

Summary

The landscape in which school leaders serve is rapidly changing and requires a different kind of school leader than was needed in the past. The recently adopted ISLLC standards provide a conceptual framework for visualizing and understanding this new paradigm of leadership. These standards also provide guidance in the preparation and evaluation of future school leaders. Embedded throughout these standards are several themes or strands. One embedded theme includes legal and ethical standards for leadership, a focus of this text.

School leaders are expected to make rational decisions in an open system that is constantly buffeted by internal and external demands for school improvement and school safety while maintaining a caring and humane environment. The constant demands and the conflict surrounding these demands challenge even the most experienced school leaders to make reasoned decisions. Legal principles do provide guidance in decision making. However, an understanding of the types of legal principles and the ethical application of these principles is necessary for effective leadership.

CONNECTING STANDARDS TO PRACTICE

DISCRIMINATION OR BACKGROUND KNOWLEDGE, PART I

During Sharon Grey's first weeks as assistant superintendent, she was approached by a delegation of minority parents representing two of the three middle schools in the district. The parents politely explained that their children in Pocono and Jefferson Middle Schools were routinely denied access to Pre-Advanced Placement courses in both schools. After the parents left, Sharon reviewed the demographics of Pocono and Jefferson. She than reviewed the previous year's enrollment in eighth-grade Pre-AP courses for both middle schools. Previous-year Pocono

Middle School eighth-grade demographics consisted of 35% African American, 12% Hispanic, 5% Asian, and 48% White students. Eighth-grade Pre-AP course demographics consisted of 72% White, 5% Asian, 6% African American, and 6% Hispanic students. Jefferson Middle School demographics consisted of 20% African American, 40% Hispanic, and 40% White students. Eighth-grade Pre-AP course demographics consisted of 75% White, 10% African American, and 15% Hispanic students. Sharon called each of the middle school principals to inquire about the underrepresentation of students of color in eighth-grade Pre-AP courses. She was informed that Pre-AP teachers contended that many students of color did not have the study skills or background knowledge necessary for success in these courses.

Question

1. Does this case study represent a structured or ill-structured problem? What characteristics of the case study support your conclusion?

2. Does this case study present Sharon Grey with an ethical dilemma? Are there potential legal issues hidden in this case study?

3. What ISLLC standards are applicable to this case study?

4. Using the decision-making model presented in this chapter, develop a step-by-step approach to address this case study.

CHAPTER **2**

The Law of Education

INTRODUCTION

This chapter describes the various agencies and types of law that affect education. It also discusses the organization and functions of the various judicial bodies that have an impact on education. School leadership candidates are introduced to standards of review, significant federal civil rights laws, the contents of legal decisions, and a sample legal brief.

FOCUS QUESTIONS

1. How are federal courts organized, and what kind of decisions do they make?
2. What is law? How is law different from policy?
3. From what source does the authority of local boards of education emanate?
4. How can campus and district leaders remain current with changes in law and policy at the national and state level?

KEY TERMS

Common (case) law	Legal brief	*Stare decisis*
Constitutional law	Plaintiff	State boards of education
Defendant	Qualified immunity	Statutory law
En banc	Regulations	Strict scrutiny
Federalism	Standing	Writ of certiorari (writ)

CASE STUDY

Confused Yet?

As far as Elise Daniels was concerned, the monthly meeting of the 20 River County middle school principals was the most informative and relaxing activity in her school year. Twice per year, the principals invited a guest to speak to the group. Elise was particularly interested in the fall special guest speaker, the attorney for the state school boards association. Elise had heard him speak several times, so she was aware of his deep knowledge of school law and emerging issues. As the attorney, spoke Elise found herself becoming more anxious. It was as if the attorney was speaking a foreign language. *Tinker* rules, due process, Title IX, Office of Civil Rights, and the state bullying law. Elise found herself thinking, "The Americans with Disabilities Act has been amended? How am I supposed to keep up with all of this?"

LEADERSHIP PERSPECTIVES

Middle School Principal Elise Daniels in the case study "Confused Yet?" is correct. School law can be confusing. Educators work in a highly regulated environment directly and indirectly impacted by a wide variety of local, state, and federal authorities. When P–12 educators refer to "the law," they are often referring to state and/or federal statutes enacted by legislatures (Fowler, 2009). This understanding is correct. The U.S. Congress and 50 state legislatures are active in the law-making business. To make matters more difficult, the law is constantly changing and evolving as new situations arise. For example, 10 years ago few if any states had passed antibullying laws. By 2008, however, almost every state had some form of antibullying legislation on the books. Soon after, the phenomenon of cyberbullying emerged, and state legislators rushed to add cyberbullying and/or electronic bullying to their state education laws. One can only guess at what new real or perceived problem affecting public P–12 schools will be next.

P–12 educators also refer to school board policy as "law." However, law and policy are not necessarily identical. Fowler (2009, p. 4) defines policy as "one way through which a political system handles a public problem. It includes a government's expressed intentions and official enactments." For example, a school board policy regarding teacher attendance is not a law, but rather a school board's attempt to address a public problem. Thus, school boards are *policy actors*, defined as individuals or groups of individuals who directly or indirectly influence public policy.

School boards are not the only education policy actors. Policy actors also include (1) federal and state legislative bodies, federal and state judges, federal and state departments of education, state governors, chief state school officers, local school boards, superintendents, and campus administrators; (2) federal agencies such as the Office for Civil Rights and the Equal Employment Opportunity Commission; (3) professional associations such as the National School Boards Association, the National Association of Secondary School Principals, and the American Association of School Administrators; and (4) various lobbying and other advocacy groups such as the American Civil Liberties Union. These professional association and advocacy groups try to influence policy in various ways, including the filing of *amicus curiae* (friend of the court) briefs presenting their view of how a court should rule in certain cases. There is little wonder that Elise Daniels feels somewhat overwhelmed by the number of policy actors that affect public education and the constant challenges presented by new and sometimes unfamiliar laws. This chapter presents a brief overview of the types of law that affect education, introduces the primary federal constitutional and statutory laws presented in this text, and outlines the importance of understanding state law and school board policy.

EDUCATION AND THE LEGAL ARENA

An understanding of education and the legal arena starts with a discussion of the United States federalist political system. Frances Fowler (2009) finds that the best way to define a federalist system is to contrast it with unitary government, the other common form of democracy. In a unitary system, only one government in the country has the power to pass laws, raise taxes, and so forth. Local government exists, but can be overruled by the national government. France, Japan, and the United Kingdom are examples of unitary government. In contrast, the United States is a federalist system. A federalist system consists of several sovereign (autonomous) governments sharing powers. In the United States system there are 51 governments: 1 national government and 50 state governments. The federal government cannot abolish state governments, and state governments cannot abolish the federal government. It is generally acknowledged that a federalist system is more difficult than a unitary system of government. However, the design seems to fit well with the Founding Fathers' fear of dominant central government and with the strong regional ties of the original 13 colonies.

Within the backdrop of *federalism*, the Founding Fathers' concern about overly powerful central government led to the idea of separation of powers rather than to a fused or unified government at the national level. Thus, the Founding Fathers constitutionally delegated certain powers to each of the three branches of government (executive, legislative, and judicial) that serve as a balance or check on the powers of the other branches. This seemed like such a good idea that the concept of separation of powers is built into every state constitution (Fowler, 2009). Separation of powers is designed to create conflict as the separate branches of government vie for power. However, the conflict between the legislative and judicial branches can be particularly intense. For example, courts, especially the U.S. Supreme Court and the various state supreme courts, can declare a law or governmental action to be unconstitutional. Thus, a state school finance formula developed by the state legislature, signed into law by the governor, and applied by the state department of education can be declared unconstitutional by the state supreme court. This action by a small group of individuals, often with lifetime appointments, can create considerable heartache as the legislative and executive branches attempt to develop a sound school finance formula within the larger political arena of taxes and allocation of public monies.

Education Law in a Federalist Political System

The contemporary philosopher Jurgen Habermas (2001) presents the following definition of modern law:

> Modern law is formed by a system of norms that are coercive, positive, and . . . freedom guaranteeing. The formal properties of coercion and positivity are associated with the claim to legitimacy: the fact that norms backed by the threat of state sanction stem from the changeable decisions of a political lawgiver is linked with the expectation that these norms guarantee the autonomy of all legal persons equally. (p. 447)

Thus, modern law is designed to bring order to chaos by forming a system of forced norms or policies that regulate much of the behavior and actions of citizens. These policies are viewed, at least by Habermas, to be positive in that they enable campus and district leaders to regulate teacher and student behavior in a way that promotes learning while at the same time they promote equity, fairness, and safety. For example, school structures allow for the placement of students in classrooms, teacher handbooks require that teachers supervise students assigned to their classrooms, and school rules outline unacceptable student behaviors that interfere with learning. Boards of education are required to provide a free and appropriate public education for all children regardless of economic status or handicapping condition; administrators are charged with maintaining good order and discipline in schools; and parents may choose to educate their children at home. As Elise Daniels in the opening case study "Confused Yet?" is beginning to understand, a significant amount of ambiguity exists in all phases of modern law (Sperry, 1999). Educators function daily in this ambiguous legal arena, which simultaneously forces compliance by, empowers, and limits the actions, behaviors, and choices of students, teachers, and administrators. **ISLLC Standard 5** calls for candidates to promote the success of every student by acting with integrity, fairness, and in an ethical manner. For example, local school boards are empowered to dismiss incompetent teachers and to suspend or expel unruly students. At the same time, teachers and students possess certain rights that limit the power of school boards to dismiss or suspend them. It is the naturally existing tension between the rights of school boards to regulate teacher and student conduct and the legal protection provided to teachers and students that creates the basis for much of the legal conflict in public education. These rights, obligations, and limits weave a multihued tapestry whose design is clear in some places and not in others.

ISLLC Standard 6 calls for candidates to have knowledge of policies, laws, and regulations enacted by state, local, and federal authorities that affect schools. For all practical purposes, five forms of federal and state law and policy are the threads from which the tapestry of policies, laws, and regulations enacted by these authorities is woven. These five forms of law include:

- Federal and state constitutional law
- Federal and state statutory law
- Federal and state regulations
- Federal and state common (case) law
- State and local school board policy

Federal and State Constitutional Law

The Constitution of the United States, and more specifically the Bill of Rights, was designed primarily to protect citizens from excesses of government and provides the framework for all legal actions. The U.S. Constitution empowers the executive and legislative branches of government to make and enforce certain types of laws and policies and the court system (judicial branch) to interpret and apply these laws and policies to various situations. These interpretations of law by various courts create legally binding opinions or precedents within a particular court's span of authority (Hilyerd, 2004). All laws passed by federal and state bodies, all state constitutions, all regulations, and all school board policies are subject to the provisions of the U.S. Constitution. There are 24 amendments to the U.S. Constitution (see the Appendix). The amendments most applicable to educational law and featured throughout this text are the First Amendment, the Fourth Amendment, the Fifth Amendment, and the Fourteenth Amendment.

> *First Amendment:* Ratified with the Bill of Rights in 1791; guarantees the freedoms of religion, speech, press, association, assembly, and petition. The First Amendment is considered so important to our democracy that surprisingly few restrictions apply.
>
> *Fourth Amendment:* Ratified with the Bill of Rights in 1791; prohibits unreasonable searches and seizures and the issuance of warrants without probable cause.
>
> *Fifth Amendment:* Ratified with the Bill of Rights in 1791; provides (among other things) that a person may not be deprived of life, liberty, or property without due process of law.
>
> *Fourteenth Amendment:* Ratified in 1868; extends citizenship status to all persons born or naturalized in the United States and effectively applies the Bill of Rights to the states by prohibiting states from denying due process and equal protection and from abridging the privileges of U.S. citizenship. This amendment also gave Congress the power to enforce these provisions, leading to legislation such as the Civil Rights Act (Garner, 2006).

Statutory Law

Statutory law is conceived, debated, and enacted by the U.S. Congress or by state legislative bodies, subject only to the limitations established by state or federal constitutions. More than any other form of law, statutory law represents the nexus between politics and public education. Federal statutes must be consistent with the U.S. Constitution, and state law must be consistent with the state constitution, federal statutory law, and the U.S. Constitution.

FEDERAL LAW   The federal government has no authority to interfere with the educational systems within the individual states (Hilyerd, 2004). Consequently, federal statutes are often *spending clause* laws. These laws are enforced by the threat of the withholding of federal funds unless statutory requirements are met. The Missouri Supreme Court recently reviewed a spending clause provision that protects teachers from liability under certain circumstances (*Dydell v. Taylor*, 2011). The court concluded that spending clause legislation is "all carrot and no stick." All a state must do that objects to provisions of the federal government is pass a law saying no to federal money. Naturally, this may be easier said than done. Saying no would mean loss of federal money for, among other things, special education, Title I, Title II, Title IV, and free and reduced lunch reimbursement.

The most significant federal laws impacting education are the civil rights laws, Title IX, No Child Left Behind (NCLB), and various equal employment opportunity laws such as the Americans with Disabilities Act (ADA). Equal employment opportunity laws are discussed in detail later in the text.

The Civil Rights Act is a series of federal statutes enacted after the Civil War and, much later, during and after the civil rights movement of the 1960s. These statutes were implemented to give further force to the concept of personal liberty and equal protection. The Act is particularly germane to the prohibition of discrimination in educational opportunities for students based on race, sex, religion, or color (Garner, 2006). All Civil Rights Acts are enforced by the *Office for Civil Rights* (OCR). A brief overview includes the following:

Civil Rights Acts of 1866 and 1870 (42 U.S.C. § 1981): Provides the "full and equal benefit of all laws . . . for the security of persons and property as is enjoyed by white citizens."

Civil Rights Act of 1871 (42 U.S.C. § 1983): Sometimes called *§ 1983* in judicial decisions, this act allows citizens (including students) to bring suit against state actors (school boards, school leaders, and teachers) who deprive them of any rights under law.

Civil Rights Act of 1964, Title VI: Prohibits exclusion or discrimination under federally funded or assisted programs because of race, color, or natural origin.

Civil Rights Act of 1964, Title VII: Prohibits discrimination in employment due to race, color, religion, sex, or natural origin. Title VII may well be the most significant antidiscrimination legislation ever passed by the U.S. Congress.

Civil Rights Act of 1991 (P. L. 102-166): Designed to strengthen and improve federal civil rights laws prohibiting discrimination because of race, color, or natural origin. This act provides for damages in cases of deliberate violation of civil right laws. This act also establishes the concept of disparate impact and student discipline, tracking by race, color, or natural origin, and other disparate treatment based on race, color, or natural origin.

Other federal laws affecting education include the following:

Title IX. Part of the Education Amendments of 1972, this act was designed to protect students from being denied the benefits of any educational program or activity because of sex. Title IX applies to admissions, athletic programs, course offerings, student-on-student or employee harassment based on sex, physical education, educational programs and activities, and employment. OCR is also responsible for the enforcement of Title IX.

Equal Educational Opportunities Act (EEOA, 1974). This act was designed to require school districts to establish language programs and eliminate language barriers in schools.

No Child Left Behind (NCLB) of 2001: The reauthorization of the Elementary and Secondary Education Act, the central federal law in P-12 education. NCLB contains a number of controversial measures intended to improve student achievement and hold states and schools accountable for these improvements. The act is in the process of reauthorization by Congress.

STATE LAWS The U.S. Constitution does not mention education. The Tenth Amendment ("The powers not delegated to the United States by the Constitution, nor prohibited by it to the States, are reserved to the States respectively") delegates to the individual states the power to establish and regulate public educational systems.

Consequently, public education systems are established by individual state constitutions. State constitutions require their respective state legislative bodies to establish systems of public education. For example, Article XI Section 1(a) of the Missouri constitution reads, "A general diffusion of knowledge and intelligence being essential to the preservation of the rights and liberties of the people, the *general assembly shall establish and maintain free public schools* [italics added] for the gratuitous instruction of all persons in this state within ages not in excess of twenty-one years as prescribed by law."

Other state constitutions have similar provisions requiring the establishment of a public education system within the state. Although some variety does exist, the public education systems for the 50 states and the District of Columbia are remarkably similar. Consequently, some commonalities in state educational law and policy are apparent. For example, state education codes (1) create local school districts and boards of education, (2) define how school districts may consolidate and/or reorganize, (3) define who may and who must attend school, (4) provide guidance for student discipline, (5) designate qualification for public school employees including teachers, principals, and superintendents, (6) outline guidance for the termination of employees, (7) define the number of days and hours students must be in attendance, and (8) set graduation requirements.

State Actors

The key state actors of the PK–12 public education governance system are state governors, legislators, state boards of education (SBEs), chief state school officers (CSSOs), state education agencies (SEAs), and local boards of education (Education Commission of the States, 2005). *State boards of education* are policy-making bodies that function immediately below the state legislature. According to the Education Commission of the States (2005), most state boards share six common legal powers: (1) establishing certification standards for teachers and administrators, (2) establishing high school graduation requirements, (3) establishing state testing programs, (4) establishing standards for accreditation of school districts and preparation programs for teachers and administrators, (5) reviewing and approving the budget of the state education agency, and (6) developing rules and regulations for the administration of state programs. In 32 states, the members of the state board of education are appointed (usually by the governor); boards in 11 states are composed of elected members; and 5 states have a combination of appointed and elected state board members. Minnesota and Wisconsin do not have state boards.

The general supervision and administration of the state's public education system are delegated to the chief state school officer. The CSSO is an elected position in 14 states. In the other 36 states, the CSSO is appointed either by the governor or by the state board. These individuals head the state education agency, usually called the state department of education. The state departments of education are charged with the administration and enforcement of state board of education policy and statutory law and are responsible for the supervision of all PK–12 educational institutions in a state (Education Commission of the States, 2005).

Regulations

Regulations are developed by various federal and state agencies empowered to interpret, disseminate, and enforce statutory law and state school board policy. As long as the agency stays within the boundaries of the statute or policy, their decisions have the force of law. Two agencies that affect public schools are the federal Department of Education and the departments of education housed at the state level. For example, the U.S. Department of Education is charged with the interpretation, dissemination, and enforcement of the congressional intent that served as the guiding force behind the enactment of the Individuals with Disabilities Education Act (IDEA), the Safe and Drug-Free Schools and Communities Act, and NCLB. These programs are administered at the state level; however, the federal Department of Education establishes the basic guidelines.

In addition to administering federal programs, state departments of education, overseen by the state board of education and the CSSO, are charged with the duty to interpret, disseminate, and enforce state law and state board policy. For example, state departments of education traditionally issue teaching certificates, provide guidelines for the collection and expenditure of public funds, and oversee mandated state testing programs. Regardless of the source, regulations carry the force of law and are backed by the threat of sanctions, usually in the form of loss of funding or accreditation.

School Board Policy

In principle, local boards of education are designed to represent the beliefs and values of the community, oversee the expenditure of public funding, and serve in a direct supervisory capacity for the local school districts. According to the Educational Commission of the States (2005), there are more than 14,000 local school boards operating in the United States. Of these, the vast majority are composed of citizens elected by the registered voters in their particular political subdivision. Several urban areas, however, are moving to have some or all of their school board members appointed by the mayor of the city. Local boards of education can be either fiscally independent or fiscally dependent. Fiscally independent boards (about 90% of the school boards in the United States) are autonomous with respect to local city or county government. Independent boards may raise taxes, set and approve budgets, and allocate resources separately and independently from city or county government boards. Dependent boards are actually an education agency operated by a unit of local government. These boards are dependent on the local government to raise taxes, allocate resources, and approve budgets (Fowler, 2009).

Boards of education are simultaneously empowered and limited by their state constitution, the federal Constitution, state board of education policy, regulations developed by either the state or federal education department, and statutory law. For example, local boards of education are generally empowered by state statute to establish and oversee the public schools in their district, collect and spend public funds, and establish attendance boundaries within their district. Policies of local boards of education must meet the minimum guidelines established by the state legislature or state board of education. Board authority is also limited. For example, boards may collect and spend public funds only in accordance with state law, and they may not violate the basic constitutional rights of teachers or choose to purposefully segregate schools by race. In addition, boards of education may not purposefully disregard federal statutory requirements such as IDEA, state statutory requirements such as tenure laws, or state board of education policies such as graduation requirements.

Boards of education codify and exercise their authority through a set of written policies. As long as a written and legally adopted policy does not violate statutory, regulatory, or **constitutional law**, it is enforceable, and teachers, students, and administrators must abide by it. Boards enjoy considerable authority and often serve as the final arbiter of disputes within a district. Violating school board policy or authority can be grounds for termination of employment (see, for example, *Hearn v. The Board of Public Education* [1999] and *Lacks v. Ferguson Reorganized School District* [1998], affirming a school board's authority to terminate the employment of a teacher for violation of school board policy).

School board policy, actions, and decisions are open to the public under state "sunshine" or "open records" laws. Every state provides for the dissemination of school board actions, notice for the time and place of school board meetings, the legitimate reasons for closed session, and the process for closing school board meetings to the public. For example, Missouri state law requires that "all public meetings of public governmental bodies shall be open to the public (and) all public records of public government bodies shall be open to the public for inspection and copying" (RSMo 610.020). In addition to school board decisions, individual administrator and teacher salaries are available to the public. A few states are discussing using student test scores to "rate" or "rank" teachers into quartiles. It can be assumed that aggregate test scores for individual teachers as well as their individual rankings would be available under state open records laws. Naturally some items remain private and are not open to the public. For example, discussions regarding legal issues with the school board attorney, the purchase or lease of property, termination or discipline of employees, and identifiable students or minors are exempt from public disclosure. In addition, school boards must give the public adequate notice of the time, date, and place of each meeting, and agenda items for a legally constituted meeting of the board. For example, a Massachusetts state court held that e-mail communications between school board members regarding the professional competency of the superintendent constituted a meeting of the board and therefore violated the state open records law (*District Attorney v. School Committee*, 2009).

THE JUDICIAL SYSTEM

Judges in the United States are powerful policy actors. Federal courts can declare a state or federal law unconstitutional, overrule a school board decision, or interpret laws. For example, the U.S. Supreme Court has interpreted Title IX to mean that school districts can be held liable for student-on-student sexual harassment under certain conditions (*Davis v. Monroe County Board of Education*, 1999). State courts are also important policy actors. State courts play an important role in school finance policy in that several state courts have declared state school finance systems to be unconstitutional (Fowler, 2009). State and federal court decisions result in common or case law.

Common Law

Common (case) law develops from various court decisions that *interpret or apply* constitutional, statutory, regulatory law, or school board policy to a particular situation.

The common law concept has its genesis in the English legal system, dating back to the late Middle Ages. The common law concept is based on the premise that not all legal problems can, or should, be covered by a statute. Consequently, in the English system judges are allowed to create solutions to problems. Later, these decisions are written down and establish precedent for future decisions, unless they are overruled by a new law, statute, or higher court. Because the United States started as an English colony, this system was naturally adopted by the colonies and became the model for the current legal system (Hilyerd, 2004).

Although fraught with ambiguities, common law is especially important to school administrators. For example, the Fourth Amendment to the Constitution provides citizens protection from unreasonable search of their persons and property. The Fourth Amendment does not prohibit all searches, just *unreasonable* ones. The problem is defining an "unreasonable" search. If a search is unreasonable in one situation, is a similar search unreasonable in every situation?

Consequently, one of the primary functions of the court system is to interpret the legality of actions as applied to specific situations. This body of decisions becomes common law and determines the powers and limitations of official actions for the educational leaders who reside within the jurisdiction of that particular court. Previous decisions set precedents for future decisions of that particular court (***stare decisis***). These decisions serve as precedents and are law for that particular jurisdiction. Decisions from other state or federal courts are persuasive and provide guidance only for that particular jurisdiction.

Many educators assume that the law is stable and that courts establish what can and cannot be done. However, courts decide on the facts of a case only in a particular situation. It cannot always be assumed that a particular decision will apply in all other situations. David J. Sperry (1999) succinctly captures this concept as he explains:

> The great myth of the law is that the law is certain, exact, and fixed. The law is not stationary; it is continually evolving as courts reinterpret constitutional and statutory provisions and legislatures enact new laws. This is why best practices in educational law should not be based solely on knowledge of a specific statute, administrative regulation, or court case, but rather on an understanding of the lawmaking process. (p. 11)

Common law represents the dynamic nature of educational law and is the nexus where the tensions between school board authority and the rights of students and teachers converge. It is at this nexus that the questions of ethical and legal decision making often become the lightning rod of controversy. However, common law has established over time some fundamental concepts that school administrators should consistently apply to decision making. Failure to abide by or honor these established principles can lead to serious legal troubles. These principles are discussed in greater detail throughout the remainder of the text as they apply to various legal topics and leadership dilemmas.

The U.S. Legal System

In the U.S. legal system there are two overlapping judicial systems, one state and the other federal. Thus, there are 51 legal systems: 1 federal system and 50 state systems.

State legal systems have jurisdiction over matters involving the state constitution and state statutes. The federal system has jurisdiction over legal matters involving the U.S. Constitution, controversies between the U.S. government (in education law this includes school boards and school employees) and citizens (administrators, teachers, students, and parents), and disputes between states or between parties from different states. The two types of systems are similar in organization and function, but vary somewhat in the types of cases considered and the decisions that are rendered. Both state and federal courts are organized in a similar manner. Trial courts function at the entry level. Trial courts hear cases where facts are presented and disputed by both sides. The next level is a series of intermediate courts of appeal. The highest state court and the U.S. Supreme Court serve as the final arbiters of law for their respective jurisdictions.

All court systems are similar in that judges may not solicit or create cases or disputes for judgment. A judge or a panel of judges may not rule a school policy or administrative practice unconstitutional or in violation of a state statute unless someone affected by the policy or practice brings the issue before the court. Persons affected by a practice or policy are said to have **standing**. For example, suppose that a classroom teacher searches two students for an allegedly stolen ring. The ring is not found, and a question arises as to the reasonableness of the search. Only the parents of the students who were actually searched (or the students themselves, if considered adults) have standing to question the practice before a court.

The legal system hears two types of cases: *criminal cases* and *civil cases*. The difference is significant. In criminal cases a jury must use a "beyond a reasonable doubt" standard of proof. This means that the evidence is so strong that there is no reasonable doubt that the defendant committed the crime (Administrative Office of the U.S. Courts, 2003). Civil cases are decided by "a preponderance of the evidence," meaning whether it is more than likely that the defendant committed the crime or wronged the plaintiff. Local school boards are bound by the preponderance of the evidence standard of proof.

The vast majority of school law cases are civil cases. In civil cases, one person files a complaint with a state or federal court with jurisdiction to hear the case. The court serves a copy of the complaint on the person or school district being accused of some injury. The example of a classroom teacher searching two students would be a civil case. Assume in our example that the parents of the students file a complaint against the teacher (and probably the school district). The complaint is "served" on the teacher. To prepare for trial, both parties engage in *discovery*, meaning that the two sides must provide information to each other. One common method of discovery is the deposition. In the deposition, a witness is required to answer questions under oath about the case. The answers to the questions are recorded by a court reporter. The written record is provided to both sides (Administrative Office of the U.S. Courts, 2003). There are very few questions of "limits" during discovery. For example, the student attorney may ask the teacher about medications she is taking, about her medical history, or whether she has ever searched a student before. Judges encourage the two sides to try to reach an agreement without going to trial. When the two sides reach an agreement, it is known as a *settlement* (Administrative Office of the U.S. Courts, 2003). In fact, most education disputes between parents and school boards are settled before going to trial.

FEDERAL COURTS   Article III of the United States Constitution establishes the judicial branch as one of the three separate branches of the federal government. Federal courts do not make laws. That is the responsibility of the legislative branch of government. Congress, not the judiciary, controls the types of cases that may be addressed in federal courts. Congress decides how many judges there should be, determines which of the president's nominees ultimately become federal judges, approves the federal courts' budget, and appropriates money for the judiciary to operate. At the same time, the Founding Fathers considered an independent judiciary essential to ensure fairness and equal justice for all citizens. Thus, federal justices have lifetime appointments, Congress cannot reduce their salaries, and federal justices can be impeached only for "high crimes and misdemeanors."

Federal courts deal almost exclusively with questions involving the U.S. Constitution, federal laws, or controversies between states (Administrative Office of the U.S. Courts, 2003).

The areas of most concern to educators are questions involving the U.S. Constitution and federal statutes as these issues apply to the educational arena. It is interesting to note that the federal court system has not always been active in constitutional disputes regarding public education. This changed in 1943 when the U.S. Supreme Court found that the U.S. Constitution "protects the citizens against the State itself and all of its creatures—*Boards of Education not excepted*" [italics added] (*West Virginia State Board of Education v. Barnette,* 1943). This ruling serves as one foundation for the principle that boards of education, school administrators, and teachers are bound by the U.S. Constitution.

The federal court system is hierarchically organized around 94 trial courts called federal district courts, 12 courts of appeal called circuit courts or appellate courts, and one Supreme Court. Each state has at least one district court, and more populous states have more than one. For example, there are two federal district courts in Missouri. The Eastern District Court is housed in St. Louis, Missouri and the Western District Court is housed in Kansas City, Missouri. The primary function of these courts is to hear evidence in order to build a factual record of the case, and from this record, to apply the applicable constitutional, statutory, regulatory, or common law to the dispute (Administrative Office of the U.S. Courts, 2003).

The intermediate appellate courts are the 13 multimember Circuit Courts of Appeal. Eleven of these courts have jurisdiction over a group of states (see Figure 2–1). In the foregoing example, the U.S. Court of Appeals for the Eighth Circuit serves Missouri and six other states. Consequently, an appeal from either the Eastern or Western District Court of Missouri would be made in the Eighth Circuit Court of Appeals. The primary function of the circuit courts is to decide issues of law. These courts do not hear new evidence, hear from witnesses, or refer decisions to juries. However, these courts may elect to hear oral arguments from attorneys representing both sides of the issue. The panel of judges (usually three, although sometimes circuit courts elect to hear a case *en banc*, meaning that all of the justices in that circuit hear the case) reviews the written record and hears oral arguments, votes, reaches a decision, and writes an opinion.

THE U.S. SUPREME COURT   The U.S. Supreme Court consists of the Chief Justice of the United States and eight associate justices. The U.S. Supreme Court is the final arbiter

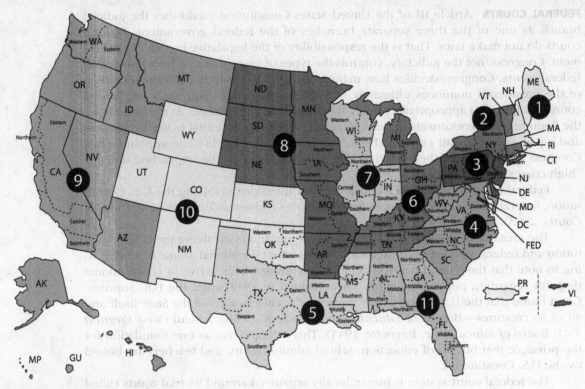

FIGURE 2–1   Geographic Boundaries of United States Courts of Appeal and United States District Courts.

of questions involving the U.S. Constitution and federal statutes. The Court hears appeals from circuit courts and from the highest state courts on issues involving federal questions. A person who loses in a federal court of appeals or the highest court in a state (a state supreme court, for example) may file a petition for a ***writ of certiorari (writ)***, which is a document asking the Supreme Court to review the case (Administrative Office of the U.S. Courts, 2003). The U.S. Supreme Court can hear only cases that are appealed. In other words, a lower court ruling may be of particular interest to several justices on the Court, but these justices may not get involved until the case is appealed. However, the Court is not required to hear or consider every case that is appealed. At least four justices must agree to grant an appeal before a case can be heard and adjudicated by the full Court. The Court usually selects the cases it will consider with great care.

When the court decides to hear a case, the Chief Justice will appoint one of the justices (or him- or herself) to write the opinion. A majority of the members must agree on a decision and the rationale for the decision before the opinion becomes applicable. This agreement among at least five justices forms a majority opinion. Justices who disagree with the majority may elect to issue a dissenting opinion. A concurring opinion may be written by a justice who agrees with either the majority or a dissenting opinion, but for different reasons. However, it is only the majority opinion that creates a precedent and becomes binding on all other governmental institutions in the United States.

STANDARDS OF REVIEW

[*Note*. This section was written by Thomas J. Graca, Vice President, Planning and Development, Eastfield College, Dallas County Community College District, Mesquite, TX. The author gratefully acknowledges Tom's invaluable contribution.]

In certain cases, particularly First Amendment and **equal protection** cases in school law, courts apply various standards of review to guide their decisions. Three standards of review apply in different situations: (1) strict scrutiny, (2) middle-tier scrutiny, and (3) rational basis.

The first standard of review is called strict scrutiny. **Strict scrutiny** applies in cases involving (1) First Amendment rights, (2) the suspect classifications of race, lineage, and national origin, and (3) when the rights of voting, travel, or privacy are implicated. When a court determines that strict scrutiny is the standard that applies, the state (or school district) will almost always lose. In order to prevail, the state must prove that the law or regulation is necessary to achieve a *compelling state interest*. For example, were a state to require that African American teacher applicants score "x" on the state teacher certification exam, and White teacher applicants score "y" on the state teacher certification exam, most courts would likely use the strict scrutiny standard because race is a suspect classification. Then the state would have the burden of proving that there was no less restrictive means (necessity) to achieve some compelling governmental interest (e.g., diversity in the teaching force). But the argument would need to be *compelling*. In another example, courts apply strict scrutiny to school district policies that promote racial balances between schools within the district. When courts apply this standard to these policies, the district almost always loses. In other words, their argument is not compelling.

The second standard of review is called either *middle-tier scrutiny* or intermediate scrutiny. This second standard of review applies to gender classifications and illegitimacy (in lineage). In order to prevail under this middle tier, the state would have to prove that the law or regulation was *substantially* related to an important interest (juxtapose with *necessary* and *compelling* in strict scrutiny earlier). So, in an analogous example to the race example just given, if women had to score "a" on the exam, and men had to score "b" on the exam, the state would have to prove that there is a substantial relationship between the difference in requirements based on gender and an important interest. You should observe that the state would be more likely to win the gender case than the race cases. Do you see why? The difference between *compelling* and *important* and the difference between *necessary* and *substantially* are key language.

The third standard of review is called rational basis. *Rational basis review applies in all other equal protection cases.* Some examples of specific cases where rational basis was applied include wealth, age, and mental capacity. In order to prevail under rational basis review, the plaintiff must prove (note that burden has shifted from the state) that the law or regulation is not rationally related to any legitimate interest. When rational basis is applied, the state almost always wins. Consider our teacher certification exam. Imagine that the fee for taking the state's test was $10,000. Not all people can afford to take a $10,000 test. So, the state is discriminating against people who can't afford the test. Wealth, however, is not a suspect classification. So, a poor certification candidate would have to prove that there was no relationship between the fee and any legitimate interest. The state would likely argue that the fee pays for a really good test, with really good test security, that will identify really good teachers and that the burden of the fee is rightfully placed on the test taker. Whether you agree with the argument or not, you must admit that it is rational. Whether or not a $10,000 test fee is good policy does not matter. Wealth is not a suspect classification, so the state may discriminate all it likes, as long as it does so rationally to achieve any legitimate government purpose. In other words, *school districts must be particularly discriminatory to fail under a rational basis review.*

STATE COURTS State courts are an important policy actor in school law, because the vast majority of school law cases are decided by these courts. State courts hear cases involving state law and state constitutional issues. State court decisions, like state laws, have no meaning in other states. Each state court system is similar in arrangement and is organized much like the federal system into trial courts, intermediate appellate courts, and a court of final arbitration, in most cases a supreme court. However, each state court system is somewhat different. The names and numbers of courts vary from state to state.

In approximately 36 to 38 states, judges are elected by popular vote. In the other states, judges are appointed by the governor and approved by the state senate. Most state court systems and laws are based on the English model. Louisiana created a legal system based on the French civil law system (Hilyerd, 2004).

ELEMENTS OF A COURT DECISION

School leaders are expected to know and remain current with various legal rulings and trends that affect education, especially rulings that define the rights of teachers and students. Unfortunately, accessing, reading, and understanding court opinions can be difficult, especially for school administrators, who usually do not have formal legal training. However, an understanding of the organization of most court decisions can aid in this effort. A typical federal court opinion contains the following elements: case name, facts of the case, a review of the procedural history, legal questions, a ruling, justification for the ruling, and the disposition of the case.

CASE NAME Cases are usually named after the parties or people involved. The person who brings the suit is the **plaintiff** and is listed first. The person or governing body being sued is the **defendant** and is listed second. For example, if teacher Jones brings suit against Consolidated School District, Jones is the plaintiff and Consolidated School District is the defendant. The case would be published as *Jones v. Consolidated School District*. If Jones prevails at the trial court and the Consolidated School District decides to appeal the ruling or verdict, the School District becomes the appellant (or petitioner) and Jones is considered the appellee (or respondent). The case now lists the appellant first and becomes *Consolidated School District v. Jones*. In addition to the parties involved, the case name should also contain the proper citation.

FACTS OF THE CASE The facts of the case are a review of the information, written record, and history of the case. The facts of the case should explain who allegedly did what, when, and why.

LEGAL QUESTIONS The legal questions establish what the court is considering. Assume Jones is bringing suit against Consolidated School District alleging that an illegal search of her personal laptop computer at school by school officials resulted in termination of employment. The question before the court becomes, "Was the search of the personal laptop that led to Jones' termination reasonable under the circumstances in this situation?" If the search was determined to be reasonable, the termination of Jones would probably stand. If the search is determined to be unreasonable, the termination may be reversed.

REVIEW OF PROCEDURAL HISTORY This part of the opinion traces the legal history of the case. For example, in *Consolidated School District v. Jones,* the procedural history would include a summary of the ruling of the trial court. If the case were one of the few selected for review by the U.S. Supreme Court, the procedural history would also include a summary of the circuit court ruling.

COURT RULING The judgment of the court answers the legal question.

RATIONALE Judicial decisions must be based on reason and past decisions, not personal opinion. This section of the opinion outlines the rationale behind the decision and usually contains several previous similar rulings to justify the current decision.

DISPOSITION OF THE CASE After justifying and issuing a ruling, the court must dispose of the case. If the court finds that the Jones search was not justified under the circumstances, the court will determine a remedy for the injustice. Depending on the situation, this remedy could include back pay, reinstatement, or possibly a monetary award or attorney's fee. If the Jones search was justified, then the case is dismissed. Appellate courts (circuit courts) and the Supreme Court usually dispose of a case by electing to affirm or uphold the lower court, reverse the lower court ("remand for retrial consistent with this opinion"), or modify (affirm in part, reverse in part). Occasionally a court will find an action by a school official to be unconstitutional but grant qualified immunity.

   Qualified immunity may be defined as "immunity from civil liability for a public official who is performing a discretionary function, as long as the conduct does not violate clearly established constitutional or statutory rights" (Garner, 2006, pp. 330–331). The U.S. Supreme Court has established a two-pronged test for qualified immunity: (1) whether a federal constitutional right has been violated based on the alleged facts, and (2) assuming that a violation of constitutional rights is established, whether the constitutional right was clearly established at the time of the alleged incident and a reasonable defendant would have understood that the conduct was unlawful (*Saucier v. Katz*, 2001). For example, assume that the search of Jones's personal computer did violate her Fourth-Amendment rights. If the search did not violate an established law or court ruling that a reasonable school official would or should have knowledge of, then it is possible that the school official will be granted qualified immunity.

Writing Legal Briefs

Unfortunately, court rulings are often ambiguous, and even experienced school attorneys and judges often disagree on the interpretation of the court ruling. It is important, however, to consider the implications of legal decisions for school administration. One effective way to see these implications is to read the legal brief.

EXAMPLE 2–1   Case: Hazelwood School District v. Kuhlmeir

Citation: 484 U.S. 260 (1988)

1. ***Facts of the Case***

    Former student staff members of a high school newspaper alleged violation of their First Amendment rights when the school principal deleted two pages from one issue of the newspaper that included articles describing the impact of teen pregnancy and divorce on students.

2. ***Question***

    To what extent may educators exercise editorial control over the contents of a school newspaper produced as part of a journalism class?

3. ***Rulings***

    Trial Court held that no violation of student rights had occurred. The Eighth Circuit Court of Appeals held that a violation of student rights had occurred. The Supreme Court reversed and remanded. Educators may exercise editorial control over student speech that could responsibly be interpreted as school sponsored as long as the control is responsibly related to legitimate educational concerns.

4. ***Rationale***

    Students do not leave all of their Constitutional rights at the schoolhouse gate (*Tinker v. Des Moines*). However, students have a lesser expectation while in school and student speech that is inconsistent with the educational mission of the school need not be tolerated (*Bethel v. Fraser*). The Court acknowledged that the manner of speech in classrooms is best determined by the school board, rather than federal courts. In this particular case, the school newspaper was part of the curriculum, a supervised learning experience for students, and the school had by past policy and practice expressed editorial control over the content of the paper.

5. ***Implications***

    Educators may express editorial control over student curricular expression in the classroom, school theatrical productions, co-curricular activities, or other venues that could be reasonably linked to the school. However, educators may not censor student speech without a valid educational purpose.

The **legal brief** summarizes the elements of a court opinion into a usable document for further study and referral. Example 2–1 is a legal brief of a U.S. Supreme Court case involving a high school newspaper. This suggested format combines some of the elements of a typical decision into a one-page summary. This format also recommends an *implication section* to provide educational leaders and current leadership candidates with an opportunity to analyze and apply the rulings of a particular case in decision making (see Example 2–1).

LEGAL CITATIONS

All legal citations follow a similar format and include the name of the case, the court deciding the case, the publication source (in volumes called *Reporters*), the page number in the *Reporter*, and the year the case was decided. U.S. Supreme Court cases are published in the *U.S. Reports* (U.S.), circuit court decisions in the *Federal Reporter* (F., F.2d for the second series, or F. 3d for the third series), and district court cases in the *Federal Supplement* (F. Supp.). Several examples follow. However, for a complete guide to citations and the meanings of abbreviations, please refer to the *Publication Manual of the American Psychological Association*, 6th ed. (2009, pp. 216–223).

U.S. Supreme Court Citation

Davis v. Monroe County Bd. of Education, 119 U.S. 1661 (1999)

Circuit Court of Appeals Citation

Todd v. Rush County Schools, 133 F.3d 984 (7th Cir. 1997). Cert denied.

Federal District Court Citation

Adler v. Duval County School Board, 206 F.3d 1071 (11th Cir. 2000).

State Court

Trinidad School District v. Lopez 963 P.2d 1095 (Colorado Supreme Court, 1998).

SOURCES OF LAW

The proliferation of several reliable law-related Internet sources has made it much easier for busy administrators to remain current and research law-related issues. A note of caution: Internet sources are subject to change, and many sources are not regulated. Consequently, it is advisable to rely on established sources. However, many of these sites have gained in popularity and reliability enough to be recognized as acceptable sources by the *Publication Manual of the American Psychological Association* (2009). Some of these sources include:

Internet Databases

Findlaw: (www.findlaw.com) A free search service for U.S. Supreme Court cases and recent circuit court cases. Links U.S. Supreme Court cases with other court citations.

LexisNexis: A subscription service available in some university libraries. Provides full text searching and retrieval of published cases from several jurisdictions including U.S. Supreme Court, federal circuit and district courts, and state supreme courts.

The Cornell Legal Information Institute (www.law.cornell.edu/statutes.html). Internet links to statutory sources, both federal and state.

U.S. Supreme Court (www.supremecourtus.gov). Provides information, opinions, transcripts of oral arguments, and docket summaries for the U.S. Supreme Court.

Associations

American Association of School Administrators (www.aasa.org). AASA is primarily an association for school superintendents. The association journal (*AASA Administrator*) contains articles of interest to school administrators at both the campus and the district level. Membership is required for publications.

Education Commission of the States (www.ecs.org). Policy makers who are interested in particular education topics can usually find what they need on the

ECS website. For further access to timely education policy news, ECS has two flagship electronic publications: *e-Clips*, a daily roundup of the nation's top education news, and *e-Connection*, a weekly bulletin that highlights state policy trends, new reports, upcoming meetings and events, useful websites, and ECS news. Policy information is available for download free of charge.

Education Law Association (www.ela.org). ELA is generally acknowledged as the premier education law association. ELA provides a bimonthly update of legal decisions from state and federal courts pertaining to education. The association holds an annual meeting that includes presentations on a variety of legal issues of concern to P–12 educators and administrators and publishes numerous and affordable monographs and books on school law. Membership is required for bimonthly updates.

National Association of Secondary School Principals (www.nassp.org). NASSP sponsors a free electronic mailing list on topics of interest to middle school and high school principals. The association publishes numerous books and monographs on various topics, including school safety. Membership is required for publications.

National School Boards Association (www.nsba.org). NSBA provides a free weekly electronic mailing list that includes legal issues of interest to educators and school board members. The association publishes the *School Board Journal*, which contains practical tips and advice for school board members including legal issues. Membership is required for publications.

The First Amendment Center (www.firstamendmentcenter.org). Provides information about First Amendment issues including religion.

Blogs and Online Newsletters

eSchool News (www.eschoolnews.com). This provides timely information on legal issues regarding technology in schools, network safety information, and trends in the use of technology to improve school safety.

The Edjurist (www.Edjurist.com). Provides a wide range of information, including links to state departments of education websites and searchable school law databases.

The School Law Blog (http://blogs.edweek.org/edweek/school_law/). Written by Mark Walsh, a respected education law attorney, this blog provides a synopsis of school law cases from around the nation.

Linking to PRACTICE

- Administrative decision-making authority flows from the board of education. Know and respect the limits of your authority.
- Remain current with federal and state law and regulation that affect education. These laws and regulations are available from a variety of Internet sources.
- Learn to read and understand the reasoning behind judicial decisions at the state and federal level.
- Do not assume that the only guide to decision making is knowledge of law. This is simply not true.

Summary

The legal principles of educational leadership form a multihued tapestry whose design is clear in some areas and blurred in others. The threads from which this tapestry is woven include constitutional law, state and federal statutes, state and federal regulations, school board policy, and common law.

One common misunderstanding is the belief that laws are static and immutable and guide all decision making. Nothing could be further from the truth. Significant ambiguity does exist, and legal requirements and interpretations of law are constantly changing form, function, and shades of color. Correctly applying the mandatory and enabling requirements of law requires an understanding of how laws are created and the limits and obligations of law. Remaining current is necessary for effective school leadership.

CONNECTING STANDARDS TO PRACTICE

LEGAL CHALLENGES AT RIVERBOAT SCHOOL DISTRICT

Assistant Superintendent Sharon Grey assembled district principals to discuss the three ongoing lawsuits in the district. The purpose of the meeting was to clarify the reasons for the suits and to dispel any false information. Sharon outlined the lawsuits one at a time.

Suit One

Riverboat Superintendent Paula Gibbs had 2 years left on her 3-year contract. By policy and practice, the board reviewed the superintendent at least once per year, discussed their evaluation with the superintendent in closed session, and provided the superintendent an opportunity to dispute any of the findings. Starting in November, the school board president created a Google document with the superintendent evaluation criteria approved by the district. Each board member was given access to the document. Board members added, deleted, and debated the evaluation language from November to January. Two weeks before the scheduled meeting to discuss the evaluation with the superintendent, the school board president asked for a roll call vote at the end of the Google document. The vote was 4-3 to terminate her contract as superintendent. Unable to reach a settlement, Paula's attorney brought suit claiming that the evaluation and the school board vote to terminate her was not held at a legally called meeting and the ongoing discussions on Google documents constituted a meeting of the board without proper notice to the public.

Suit Two

The Riverboat High School boys' basketball team was the pride of the community. After the team's most recent state championship, voters approved a large bond issue to build a new field house with state-of-the-art equipment, weight room, and basketball playing surface. Against Sharon Grey's advice and without consulting with the school district attorney, the athletic director scheduled all the junior varsity and varsity girls' basketball games and practices at the old facility and reserved the new field house exclusively for the boys' team practices and games. A group of parents brought suit against the district.

Suit Three

Several Jefferson Middle School students had taken ill, apparently from taking contraband pills fellow students were bringing to school and selling at lunch. Needless to say, Jefferson Middle School administrators were under considerable pressure to stop the flow of pills into the school. A student told Assistant Principal Marsha Jefferson that eighth-grader LaDonna Jones had offered to sell her a couple of prescription Tylenols at lunch for $10. AP Wilson went immediately to the gym where LaDonna was playing basketball in physical education class and took her to the dressing room. Once in the dressing room, Wilson searched LaDonna's school clothes, her jacket, her purse, and her book bag. Two Midols were found in LaDonna's purse. AP Wilson asked LaDonna to remove her gym clothes and pull out her bra and underwear in such a way that any hidden contraband would fall out. No pills were found. LaDonna's parents were not happy and hired an attorney. Unable to reach a settlement with the school district, LaDonna's attorney filed suit against the district asking for $100,000 in damages.

Questions

1. Which type of law does each of the scenarios represent? State law, federal law, or constitutional law?

2. Is the scenario criminal or civil?

3. What is the legal question in each of the scenarios?

4. Cite two ISLLC standards pertaining to each scenario.

CHAPTER 3

Education, Religion, and Community Values

INTRODUCTION

This chapter discusses one of the most controversial issues school leaders face: the role of religion in the public school. Regardless of personal viewpoint, religious issues elicit strong emotions. There also seems to be very little room for compromise. In addition to community pressure, many teachers, students, school administrators, and school board members have strong beliefs regarding the place of religion in public schools. This chapter addresses some of the legal guidelines regarding religious expression in public schools and presents an ethical model illustrating the importance of effective communication when issues of conflicting interest arise.

FOCUS QUESTIONS

1. How may school leaders use ethical models to improve communication and decision making?
2. Are public schools "religion-free" zones?
3. Should students be allowed to express their religious beliefs at school? Under what circumstances?
4. Should teachers and other adults express their religious beliefs at school? Under what circumstances?

KEY TERMS

Discourse ethics	Establishment Clause	Free Exercise Clause
Equal Access Act	Forum	Viewpoint discrimination

CASE STUDY

Candy Canes

On Monday before the winter break, Edgewood Elementary School principal Joyce Smith called Flora Norris, Assistant Superintendent of Elementary Education in North Suburban School District. "Dr. Norris," Joyce began, "It has come to my attention that several third- and fourth-grade students who attend East Unity Church are handing out candy canes to their teachers and classmates. The peppermint candy canes have several religious messages on them. One reads, 'Jesus is the Reason for the Season.' The rest have similar messages. All of the candy canes are tied with a green ribbon inviting students and their parents to attend East Unity Church for Christmas Eve services. What should we do?"

Flora thought for a moment. She knew the minister at East Unity quite well. He had a reputation for pushing the envelope when it came to religion and school district policy. "You know the policy, Joyce. Students may hand the candy canes out before school, after school and during lunch, but not in class. Caution your teachers not to allow students to hand out the candy canes in class and not to accept the candy canes from students or comment on them."

It was not long before the East Unity minister called to state his concerns about students not being able to share their Christian message with other students in their classes. Soon afterwards the school board president called to ask Flora why all of a sudden the district had stopped cooperating with local churches. Sensing a problem, Flora immediately notified the superintendent. After her brief overview of the issue, the superintendent interrupted and stated, "I know. I already have had a call from a couple of board members. Apparently the Reverend enlisted all the elementary students that attend his church to hand out the candy canes. Now he is complaining to school board members about our policy."

LEADERSHIP PERSPECTIVES

The case study "Candy Canes" illustrates the conflict generated by the role of religion in public schools. Unfortunately, the controversy has also become one of extremes. At one end of the continuum are those who advocate the promotion of religion (usually their own) in public schools. At the other end of the continuum are those who view public schools as religion-free zones. The stage for this controversy is found in the first 16 words of the First Amendment to the U.S. Constitution: "Congress shall make no law respecting an establishment of religion, or prohibiting the free exercise thereof." The first clause, the ***Establishment Clause***, requires neutrality from government (state legislative bodies, school employees, and school boards) and prohibits public school *advancement of religion*. The second clause, the ***Free Exercise Clause***, prohibits school officials from *interfering with religious expression*. The crux of the problem in balancing these two imperatives is this: Enforcing one clause often seems to violate the other. For example, in "Candy Canes," the Free Exercise Clause clearly establishes the participating students' right to religious expression. But, at what point does their free exercise violate the Establishment Clause? It is at this point, where one person's Establishment Clause inhibits another person's Free Exercise Clause and vice versa, that the seeds of controversy are sown. Part of the problem is that legal scholars, federal judges, and U.S. Supreme Court justices often disagree on when to apply which clause in the context of the public school. Is it permissible for public schools to place restrictions on a grade school student's religious messages? Does restricting the message send the message that the student's religious views are not welcome? Is it permissible to hang the Ten Commandments in the hallway of a public high school where the vast majority of teachers and students are Christian? Should it be permissible for student speakers to pray or proselytize during high school graduation ceremonies? These and other questions illustrate the difficulty in balancing the free exercise and establishment clauses. These questions also illustrate the ongoing culture wars over the role of religion in public education.

Steven Waldman, in his excellent book *Founding Faith* (2008), tells the story of the evolution of the religion clauses in the First Amendment. Much of the following is adapted from his book. In the late 1700s, 11 of the 13 colonies had a state-sponsored religion. Yet Article VI, Clause 3 of the U.S. Constitution reads, "No religious test shall ever be required as a qualification to any office or public trust under the United States." It is easy to see why this provision passed without much dissent. The framers of the Constitution were not thinking or contemplating the role of "government" in religion. They were debating the role of "the national government in religion" (Waldman, 2008, p. 131). In other words, the framers were not thinking of state-sponsored religion, but rather thinking about the federal government sponsorship of religion. It is true that many of the framers were very religious men. It is also true that when the framers met for the first time, many of them found themselves in the most religiously diverse group they had ever been in. So, what religion would the national government sponsor? This may be why the U.S. Constitution is a "stunningly secular (document). It does not mention Jesus, God, the Creator, or even Providence. The rights, we are told in the first three words, come from 'we the people,' not God the Almighty" (Waldman, 2008, p. 130).

The Bill of Rights, however, was not written by the federal Constitutional Convention, but by the newly created Congress. The Bill of Rights is therefore a product of the "sausage grinder" of debate and political compromise. As one of the primary intellects behind the Bill of Rights, James Madison pushed to give the federal government the power to protect citizens from the "state tyranny" of a sponsored religion, and he argued unsuccessfully to apply the First Amendment to the states. As often happens in politics, Madison ended up completely reversing course and found himself having to convince members of Congress that the beauty of the First Amendment was that it continued to allow state governments to support religion (Waldman, 2008). Thus, the basis for the culture wars over religion and public education rests on a political compromise made more than 200 years ago.

By the 1800s, most states had abandoned sponsorship of a particular religion. However, the controversy continues, and public school leaders often find themselves caught between those who wish to bring religion back into public schools and those who believe that public schools should be religion-free zones. Confronting these challenges requires not only an understanding of the applicable legal concepts, but also an understanding, appreciation, and use of the community's diverse cultural, social, and religious resources. These challenges may also require   ISLLC Standard 4B

ISLLC Standards 5B
and 5D

the ability to put aside one's own often deeply held beliefs and seek to understand the perspectives of others. The discourse ethics of Jurgen Habermas can provide guidance.

DISCOURSE ETHICS: RESOLVING ISSUES OF CONFLICTING INTERESTS

In the case study "Candy Canes," Flora Norris is confronted with the conflicting demands of a variety of individuals, which could challenge the skills of even the most experienced school leader. However, the ISLLC standards require that she not only respond legally and decisively to the challenge, but also demonstrate sensitivity and impartiality and respect the rights of others. In other words, Flora's ethical and legal responsibility is to lead the board of education to "make a conscious choice, rather than permitting the current practice to continue without justification" (Rebore, 2001, p. 242).

ISLLC Standards 5B,
5C, 5D, and 5E

In his book *Moral Consciousness and Communicative Action* (1990), the contemporary philosopher Jurgen Habermas proposes **discourse ethics** as a model of communication that may lead to the types of school cultures based on effective communication, collaboration, and mutual agreement outlined in **ISLLC Standards 2A, 5B, and 5C**. Discourse ethics is not designed to eliminate impartiality of judgment. Rather, it is a model designed to encourage active communication, an understanding of the perspectives of others, empathy, and rational argumentation instead of simply suggesting or imposing a solution on others.

ISLLC Standards 2A,
5B, and 5C

Discourse ethics is premised on active communication. In other words, in the case study "Candy Canes," Flora Norris cannot *assume* that she understands the minister's complaints, the position of several board members, or even Principal Smith's concerns. To this end, discourse ethics is designed to create opportunities for open discussion and communication that provide a potential for understanding the perspectives of others, mutual agreement, and collective responsibility characteristic of cooperative school cultures. Seeking to understand the perspectives of others does not necessarily mean agreeing with those perspectives. However, seeking to understand serves as the foundation for the empathy necessary for rational arguments, for or against a particular normative practice or policy decision. In short, discourse ethics is a model that promotes the type of understanding necessary for cooperative school cultures characterized by collaboration, mutual agreement, and acceptance, rather than simple enforcement by policy. Reaching understanding, and thus validity, requires an element of unconditional acceptance of the views, needs, and wants of all concerned. It is this unconditional acceptance of the views of others that provides the background for the establishment of the validity of a norm or action rather than the mere de facto acceptance of a practice or action. In other words, what is justified is not necessarily a function of custom (the way things have always been done) but a question of justification.

Discourse Ethics and Cooperative School Culture

ISLLC Standards 2A,
4C, and 4D

In discussing discourse ethics, Ronald Rebore (2001) makes a distinction between mediation and arbitration that provides guidance in the development of the type of cooperative school cultures called for in **ISLLC Standards 2A, 4C, and 4D**. *Mediation* is designed to seek understanding of the perspectives of others in order to facilitate,

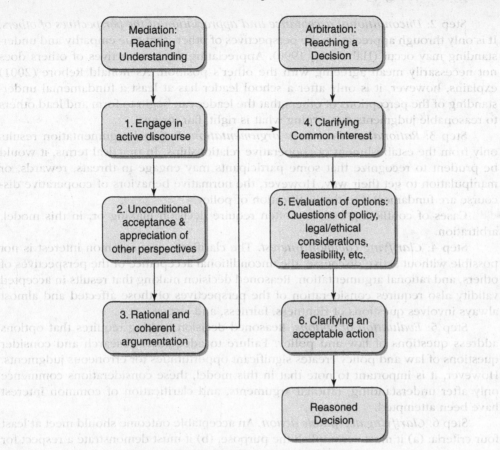

FIGURE 3–1 Discourse ethics: Resolving questions of conflicting interests.

Mediation can be viewed as participants *striving to reach understanding. Arbitration* is designed to give an answer, or in other words, to reach a decision. Arbitration can be viewed in the same way as negotiating a compromise, where the participants try to *strike a balance between conflicting interests* to reach an equitable solution. The distinction between mediation (*seeking to understand*) and arbitration (*reaching a reasoned decision*) can provide a model for school leaders to use when faced with issues of conflicting interest (Figure 3–1).

The case study "Candy Canes" can serve as an illustration of this model. Flora Norris faces several issues of conflicting interest and is charged by her position as assistant superintendent to attempt to lead the board to a conscious choice that is reasonable and justifiable. In this model, Flora's efforts would begin with mediation.

Step 1: *Engage in active discourse.* Discourse ethics rest on the assumption that justification of norms or decisions requires real discourse. In other words, Flora Norris cannot assume that she knows the views, claims, and perspectives of all individuals involved. Therefore, she must begin the process by actively seeking and engaging others in verbal communication.

Step 2: *Unconditional acceptance and appreciation of the perspectives of others*. It is only through appreciating the perspectives of others that true empathy and understanding may occur (Habermas, 1990). Appreciating the perspectives of others does not necessarily mean agreeing with the other's position. As Ronald Rebore (2001) explains, however, it is only after a school leader has at least a fundamental understanding of the perceptions of others that the leader can begin to form and lead others to reasonable judgments concerning what is right, fair, or just.

Step 3: *Rational and coherent argumentation*. Rational argumentation results only from the establishment of cooperative relationships. In practical terms, it would be prudent to recognize that some participants may engage in threats, rewards, or manipulation to get their way. However, the normative behaviors of cooperative discourse are fundamental to the justification of policy.

Cases of conflicting interests often require decision making or, in this model, arbitration.

Step 4: *Clarifying common interest*. The clarification of common interest is not possible without active discourse, the unconditional acceptance of the perspectives of others, and rational argumentation. Reasoned decision making that results in accepted validity also requires consideration of the perspectives of those affected and almost always involves questions of rightness, fairness, and justice.

Step 5: *Evaluation of options*. Reasoned decision making requires that options address questions of law and policy. Failure to adequately research and consider questions of law and policy creates significant opportunities for erroneous judgments. However, it is important to note that in this model, these considerations commence only after understanding, rational arguments, and clarification of common interest have been attempted.

Step 6: *Clarifying acceptable action*. An acceptable outcome should meet at least four criteria: (a) it must accomplish the purpose, (b) it must demonstrate a respect for the rights of others, (c) it must be legally and ethically defensible, and (d) it must benefit students and their families.

As Habermas (1990) points out, it is very difficult and often impossible to resolve conflicts of deeply held moral beliefs. "Candy Canes" may be such a case. Failure to reach understanding and at least an acceptable compromise perceived as fair by all concerned is the primary reason some disagreements of conflicting interests are referred to the judicial system in the first place. Consequently, learning to develop and sustain cooperative relationships as outlined in **ISLLC Standards 2A, 4C, 4D, 5B, 5D, and 5E** and to appreciate the perspectives of others is a difficult but necessary educational leadership task in a diverse society.

ISLLC Standards 2A, 4C, 4D, 5B, 5D, and 5E

Linking to PRACTICE

Do:
- Collaborate with school and community members to develop proactive policies and practices that establish parameters of student religious expression at school.

This dialogue may also neutralize some of the criticism that public schools are "antireligion."
- Understand that school cultures become normative. Use the "Resolving Issues of

Conflicting Interest" model presented in this chapter (or similar communication model) to develop normative practices of cooperative school cultures.

• Train faculty and others (such as a site-based team) in the communication model. Create opportunities to use the communication model in various situations. Begin meetings by sharing guidelines for mediation and arbitration. Make the focus of the meeting clear. Articulate the transition from seeking input, acceptance, and reasonable argumentation and

the time for selecting a solution from alternatives.

• Know that decisions that lead to conscious choices are often much easier to defend from a legal and ethical point of view than those imposed by a policy-making authority.

Do Not:

• Assume that knowledge of law and policy is all a school leader needs to make reasoned and generally accepted decisions.

PUBLIC SCHOOLS AND RELIGION

There have been thousands of battles similar to the case study "Candy Canes" in local school districts all over the country about the proper role of religion in public schools. Although these battles have ebbed and flowed, Steven Waldman (2008) points to a few "seismic shifts" that stand out, including (1) the Civil War, (2) U.S. Supreme Court rulings that applied the First Amendment to the church–public school battle, and (3) Charles Darwin's *The Origin of Species*. It is also difficult to argue that the passage of the Equal Access Act in 1984 and the application of forum analysis and viewpoint discrimination to religious expression in public schools have not had a similar impact on the church–public school debate.

The Civil War

At the end of the Civil War, the Northern victors concluded that the basic relationship between the federal government and the states needed to change (Waldman, 2008). Up until this time, the Bill of Rights had applied only to the national government and not to the states. After the war, the Northern victors decided that perhaps James Madison was correct: The Bill of Rights should also apply to state governmental action. The Fourteenth Amendment was ratified in 1866. The purpose of the amendment was to protect citizens by applying the protections of the Bill of Rights to state action. The men who ratified the Fourteenth Amendment most likely did not envision how this amendment would change the dynamic between religion and public schools.

The U.S. Supreme Court and Religion

The U.S. Supreme Court (and federal courts in general) applies strict scrutiny to First Amendment cases. This means that the court does not consider if some religious expression in public schools is permissible, but if there is some *compelling reason* why it is *not permissible*. It should also be noted that many—if not most—of the significant Supreme Court cases affecting religion in public schools were brought by religious people (Waldman, 2008). It is through this lens that we view the following summaries of important U.S. Supreme Court cases.

***Engel v. Vitale* (1962):** Held that school officials in New York State could not compose a prayer for students to recite.

***Abington Township School District v. Schempp* (1963):** The Court made it clear that study about religion, as distinguished from espousing or sponsoring religious expression, is constitutional. In other words, teaching about religions objectively or neutrally to educate students about a variety of religious traditions is permissible.

***Epperson v. Arkansas* (1968):** The U.S. Supreme Court invalidated an Arkansas law that forbade the teaching of evolution in public schools.

***Lemon v. Kurtzman* (1971):** The legal question in this case addressed whether or not government aid to religious schools was constitutional. In answering this question, the Court devised a three-pronged test. In order to pass constitutional muster, the governmental action or policy must: (1) have a secular purpose, (2) neither advance nor inhibit religion, and (3) not cause excessive entanglement between government and religion. If the action or policy fails any one of the prongs, then it does not pass constitutional muster.

***Stone v. Graham* (1980):** A Kentucky statute required the posting of a copy of the Ten Commandments, purchased with private contributions, on the wall of each public classroom in the state. The court held that Kentucky's statute had no secular purpose and was therefore unconstitutional.

***Lynch v. Donnelly* (1984):** The Court considered whether the inclusion of a crèche in the city's Christmas display violated the Establishment Clause. The court found that the display was not an effort to advocate a particular religious message and had "legitimate secular purposes." More important to the discussion of religion and education was Justice O'Connor's concurring opinion, where she established what is referred to as the *Endorsement Test*. Endorsement is a practice that endorses religion or religious beliefs in a way that indicates to those who agree that they are "favored" insiders. The other side of the coin is the "disapproval" of religion or religious beliefs in a way that indicates that believers are disfavored outsiders.

***Aguilar v. Felton* (1985):** The use of Title I funds to pay salaries of parochial school teachers violated the Establishment Clause.

***Wallace v. Jaffree* (1985):** A 1978 Alabama state law authorized a 1-minute period of silence in all public schools. Over the next few years, this statute evolved to authorize teachers to lead "willing students" in a prescribed prayer. The Court took care to protect the right of students to engage in voluntary prayer during a moment of silence contained in the original legislation, but found the 1982 legislation unconstitutional because of the clear intent to "return voluntary prayer" to the public schools.

***Board of Education v. Mergens* (1990):** The Court found that the Equal Access Act did not violate the Establishment Clause. Schools that have established a limited open forum must allow student-led religious groups the same access to facilities, newspapers, bulletin boards, public address systems, and so forth that is given to other student clubs and activities.

***Lee v. Weisman* (1992):** Prayers at graduation exercises and baccalaureate services have been a long-standing tradition at public schools throughout the United States. A Rhode Island student and her father challenged a school principal's policy of inviting local clergy to offer an invocation and benediction at graduation. The Court reasoned that high school graduation is of such significance in the lives of many students that the inclusion of prayers at a public school graduation ceremony effectively "coerced" students to participate in religious exercise and resulted in governmental endorsement of religion (coercion test).

***Lamb's Chapel v. Center Moriches Union Free School District* (1993):** A unanimous U.S. Supreme Court decision that found religious speech in public schools to be a fully protected subset of free speech.

***Agostini v. Felton* (1997):** In partially overruling *Aguilar v. Felton,* the Court found that it was not a violation of the Establishment Clause to use federal Title I funds to allow public school teachers to teach at religious schools. The instructional material must be secular and neutral in nature, and no "excessive entanglement" between religion and public schools was apparent.

***Edwards v. Aguillard* (1987):** The most recent U.S. Supreme Court decision involving teaching of creation science along with evolution involved a Louisiana statute named the Creationism Act. The act forbade the teaching of the theory of evolution in public elementary and secondary schools unless accompanied by instruction in the theory of "creation science." The act did not require the teaching of either concept unless the other was also taught. The Supreme Court found that the act did not further its stated purpose of "protecting academic freedom" and that it impermissibly endorsed the religious belief that a supernatural being created humankind.

***Santa Fe Independent School District v. Doe* (2000):** The U.S. Supreme Court held a Texas District School Board policy allowing student-initiated prayers at football games to be unconstitutional. The policy titled "Prayer at Football Games" limited the message to those deemed "appropriate" by the school administration. The school district argued that students were not required to attend football games and that the student elections served as a "circuit breaker" to state endorsement of religion. However, the majority opinion pointed out that (1) students are subjected to only approved messages broadcast over the school's public address system, (2) the process does nothing to protect minority views, and (3) many students, such as cheerleaders, band members, and certainly the players, are required to attend. These issues, and the long history in the school district of prayer at athletic events, led the Court to conclude, "The District . . . asks us to pretend that we do not recognize what every Santa Fe High School student understands clearly—that this policy is about prayer."

***Good News Club v. Milford Central School* (2001):** The Court held that it is viewpoint discrimination when school districts by policy or practice allow non-sectarian groups to use school facilities and disallow religious groups' equal access. The Court was very careful to point out, however, that not all speech is protected in a limited open forum.

Darwin's Theory of Evolution

Darwin's theory of evolution dramatically affected the culture wars in the United States. Rightly or wrongly, many religious people came to fear that the advance of science undermined their faith. Furthermore, many religious people believe that science and secularism have undermined morality and that secularism is at least indirectly responsible for discipline problems, disrespect of authority, and violence in public schools (Waldman, 2008). As a result of *Edwards v. Aguillard* (1987), there have been several efforts to counter the teaching of Darwin's theory of evolution in public schools by requiring the addition of a disclaimer in science books. In a recent example, the Tangipahoa Parish School Board (TPSB) in southeastern Louisiana passed a resolution that required teachers to read a disclaimer immediately before the teaching of evolution. This disclaimer, in part, read:

> The Scientific Theory of evolution . . . . should be presented to inform students of the scientific concept and not intended to influence or dissuade the Biblical version of Creation. . . . It is further recognized . . . that it is the basic right and privilege of each student to form his/her own opinion and maintain beliefs taught by parents. . . . Students are urged to exercise critical thinking.

The Fifth Circuit Court of Appeals affirmed a district court ruling that this disclaimer violated the Establishment Clause (*Freiler v. Tangipahoa Parish Board of Education,* 1999). In applying the coercion test, the court found the board's disclaimer devoid of secular purpose and called the school board's stated purpose to promote critical thinking a "sham." The TPSB's request for an *en banc* hearing before the Fifth Circuit Court was denied by an 8–7 vote. In addition, the U.S. Supreme Court denied certiorari by a vote of 6–3. In a rare written dissenting opinion of the denial of certiorari, Justice Scalia (joined by Chief Justice Rehnquist and Justice Thomas) stated the opinion that *Lemon* lacked credibility and "we stand by in silence while a deeply divided Fifth Circuit bars a school district from even suggesting to students that other theories besides evolution—including but not limited to, the Biblical theory of creation—are worthy of their consideration" (Stader, Armenta, & Hill, 2002).

In another challenge to the teaching of evolution in high schools, a Pennsylvania school board passed a resolution stating that "students will be made aware of gaps/problems in Darwin's Theory and other theories of evolution, including . . . intelligent design" (quoted in Armenta & Lane, 2010, p. 78). The policy references intelligent design and the book *Of Pandas and People.* After a lengthy trial, Judge John E. Jones applied both the *Lemon* and endorsement tests and issued a sharply worded ruling in which he held that "intelligent design" was, as the plaintiffs argued, a form of creationism, and therefore unconstitutional (*Kitzmiller v. Dover Area School District,* 2005). Debates at the state level in Kansas, Utah, Texas, and several other states as well as intelligent design and evolution debates at local school boards across the country demonstrate the continued intensity generated by this issue (Armenta & Lane, 2010).

THE EQUAL ACCESS ACT AND RELIGIOUS EXPRESSION

During the 1970s and early 1980s, courts generally supported the right of school districts to prohibit student-led religious clubs or groups on campus. The **Equal Access Act** (20 U.S.C. 4071-74) was passed in 1984 in response to public pressure and lobbying by Christian groups. The law applies only to *public secondary schools* that allow noncurricular clubs to meet outside of the school day or during other noninstructional time. An understanding of the Equal Access Act begins with forum analysis. A *forum* is simply a place, and speech rights can be determined by the nature of the place. Courts have referred to nonpublic fora, public fora, designated fora, limited public fora, and open fora. Community and federal parks are generally considered public or open fora. Restrictions on speech in a public forum require that the state demonstrate a compelling interest in suppressing the speech. Schools are usually considered to be either limited open fora or closed fora, depending on the circumstances. A *closed forum* is created when a school district does not allow noncurricular groups or clubs to meet during noninstructional time. Restrictions on all noncurricular speech are permissible in a closed forum. A *limited open forum* is created when schools allow noncurricular clubs or groups to meet during noninstructional time. Restrictions on speech are permissible in a limited open forum as long as the restrictions are reasonably related to the educational mission of the school and are viewpoint neutral. For example, a city government may not be able to ban certain activities in a public park (open forum) that a school district (limited open forum) may be able to ban on school property.

The Equal Access Act applies to schools that have created a limited open forum by allowing at least one student-led, noncurriculum club to meet outside of class time. The language in the Equal Access Act is fairly straightforward. A secondary school that has created a limited open forum must allow additional clubs to be organized, as long as:

- The meeting is voluntary and student-initiated
- Teachers or other school employees do not sponsor the group
- School employees do not promote, lead, or participate in a meeting
- School employees are present at religious meetings only in a supervisory or non-participatory capacity
- The meeting does not materially and substantially interfere with the orderly conduct of educational activities within the school
- Nonschool persons may not direct, conduct, control, or regularly attend activities of student groups

Viewpoint Discrimination

The Equal Access Act creates a statutory right for equal access to school facilities and vehicles of expression designated as a limited open forum. The extent of these rights is determined by policy and past practice. If a school allows noncurricular clubs to meet at lunch, during an advisory period, or after school, a limited open forum has been created *during these times and places*. If a school allows noncurricular student groups access to announcements or bulletin boards, for example, then these *venues are now considered limited open fora* ("Guidance on Constitutionally Protected Prayer," 2003). *Viewpoint discrimination* occurs when some groups such as an after-school chess club are allowed to meet or use school bulletin boards, school announcements, or other means of school-sponsored communication and other groups such as the Fellowship of Christian Athletes are denied access on an equal basis (see *Donovan v. Punxsutawney,* 2003, as an example).

This same logic applies when school districts have a policy or practice of allowing nonprofit groups access to school bulletin boards, take-home flyers, or other means of communication. For example, several school districts allow nonprofit groups to furnish flyers advertising activities of interest to children for students to take home to their parents. This policy or practice creates a limited open forum ("Guidance on Constitutionally Protected Prayer," 2003). Consequently, religious groups must be treated the same as nonreligious groups (see *Child Evangelism Fellowship of Maryland, Inc. v. Montgomery County Public Schools,* 2002, and *Hills v. Scottsdale,* 2003, as examples). Courts use the same logic when considering district facility use by community groups after school. If, for example, by policy or by past practice a board has allowed the YMCA or city council to use school facilities, a limited open forum has been created and religious groups must be treated the same as nonreligious groups (*Good News Club v. Milford Central School,* 2001).

Student Challenges to Equal Access

One of the unintended consequences of the Equal Access Act was to create a venue by which more controversial groups, such as gay and lesbian support groups, could gain access to school facilities. If the school has created a limited open forum by allowing other noncurricular groups to meet during noninstructional time, the Equal Access Act prohibits schools from denying the same access (facilities, bulletin boards, hallways, and announcements, for example) to these groups (*Colin v. Orange Unified School District,* 2000; *East High School Prism Club v. Seidel,* 2000; *Straights and Gays for Equity v. Osseo Area Schools,* 2006, reaffirmed in 2008; and *White County High School Peers Rising in Diverse Education v. White County School District,* 2006, are examples of federal court equal access decisions supporting gay and lesbian support groups). In an exception to this trend, a Texas federal district court sided with the school's decision to ban a gay–straight support group in *Caudillo v. Lubbock* (2004). This case differs from the other cases cited in at least one significant way: The gay–straight group allied itself with an outside advocate whose website linked information about safer sex practices. The school and the court viewed this information as "sexually explicit" and "obscene."

Unfortunately, supporting lesbian, gay, bisexual, and transsexual support groups' petition for inclusion is sometimes not as easy as it sounds. For example, controversy followed when the Gay–Straight Alliance (GSA) petitioned the Boyd County (Canonsburg, Kentucky) High School to meet during noninstructional time, to use hallways and bulletin boards, and to make club announcements during homeroom as other student groups did. Controversy surrounding the GSA petition included a student walkout, open hostility from opponents, an acrimonious school board meeting, and a protest from local ministers (*Boyd County High School Gay Straight Alliance v. Board,* 2003). The district court had little trouble determining that Boyd County High School had created and continued to operate a limited open forum during noninstructional time and homeroom. Denying GSA the same opportunities violated the Equal Access Act. Next the court considered the uproar and disruption surrounding GSA. The court acknowledged that schools could ban groups that created "material and substantial disruption" to the educational process (*Tinker v. Des Moines,* 1969). However, the *disruption was caused by GSA opponents,* not GSA club members. This is an important point. The court interpreted *Tinker v. Des Moines School District* (1969) and the "heckler's veto concept" (*Chaplinsky v. New Hampshire,* 1942) as designed to prevent school officials from punishing students for unpopular views instead of punishing the students who respond to the views in a disruptive manner. Consequently, the district must furnish the same opportunities to GSA as other noncurricular student groups. In short, "the values underlying the First Amendment demand that the conduct of hecklers not be permitted to quash the legitimate, non-disruptive, appropriately timed, appropriately mannered, and appropriated placed expression of students in public schools" (Stader & Graca, 2010).

Boy Scouts of America Act

The Boy Scouts of America Equal Access Act (Boy Scouts Act) is part of the No Child Left Behind Act of 2002. Under the Boy Scouts Act, school districts that have created a limited open forum by allowing one or more outside youth or community groups to meet on school premises or use school facilities before or after school hours may not deny equal access to the Boy Scouts or any other youth groups listed as a patriotic society. According to this act, school districts may not deny access or discriminate against the Boy Scouts or other patriotic youth groups for reasons based on membership or leadership criteria or oath of allegiance to God and country. The act does not require that schools sponsor the Boy Scouts or other similar organizations, but does require that these groups have equal access to facilities and other means of expression.

STATE-SPONSORED RELIGIOUS ACTIVITIES

At least 35 states have legislation authorizing or requiring a moment of silence, meditation, or reflection at the beginning of each school day (Education Commission of the States, 2000). As long as the statutes does not authorize teachers to lead "willing students" in a prescribed prayer (*Wallace v. Jaffree*, 1985) or use language that seems to encourage students to use the time to pray (*Doe v. School Board of Ouachita Parish*, 2001), this type of legislation has been challenged with limited success. For example, the Fourth Circuit Court has recently affirmed a district court ruling that Virginia's moment of silence law is constitutional (*Brown v. Gilmore*, 2001). The Fifth Circuit has more recently reached a similar conclusion by declaring a Texas moment of silence law constitutional (*Croft v. Perry*, 2009).

    Challenges to the Pledge of Allegiance based on the claim that the words "one nation under God" violate the Establishment Clause have met a similar fate. The Fourth Circuit and the Seventh Circuit both ruled that the National Pledge passes constitutional muster under the Establishment Clause, even though the words "under God" were added to the pledge by Congress in 1954 (*Myers v. Loudon County Public Schools*, 2005; *Sherman v. Community Consolidated School District 21*, 1992). The Texas Pledge of Allegiance was amended in 2007 to insert the words "under God." The amended Texas Pledge reads "Honor the Texas flag: I pledge allegiance to thee, Texas, one state under God, one and indivisible." Texas state law requires students to recite the National Pledge and the Texas pledge to the state flag once during each school day. The Texas Pledge law has been upheld by the Fifth Circuit (*Croft v. Perry*, 2010).

DISTRICT-SPONSORED RELIGIOUS ACTIVITES

School districts as well as administrators, teachers, and other school employees are prohibited from sponsoring, endorsing, discouraging, or encouraging religious activity. It is permissible to release students for off-campus religious instruction during the school day, and many states have laws authorizing such practices (see *Pierce v. Sullivan*, 2004, as an example). Transportation and any expenses for instructional materials may not be supported by school district funds. It is unlikely, although not certain, that the giving of credit toward graduation for participation in off-campus religious instruction is constitutional. Released time for on-campus religious instruction is very problematic (Haynes & Thomas, 2001). For example, the Rhea County (Tennessee) school district had a long-standing practice of permitting Bryan College to conduct "Bible Education Ministry" in the county's public elementary schools. The classes were conducted by Bryan College volunteers for 30 minutes once a week during the school day. The content of the lessons was clearly religious. On judicial review, the Sixth Circuit Court had little difficulty concluding that because the instruction occurred during the school day and on school property, it sent a "clear message of state endorsement of religion—Christianity in particular—to an objective observer" (*Doe v. Porter*, 2004).

Displays and Holidays

Holiday programs, often religious in content and purpose, dominate Christian traditions. Increased religious diversity and sensitivity to the religious views of others has created some concern over these traditions. Thus, sensitivity and an understanding of other perspectives are necessary. As Mawdsley and Russo (2004) point out, however, any religious displays may be suspect. The problem is, when is a display too religious? Or conversely, when is a display not religious enough? For example, David Saxe brought suit against the State College (Pennsylvania) Area School District claiming that a table display and song program at an elementary school holiday concert were not "Christian enough" (*Sechler & Saxe v. State College Area School District*, 2000). The table display was composed of several items including a Menorah, a Kwanzaa candelabrum, and several books. The concert consisted of several nonreligious songs and a parody that apparently offended Saxe. On review, the district court found that the holiday display and song program sent a message of inclusion and were consistent with applicable U.S. Supreme Court rulings. Although seemingly frivolous, this case illustrates the fine line many school leaders walk between meeting community demands for continuing religious traditions and increased plurality and demands for neutrality.

It is permissible to include some religious selections in school concerts and even to allow performances at religious sites as long as nonreligious sites and music are also selected (Mawdsley & Russo, 2004). However, concerts dominated by religious music, especially when the concert is presented as part of a particular religious holiday, should be avoided (Haynes & Thomas, 2001). It has been clearly established that students should not be required to participate in any school activity, or part of an activity, that may be offensive to their religious beliefs. For example, two sophomore members of the school choir and their parents filed suit to prohibit the choir from rehearsing and performing "The Lord's Prayer." The district court granted the plaintiffs' request for a permanent injunction (*Skarin v. Woodbine Community School District*, 2002).

Linking to PRACTICE

Do:

- Understand the limitations on religious music and displays and where they are allowed as part of the curriculum, in concerts, and other public performances.
- Establish policies to fairly accommodate those students who wish to be excused from a concert or public performance (or possibly from a single song) because of religious reasons. The policy should be fairly administered and routinely granted. The policy should state reasonable ways for the student to make up the performance and not suffer grade penalty for failure to participate.
- Examine the selection of holiday music and displays before controversy erupts.

- Understand that any school-sponsored religious display is open to challenge (Mawdsley & Russo, 2004). Some challengers may consider the display too religious, others that the display is not religious enough.
- Including a wide range of secular, religious, and ethnic symbols as part of holiday displays may immunize schools from sponsorship concerns but possibly not from accusations of insensitivity to Christian traditions (Mawdsley & Russo, 2004).
- Become familiar with the nature and needs of the religious groups in the school community (Haynes & Thomas, 2001).

Murals, Signs, and Other School-Sponsored Speech

School-sponsored signs, literature, murals, and paintings have also generated controversy. However, courts are reluctant to second-guess the reasonable rules and regulations developed by school administrators. For example, a Wisconsin school principal invited student groups to paint murals in the school. Two student members of the Bible Club sued over the principal's refusal to approve their preliminary sketch in totality (*Gernetzke v. Kenosha Unified School District,* 2001). The proposed mural included a heart, two doves, an open Bible with a well-known passage from the New Testament, and a large cross. The principal approved all but the cross, reasoning that so salient a Christian symbol would invite other suits and force him to approve other less savory murals proposed by the Satanic or neo-Nazi elements present in the school. The Seventh Circuit Court affirmed a lower court ruling in favor of the school district. The court was careful to point out that the principal had refused all or parts of other secular murals. His reasonable concerns over litigation and disorder did not demonstrate discrimination, but were a legitimate exercise of his authority to control messages that might cause disruption or bear the imprint of the school. Similarly, the Ninth Circuit Court found a school district's decision to exclude certain advertisements on a baseball-field fence, including religious ones, reasonable (*DiLoreto v. Downey Unified School District,* 1999).

In a similar decision, the 10th Circuit Court ruled that Columbine High School officials could exercise editorial control over numerous tiles designed to be permanently attached to school hallways. Current and past students, parents, rescue and police personnel, and mental health workers involved in the 1999 Columbine shooting were among those invited to participate in the project. The guidelines specified that tiles with references to the attack, names or initials of students, Columbine ribbons, religious symbols, or obscene or offensive content would not be fired or hung. Several tiles painted by the families of the victims violated these rules. After a meeting with families, the restrictions against tiles with their children's names, dates other than 4-20, and the Columbine ribbon were relaxed, and parents were invited to repaint their tiles. The parents refused to change or repaint the tiles and brought suit. In an interesting and wide-ranging opinion, citing various fora analyses, forms of speech, and *Hazelwood School District v. Kuhlmeier* (1988), the 10th Circuit Court found that the tiles conveyed approval of the message by the school and were subject to the reasonable rules and restrictions developed by the district (*Fleming v. Jefferson County School District R-1*, 2002 cert. denied).

STUDENTS AND RELIGIOUS EXPRESSION

Students often wish to share their religious beliefs with other students in the school. Certainly, students do have this right under the Free Exercise Clause. For example, student-initiated before- and after-school activities such as "see you at the pole," prayer groups, and religious clubs are permissible. Students may read a Bible or other religious material, pray, or engage other consenting students in religious discussion during noninstructional time such as lunch, recess, or passing time between classes. School officials may impose reasonable rules and regulations to maintain order, but may not discriminate against religiously based activities. Administrators, teachers, and other school employees should refrain from encouraging, discouraging, or promoting student prayer, Bible reading, attendance at a religious club meeting, and so forth ("Guidance on Constitutionally Protected Prayer," 2003). Teachers and other school employees may not pray with students in public schools and may be terminated for doing so. Schools are not required to allow outside adults to come on campus and lead such an event. It is the rights of students, not outside adults, that are protected (Haynes & Thomas, 2001).

It is not permissible for one student's religion to determine the curriculum for all other students. Students may be excused from certain reading assignments, homework activities, and so forth on religious grounds. Schools may offer alternative assignments. However, if the requests for exemption or alternative assignments become overly burdensome for teachers, it is conceivable that a court would find the school district's refusal to continue to offer multiple alternative assignments reasonable. A reasonable number of excused absences for religious reasons seem appropriate. Makeup work may be required (Haynes & Thomas, 2001).

One area of concern to many teachers is what to do with student assignments or projects of a religious nature. Teachers may accept assignments or other student work that has a religious theme. In fact, NCLB (2002) clarifies this concept by stating that students may express religious beliefs in homework, artwork, or other written or oral assignments without penalty or reward because of the religious content. Teachers are not required to accept assignments that do not meet the established objectives of the assignment or inappropriately convey that the school sponsors the message (see *Settle v. Dickson County School Board*, 1995, and *C. H. v. Oliva*, 1997, as examples).

If policy or practice has allowed students to distribute literature to other students during noninstructional time on school grounds, school policy should be applied equally to the distribution of religious material (*Board of Education v. Mergens*, 1990; *Pope v. East Brunswick Board of Education*, 1993). For example, a Massachusetts district court held that it was viewpoint discrimination to prohibit students from (and later punish them for) distributing candy canes containing proselytizing messages sponsored by a school Bible club during noninstructional time. In this case other groups on campus were allowed to distribute literature during noninstructional time (*Westfield High School L. I. F. E. Club v. City of Westfield*, 2003).

As always, school administrators can deny the distribution of any literature, such as hate literature or literature containing gang symbols, which may cause substantial disruption. Simple disagreement with the message or undifferentiated concerns of disruption may not suffice to justify suppression of student speech.

Mawdsley and Russo (2004) provide the following guidelines regarding student religious expression in public schools:

1. Students are *private actors* and are not restricted by the Establishment Clause.
2. Students with religious messages should not be prohibited from discussing their religious beliefs with others simply because of some undifferentiated fear of disruption.
3. Students with religious messages must be treated the same as students with nonreligious messages.
4. Schools may choose to prohibit *students* from distributing religious literature during class time and at school-sponsored events.
5. Limit student distribution of religious literature to noninstructional time and before and after school.
6. In addition, school administrators can and should enforce harassment policies where student-to-student proselytizing has become unwelcome (Mawdsley, 1998).

Linking to PRACTICE

Do:
- Acknowledge the rights of students to express their religious beliefs in school assignments, during noninstructional times, and before and after school.

- Understand that murals, signs, tiles, sports programs, and advertisements at extracurricular events convey the impression of school sponsorship.

Student-Led Prayers at Graduation

Prayers at graduation exercises and baccalaureate services have been a long-standing tradition at public schools throughout the United States. However, in a hotly debated ruling, the U.S. Supreme Court found such prayers unconstitutional (*Lee v. Weisman*, 1992). In response to *Weisman*, several school districts have considered allowing students to vote on whether to select a student to deliver a message of their choosing at school events and graduation. On one side of the debate are those who believe that student religious speech at graduation ceremonies violates the Establishment Clause. The U.S. Supreme Court supported the separationist argument in *Santa Fe Independent School District v. Doe* (2000). In *Santa Fe*, the court pointed out that constitutional rights are not subject to vote. In other words, a majority of students could not vote to suspend the Establishment Clause and have organized prayer at a school-sponsored event. In this reasoning, a graduation exercise is a school-sponsored event, and students are still being coerced, however subtly, to participate in a religious activity. Even a "nonsectarian" and "nonproselytizing" prayer may not solve the problem. To some Christians, the idea of a nonsectarian prayer is offensive. In addition, the U.S. Supreme Court held in *Weisman* that even nondenominational prayers may not be established by the government. There is also the problem of school officials trying to figure out whether or not a particular student prayer is proselytizing (Haynes & Thomas, 2001).

For example, the Ninth Circuit Court upheld a school district's decision not to allow two students to deliver a message at graduation that school officials considered proselytizing (*Cole v. Oroville Union Free School District*, 2000). The Ninth Circuit was soon faced with a similar question of a school principal's censoring the proselytizing portions of a salutatorian address at graduation (*Lassonde v. Pleasanton Unified School District*, 2003). In this particular case the speech contained several personal references to God as well as several overtly proselytizing sections. Reasoning that the personal statements were acceptable, the school principal and district legal counsel censored the proselytizing comments of the speech because of Establishment Clause concerns. The student proposed a "disclaimer" stating that the views of the student speakers did not necessarily reflect the views of the district. This proposal was rejected by the district. The student reluctantly agreed to delete the proselytizing portions with the understanding that he could distribute uncensored copies of his speech outside the commencement area. One year later the student brought suit alleging that the censorship of his speech violated his First Amendment rights. The court held the actions of the district necessary to avoid a conflict with the Establishment Clause. The court reasoned that because the school district had obvious control over graduation and by past practice reviewed student speeches, any speech or actions would bear the imprint of the school.

On the other side of this debate are those who contend that not allowing students to express their religious beliefs at graduation violates the Free Exercise Clause. This view has met with some success. For example, the Fifth Circuit Court held in 1992 that student-led prayer that was approved by a vote of the students and was nonsectarian and nonproselytizing was permissible at high school graduation ceremonies (*Jones v. Clear Creek Independent School District*, 1992). In addition, the 11th Circuit Court affirmed a lower court ruling that found student-initiated, student-led prayer during graduation permissible so long as the administration and faculty were not involved in the decision-making process (*Adler v. Duval County School Board*, 2000). As Judge Hill of the 11th Circuit Court explains:

> The . . . (*Santa Fe*) . . . policy is not a *neutral* accommodation of religion. The prayer condemned there was coercive precisely because it was not *private*. (However), a policy that tolerates religion does not improperly *endorse* it. Private speech endorsing religion is . . . protected—even in school. *Remove the school sponsorship, and the prayer is private* [italics added] (*Chandler v. Siegelman*, 2000, selected quotes).

One suggestion for avoiding this controversy outlined in "Guidance on Constitutionally Protected Prayer" (2003) is a disclaimer clarifying that the speech (or views) expressed are the speaker's and not the schools. These guidelines seem to suggest that schools may remain neutral by adding a disclaimer to the program. As Haynes (2003) points out, this approach may essentially create a public forum or free speech zone that relieves school officials from prior review of commencement speeches. Schools could continue to control profane, sexually explicit, or defamatory speech. However, the speech could include political or religious views offensive to many in the audience. In addition, if the speech is not reviewed in advance, any controversial, profane, or explicit views may not be known until after the speech has begun. School officials would then be faced with the unpleasant choice of either interrupting the speech or allowing it to continue. Further, as the Ninth Circuit Court pointed out in *Lassonde* (2003), disclaimers do not protect those with minority viewpoints from being coerced into choosing between an important milestone and being subjected to an unpleasant or unwanted proselytizing speech.

Haynes (2003) suggests that the best place for prayers and sermons may be baccalaureate or other religious services scheduled after school hours during the week leading up to commencement. Baccalaureate services sponsored by private groups are permissible as long as the district is not favoring or disfavoring particular groups. For example, allowing the senior class to select the location and speakers for baccalaureate would seem permissible. If the school makes facilities available to other private groups, the Equal Access Act requires that facilities also must be made available to private groups for baccalaureate services.

Linking to PRACTICE

Do:

- Discuss the role of students as commencement speakers. Develop proactive policies before controversy erupts.
- Seek common ground where individual groups of parents and students may express their religious preferences at extracurricular events without involving a school-owned public address system. A "moment of silence" would be one example (Haynes, 2003).

Do Not:

- Create an open forum at commencement. It is difficult to understand how a disclaimer can immunize school officials from criticism for excessive proselytizing or from profane or unpopular speech at commencement services sponsored by the school.

EMPLOYEES AND RELIGIOUS EXPRESSION

It would be unreasonable—and impossible—to expect teachers, administrators, and board members not to have religious beliefs. However, when employees walk through the schoolhouse gate, they assume the mantle of state authority and are required to take a neutral position while carrying out their duties. Administrators, teachers, and other school employees are prohibited by the Establishment Clause from encouraging or discouraging prayer, and from actively participating in religious activity with students at school ("Guidance on Constitutionally Protected Prayer," 2003). For example, teachers and other school officials should not participate in or lead student prayer or use their position as respected role models to promote or encourage outside religious activities such as revivals, church outings, or other faith-based activities. In short, the rights of school employees and school representatives can be limited or curtailed where efforts at religious expression could be reasonably interpreted as implying public school endorsement (Mawdsley & Russo, 2004). For example, a Louisiana district court issued a permanent injunction prohibiting an elementary school principal from distributing Bibles to fifth-grade students (*Jabr v. Rapides Parish School Board,* 2001). Similarly, the Eighth Circuit found the orchestration of baccalaureate ceremonies by senior class sponsors to violate the *Lemon* test. The court found that the school district took an active role in the production of "a service that continued the tradition of having local clergy offer prayers and religious messages" (*Warnock v. Archer,* 2006). This case points out that baccalaureate services should in fact be student organized and led.

Administrators, teachers, and other school employees may take part in religious activities where the overall context makes it clear that they are not acting in their official capacity ("Guidance on Constitutionally Protected Prayer," 2003). For example, it would seem appropriate for school employees to participate in a religious activity held at the school during the evening and in privately sponsored baccalaureate services. Teachers and others may elect to pray or read the Bible or other religious documents during the school day, as long as students are not involved, and they may wear nonobtrusive jewelry or religious symbols such as a cross or star of David.

Teachers and other employees may be disciplined and even terminated for promoting religious participation, even subtly. For example, fifth-grade teacher Roberts read silently from a Bible he habitually kept in plain view on his desk. In addition, a Christian poster was displayed in the classroom, and the classroom library contained two Christian books. Roberts did not read aloud or overtly proselytize to students. When a parent complained to the principal about Roberts's poster and the two books, the teacher was instructed to remove the Bible from his desk, not to read from the Bible during school time, and to remove the poster and two Christian books from the classroom. On appeal, the 10th Circuit Court affirmed the trial court ruling, reasoning that the school district acted properly in taking action to disapprove of classroom activity that appears to promote a particular religion (*Roberts v. Madigan,* 1990). Similarly, a district court in Florida upheld the dismissal of a teacher for consistently refusing to follow a corrective action plan that prohibited her from distributing Bibles and posting religious posters in her classroom (*Tuma v. Dade County Public Schools,* 1998).

Linking to PRACTICE

Do:

- Develop proactive policies that outline the religious rights and responsibilities of public school employees while on campus or representing the school at extracurricular events, field trips, or other off-campus school-sponsored activities.

Do Not:

- Permit school employees to lead, encourage, hinder, or participate in student religious expression on school grounds.

PRAYER AT SCHOOL BOARD MEETINGS   In *Lemon v. Kurtzman,* the U.S. Supreme Court articulated a three-pronged test to determine whether or not a governmental action is constitutional. Assuming that a school board has an obvious connection to public education, the Sixth Circuit found that prayer before a school board meeting violated all three prongs of *Lemon* (*Coles v. Cleveland Board of Education,* 1999). In a more recent example, a Tangipahoa Parish (Louisiana) School Board practice of starting board meetings with a sectarian prayer delivered by a board member, the superintendent, or a local minister was challenged by a parent (*Doe v. Tangipahoa*, 2005). The federal district court for eastern Louisiana noted that this and similar cases sit between two competing concepts: State-endorsed prayer is not permissible in public schools, but is permissible at the opening of a legislative session. The court also noted that school boards hold both a legislative and an educational function. Following the lead of the Sixth Circuit Court in *Coles,* the district court reasoned that a school board has an intimate relationship with the public school system. Therefore, the school board prayer violated *Lemon* and was thus unconstitutional.

On appeal, the Fifth Circuit determined that the 1983 U.S. Supreme Court case *Marsh v. Chambers* applied to school board prayers (*Doe v. Tangipahoa*, 2006). In *Marsh*, the court considered a challenge to a Nebraska practice of employing a chaplain to deliver religious invocations during legislative sessions. The court reasoned that historically the framers established a paid chaplain position for federal legislative sessions. Therefore, if the framers did not see a problem with federal legislative prayer or chaplaincy, why should this be a problem for a state legislative body? On review, the district court abandoned *Lemon* and applied the *Marsh* test to the prayer practice (*Doe v. Tangipahoa*, 2009). Using *Marsh* as a guide, the court concluded that despite numerous prayers that referenced Jesus specifically, the Tangipahoa school board prayers fell within the scope of legality under the Establishment Clause (Fetter-Harrott, 2010).

PUBLIC MONEY AND PRIVATE SCHOOLS

For the past half century, the U.S. Supreme Court and several circuit courts have drawn a relatively well-defined line in the sand between public money and aid to private schools. However, several recent decisions have significantly blurred this line and in some cases erased it altogether. This transition essentially began with *Agostini v. Felton* (1997), where a Supreme Court majority determined that several past decisions were "no longer good law." In *Agostini* the Court determined that Title I monies could be used to provide public employees to teach remedial classes at private schools, including religious schools. In doing so, the Court established two basic criteria for determining the constitutionality of such aid: (1) Can any religious indoctrination that occurs in those schools be reasonably attributed to governmental action, and (2) does the aid program have the primary effect of advancing or inhibiting religion? The Court followed this same logic in *Mitchell v. Helms* (2000) in upholding the constitutionality of the use of Title VI monies to purchase equipment for private schools in Jefferson Parish, Louisiana.

Vouchers

One of the more controversial topics is the use of public money to fund student attendance at private and parochial schools through the use of tax credits/deductions or vouchers. A *voucher* is a "payment the government makes to a parent, or an institution on a parent's behalf, to be used for a child's education expenses" (Education Commission of the States, 2002, p. 1). A *tax credit* provides a direct reduction to the tax liability of a qualifying individual, and a *tax deduction* is a reduction in taxable income made prior to calculating tax liability (Education Commission of the States,

2002). The constitutionality of publicly funded vouchers has been established at the federal level by the U.S. Supreme Court in *Zelman v. Simmons-Harris* (2002). In this case, the Court upheld a voucher program in Cleveland by concluding, "The Cleveland voucher program affords parents of eligible children genuine nonreligious options." The Court did not dispute that the program was established for the valid secular purpose of providing educational support for poor children in an admittedly failed school system. Rather, the Court focused on the single legal question of whether the Ohio program advances or inhibits religion. To answer this question, the Court considered the distinction between governmental programs that provide aid directly to religious schools and those programs in which state funds reach religious schools indirectly through the independent choices of numerous parents and students. In the latter case, the public funding is attributed to the student, who may choose to remain at a public school that receives funding according to average daily enrollment or to attend a religious school that receives funding by tuition. A majority of the Court had little trouble making this distinction and held that the Ohio voucher system did not violate the Establishment Clause of the First Amendment.

The U.S. Supreme Court has also considered the question of tax credits for contributions to support scholarships for private schools, many of which are religious in nature (*Arizona Christian School Tuition Organization v. Winn,* 2011). Arizona provides tax credits for contributions to school tuition organizations, or STOs. STOs use these contributions to provide scholarships to students attending private schools, many of which are religious. A group of Arizona taxpayers challenged the STO tax credit as a violation of Establishment Clause. The Court opined that a tax credit allows dissenting taxpayers to use their own funds in accordance with their own consciences. In this case, the STO tax credit does not "extrac[t] and spen[d]" a conscientious dissenter's funds in service of an establishment or "force a citizen to contribute" to a sectarian organization. Rather, taxpayers are free to pay their own tax bills without contributing to an STO, to contribute to a religious or secular STO of their choice, or to contribute to other charitable organizations.

With the federal question answered, the battleground now moves to the various states. In several states, voucher proponents face more restrictive state constitutional clauses than found in the federal Establishment Clause. These clauses are commonly referred to as "Blaine amendments" and effectively bar the use of public money for religious causes. Other state constitutions have provisions that protect individuals from being compelled to support any religious group without their consent. Currently 36 states have Blaine amendments; 18 states have both Blaine amendments and a consent clause. Only Louisiana, Maine, and North Carolina have neither (Darden, 2002).

Summary

In the past decade the legal battle between two equally determined segments of our society has intensified. On occasion, public school employees and students are vocal advocates of one segment or the other, often simultaneously in the same school. On other occasions, community groups create significant pressure on local schools to accommodate their particular religious preferences. Students, teachers, and community groups do have a legal right to practice and advance their religions, but not at the expense of others. Finding this balance in this emotional arena is exceedingly difficult. However, as America's schools become more ethnically and religiously diverse, failures to recognize, respect, and accommodate this increased diversity hold the potential of needlessly Balkanizing an already challenged public school system.

CONNECTING STANDARDS TO PRACTICE

LET US PRAY

Assistant Superintendent Sharon Grey was well aware of the religious views of new school board member Alison Watts. Consequently, Sharon was not surprised when Alison introduced a new policy for the board to consider. The proposed policy, entitled "Student Expression of Religious Viewpoints," would create a limited open forum at football games and commencement activities and allow students to speak at these events. The policy would require Riverboat High School administrators to put disclaimers in graduation and football programs that the student speech is not school sponsored. It also required the administration to consult with the student council membership and create a process for the neutral selection of students to speak at such events.

The proposed policy read, in part:

> To ensure that the school district does not discriminate against a student's publicly stated voluntary expression of a religious viewpoint and to eliminate any actual or perceived affirmative school sponsorship or attribution to the district of a student's expression of a religious viewpoint Riverboat School District shall adopt a policy, which must include the establishment of a limited open forum for student speakers at commencement activities and all high school home football

games. The policy regarding the limited open forum must also require the high school administration in consultation with the student council membership to: (1) Provide the forum in a manner that does not discriminate against a student's voluntary expression of a religious viewpoint or on an otherwise permissible subject; (2) Provide a method, based on neutral criteria, for the selection of student speakers at high school football games and graduation ceremonies; (3) Ensure that a student speaker does not engage in obscene, vulgar, offensively lewd, or indecent speech; and (4) State, in writing, that the student's speech does not reflect the endorsement, sponsorship, position, or expression of the district.

Question

Argue for or against the proposed policy to create a limited open forum at football games and commencement. Clarify the legal question. Cite ISLLC standards and case law (i.e., *Lee v. Weisman, Lamb's Chapel v. Center Moriches, Jones v. Clear Creek*, etc.) to support your answer. Write a letter or memorandum to the superintendent or school board president justifying your position.

CHAPTER 4

Student Privacy and First Amendment Rights

INTRODUCTION

The First Amendment protects the freedoms of religion, the press, association, and to petition the government for redress of grievances. This chapter addresses speech and association rights as they apply to public school students on and off campus. Students do have some rights to express their ideas and opinions in schools. However, student rights to expression in school are limited. Achieving the right balance between student freedom of expression and maintaining order is often difficult. But, understanding the importance of student rights to expression is part of being an ethical and humane school leader. Student rights to privacy of personal and academic records are defined by federal law. Understanding these rights is also part of effective school leadership. This chapter presents selected ethical and legal guidelines to aid in this understanding.

FOCUS QUESTIONS

1. Should there be a balance between providing a safe and efficient school and the rights of students to express an unpopular viewpoint?
2. What are the rights of students to confidentiality of their personal and academic records?
3. What rights to expression do students have?
4. When may student rights be suppressed?
5. What is meant by the term *true threat*?

KEY TERMS

Culture	Lifeworld	Systemsworld
Directory information	School culture	Threat assessment
FERPA	Social capital	

CASE STUDY
Shanna's Shirt

Ethan Miller finished his phone conversation with the superintendent with a sigh. The case of the Gay–Straight Club and Shanna's Shirt had turned into a real challenge. Ridge Woods High School served a rural Missouri community with an enrollment of 850 students. In September a group of students petitioned the school board to allow a "Gay–Straight Club" (GSC) to meet during the same times and places and have access to the same communication as the long-established Bible Club. After considerable community uproar, threatened lawsuits, and a dozen emotional meetings, the board of education decided to allow the club to meet during noninstruction time. After the first GSC meeting, two male and three female members of the GSC reported being sexually harassed by other students on campus based on their perceived sexual orientation. At least two parents of the students claiming to be harassed filed suit in federal court. The female teacher who was the GSC sponsor reported being taunted by students in the hallway and receiving harassing phone calls at home. The school district insurance company believed the school district was at risk of a significant jury award and encouraged a settlement with the student-plaintiffs and the sponsor.

The day after the school board agreed to settle, Shanna Tyler wore a T-shirt to school with the imprint "Homosexuality is Shameful. Romans 1:27" on the front and "Be ashamed. Our school has embraced what God has condemned" on the back. The district dress code states only that clothing may not advocate or advertise drugs, alcohol, or tobacco and may not contain lewd, profane, or vulgar language or symbols.

Apparently, several community groups were supporting Shanna's shirt and her message. Ethan's conversation with the superintendent had reinforced the point that many community members believed that homosexuality is sinful and were unhappy. At the same time, several members of the Gay–Straight Club reported to teachers and others that they were offended by the message. A few teachers had expressed to Ethan that he should send Shanna home until she agreed not to wear the shirt at school. Angry with the board settlement, several teachers supported Shanna's right to wear the shirt.

LEADERSHIP PERSPECTIVES

All schools are composed of complex student societies that have one thing in common: The "accepted" behavior in a school is normative and determined to a great extent by a clique of students, especially in middle school and high school, who formulate, model, and enforce the unofficial norms for acceptable dress and behavior by the rest of the student body. Lyle E. Schaller (2000) summarizes the importance of this point: "Students' perceptions of their school environment are more likely to influence their behavior than the perceptions of that same environment held by a principal or a school board member or a teacher or a parent or a taxpayer" (p. 14).

As important as student perceptions may be, school leaders have an obligation to maintain good order. In the opening case study, "Shanna's Shirt," Ethan Miller must decide to either allow Shanna to wear the shirt or to ban the wearing of the shirt on school grounds. Regardless of his choice, **ISLLC Standard 5B** requires that Ethan apply self-awareness, reflective practice, transparency, and ethical behavior to the problem of Shanna's shirt. He also needs knowledge of the various policies, laws, and regulations enacted by state, local, and federal authorities that guide his decision. The conflict presented in "Shanna's Shirt" is relatively clear. Shanna is expressing her displeasure with what she perceives as an unfair and unwise decision by the school board. She is also expressing her religious view that homosexuality is sinful. Several community members and teachers are supportive of Shanna's message. Other students report being offended by the message. Ethan Miller is correct in considering balancing the legal rights of students with the need to maintain good order and harmony in the school. Both good order and Shanna's First Amendment rights are important, but which should prevail? What rights do students have to express their growing independence? What rights do school leaders have to suppress unpleasant or critical speech in order to maintain a "safe, efficient, and effective learning environment"? What ethical principles should guide Ethan's considerations? This chapter is designed to provide guidance in the often difficult choices inherent in this balance.

LIFEWORLDS AND SYSTEMS: POLICIES, PEOPLE, AND SCHOOL CULTURE

ISLLC Standard 2 calls for school leaders who "promote the success of every student by advocating, nurturing, and sustaining a school culture . . . conducive to student learning." There should be little doubt that understanding the importance of school culture is a significant part of effective school leadership. Sergiovanni (2000) states, "Most successful school leaders will tell you that getting the culture right and paying attention to how parents, teachers, and students define and experience meaning are two widely accepted rules for creating effective schools" (p. 1). But, what is school culture, and how do we recognize it when we see it? Rebore (2003) says that school cultures "consist of those attitudes, beliefs and values, feelings, and opinions that are shared by a significant number of their influential members and that are communicated to others" (p. 145). In other words, *school culture* is the *normative* glue that holds a particular school together by defining and perpetuating how administrators, teachers, parents, and students interact with one another (Sergiovanni, 2000). The significance of this normative glue is that teachers, students, and parents who are new to the campus are soon influenced and invariably engulfed by the campus culture.

The German philosopher Jürgen Habermas (1987) provides a theoretical framework and language system for understanding school culture. Habermas views all social systems, including corporations, football teams, and families, as existing simultaneously as a *systemsworld* and as a *lifeworld*. Viewing school districts, schools within a district, and classrooms within a school as social systems is quite compatible with Habermas's concepts of lifeworlds and systems. The *lifeworld* is represented by the normative behavior determined and perpetuated by the individuals (employees, students, players, parents, and children) who make up a particular environment. The lifeworld is symbolized by culture, community, and person. *Culture* represents the *learned* ways of believing, valuing, and behaving that bind people together (Gollnick & Chinn, 2004). These shared cultural patterns create and normalize a general agreement among the participants that becomes a natural and accepted way of communicating, behaving, and reacting to one another and to the environment. One's own culture is viewed as natural, correct, and superior to other ways of thinking, believing, and behaving. Consequently, cultural influences become an unconscious blinder and a lens through which participants view and judge the world.

Community is the heart of a school's lifeworld (Sergiovanni, 2000). Communities generally have four common elements: styles of dress, music, language symbols, and ritual. Students may be members of several communities including a religious organization, a school volleyball team, and a Boy Scout troop. Students are also members of a school community who often share a common style of dress, have similar tastes in music, communicate in sometimes indecipherable language (at least to the uninitiated adult ear), and have well-understood rituals that govern how students interact with one another.

Community membership is important because the participants know that they are connected to others, feel known and cared for by others, and are part of a social group that is valuable (Sergiovanni, 2000). In short, community membership develops social capital. ***Social capital*** refers to the resources, social support networks, and trust that are generated by positive relationships among people (Sergiovanni, 2000). Two potential sources of student social capital are family and school. Access to social capital is particularly important in reducing school violence. As Payne, Gottfredson, and Gottfredson (2003) state:

> Supportive and collaborative relationships and common norms and goals reported by teachers [are] internalized by . . . students, resulting in higher levels of student bonding. These higher bonding levels . . . lead to less delinquency. With improvements in communal school organization and student bonding, schools . . . experience a reduction in disorder. (pp. 772–773)

Review the case study "Shanna's Shirt." Membership in clubs such as the Bible Club and Gay–Straight Alliance can be sources of social capital for students and promote student bonding. Communal school organization and student bonding are the foundations for providing school personnel, students, and visitors with the safe and secure building environment called for in **ISLLC Standard 3**. In this case study, communal organization and student bonds are being stressed. At least some teachers and students are supporting Shanna. Others are offended by the message. Ethan Miller is faced with a difficult choice. If he bans the shirt, some members of the school community will be unhappy. If he allows Shanna to continue to express her antihomosexual views, those members opposed to or offended by this view will be unhappy. Such is the life of a school principal.

▶ ISLLC Standard 3

Person is represented by the significance, identity, and personal value individuals derive from their community memberships (Habermas, 1987; Sergiovanni, 2000). The important point is this: Membership in various subcultures or communities creates and perpetuates the significance, identity, and personal value that all human beings crave. This is an important point. In a school community that promotes social capital, student bonding, and a sense of community, the students and the teachers derive individual value as a person from the interaction of the larger school culture and the various subcultures of which they are members (Stader, 2011).

Membership in one subculture or community can conflict with that in other subcultures (Gollnick & Chinn, 2004). Membership in a community religious organization may conflict with district policy regarding the organization of a Gay–Straight Club. This conflict between school communities sometimes results in harassment, ostracism, and abuse. Such conflict is almost always at odds with good order and discipline in a school. For example, according to a recent National Center for Education Statistics report on school violence, the most common reason reported by students for bringing guns, knives, or other weapons to school is because of bullying by other students or for protection from gangs (Addington, Ruddy, Miller, Defoe, & Chandler, 2002).

In schools, culture is represented by the norms, behaviors, and traditions transmitted from one generation of students and teachers to subsequent generations. School culture defines and perpetuates all student–student and student–teacher interactions on that campus. However, *the normative culture of every school is slightly different, and no two school cultures even within the same district or town are exactly alike*. It is the differences in individual school cultures that establish and perpetuate the normative behaviors of students, teachers, and administrators in that school.

The *systemsworld* consists of the management designs, rules, accounting systems, and schedules that provide a framework for teachers and students to engage in the practice of teaching and learning (Sergiovanni, 2000). The systemsworld provides the enforced norms that allow schools to function in a relatively calm and orderly manner. How students are grouped, the lunch schedule, the procedures for checking out of school, and rules against fighting, bullying, and intimidation are examples of school systemsworlds. In other words, the systemsworld is represented by the *policies* necessary for schools to function.

ISLLC Standards 3, 3A, and 3B

The interrelationship between the lifeworld and the systemsworld establishes the written and unwritten rules that create and perpetuate the normative environment of the school. This relationship is symbolized in Figure 4–1.

The important point is this: *Both the systemsworld (policy designed to promote order) and lifeworld (the needs of people for a sense of belonging and identity) are essential to a positive school culture*. When in balance, the lifeworld and systemsworld

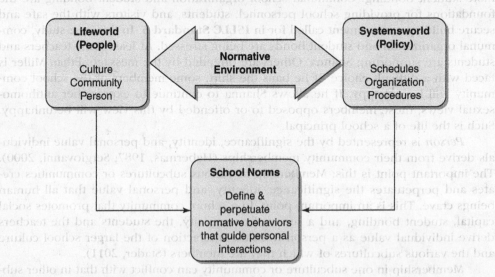

FIGURE 4–1 The lifeworld–systemsworld relationship.

function cooperatively for a positive and engaging school culture. However, the systemsworld and the lifeworld are perpetually in competition for dominance of the school culture (Habermas, 1987; Sergiovanni, 2000).

People and Policy: A Fight for Dominance

Habermas (1987) contends that much of the controversy concerning school policy can be understood as a fight for or against the system domination (or colonization) of student lifeworlds. Habermas points to the trend toward litigation-proof policy and the overregulation of the curriculum as examples. Rather than leading to a positive school culture, this overregulation leads to depersonalization, inhibition of innovation, breakdown of responsibility, and immobility. This happens because these enforced norms are implemented without consideration of the persons concerned, or of their needs and interests. Overregulation and reliance on systems solutions (policies and rules) result in a dominant systemsworld. Domination by the systemsworld, which Sergiovanni (2000) contends is common, creates an oppressive, dysfunctional, and alienating school culture. In systems-dominated schools, the rules and procedures become a means to an end with little regard for lifeworld issues. In these schools, student lifeworlds are viewed negatively, and social order is constructed exclusively from the system perspective (Habermas, 1987). What is often overlooked in these schools is that culture, community, and person are basic needs. When these needs are not met, students turn to their own subculture, usually at odds with school purposes, in search of belonging and meaning (Schaller, 2000; Sergiovanni, 2000). In short, *the failure to understand and appreciate the importance of student lifeworlds often undermines the very purpose of the policies designed to promote order.*

The relationship between lifeworlds and systems in the normative environment is illustrated in Table 4–1.

TABLE 4–1	The Impact of the Normative Environment on Student Lifeworlds*	
Lifeworld Components	**Balanced Lifeworld and System**	**Systems-Dominated School**
Culture	Productive and well-ordered culture, shared goals, legitimate authority.	Loss of cultural meaning, challenges to authority common, legitimacy of authority questioned.
Community	Positive and well-ordered student/faculty and student/student interpersonal relationships.	Lack of purpose, fractured student/student and student/faculty interpersonal relationships.
Person	Sense of personal worth and belonging. Motivation to conform to written and unwritten school norms, sense of purpose, importance, and individual value gained from positive social interactions in the school.	Sense of anonymity and hopelessness. Withdrawal of motivation to conform to written and unwritten school norms; individual value gained from student-generated lifeworlds. Rule compliance by coercion.

Note: Based on Habermas, J. (1987). *The theory of communicative action: Vol. 2. Lifeworld and system: A critique of functionalist reason* (T. McCarthy, Trans.) (pp. 142–143). Boston, MA: Beacon Press.

A thin line often separates orderly and positive schools from negative and toxic schools or, at the other extreme, overly permissive school cultures. Make no mistake: There is a time for decisive action, just as there should be times for understanding, compassion, and reasonableness. The leadership challenge is determining when and under what circumstances it is appropriate to choose which action. As illustrated by **ISLLC Standard 3**, Ethan Miller must balance the needs of the student lifeworld with his obligation to provide a safe and efficient school facility.

ISLLC Standard 3 ▶

Linking to PRACTICE

Do:

- Develop objective measures of the relative health of school and classroom culture. For example, student attendance, frequency of office referrals, and levels of cooperativeness of student interpersonal interactions are good measures of the relative health of school culture.
- Develop annual measurable objectives to improve school culture. Use research/literature-based strategies and measurable evaluative criteria.

- Recognize that a balance between people and policy is necessary for a healthy school culture.
- Understand that student lifeworlds will exist, either supported by school policies or at cross purposes to them.

Do Not:

- Become overly dependent on rules and policy to maintain order. A well-ordered, positive school culture results from a combination of rules and personal interactions, not from rigid rule compliance.

STUDENT RIGHTS

ISLLC Standard 3 ▶

The legal authority of school leaders to develop, implement, and enforce rules, regulations, and policies designed to establish and maintain good order and discipline is well established. This responsibility is reflected in **ISLLC Standard 3**. At first glance, students may seem to enjoy a broad array of rights. However, court decisions and administrative agency interpretations of statutes typically limit many of these rights to narrow sets of circumstances. The following sections consider these rights.

STUDENT RECORDS

The Family Educational Rights and Privacy Act (*FERPA*) is an example of spending clause legislation designed to protect student educational records. FERPA (20 U.S.C. 1232) was enacted in 1974 by Congress in response to concerns expressed by educators, parents, students, and institutions regarding student academic and personal information. FERPA affects all public and private schools that receive federal funds. *Balancing Student Privacy and School Safety: A Guide to the Family Rights and Privacy Act for Elementary and Secondary Schools* is available free of charge from http://edpubs.ed.gov. This excellent guide, from which much of this information was taken, presents an overview of student privacy as defined by FERPA. Informal e-mail responses to questions about FERPA are available from the Family Policy

Compliance Office. The most germane provisions of FERPA can be summarized as follows:

- Parents have the right to inspect and review their child's education records, defined as all records, files, documents, and other materials related to a student and maintained by the school. All records regardless of medium including handwriting, videotape, computer files, print and so forth are subject to FERPA. This right transfers to the eligible student at 18 years of age.
- Parents or eligible students have the right to ask for a review of records that they believe to be inaccurate or misleading. Schools must respond promptly to such requests. A formal hearing may be requested if the school refuses to amend disputed records.
- Schools must have written permission from the parent or eligible student in order to release any information from a student's educational record without consent, *except:*
  - School officials with legitimate educational interest
  - Other schools to which a student is transferring
  - Specified officials for audit or evaluation purposes
  - For compliance with a judicial order or subpoena
  - Appropriate officials in cases of health and safety emergencies
  - State and local authorities
- Schools must retain a written log with the educational records of each student indicating all individuals, agencies, or organizations that have requested or obtained access to a student's educational records, including the interest that each has in obtaining the information.

Directory Information

FERPA permits schools to designate certain information, such as names, addresses, telephone numbers, degrees and honors received, major field of study, participation in officially recognized activities and sports, dates of attendance, and weight and height of athletic team members, as *directory information*. Schools are required to provide a yearly notice to parents and eligible students of any designated categories of directory information and allow a reasonable time for parents or eligible students to refuse to allow release of this information without prior consent. Once this information has been designated as directory information, the school may release this information regarding nonobjecting students to any agency or requesting party. For example, schools routinely release honor roll lists, scholarship awards, and individual athletic statistics to local newspapers. Congress now requires public and private secondary schools to release to requesting military recruiters lists of the names, addresses, and telephone numbers of nonobjecting students.

The Supreme Court and FERPA

During the 2002 term, the U.S. Supreme Court heard two FERPA cases. The first, *Owasso Independent School District v. Falvo* (2002), considered peer grading. The Supreme Court granted certiorari to consider only the legal question "Does peer grading violate FERPA?" The Court held that it does not (*Owasso Independent School District v. Falvo,*

2002). The Court reasoned that student papers being graded by another student are not at this stage maintained by the teacher and that each student grader is not a person acting for an educational institution. *Gonzaga University v. Doe* (2002) considered whether or not a FERPA violation by an institution creates a private right of action (i.e., the legal right to sue). The case involved a student enrolled in the teacher certification program at Gonzaga University. Washington state law required that all teacher candidates be certified by the graduating college to be of "good moral character." A Gonzaga official, after overhearing a conversation between two students, revealed to the state agency that student Doe was suspected of sexual misconduct. Doe was denied certification by the state agency. Doe learned of the allegation, brought suit under FERPA, and was awarded $1.155 million by a jury in state court (*Doe v. Gonzaga University,* 2001). On review, however, the U.S. Supreme Court held that FERPA created no personal rights to enforcement. Consequently, individual students whose FERPA rights have been violated seem to have little recourse to remedy the situation (Daggett, 2002).

Linking to PRACTICE

Do:

- Develop clear district and campus policies concerning the privacy of student records.
- Beware of blanket parental consent forms. These forms may be appropriate for such publications as school sports programs, band/choir memberships, or honor roll lists. However, any publication such as a school newspaper or newsletter that may reveal more personally identifiable information should have parental approval before publication.
- Communicate to parents, students, and teachers the importance of confidentiality, the rights of students and parents,

and under what circumstances records will be shared.
- Clearly outline and regularly communicate to parents and students what directory information may be included in school publications.
- Ensure that student records are accessed only for educationally legitimate reasons.
- Develop a system of accurately logging requests for records and the disposition of each request.
- Consider separating discipline files from academic files. Both are covered by FERPA, but separate files provide another layer of protection for students.

STUDENTS AND THE FIRST AMENDMENT

The freedom of speech is considered so important in our society that some *compelling* interest must be present before that right can be suppressed. With this high standard of review, there are surprisingly few cases where courts have found that the speech rights of *private citizens* are not protected. For example, almost 100 years ago, Justice Holmes of the U.S. Supreme Court opined that "falsely shouting fire in a theater" is not protected speech (*Schenck v. United States,* 1919). Later, the U.S. Supreme Court has held that "fighting words" (*Chaplinsky v. New Hampshire,* 1942) and "true threats" (*Watts v. United States,* 1969) are not protected by the First Amendment. Most recently, the Court has held that "hate speech" (*R. A. V. v. City of St. Paul,* 1992) and intimidating symbols such as cross burnings (*Virginia v. Black,* 2003) are not protected. With these few exceptions (fighting words, true threats, hate speech, and intimidation) the

First Amendment is designed to protect unpopular speech—including student. As District Court Justice Sippel states in *Beussink v. Woodland* Schools (1998):

> Indeed, it is provocative and challenging speech . . . which is most in need of the protections of the First Amendment. Popular speech is not likely to provoke censure. It is unpopular speech that invites censure. It is unpopular speech which needs the protection of the First Amendment. The First Amendment was designed for this very purpose.

Establishing Student First Amendment Rights

The U.S. Supreme Court first recognized student First Amendment rights in *West Virginia Board of Education v. Barnette* (1943). The West Virginia Board of Education required students to salute the flag while reciting the Pledge of Allegiance. After several Jehovah's Witnesses were expelled for refusing to salute the flag, the court recognized that as a state actor public schools were bound by the Fourteenth Amendment to respect students' First Amendment rights. However, the U.S. Supreme Court has carved out an entirely different body of First Amendment law for public school students in a series of four cases: *Tinker v. Des Moines School District* (1969), *Bethel School District No. 403 v. Fraser* (1986), *Hazelwood School District v. Kuhlmeier* (1988), and, most recently, *Morse v. Frederick* (2007).

The trend toward respecting student First Amendment rights on school grounds continued in *Tinker v. Des Moines School District* (1969). This is the famous "black armband" case. Several students, including John and Mary Beth Tinker, planned to wear black armbands to school to protest U.S. involvement in the Viet Nam war. After hearing of these plans, principals in the district met and adopted a policy that prohibited the wearing of armbands to school. John Tinker wore his armband the next day, refused to remove the armband, and was suspended from school (Stader, 2001a). In a well-written decision containing probably the most often quoted citation in education law, Mr. Justice Fortas established the concept that

> it can hardly be argued that either students or teachers shed their constitutional rights to freedom of speech or expression at the schoolhouse gate . . .
> the constitution says that Congress (and the States) may not abridge the right to free speech. This provision means what it says.

First and foremost, the Supreme Court attempted to validate the First Amendment rights of students while deliberately recognizing that students do not have the same expressive rights inside the schoolhouse gate as they do outside the gate. The Court recognized that unabridged student speech would likely result in chaos. Justice Fortas tempered student First Amendment rights as follows:

> [A student] may express his [or her] opinions, even on controversial subjects . . . . if he [or she] does so without *materially and substantially interfering with the requirements of appropriate discipline in the operation of the school and without colliding with the rights of others.* But conduct by the student, in class or out of it, which for any reason—whether it stems from time, place, or type of behavior—*materially disrupts classwork or involves substantial disorder or invasion of the rights of others is,* of course, not immunized by the constitutional guarantee of freedom of speech.

The first prong of *Tinker* is the material and substantial disruption test. The decisive factor in *Tinker* was the lack of evidence of disruption caused by the armbands. It is certainly appropriate for students to express their opinions, and some tolerance for minor disruption to the school day seems justifiable. However, at some point it certainly might be appropriate to take action to maintain good order, discipline, and harmony. The problem, of course, is how much disruption must occur to justify taking action? It is clear that school leaders need not wait until complete chaos before acting. In addition, past evidence of unrest or disruption can often suffice as justification for suppressing student speech on school grounds.

The second prong of *Tinker* considers the collision with the rights of others. The *Tinker* Court established the concept that schools should be a forum for ideas and that these ideas and expressions should not be suppressed simply because they make school officials uncomfortable. This is particularly important when students peacefully express opinions that are counter to the beliefs or views of others within the school and community. The question then becomes, who is causing the disruption? For example, controversy followed when Aaron Fricke was denied permission to bring a male date to the school prom based on widespread student and community uproar. Justice Pettine stated, in part:

I have concluded that even a legitimate interest in school discipline does not outweigh a student's right to peacefully express his views in an appropriate time, place, and manner. The First Amendment does not tolerate mob rule by unruly school children. (*Fricke v. Lynch*, 1980)

There is little doubt that *Tinker* is ambiguous. For example, assume that a student takes an unpopular viewpoint that creates some controversy among community members, teachers, and some students. Schools are supposed to be forums for ideas, and these ideas are not to be suppressed simply because some individuals do not want to hear the message, right? The questions then become: (1) At what point does the controversy become "substantially disruptive," and (2) who is causing the disruption, the student or those opposed to her views? The answer, of course, is that it depends. The fundamental protections of the First Amendment and the ambiguity of *Tinker* make balancing the rights of students with good order and discipline to be particularly challenging. One thing is clear: Students do have the right to express unpopular opinions; they just do not have the right to disrupt the school or invade the rights of others.

Lewd or Profane Speech

Student free expression rights do not extend to derogatory, disrespectful, profane, or vulgar speech. Restrictions on this type of student expression were clarified by the U.S. Supreme Court in *Bethel School District No. 403 v. Fraser* (1986). Student Fraser, in spite of the warnings from two of his teachers, delivered a sexually explicit nominating speech at an assembly for a fellow student running for elective school office. During his speech, Fraser repeatedly referred to his candidate "in terms of an elaborate, graphic, and explicit sexual metaphor." Fraser was suspended from school for 3 days. Fraser and his parents, citing a violation of his First Amendment rights, sought judicial relief. On appeal, the Supreme Court ruled in favor of the district. The Court held that schools can discipline students for indecent speech and "nothing in the Constitution prohibits (schools) from insisting that certain modes of expression are inappropriate and subject to sanctions." In *Fraser,* the Court established that school officials' legitimate need to suppress lewd or vulgar speech or speech that runs counter to the educational mission of the school at *school-sponsored* events outweighs the First Amendment rights of students. The Court was careful to point out that the same speech off-campus would be protected.

School-Sponsored Speech

The extent of student freedom of expression related to curricular speech or speech that may reasonably be viewed as sanctioned by the school was defined in *Hazelwood School District v. Kuhlmeier* (1988). In this case, members of the school newspaper wrote two articles, one concerning divorce, the other teenage sexuality. Principal Reynolds, under pressure of time, elected to delete the articles because he was concerned that the students and parents in the articles could be easily identified. In the process, several other articles were also deleted from the paper. Students petitioned the courts that this censorship violated their First Amendment rights. In a 5–4 decision, the Court held that "educators do not offend the First Amendment by exercising editorial control over the style and content of student speech in school-sponsored expressive activities." In short, school personnel control expression that could reasonably be seen as bearing the stamp of approval of the school. The *Hazelwood* ruling further expanded administrative control of student expression by finding schools to be a nonpublic forum. Lower courts have been relatively consistent in applying this standard to any student speech that could reasonably be viewed as bearing the imprimatur of the school.

Speech Promoting Drug Use

The most recent U.S. Supreme Court review of student speech rights at school-sponsored events was *Morse v. Frederick* (2007). During a school-sponsored outing to watch the Olympic Torch Relay pass through Juneau, Alaska, Joseph Frederick, a high school senior, unfurled a banner reading "Bong Hits 4 Jesus." Principal Deborah Morse asked Joseph to take the banner down. When Joseph refused, Morse confiscated the banner and suspended Joseph. The Ninth Circuit Court held that Joseph's speech was protected and that Morse violated Joseph's free speech rights by confiscating the banner and punishing Joseph. On review, the U.S. Supreme Court held that school authorities may "restrict student speech at a school event, when that speech is reasonably viewed as promoting illegal drug use." It is important to note that the court refused to go any further and allow the restriction of any speech on school grounds that could plausibly be interpreted as commenting on a political or social issue. In his concurring opinion, Justice Alito (joined by Justice Kennedy) clearly stated that he joined the opinion of court on the understanding that (1) it goes no further than to hold that a public school may restrict speech that a reasonable observer would interpret as advocating illegal drug use and (2) it provides no support for any restriction of speech that can plausibly be interpreted as commenting on any political or social issue such as speech about "the wisdom of the war on drugs or of legalizing marijuana for medicinal use." This type of speech would be protected. It is also clear that Frederick's banner is protected speech outside school.

Hate Speech

Hate speech is a common problem on many campuses, regardless of location. In 2007, 10% of students ages 12 to 18 reported that someone at school had used hate-related words against them, and 35% reported seeing hate-related graffiti at school during the school year (Robers, Zhang, & Truman, 2010). Hate speech is not protected speech, and school leaders have little difficulty justifying disciplinary action. Some speech and symbols are easy to identity as hate speech and generally acknowledged as unacceptable at school. Other speech and symbols, such as the Confederate flag, may be more difficult. However, courts have been supportive of school rules banning the Confederate flag and other symbols from school grounds and school-sponsored activities when school leaders can show that similar symbols in the past have resulted in disruption (see, for example, *B. W. A. v. Farmington R-7 School District*, 2009; *Barr v. Lafon*, 2008; *Defoe v. Spiva*, 2010; *Scott v. School Board of Alachua County*, 2003; *West v. Derby Unified School District No. 260,* 2000, cert. denied).

Although courts have virtually unanimously supported bans on Confederate flags and other similar symbols when districts can reasonably forecast disruption, anti-homosexual speech as hate speech that invades the rights of sexual-minority and questioning youth is an area of law that continues to emerge. For example, the Ninth Circuit used social science research to support a Poway School District ban on a T-shirt that read "*Homosexuality is Shameful. Romans 1:27*" (*Harper v. Poway*, 2006; note that this ruling was later vacated as moot by the U.S. Supreme Court, 2007). Student Harper wore the shirt after a student-led Day of Silence activity in support of sexual-minority youth in the school. The court reasoned that the language of the shirt was especially hurtful to sexual-minority and questioning youth. Consequently the message violated the second prong of *Tinker* by colliding with the rights of others in the school. However, in a similar set of circumstances, the Seventh Circuit Court of Appeals used comparable research and logic to conclude that a "Be Happy, Not Gay" message was not "fighting words," did not create material and substantial disruption, and did not collide with the rights of sexual-minority and questioning youth in the school. The court concluded that there is no legal right to prevent criticism or "hurt feelings" defense (*Nuxoll v. Indian Prairie School District*, 2011).

Regardless of the circumstances and/or place of student speech, courts always use the principles that have been set forth on speech in general (fighting words, true threat, hate speech, and intimidation) and the special circumstances of schools (*Tinker, Fraser, Hazelwood,* and *Morse*) to reach a decision. Courts consider the amount of the disruption caused by the speech, the content of the speech (lewd or profane or promoting drug use), whether or not the speech is school sponsored, and whether or not any restrictions on speech are viewpoint neutral. Review the case study "Shanna's Shirt" again. The message on her shirt is not a threat, is not lewd or profane, at least according to the Seventh Circuit is not fighting words, cannot reasonably be viewed as promoting illegal drug use, and one can assume the message is not school-sponsored speech. Therefore, *Tinker* applies, right?

Now, think about the two prongs of *Tinker*, "material and substantial disruption" and "collides with the rights of others." Has enough disruption occurred? Does the message collide with the rights of others? As pointed out, courts are divided on whether or not antihomosexual speech collides with the rights of sexual-minority or questioning youth and their supporters. Some general guidelines exist, but significant areas of ambiguity also exist.

STUDENT DRESS

As of 2008, 22 states authorized schools and districts to implement dress code and/or uniform policies (Colasanti, 2008a). The U.S. Supreme Court has not ruled on a dress code case and, in spite of several opportunities, seems at this point unlikely to do so. However, since the mid-1980s, and particularly in the wake of the school violence outbreak in 1999, lower courts have consistently empowered school administrators to exercise a great degree of control over student dress (DeMitchell, Fossey, & Cobb, 2000). Unless specifically prohibited by state law (Massachusetts, for example, prohibits dress codes except for health and safety reasons), it can be assumed that school districts may adopt reasonable and viewpoint-neutral student dress codes. For example, the Sixth Circuit Court recently indicated that three criteria were critical in determining the legality of school dress code policies: (1) a higher level of scrutiny is appropriate only for viewpoint-specific cases, (2) school officials have greater discretion in prohibiting obscene, vulgar, and/or disruptive clothing, and (3) even more discretion is allowed if the speech or dress can be considered school sponsored (*Castorina v. Madison County School Board*, 2001; also see *Blau v. Fort Thomas*, 2005, for similar logic).

Controversial dress usually involves symbolic expression such as choice and style of wearing apparel or T-shirt messages. Unfortunately, guiding case law is significantly intertwined and does not provide clear guidance. Courts have supported bans on "sagging pants" (*Bivens v. Albuquerque Public Schools*, 1995), the wearing of "Drugs Suck" T-shirts (*Broussard v. School Board of City of Norfolk*, 1992), and the banning of Marilyn Manson T-shirts (*Boroff v. Van Wert City Board of Education*, 2000). Clothing or symbols linked to gang membership can usually be banned when the district can demonstrate a gang problem or when the dress or symbol can be linked with disruptive behavior (*Chalifoux v. New Cancy Independent School District*, 1997; *Jeglin v. San Jacinto Unified School District*, 1993).

Other courts have supported student rights. The Western District Court of Oklahoma, in recognizing that the banning of wearing apparel advertising alcoholic beverages was not unconstitutional, held that a school district ban on apparel with alcohol symbols did not apply to a senior class T-shirt that read, "The Best of the Night's Adventures are Reserved for People With Nothing Planned." This slogan was for Bacardi rum (*McIntire v. Bethel School District*, 1992). In another example of supporting student rights, the Third Circuit Court held that a Jeff Foxworthy T-shirt did not violate a "racial harassment policy" established in response to a history of racial disturbances at a high school (*Sypniewski v. Warren Hills Regional Board of Education*, 2002).

A similar line of reasoning was applied by the Eastern District Court of Michigan to a T-shirt with a message critical of President George W. Bush. Using *Tinker v. Des Moines* (1969), the court held that the banning of the shirt based on an unsubstantiated fear that a minority viewpoint may create opposition does not justify a preemptive ban on a clearly political message (*Barber v. Dearborn*, 2003). Following the same logic of lack of evidence of disruption, the District Court of Minnesota ordered an injunction barring a school principal from banning a "straight pride" sweatshirt in a Minnesota high school. The court refused to state that such a message could not be legally banned. But, absent any evidence that the decision was based on a reasonable belief of disruption other than a few complaints from students, the court had no option but to issue the injunction (*Chambers v. Babbitt*, 2001).

The concept of school uniforms has also gained acceptance and judicial support. Numerous states allow districts to implement school uniform policies, but no state requires that districts do so (Colasanti, 2008a). Proponents believe school uniforms (1) decrease violence, (2) prevent gang-related attire, (3) instill discipline, (4) help students concentrate, and (5) aid in the recognition of intruders. Regardless of the efficacy of these benefits to schools, courts have consistently supported school uniform policies. For example, a district court in Texas concluded that choice of clothing in school is not protected by the First Amendment (*Littlefield v. Forney Independent School District*, 2000). In a similar decision, the Fifth Circuit Court concluded that school boards, not the federal courts, have the authority to decide what constitutes appropriate dress in schools (*Canady v. Bossier Parish School Board*, 2001).

Linking to PRACTICE

Do:

- Create opportunities for open discussion with parents, community members, teachers, and students regarding appropriate school attire.
- Honor diverse views. Beware of viewpoint discrimination.
- Maintain accurate records documenting disruption created by various symbols. These records may be invaluable in justifying decisions to ban certain expressive items.
- Develop policies that address clothing items with symbols that are profane, vulgar, sexually suggestive, or advocate alcohol, tobacco, and other drug use. These policies are almost always defensible.
- Consider dress code and uniform policies as part of a comprehensive plan to promote a safe, orderly, and positive school culture.

- Understand that dress code and uniform policies are not "silver bullets" to solve all school discipline and safety concerns.
- Objectively evaluate the effectiveness of dress code and uniform policies.
- Beware of dress code and uniform policies that can become troublesome enough (significant enforcement time, student time out of class, disagreements among faculty, and parent dissatisfaction, to name a few) to outweigh the potential or actual benefit gained from having the policy in the first place.

Do Not:

- Overreact.
- Suppress the peaceful expression of minority viewpoints simply because some individuals do not wish to hear the message.
- Wait for complete chaos before banning disruptive speech.

LIBRARY BOOKS

The U.S. Supreme Court considered the balance between the authority of a school board to determine the content and subject matter of books in a school library and the First Amendment rights of students in *Board of Education v. Pico* (1982). In 1975, Three Island Trees School District sought removal from the high school library of several books that a politically conservative organization had determined to be objectionable. The board appointed a review committee. The committee recommended returning several of the books, placing a few on restricted shelves, and removing two from the library. The board voted to remove all but one book. The U.S. Supreme Court upheld the challenge to the board action by declaring,

> Local school boards may not remove books from school library shelves simply because they dislike the ideas contained in those books and seek by their removal to prescribe what shall be orthodox in politics, nationalism, religion, or other matters of opinion.

Using *Pico* as a guide, an Arkansas federal district court reached a similar decision in *Counts v. Cedarville School District* (2003). The district board had voted to restrict students' access to the Harry Potter books. The court ordered the return of the books to the unrestricted section of the library on the grounds that the restrictions violated students' First Amendment rights to read and receive information. The court noted that school boards do have considerable discretion in the operation of the school district. However, the school board is still bound by the Bill of Rights.

THREATS

In light of recent acts of school violence, statements or writings that could once be passed off as adolescent braggadocio must be taken seriously (Stader, 2000). The U.S. Supreme Court has established that a threat that is not true is protected speech (*Watts v. U.S.*, 1969). The Court later defined true threats in *Virginia v. Black* (2003) as follows: "True threats encompass those statements where the speaker means to communicate a serious expression of intent to commit an act of unlawful violence to a particular individual or group of individuals." The most common approach taken by the courts is based on the vantage point of the speaker and/or the vantage point of the recipient (Hyman, 2006). In student threat cases, courts use the "reasonable person" standard. For the speaker's vantage point, if a reasonable person could foresee that his or her words could be taken as a threat, then it is a threat. For the recipient's vantage point, if a reasonable person could perceive the statement as a threat, then it is a threat.

Let us take a brief look at two cases that illustrate these two vantage points. A good example of the vantage point of the speaker may be *Lovell v. Poway Unified School District* (1996). At the end of a long day, in an effort to change her schedule, student Lovell (then 15) arrived before the school counselor. The counselor informed Lovell that the classes she had finally arranged were overloaded and refused to change Lovell's schedule. At this point Lovell either said, "I'm so angry, I could just shoot someone" (Lovell's version) or, "If you don't give me this schedule change, I'm going to shoot you" (counselor's version). Both parties agree that Lovell immediately apologized, and the counselor made the schedule changes. In upholding the suspension of Lovell, the court reasoned that the central issue is not whether the student actually meant what he or she said; rather, the entire factual context, including the reaction of listeners, must be considered. Basically, the result turns on whether a reasonable person under the circumstances *should have foreseen that her words would appear threatening*.

In a rare *en banc* review using the vantage point of the recipient, the Eighth Circuit Court supported the expulsion of a middle school student (Doe) for writing a threatening letter at home describing the rape, sodomy, and murder of his ex-girl-friend. The letter remained at home and was allegedly not meant to become public. When a third party delivered the letter to the girl, she became frightened, went home early from school, and slept with the lights on for several nights. Doe was expelled for the remainder of his eighth-grade year. The trial court concluded that the letter was not a "true threat" and ordered Doe reinstated. On appeal, a divided panel of the Eighth Circuit Court affirmed the district court's decision. On further review, this ruling was vacated and the entire Eighth Circuit Court conducted an *en banc* rehearing. Citing the *Lovell* reasonable person standard, the court concluded that based on the tone of the letter, they were not surprised that those who read it interpreted it as a threat. Considering the facts and the reaction of the girlfriend, the court upheld the expulsion of Doe (*Doe v. Pulaski County Special School District,* 2002). The important point is that *the reaction of the recipient clearly established that the letter was perceived as a true threat.* As Stader (2011) writes, "In reality, it is the reaction of the participants and the impact of the statement on others that is important. If it sounds like a threat, if the speaker appears threatening, or if others react as if a threat has been made, then it is a threat" (p. 145).

A general decision-making guide is presented in Figure 4–2.

Threat Assessment

Regardless of the circumstances, even frivolous threats can create considerable apprehension among students, teachers, and parents. The stakes are high. Failure to properly remove a student who is a true danger from the school setting is a recipe for disaster on several fronts. Yet depriving a student of a public education when he or she is guilty of nothing more than poor judgment creates several legal and ethical dilemmas. A proper decision is often difficult. However, a threat assessment policy can provide guidance (Fein et al., 2004). *Threat assessment* starts with determining whether or not a true threat has been made. If, for example, a reasonable person would not view the action as a threat, this model recommends contacting parents to explain the situation. Some disciplinary action may be warranted to address the behavior. If, on the other hand, a reasonable person and the reaction of others indicate a potential threat, then contacting parents is mandatory. Short-term or emergency suspension or expulsion should be considered. At this point, Fein et al. (2004) and Stader (2000, 2001a) recommend that the student (or students) be referred to local law enforcement and to a local counseling or mental health agency with experience working with students of a similar age. At the same time that these agencies are making their independent assessments, this model recommends an internal school-based assessment that gathers as many facts as possible. The evidence and assessments of law enforcement and mental health professionals, and the facts and information gathered by school personnel, should be objectively considered to support either further suspension or expulsion or a return to school. The central question of a threat assessment is whether a student poses a threat, not whether the student made a threat. Threats should never be taken lightly. However, all threats may not be created equal.

In a case illustrative of this approach, the Ninth Circuit Court held the emergency suspension of Washington high school student Bruce LaVine to be sufficiently justified (*LaVine v. Blaine School District,* 2001). Bruce wrote a poem describing scenes of

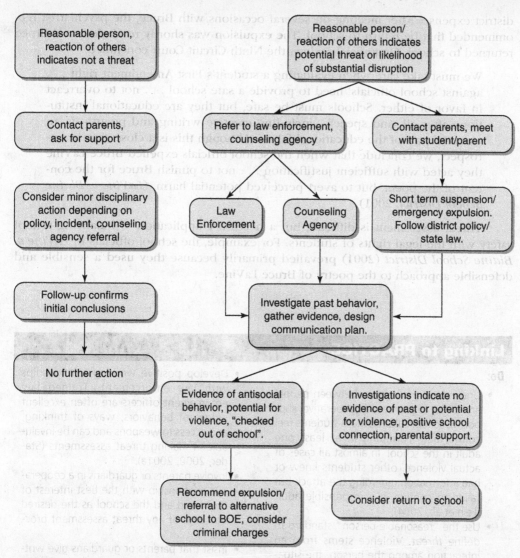

FIGURE 4–2   Responding to threats.

violence in his high school. His mother warned him not to take the poem to school, fearing overreaction on the part of teachers and administrators. Bruce did not follow his mother's advice, and on a Friday he submitted the poem to his English teacher for her comments. When his teacher read the poem that evening, she decided to contact school officials. The principal decided to invoke a provision of Washington state law providing for emergency expulsions. The principal informed Bruce and his parents of the expulsion on Monday morning. Both Bruce and his father became angry, belligerent, and profane. After Bruce was expelled, his parents hired an attorney, who immediately began communicating with the school district's attorney. After several conversations, it was agreed that Bruce should be evaluated by a psychiatrist at school district expense. After meeting on several occasions with Bruce, the psychiatrist recommended that he return to school. The expulsion was shortly rescinded, and Bruce returned to school. On judicial review, the Ninth Circuit Court concluded:

> We must take care when evaluating a student's First Amendment right . . . against school officials' need to provide a safe school . . . not to overreact in favor of either. Schools must be safe, but they are educational institutions after all, and speech—including creative writing and poetry—is an essential part of the educational fabric. Although this is a close case in retrospect, we conclude that when the school officials expelled Bruce LaVine they acted with sufficient justification . . . not to punish Bruce for the content of the poem, but to avert perceived potential harm. (*LaVine v. Blaine School District*, 2001)

Threat assessment is difficult, but a necessary application of balancing school safety with the legal rights of students. For example, the school officials in *LaVine v. Blaine School District* (2001) prevailed primarily because they used a sensible and defensible approach to the poetry of Bruce LaVine.

Linking to PRACTICE

Do:

- Understand the balance between people and policy to promote a cooperative, supportive school culture where students feel comfortable confiding in at least one adult in the school. In almost all cases of actual violence, other students knew or had information regarding the attack but failed to confide in a responsible adult (Fein et al., 2004).
- Use the "reasonable person" standard to define *threat*. Violence stems from an interaction among the person, the situation, the setting, and the target (Fein et al., 2004).
- Use the reactions of others as a predictor of the likelihood of disruption.
- Consult outside professionals. Violence is the end result of an understandable, and oftentimes discernible, process of thinking and behavior (Fein et al., 2004). Most educators are not qualified to make this assessment. Develop positive working relationships with qualified mental health professionals willing to provide such assessments of K–12 students.

- Develop positive working relationships with law enforcement. Trained law enforcement officers are often excellent judges of behaviors, ways of thinking, and access to weapons and can be invaluable in making threat assessments (Stader, 2000, 2001a).
- Involve parents or guardians in a cooperative relationship with the best interest of their child and the school as the desired outcome of any threat assessment process.
- Insist that parents or guardians give written permission for a sharing of information among school, law enforcement, and mental health professionals.
- School districts should provide training for at least one person to serve as a "threat assessor" for the district.

Do Not:

- Overreact. Not every adolescent utterance, poem, or drawing is a precursor to school violence.
- Fail to follow school board policy and state law.

STUDENT OFF-CAMPUS SPEECH

Student speech off campus receives more protection than student speech on campus (Hyman, 2006). As Justice Brennan (citing *Cohen v. California,* 1971) cautioned in *Fraser,* just because profane speech can be banned on campus does not mean that the same speech conducted off-campus is subject to censorship by school authorities. For example, a federal district court held that school officials lack authority to punish a student for conduct that does not occur on school grounds or during the school day when the district cannot establish that the conduct would adversely affect the orderly operation of the school (*Smith v. Klein,* 1986).

Underground newspapers created off-campus have similar protections (see *Thomas v. Board,* 1979, for example). However, if the publication can be linked to substantial disruption in the school, then it could be banned. The Seventh Circuit Court took this approach when a Wisconsin school district expelled Justin Boucher for 1 year after Justin wrote an article in an unofficial school newspaper distributed on campus describing how to "hack" school computers (*Boucher v. School Board,* 1998). The article, according to school officials, provided instruction on unauthorized access to the school district computers. Boucher argued that his speech was created off-campus and was innocuous. The Seventh Circuit Court was not impressed by these arguments, finding that school officials had legitimate concerns over disruption. The court upheld Boucher's 1-year expulsion.

The Second Circuit Court recently upheld the banning of an independent student newspaper being distributed on campus containing a sexually explicit cartoon. The school newspaper sponsor had earlier banned the cartoon from the official school paper. The court, citing *Bethel v. Fraser* (1986), concluded that the cartoon was "unquestionably lewd" and therefore banning the distribution of the newspaper on campus did not offend the First Amendment (*R. O. v. Ithaca,* 2011).

Student Internet Speech

Speech on the Internet is entitled to the same First Amendment protections as other speech (*Reno v. ACLU,* 1997). Not only has the proliferation of the Internet in schools and homes empowered students and citizens to freely access information, it has also created an unfettered and uncensored forum for expression. Expression that was at one time limited to relatively small groups of people can now be almost instantaneously and indiscriminately broadcast worldwide. Although this power holds great potential, it also holds particular challenges for school leaders when students use the Internet to engage in controversial speech. Justice Cappy succinctly captured the challenge the Internet creates for school leaders: "Tinker's simple armband, worn silently and brought in to a Des Moines, Iowa classroom, has been replaced by [a] complex multi-media website, accessible to fellow students, teachers, and the world" (*J. S. v. Bethlehem Area School District,* 2002). This challenge is compounded by the emergence of communication technologies such as Twitter, Facebook, and MySpace that make access to student comments almost instantaneous anywhere, including school hallways, lunch rooms, playgrounds, and classrooms.

Unfortunately, the U.S. Supreme Court has not ruled on a student online speech case, and lower courts have been inconsistent. Consequently, student off-campus online speech cases are usually decided along two lines of reasoning: (1) true threats (serious expression of intent to commit violence) are not protected speech, or (2) the material and substantial disruption standard of *Tinker* apply. In other words, simply disliking the message or fearing disruption is not enough to trump student off-campus speech rights. Thus, school authorities must either demonstrate that the off-campus communication is a true threat, or show a direct link between the off-campus speech and substantial disruption at school (Graca & Stader, 2007).

Regardless of the off-campus communicative medium, courts usually start with a threat analysis. If the speech can be considered a threat, the court usually stops the inquiry and supports banning the speech and whatever punishment the school district elects to apply. For example, the United States Northern District Court of New York supported the one-semester suspension of Aaron Wisniewski for posting on the Internet a threat to kill one of his teachers (*Wisniewski v. Board of Education*, 2006). The posting included an icon depicting a gun pointing to a head, a bullet leaving the gun, and blood splattering from the head. The message was "Kill Mr. VanderMolen." The court had little trouble recognizing the message as a true threat. Similarly, a high school student sent several instant messages to a classmate threatening to get a gun and kill everyone he hated, then kill himself. The student receiving the messages forwarded the messages to school administrators. The student sending the messages was suspended. The federal court had little difficulty determining that the message constituted a true threat (*Mardis v. Hannibal School District*, 2010).

If the message is not considered a true threat, courts generally turn to the substantial disruption prong of *Tinker*. Numerous examples are available. The Supreme Court of Pennsylvania upheld the expulsion of an eighth-grade student who created a website titled *Teacher Sux* (*J. S. v. Bethlehem Area School District*, 2002). The website, developed at the student's home, consisted of several pages that made derogatory comments about the student's math teacher and his principal. The website solicited $20 contributions for a "hit man," and contained a picture of the math teacher with a severed head dripping with blood, and her picture morphing into Adolf Hitler. The math teacher reported fear, short-term memory loss, an inability to mingle with crowds, and headaches, and she was required to take anti-anxiety medication. She was unable to continue in her position, forcing the school to hire a variety of substitute teachers with sometimes less than stellar results. On judicial review, the Pennsylvania Commonwealth Court concluded that, though it was offensive, the website was simply a "sophomoric . . . highly offensive and misguided attempt at humor." Consequently, the website created by J. S. did not rise to the level of a true threat and was protected by the First Amendment. The court next considered the impact of the website on the school. Given the effect the website had on the math teacher, student learning, and school morale, the school district was within its rights to expel the offending student.

Not all off-campus speech results in disruption. Joshua Mahaffey was referred for expulsion from Waterford Kettering (Michigan) High School for contributing to a website entitled *Satan's web page* (*Mahaffey v. Aldrich*, 2002). As part of his contribution to the web page, Joshua listed "People I wish would die" as well as "People that are cool." A parent notified the local police about the website. The police then notified school authorities. School authorities notified Joshua that he was being recommended for expulsion from Waterford School District. On judicial review, the district court concluded that a reasonable person in Joshua's place would not foresee that the statements on the website would be interpreted as threatening harm to anyone. Simply stated, Joshua's list of "people I wish would die" did not constitute a threat any more than his list of "people who are cool" made them more attractive. In a similar case, the Western District Court of Washington prohibited Kent School District from enforcing an emergency expulsion for intimidation, harassment, and disruption to the educational process against Nick Emmett after he created "mock obituaries" of some of his friends (*Emmett v. Kent School District,* 2000).

Messages Critical of School Policy or Individuals

Students have been critical of teachers, administrators, and school policy since the first public school was made available. Fortunately for everyone involved, these critical messages remained off-campus. Technology has changed this. Evaluating messages critical of school policy, parodies of school personnel, and so forth follows the same general format of determining whether the message is a true threat, and if not, whether the message created material and substantial disruption and/or interfered with good order and discipline. For example, Zachariah Paul compiled a "Top Ten" list about the school athletic director and track coach on his home computer containing rather sophomoric derogatory comments about the athletic director's weight, the size of his genitals, and his lack of success with women. Paul was suspended by the principal for 10 days for "verbal/written abuse of a staff member." The Western District Court for Pennsylvania held that the failure to demonstrate substantial disruption violated Paul's First Amendment rights under *Tinker*. The court pointed out that the speech was not threatening and, unlike *J. S. v. Bethlehem,* did not cause anyone to take leave (*Killion v. Franklin,* 2001). In a similar case, the Eastern District Court in Missouri held that "disliking or being upset" by the content of a student's Internet speech created off-campus is not an acceptable justification for limiting student speech under *Tinker* (*Beussink v. Woodland R-IV School District,* 1998).

Not all critical messages are protected. As junior class secretary and a member of student council, Avery Doninger was responsible for coordinating "Jamfest" (*Doninger v. Niehoff,* 2008). In response to multiple postponements of "Jamfest," Doninger and three other students sent e-mails to school district patrons. After a confrontation with Principal Niehoff over the e-mails, Avery created that evening a post on an Internet weblog that lamented the school's decision to not allow Jamfest to occur as scheduled, referred to the principal as a "douchebag" and solicited assistance from the community. Some community members did in fact contact the principal and/or superintendent. Not surprisingly, when the principal learned of the post, she took disciplinary action against Doninger, prohibiting the student's involvement in a number of cocurricular/extracurricular activities. Seemingly offended by the language of the posting, a Second Circuit panel determined that "the language with which Avery chose to encourage others to contact the administration was not only plainly offensive, but also potentially disruptive of efforts to resolve the ongoing controversy."

As a result of the controversy surrounding Jamfest, Doninger was prohibited by the principal from running for senior class secretary because of her off-campus postings. Doninger and other students were also prohibited from wearing "Team Avery" shirts to a school assembly where senior class officer candidates presented their speeches. On review, the Second Circuit Court considered two legal questions: Did the district violate Doninger's First Amendment rights by (1) preventing her from running for senior class secretary, and (2) prohibiting her from wearing a homemade printed shirt at a school assembly? The Court found that the district did not violate Doninger's First Amendment rights by prohibiting her from running for Senior Class secretary. The district did violate Doninger's right to wear the homemade shirt. However, the court held that this right was not clearly established and granted qualified immunity to the district. The court opined that qualified immunity protects school leaders when they make reasonable mistakes about the reasonableness of their actions. In this case, Principal Niehoff had a legitimate concern that the shirt would create disruption (*Doninger v. Niehoff*, 2011).

Similarly, a U.S. district court in Washington state found that the posting of a video of a teacher on the Internet after secretly filming her during class was not protected speech. The court held that the filming of a student making "rabbit ears" and pelvic thrusts behind the teacher constituted a material and substantial disruption (*Requa v. Kent School District*, 2007).

Fake MySpace and Similar Social Networking Sites

The issue of students creating fake MySpace or similar social networking sites of teachers and school leaders seems to becoming more common. Unless the fake social networking site creates material or substantial disruption or is a true threat, school officials have not been overly successful in punishing the creator of the sites. In *Draker v. Schreiber* (2008), a Texas high school assistant principal unsuccessfully sued two students for defamation based on their creation of an offensive online profile impersonation on MySpace. This case demonstrates the difficulty school officials may have in establishing a successful defamation suit against students who create fake social networking sites (Brady, 2010). In *A. B. v. State* (2007), the Indiana Court of Appeals held that a student's fake MySpace profile of the student's former middle school principal was protected political speech.

Sitting *en banc*, the Third Circuit Court of Appeals considered two fake MySpace profiles of school principals created off-campus. In *Layshock v. Hermitage* (2011), a student set up a parody profile of his principal on MySpace. Once the district learned of the profile, Justin Layshock was referred to the Alternative School, was banned from all extracurricular activities, and was not allowed to participate in his graduation ceremony. The Layshocks were also informed that the district was considering expelling Justin. The Court concluded that "a sufficient nexus between Justin's speech and a substantial disruption of the school environment" was not present. The school district did not dispute the court's holding that its punishment of Justin was not appropriate under *Tinker*. Rather, the school district argued that Justin's speech was "unquestionably vulgar, lewd and offensive, and therefore not shielded by the First Amendment." The Third Circuit Court of Appeals rejected this argument: "*Fraser* does not allow the School District to punish Justin for expressive conduct which occurred outside of the school context."

In the second case, eighth-grader J. S. created a MySpace profile making fun of her middle school principal. The profile contained adult language and sexually explicit content (*Synder v. Blue Mountain*, 2011). For example, the profile included references to sexual activity in the principal's office and hitting on students and their parents, and it made derogatory comments about the principal's son and wife. J. S. was suspended from school for 10 days by the middle school principal. Though the profile was disturbing, the record indicated that it did not cause a substantial disruption in the school. The court stated, "If anything, (Principal's) response to the profile exacerbated rather than contained the disruption in the school." In addition, "Neither the Supreme Court nor this Court has ever allowed schools to punish students for off-campus speech that is not school sponsored or at a school-sponsored event and that cause not substantial disruption at school." However, several justices dissented. The dissenting justices were concerned that the majority had left schools defenseless to protect teachers and school officials against personal, vulgar, and obscene attacks and to discipline students for these acts.

As these and other student Internet First Amendment cases illustrate, a very fine line exists between the authority of school leaders to punish students for off-campus parodies and non-threatening messages and students' First Amendment rights to freedom of expression. The law governing student speech is difficult and confusing even for judges. Student off-campus speech has the same protections as any citizen. As the Justices in *Doninger, Synder*, and *Layshock* make clear, school district authority to punish students for their off-campus expression is generally limited to those cases were a clear nexus between the speech and material and substantial disruption to good order and discipline inside the schoolhouse gates exists.

Linking to PRACTICE

Do:

- Communicate to students, teachers, and parents that Internet speech created off-campus that substantially disrupts the school may be subject to disciplinary action including expulsion.
- Remember that student speech created off-campus enjoys a higher level of protection than on-campus speech. Off-campus speech that is uncomfortable, embarrassing, or unpleasant may not rise to the level of substantial disruption.
- Establish that the speech is a true threat or a clear nexus between the off-campus speech and "material and substantial" disruption to the school before taking disciplinary action. In cases where the school district prevailed in suppressing student off-campus Internet speech, this nexus was clear. Students prevailed when this nexus was not established.
  - Student-created fake online profiles should be reported immediately to the social networking vendor. These vendors are increasingly responsive to concerns about safety, abuse, and defamation (Brady, 2010).

- Update Internet Acceptable Use policies to include issues and language unique to social networking including online profile impersonation and defamation (Brady, 2010).
- Spend more time educating and training students and parents on the responsible use of social networking technology (Brady, 2010).

Do Not:

- Overreact. Simply calling or meeting with the parents of the offending student and asking for their help may be all that is necessary.
- Wait until total chaos erupts before taking action. For example, the Pennsylvania court used the school district's delay in punishing J. S. as one rationale for determining that J. S.'s website was not a true threat (*J. S. v. Bethlehem School District,* 2002).
- Attempt to discipline students with a policy that is vague or overbroad.
- Fail to carefully follow school district due process policy.
  - Focus exclusively on punishment policies or restrict student online speech and expression (Brady, 2010).

Summary

Students often wish to express their desire for independence from parental and school authority in a variety of ways, including choices of dress, language, and symbols. However, this naturally occurring desire for expressive freedom can collide with the need to maintain order and discipline in the school. Legal guidelines can be ambiguous, and finding the right balance among student rights, a positive school environment, and the obligation for order and discipline can be difficult.

The interaction of the systemsworld and lifeworld determines the normative environment of the school. However, the systemsworld and the lifeworld continuously vie for dominance, creating a tension between freedom and order. The proper balance is required for a well-ordered and positive school culture. However, in many schools the systemsworld dominates student lifeworlds, resulting in loss of significance, alienation, and hopelessness. Consequently, decisions involving student expression should be made with great care.

The basic expressive rights of students were established in four U.S. Supreme Court cases. *Tinker v. Des Moines School District* (1969) considers student rights to pure speech; *Bethel v. Fraser* (1986) empowers school leaders to suppress lewd, vulgar, or profane speech; *Hazelwood v. Kuhlmeier* (1988) establishes control over student speech that could reasonably be considered as bearing the sponsorship or imprimatur of the school; and *Morse v. Frederick* confirms that school districts may ban messages that could reasonably be viewed as promoting drug use at school or school sponsored events.

School officials have considerable leeway in establishing viewpoint-neutral dress code or uniform policies that are reasonably related to educational purposes. Student expression that a reasonable person would perceive as threatening or that actually constitutes a threat can be suppressed.

CONNECTING STANDARDS TO PRACTICE

STUPID CUPID

As the former principal of Riverboat High School, Sharon Grey was well aware of the "Unofficial Riverboat High School Newspaper" website. The motto of the website was "All the news your official RHS newspaper can't or won't print." True to the motto, the website had published several controversial articles lampooning Homecoming and school district dress code policies. Consequently, Sharon was not overly surprised when new Riverboat principal Tara Hills asked for an appointment to seek her advice on an "Unofficial Newspaper" problem. Tara had spoken with the editors. They had agreed that some comments were a little out of line and promised to more carefully edit the website. However, several teach-

ers were beginning to openly criticize Tara for not punishing the student editors and those responsible for contributing to the online newspaper.

The criticism intensified with the latest editorial. Written under the byline *Stupid Cupid* and entitled "Love Makes Butt Faces Out of Two Riverboat Teachers," the editorial focused on rumors of an extramarital love affair between Kaycee Morning and Coach Nathan Lawrence. The editorial presented detailed allegations of liaisons between the two teachers, including one in a school office while Coach Lawrence was supposedly at basketball practice. The editorial also detailed an alleged altercation between Coach Lawrence's wife and Kaycee Morning at a local tavern. Sharon wondered how the editorial writers could possibly have that much detail.

Naturally, both Kaycee and Nathan were not happy about the editorial. Kaycee and Nathan had enlisted several teachers in their efforts to increase the pressure on Tara to punish the editorial writers. Kaycee and Nathan complained that the editorial was disrespectful of their authority as teachers, causing problems in their classes, and problems with their spouses.

Question

Argue for or against punishing the editors of the newspaper. Clarify the legal question. Cite ISLLC standards, legal guidelines governing student speech, and ethical principles (discourse ethics, lifeworlds, and systemsworlds) that we have read about so far to support your answer. Write a memo to the superintendent or board of education president justifying your decision.

CHAPTER 5

Due Process, Student Discipline, Athletics, and Title IX

INTRODUCTION

Administrators are empowered by a wide variety of federal, state, and local laws and policies to maintain orderly and safe schools. However, students do not forfeit all of their constitutional rights. This is especially true when students are off-campus. For many secondary school leaders, extracurricular activities, especially athletics, are also an important responsibility. Title IX is designed to protect students from being denied the benefits of any educational program or activity, including athletics, because of sex. Basic fairness and a healthy respect for these rights is part of being an ethical and humane school leader. This chapter considers the balance between the obligation to maintain order and safety while respecting the rights of students. The Justice as Fairness principles of the American political philosopher John Rawls, the due process rights of students, corporal punishment, excessive force, and extracurricular activities are presented here.

FOCUS QUESTIONS

1. What is a "well-ordered" school, and how is this concept related to due process and student discipline?
2. Can, and should, students be disciplined for off-campus behavior?
3. Is consistency in student discipline always rational?
4. Should schools use corporal punishment to control student behavior? What standards should courts use when reviewing charges of excessive force during corporal punishment?

KEY TERMS

Corporal punishment	Procedural due process	Substantive due process
Due process	Property interest	Title IX
Liberty interest	Shocks the conscience	Well-ordered school

CASE STUDY
The Case of the Powdered Aspirin

As principal of Medford Elementary School, Charlene Daniels was quite concerned about the rumors that several students had been bringing powdered aspirin to school and "huffing" the powder in the restroom after lunch and after recess. At the last faculty meeting, Charlene had discussed her concerns with the faculty and asked them to be more vigilant than usual as students left the cafeteria and returned from recess. It was this vigilance that led sixth-grade teacher Ralph Smith to her office. "Ms. Daniels, I just saw sixth-grader Lasiandra Davis go into the girls' restroom next to the cafeteria. I just caught a glimpse, but I am sure I saw a brown paper bag in her hand. I could not follow her into the restroom, but I sent Mrs. Hale to go check."

Mrs. Hale came out of the restroom just as Charlene and Ralph arrived holding a brown paper bag covered with a white powdery substance. "I found this in the trash can under some papers. When I arrived Lasiandra Davis was the only one in the restroom. She saw me searching the trash can and left the restroom before I could stop her."

Charlene immediately placed the brown bag with the white substance in a plastic container, called the police, and started her own investigation. The investigation lasted all afternoon, interrupted several classes, and caused several students to miss significant time in the classroom. All five of the sixth-grade teachers spent considerable time talking to their students trying to get more information. By the end of the day, Charlene was fairly convinced that Lasiandra had indeed been in possession of the paper bag. She based her conclusions on a couple of students' testimony that they had seen Lasiandra with a paper bag right before lunch, Lasiandra's teacher's observation that Lasiandra had seem "agitated" after lunch the past several days, and Mr. Smith's belief that he had seen Lasiandra take a brown paper bag into the restroom.

Charlene called Lasiandra to the office and confronted her with the allegations. Lasiandra denied that she had brought powdered aspirin to school. She said that she was not in possession of a paper bag after lunch as Mr. Smith had said, and that she knew nothing about the bag found in the trash. Charlene informed Lasiandra that she was suspending her for 5 days for "disturbing instruction." She based this finding on the fact that all sixth-grade classes had been disrupted, that all five of the sixth-grade teachers had participated in the investigation rather than teach their classes, and that she as principal spent all afternoon investigating the incident.

Lasiandra's mother and father were not happy with Charlene's decision. Both parents had called Superintendent Johanson. Charlene's parents and the superintendent had agreed to meet the next day to appeal the suspension.

LEADERSHIP PERSPECTIVES

A reasonably orderly school promotes and protects the welfare and safety of students and staff and provides the foundation for a safe and effective school environment (**ISLLC Standards 3 & 3C**). A reasonably orderly building environment also promotes social justice, equity, and accountability as called for in **ISLLC Standard 5E**. However, not all orderly schools are good schools. Not all orderly classrooms promote efficient

ISLLC Standards 3 & 3C

ISLLC Standard 5E

and effective learning (**ISLLC Standard 3**). As in a maximum-security prison, order in schools and classrooms can be obtained by rigid rules and punishment. As discussed in the previous chapter, schools and classrooms that achieve order in these ways often create a hostile, alienating, and toxic environment that is not conducive to the types of teaching and learning for which "good" schools are noted (Skiba & Peterson, 2000). There is little question, however, that effective schools and classrooms must have a system of enforced rules in place to provide the foundations for orderly and safe school cultures that promote learning. Unfortunately, a very fine line sometimes exists between maintaining order and creating overly punitive school cultures.

The opening case study "The Case of the Powdered Aspirin" illustrates this. **ISLLC Standard 2A** calls for school leaders to develop and sustain a culture of collaboration and trust. Principal Daniels has exemplified this standard by enlisting faculty in support of her efforts to maintain a substance-free environment. There is no question that students bringing powdered aspirin to school and "huffing" it is a significant school safety and student health concern. Principal Daniels is correct in being concerned about the welfare and safety of students in her school (**ISLLC Standard 3C**). She is also correct in accepting Mr. Smith's assertion that he had seen Lasiandra Davis take a brown paper bag into the girl's restroom after lunch. Principal Daniels may be correct in her belief that Lasiandra Davis is at least one of the students bringing powdered aspirin to school. As principal she is empowered by a wide variety of state laws and school board policies to enforce reasonable rules designed to maintain a safe and substance-free environment. As principal, she also has a responsibility to treat students, teachers, and others fairly and in an ethical manner regardless of the circumstances (**ISLLC Standard 5**).

Lasiandra Davis also has certain rights and responsibilities. She has the responsibility to follow reasonable rules. She also has the right to be treated fairly. School leaders' responsibility to promote good order and discipline must be balanced with student rights to be treated fairly and in an ethical manner. This balance, reflected in **ISLLC Standards 3 and 5**, is addressed in this chapter by considering the "justice as fairness" concepts of the American political philosopher John Rawls, and the legal concepts of due process, student discipline, and Title IX.

STUDENT RIGHTS AND THE WELL-ORDERED SCHOOL

John Rawls's concept of justice as fairness (2001) provides guidance when considering the balance of the sometimes conflicting principles of maintaining a reasonably orderly school that promotes learning, safety and a substance-free environment with the equally compelling requirement that all students be treated fairly. Rawls's theory of justice as fairness is a political theory, but it is applicable to schools as a concept of local justice. Rawls presents his concept in two principles of justice. The first, presented here, is particularly germane to a discussion of the relationship between student rights and the obligation to maintain order in a positive school culture.

> ***Principle One:*** Each person has the same indefeasible claim to a fully adequate scheme of equal basic liberties, which scheme is compatible with the same scheme of liberties for all. (p. 42)

Principle One assumes that all students, regardless of socioeconomic status, ethnicity, or disciplinary history, are deserving of the same liberties. The fundamental

(Left margin tags:)
ISLLC Standard 3

ISLLC Standard 2A

ISLLC Standard 3C

ISLLC Standard 5

ISLLC Standards 3 and 5

idea is the development of a school culture that exists simultaneously as a *fair system of social cooperation* that is established by *public justification*. Social cooperation requires that reasonable persons understand and honor certain basic principles, even at the expense of their own interests, provided that others are also expected to honor these principles. In other words, students can be expected to understand and honor reasonable restrictions on their freedoms. School officials can be expected to reciprocate by promoting fairness and honoring appropriate student rights. In Rawls's view, it is unreasonable not to honor fair terms of cooperation that others are expected to accept. It is worse than unreasonable to pretend to honor basic principles of social cooperation and then readily violate these principles simply because one has the power to do so. In other words, Rawls views it as unreasonable for school leaders to "talk the fairness talk" but not "walk the walk." As pointed out in Chapter 1, fairness is a difficult concept. Fairness, like beauty, is in the eye of the beholder. There is no question that walking the walk can be fraught with difficulty. But, as Rawls points out, although it may seem rational at times to violate the principle of fairness and ignore student rights, it is never reasonable.

A school culture based on social cooperation must be *publicly justified* and acceptable, not only to those who make the rules, but also to others (students, parents, teachers, etc.) who are affected by the school culture. To be effective, public justification should proceed to some form of consensus that assumes that all parties have fundamental rights and responsibilities. Rawls acknowledges that it is unlikely that all members of a diverse school with conflicting needs, values, and priorities will come to the same conclusions and the same definition of a well-ordered school. However, it is important that a reasonable consensus result from the process to serve as a basis for the justification of the need for certain rules and policies to promote order and efficiency.

The Idea of a Well-Ordered School

A school that exists as a fair system of cooperation under a public conception of justice meets **ISLLC Standards 2A, 3A, 3C, 4B, 4C, 4D, 5B, 5C, 5D, and 5E**. A school existing in this manner—a *well-ordered school*—has three defining characteristics:

ISLLC Standards 2A, 3A, 3C, 4B, 4C, 4D, 5B, 5C, 5D, and 5E

1. Everyone in the school accepts, and knows that everyone else accepts, the same concepts of justice. Moreover, this knowledge is mutually recognized as though these principles were a matter of public record. In other words, school leaders, teachers, and students acknowledge and accept that certain basic principles will be honored by everyone.
2. All personal interactions, policies, and applications of policy are designed to facilitate a system of cooperation.
3. Students, teachers, and school leaders have a rational sense of justice that allows them to understand and for the most part act accordingly as their positions in the school dictate.

These three concepts provide a mutually recognizable point of view for the development of a school culture that promotes order, safety, and security. A mutual understanding of the roles and responsibilities of administrators, teachers, and students is important. The concept of a well-ordered school characterized by a fair system of social cooperation established by public justification may seem overly theoretical. However, it is embedded in a real problem—the development of a safe, secure, and substance-free school environment that promotes student learning. For example, in a national study of crime and violence in middle schools, Cantor et al. (2001) found that in low-disorder schools, a shared sense of responsibility is present among teachers and administrators. In these schools, principals and teachers for the most part support one another and function well as a team. In contrast, this sense of shared responsibility among teachers and administrators was weak in high-disorder schools. Teachers tended to point fingers at one another, at administrators, and at school security officers for the lack of good order in the school. A school culture based on a public conception of justice provides the framework for a shared sense of responsibility by all concerned in promoting good order and discipline. Well-ordered schools characterized by a fair system of social cooperation established by public justification are most likely to have a school environment that promotes collaboration, trust, and learning (**ISLLC Standard 2A**); the welfare and safety of students and staff (**ISLLC Standard 3C**); and social justice and student achievement (**ISLLC Standard 5E**).

ISLLC Standard 2A

ISLLC Standard 3C

ISLLC Standard 5E

Linking to PRACTICE

Do:

- Develop a system of mutually acceptable and publicly justified policies designed to maintain order and promote safety.
- Involve a wide range of interested stakeholders in the formulation of school rules.
- Model and insist that teachers and other adults in the school honor basic fairness and student rights. Conversely, insist that parents and students honor basic teacher rights.
- Use the concept of a well-ordered school to reinforce feelings of emotional safety for students, teachers, and parents.
- Use data to publicly justify certain restrictions on student freedom. These data can be used to support school safety interven-

tions or conversely demonstrate that certain interventions may not be needed at this point in time.

Do Not:

- Overreact to an isolated incident or criticism and resort to more punitive policies. Defensible school discipline plans should be based on facts, not on opinions, isolated incidents, or whoever can complain the most about student disorder.
- Share identifiable student data in group settings or with individuals without a legitimate educational interest in the data. Sharing identifiable student data is a violation of FERPA and can destroy trust and erode feelings of emotional safety.

DUE PROCESS AND THE FIFTH AND FOURTEENTH AMENDMENTS

As Rawls points out, the concept of *fairness* is fundamental to a well-ordered school. The concept of justice as fairness is reflected in the legal principle of due process. **Due process** is a legal principle that considers the manner of fair and adequate procedures for making equitable and fair decisions integrated into **ISLLC Standard 5**. A constitutional right to fair procedures is established in the due process clause of both the Fifth and Fourteenth Amendments. Both amendments address the concept that persons shall not be deprived of "life, liberty, or property, without due process of law." A **property interest** is established by the state when the right to an education is extended to all individuals in a particular class. Therefore, a property interest is affected anytime a student is

ISLLC Standard 5

denied access to a public school education. A ***liberty interest*** is defined as a person's good name, integrity, or reputation. A liberty interest is created when an administrative action creates potential harm to future job or educational opportunities. There are two forms of due process: procedural and substantive. ***Procedural due process*** considers the minimum sequence of steps taken by a school official in reaching a decision, usually defined as notice and the right to a fair hearing. ***Substantive due process*** considers the fairness of a decision and involves such concepts as adequate notice, consistency of standards, how evidence was collected and applied to the decision, the rationality of the decision, and the nexus of the decision with a legitimate educational purpose.

Procedural Due Process and Out-of-School Suspension

Suspension generally refers to removal from school for a relatively short period—usually 1 to 10 days. *Expulsion* is generally defined as suspension from school for more than 10 days (Stader, 2011). Decisions for suspensions of 10 days or less are usually made by campus administrators. The maximum length of time for which campus administrators can suspend a student varies by state. For example, Missouri state law allows campus administrators to suspend students for up to 10 days (RSMo 167.171.1). Texas state law restricts campus administrators to 3 days or less (Texas Education Code 37.009). Regardless of the differences in state law, the due process requirements for out-of-school suspensions of 10 days or less were established by the U.S. Supreme Court in *Goss v. Lopez* (1975).

This case considered Ohio law empowering school principals to suspend students for up to 10 days. This law also empowered principals to expel students. Expelled students or their parents had the right to a hearing before the local board of education. However, students suspended for 10 days or less had no recourse. The Court held that students facing temporary suspension from school (defined as 10 days or less) have a property and liberty interest that qualifies them for due process protection. Based on the assumption that education is the most important function of state and local governments (*Brown v. Board of Education,* 1954), the Court reasoned that a 10-day suspension recorded on a transcript could seriously damage a student's reputation and interfere with later educational and employment opportunities. Consequently, even the temporary denial of a student's property interest in established educational benefits or potential harm to the student's liberty interest may not be constitutionally imposed without adequate due process protection. The Court established the following *procedural* guidelines for student suspensions of *10 days or less*:

- The student must be given oral or written notice of the charges. In other words, the student has the right to know what rule has been broken.
- If the student denies the charges, an explanation of the evidence the authorities have and an opportunity for the student to present his or her version of the events is required.
- These steps may be taken immediately following the misconduct or infraction that may result in suspension.

Due process procedures and practices are designed to pose a check on improperly denying a student the right to a public education. Review the opening case study, "The Case of the Powdered Aspirin." Principal Daniels is "fairly convinced" that

Lasiandra is guilty of bringing powdered aspirin to school in a brown bag and that she was in possession of the bag when she went into the restroom. Did Principal Daniels meet the requirements of *Goss* when she suspended Lasiandra? Lasiandra denied that she was in possession of the powdered aspirin. Mr. Smith was "pretty sure" Lasiandra had a brown paper bag in her possession as she entered the restroom. Lasiandra was the only person in the restroom when the female teacher followed her into the restroom. She apparently was not in possession of the bag when Mrs. Hale entered the restroom, because the bag was found in the trash can. Did Principal Daniels provide Lasiandra with the evidence she had? Why did Principal Daniels suspend Lasiandra for "disturbing instruction" rather than for possession of powdered aspirin with what one can assume the intent to "huff"? Principals (and school boards) may make decisions based on a preponderance of the evidence rather than the "beyond a reasonable doubt" requirement in criminal cases. Does a preponderance of the evidence support Principal Daniels's decision to suspend Lasiandra?

The procedural requirements established in *Goss* generally pose little problem for school administrators and should be completed *before a decision is made* to suspend the student. In cases where a student's presence endangers persons or property or threatens disruption of the academic process, administrators are justified in the immediate removal of the student from school. A preliminary decision to suspend an unruly or dangerous student may be made as long as the decision maker holds a prompt procedural hearing with the understanding that the preliminary decision to suspend can be reversed (Stader, 2001). However, the necessary notice and hearing should follow as soon as practicable (see *C.B. & T.P. v. Driscoll*, 1996 as an example). Students are usually not considered to have the same due process rights for punishments such as after-school detention or an in-school suspension (*Tristan Kipp v. Lorain Board of Education*, 2000). Traditionally, suspended students are not allowed to make up schoolwork that is missed because of the suspension. This practice has been supported by the courts (*South Gibson School Board v. Sellman*, 2002). The Fifth Circuit has recently held that a "student's transfer to an alternative educational program does not deny access to public education and therefore does not violate a Fourteenth Amendment interest (i.e. require due process)" (*Harris v. Pontotoc County School District*, 2011). In addition, courts have been consistent in finding that Miranda warnings are not required when a student is questioned by school authorities regarding possible rule violations in school (Taylor, 2002).

Substantive Due Process

Substantive due process may be defined as follows: "The doctrine that the Due Process Clauses of the 5th and 14th Amendments require legislation to be fair and reasonable in content and to further a legitimate governmental objective" (Garner, 2006, p. 228). Substantive due process usually involves four questions: (a) Does the rule or policy provide adequate notice of what conduct is prohibited? (b) Does the rule or policy serve a legitimate educational purpose? (c) Is the consequence reasonably (or rationally) connected to the offense? (d) Is the rule or policy applied equitably?

Question 1: Does the rule or policy provide adequate notice of what conduct is prohibited? This question concerns how accurately the policy or rule articulates or describes actions that would violate the rule or policy. School rules are not required to be as detailed as criminal codes. However, school rules must be written in an age-appropriate format that most reasonable students can understand. Sometimes this is difficult to accomplish. Vague or overbroad rules or policies violate substantive due process because these policies fail to provide adequate notice regarding unacceptable conduct, and they offer no clear guidance for school officials to apply the policy. In other words, school officials have wide latitude to interpret the policy at will or to do more than is necessary to achieve the desired ends. Some examples of vague or overbroad rules may include "anything that brings discredit to the school," "gang-related activities on school grounds," "misconduct," "unacceptable behavior," or behavior that "creates ill will." Refer back to the case study "The Case of the Powdered Aspirin." Although school codes need only be reasonable, is suspension for "interrupting instruction" vague or overbroad? What does "interrupting instruction" mean? However, even in incidents where some ambiguity is present, the U.S. Supreme Court has stated that federal courts should not substitute their own notions for a school board's definition of its rules (*Wood v. Strickland*, 1975, and *Board of Education of Rogers, Arkansas v. McCluskey*, 1982). These cases clarify that as long as a school board's interpretation and enforcement of rules is reasonable, courts should not interfere.

Question 2: Does the rule or policy serve a legitimate educational purpose? This question considers the balance between individual rights (freedom) of students and the need for good order, safety, and efficiency. For student rights to be restricted, the restriction must serve some legitimate educational function. As long as the rule or policy can be linked to good order, safety, or efficiency, the policy will usually pass muster. For example, the drug testing of students and policies prohibiting weapons are clearly linked to school safety. However, arbitrary or capricious actions that are unrelated to maintaining good order and discipline may violate substantive due process (*Woodard v. Los Fresnos,* 1984).

Question 3: Is the consequence reasonably (or rationally) connected to the offense? This question considers whether the consequence seems rational in light of the offense, or whether it is arbitrary or capricious. For example, referring an honor student with no disciplinary history for expulsion for being late to school would not appear rational. Think about Lasiandra Davis in the opening case study, "The Case of the Powdered Aspirin." Lasiandra may or may not be an honor student, and it is possible that she is a royal pain. However, should she be suspended for "interrupting instruction"? Is it not part of a school principal's job description to investigate potential rule violations, especially one as serious as "huffing" powdered aspirin? She was not suspended for possession of powdered aspirin, but for interrupting instruction. Was the suspension reasonably related to the offense? Courts sometimes comment about the wisdom of a rule or policy and the punishment used to enforce the rule (see, for example, *Anderson v. Milbank,* 2000). But federal courts are reluctant to substitute their judgment for school board interpretation of rules (*Wood v. Strickland,* 1975).

Question 4: Is the rule or policy applied equitably? This question can be divided into two concepts: (1) Is everyone similarly situated treated in a similar manner? (2) Does the policy have a disproportional impact on a particular identifiable group of students?

The first concept considers whether or not a policy is applied equally. A recent case involving sexual minority students may illustrate this (*C. N. v. Wolf,* 2006). Two female California high school students were disciplined for expressing affection toward each other. Heterosexual couples were not disciplined for the same behavior. In other words, policies that are applied to one group of students but not to another may violate the substantive due process rights of students. The second concept considers the intentional or unintentional impact of the policy or rule on a particular identifiable group of students. The decision by the Decatur, Illinois, school district to expel several African American students involved in a fight at a football game illustrates this (*Fuller v. Decatur*, 2000). African American students composed approximately 46 to 48% of the student body, yet 82% of the students expelled during a 2-year period were African American. However, the court found that similarly situated White students had also been expelled. In other words, the students had to demonstrate both inequitable treatment and disproportional impact. This is a very high standard to meet, especially when school safety is involved.

Long-Term Suspension and Expulsion

In most states, the authority to expel students is reserved for superintendents, school boards, or district hearing officers. In some states, such as Missouri, the school district superintendent (or a designee, in large districts) may suspend a student for up to 180 days (RsMo 167.171). This process is generally referred to as *long-term suspension*. In other states, only the board of education can suspend a student for more than 10 days.

Regardless of how expulsion is defined, due process requirements are proportional to the potential punishment. In short, the greater the potential loss of a student's property interest in attending school and the greater the threat to the student's liberty interest in not having his or her record tainted by school officials, the greater the due process requirements. Therefore, suspensions or expulsions from school longer than 10 days require more elaborate due process requirements than the rudimentary requirements established in *Goss v. Lopez* (1975). Unfortunately, the U.S. Supreme Court has not established these requirements, and student rights in long-term suspension or expulsion hearings are a conglomeration of various federal and state court rulings, state statutes, and school board policies. These patchwork requirements vary from state to state and circuit court to circuit court. At the heart of the matter, due process requires only that a student facing expulsion receive notice of the charges; notice of the date, place and time of the hearing; and a full opportunity to be heard. Some circuit courts have added further due process requirements in expulsion cases. Therefore, it is important to consult state laws and school board policy before instigating long-term suspension or expulsion. The following general guidelines—in addition to notice of charges, time of the hearing, and an opportunity to present evidence refuting the allegations—likely apply in most states to students facing expulsion from public schools:

1. Students have the right to a prompt written explanation of the facts leading to the expulsion. Expulsion cases can be challenged when a policy is "vague or over-broad." For example, "gang-related" has been found to be void for vagueness (*Stephenson v. Davenport Community School District*, 1997), as has "possession of look-alike" drugs (*Board of Education of Central Community v. Scionti*, 2000).

2. During the appeal process, students generally have the right to an evidentiary hearing, including having an attorney present. For example, a North Carolina appeals court overturned an expulsion decision because the student in question was denied the right to counsel during his appeal to the board (*In re Roberts*, 2002).

3. Students generally have the right to present and refute evidence and to cross-examine and face witnesses (*Fuller v. Decatur Public Schools*, 2000). The right to cross-examine and face witnesses, especially when the witnesses are fellow

students, is particularly controversial. However, courts have overturned the expulsion of a student because none of the student or teacher witnesses testified at the hearing (*Board of Education of Central Community v. Scionti*, 2000; *Colquitt v. Rich Township High School District*, 1998; *Nichols v. DeStefano*, 2002). The right to refute evidence is fundamental to the due process standard. The right to cross-examine witnesses varies from state to state.

4. Boards may make decisions based on a *preponderance of the evidence* rather than the "beyond a reasonable doubt" requirement of criminal trials.

5. The district should be prepared to present data demonstrating that expulsion decisions are not based on racial criteria. For example, in *Fuller v. Decatur* (2000), significantly more African American students than White students faced suspension and expulsion. However, the district was able to demonstrate that African American and White students who were similarly situated received similar punishments.

Procedural due process requirements and decision making are illustrated in Figure 5-1.

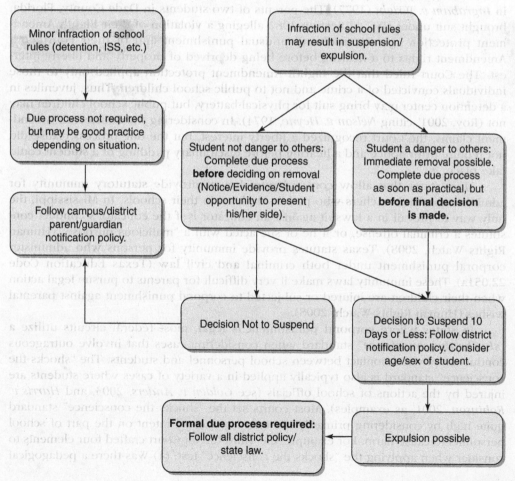

FIGURE 5-1 Procedural due process illustrated.

CORPORAL PUNISHMENT AND EXCESSIVE FORCE

Corporal punishment can be defined as "the use of physical force, including hitting, slapping, spanking, paddling or the use of physical restraint or positioning which is designed to cause pain, as a disciplinary measure" (Education Commission of the States, 1998). As of 2008, 21 states (mostly in the South and Southwest) permitted the use of corporal punishment in schools (Human Rights Watch, 2008). Twenty-nine states and Washington, DC, have banned the practice. In states where the decision to use corporal punishment is delegated to the local school board, many state school board associations recommend finding alternative means of discipline. Many school districts have taken such action. In fact, 95 of the largest school districts in the country have banned corporal punishment, including Houston, Dallas, and Memphis (Human Rights Watch, 2008). In addition, states that allow corporal punishment either establish guidelines or require local boards to establish guidelines for administering physical punishment.

The legality of corporal punishment was considered by the U.S. Supreme Court in *Ingraham v. Wright* (1977). The parents of two students in Dade County, Florida, brought suit under USC 42 Section 1982 alleging a violation of their Eighth Amendment protection against cruel and unusual punishment and of their Fourteenth Amendment rights to a hearing before being deprived of property and liberty interest. The Court ruled that the Eighth Amendment protection applied only to those individuals convicted of a crime and not to public school children. Thus, juveniles in a detention center may bring suit for physical battery, but public school children may not (Roy, 2001, citing *Nelson v. Heyne*, 1974). In considering the Fourteenth Amendment claims, the Court recognized a liberty interest, but the due process clause did not require prior notice and a hearing before disciplinary paddling of a student could take place.

Most states that allow corporal punishment provide statutory immunity for administrators and teachers who paddle students in their schools. In Mississippi, the only way to prevail in a lawsuit against an educator is if the educator's conduct constitutes a criminal offense, or if he or she acted with a "malicious purpose" (Human Rights Watch, 2008). Texas statutes provide immunity for persons who administer corporal punishment under both criminal and civil law (Texas Education Code 22.051a). These immunity laws make it very difficult for parents to pursue legal action when their children are injured or subjected to corporal punishment against parental wishes (Human Rights Watch, 2008).

In states where corporal punishment is legal, most federal circuits utilize a "*shocks the conscience*" standard when considering cases that involve outrageous conduct or physical contact between school personnel and students. The "shocks the conscience" standard is also typically applied in a variety of cases where students are injured by the actions of school officials (see *Golden v. Anders,* 2003, and *Harris v. Robinson,* 2001, as examples). Most courts set the "shocks the conscience" standard quite high by considering primarily the intent or lack of intent on the part of school personnel to cause harm. For example, the Third Circuit Court crafted four elements to consider when applying the "shocks the conscience" test: (1) Was there a pedagogical justification for the use of force? (2) Was the force utilized excessive to meet the legitimate objective in the situation? (3) Was the force applied in a good-faith effort to maintain or restore discipline, or maliciously and sadistically for the very purpose of causing harm? (4) Was there a serious injury? (*Gottlieb v. Laurel Highlands School District,* 2001).

In school discipline cases, the Tenth Circuit Court defines "shocks the conscience" as

> whether the force applied caused injury so severe, was so disproportional to the need presented, and was so inspired by malice or sadism rather than a merely careless or unwise excess of zeal that it amounted to a brutal and inhumane abuse of official power literally *shocking to the conscience.* (*Garcia v. Miera,* 1987)

The Eighth Circuit Court has established the following guidelines in considering whether or not the administering of corporal punishment shocks the consciences: (1) the need for the use of corporal punishment, (2) the relationship between the need for the punishment and the amount or severity of the punishment, (3) the extent of the injury inflicted, and (4) whether the punishment was administered in good-faith effort or done in a malicious and sadistic manner for the purpose of causing harm (*Wise v. Pea Ridge,* 1988).

Based on these definitions, it may be difficult for school personnel to shock the conscience of many federal courts, but not all behaviors are protected. For example, the Eleventh Circuit Court held that the actions of a Green County, Alabama, principal who struck a 13-year-old boy with a metal cane in the head, ribs, and back with enough force to cause a large knot on his head and migraine headaches "obviously" rise to a level that shocks the conscience (*Kirkland v. Greene,* 2003). A female high school student became quite unruly, profane, and refused to leave a classroom area (*Nicol v. Auburn-Washburn School District,* 2002). When a school security guard was summoned, he allegedly pushed the girl into a file cabinet, shoved her into another student, grabbed her in a head lock, and "pinned" her "up against [a] wall." Using the standards established in *Harris v. Robinson* (2001), the Tenth Circuit Court found that a reasonable jury could find that the actions of the security guard shock the conscience, thus violating the student's substantive due process rights.

Reaching a similar conclusion, the Second Circuit Court found the actions of a physical education teacher who grabbed a junior high school student by the throat, lifted him off the ground by his neck, dragged him across the gym floor, slammed the back of the student's head against the bleachers four times, and rammed the student's forehead into a metal fuse box to be "conscience-shocking" (*Johnson v. Newburgh School District,* 2001). The court used the following criteria to determine conscience-shocking actions: (1) Is the conduct maliciously and sadistically employed in the absence of a discernible government interest? (2) Is the conduct of a kind likely to produce substantial injury? In this particular case, the court had little difficulty answering yes to both of these criteria.

Linking to PRACTICE

Do:

- Follow school district policy and state law regarding the use—or nonuse—of corporal punishment.
- Search for alternatives in states (and districts) that allow corporal punishment. Sanctioning physical force and the intentional infliction of pain on students may create conditions that could easily escalate to "conscience-shocking" behavior.
- Investigate any incidents of physical force by faculty. For example, the physical education teacher in *Johnson v. Newburgh* (2001) had previously assaulted four other students (mostly African American). Letting this type of teacher-as-bully behavior continue unchallenged is inexcusable.
- Develop memoranda of understanding between the district and law enforcement regarding the role of school resource officers and the standards for review of behaviors that may not be appropriate in district schools.

STUDENT SUSPENSION OR EXPULSION FOR OFF-CAMPUS BEHAVIOR

Several states have passed laws allowing school districts to suspend or deny admission to students charged or convicted of serious crimes committed anywhere. For example, Missouri state law provides that no pupil shall be readmitted or enrolled to a regular program of instruction if the student has been convicted, charged with, or adjudicated to have committed a felony (RSM0 167.171.3). Many other states have similar laws that allow school districts to expel or refuse to admit students charged or convicted of serious crimes anywhere.

Courts are generally supportive of school officials' authority to develop and enforce reasonable rules for student conduct on school grounds and at school-sponsored activities, field trips, and events. However, school authority becomes more tenuous when students break school rules off school grounds. Consequently, most courts require a link between the off-campus behavior and disruption to the school environment (see *Kyle P. Parker et al. v. Board of Education of the Town of Thomaston,* 1998; *Student Alpha ID Number Guiza v. The School Board of Volusia County, Florida,* 1993).

Zirkel (2003a) and the National School Boards Association's Council of School Attorneys (2003) provide the following guidelines pertaining to the discipline of students for off-campus behavior:

1. Follow all state laws regarding the suspension or expulsion of students charged or convicted of crimes off-campus. These laws do not require a link to on-campus disruption.
2. Make clear to students and parents that accountability for proper behavior may extend beyond the schoolhouse gate when misbehavior occurs on school buses or at school-sponsored off-campus activities. Students and parents should be aware that students may be disciplined for conduct that starts at school and then extends off-campus. This is especially true when the behavior involves violence, gang activities, or drug sales (Zirkel, 2003a).
3. Discipline for off-campus behavior should be supported by a link between the behavior and disruption at school. In other words, regardless of how reprehensible the behavior may be, a relationship to the behavior and disruption in the

school should be established before taking disciplinary action (National School Boards Association's Council of School Attorneys, 2003).

4. Be sure that there is sufficient evidence to support disciplinary decisions. Avoid overreacting when considering student misconduct off-campus. Be sure to follow state and school district procedural due process requirements when suspensions or expulsions are considered for off-campus conduct (Zirkel, 2003a).

5. Follow all state laws that prohibit the enrollment or readmittance of students convicted or charged of certain crimes regardless of location.

6. If the student in question is classified as disabled under IDEA and/or Section 504, all procedural safeguards and requirements under these statutes are in force (Zirkel, 2003a).

7. Follow all state law reporting requirements to law enforcement when suspending or expelling students for offenses that are classified as felonies under state law.

EXTRACURRICULAR ACTIVITIES AND TITLE IX

Title IX is part of the Education Amendments of 1972. It is designed to protect students from being denied the benefits of any educational program or activity because of sex. Title IX applies to admissions, recruiting, course offerings, harassment based on sex, physical education, educational programs and activities, and employment. The Office for Civil Rights (OCR) is responsible for the enforcement of Title IX. OCR prefers that claims be settled in a peaceful manner without referring issues to the Department of Justice ("Secretary's Commission," 2002).

The Title IX regulations issued by the U.S. Department of Education in 1975 require equal athletic opportunities for males and females. Title IX is designed to protect all students. However, because females have been historically underrepresented in secondary school cocurricular activities, the primary focus, and thus one of the more visible impacts, of Title IX athletic enforcement has been improving opportunities for female participation in school-sponsored cocurricular activities at the P–12 level.

Although primarily designed for intercollegiate athletics, the regulations apply equally to secondary schools that accept federal money. In 1979, the U.S. Department of Education developed the following three-pronged test that provides guidance on the application of Title IX to athletics. A school may demonstrate compliance by meeting any one of the three parts:

1. The school provides opportunities for males and females in numbers that are substantially proportionate to respective enrollments; or

2. The school can demonstrate a history and continuing practice of program expansion that is responsive to the developing interest and abilities of the members of the sex that is underrepresented among athletes; or

3. The school can show that the interest and abilities of the members of that sex have been fully and effectively accommodated by the present program ("Secretary's Commission," 2002).

Currently this test applies only to colleges and universities. However, a federal district court in California held that a school district violated this test. First, the court concluded that the district did not provide girls with athletic opportunities substantially proportionate to their enrollment in the school. Second, the court found that the district failed to show a history and continuing practice of program expansion proportionate with the interest and abilities of female students, and the district had failed to fully and effectively accommodate female athletes' interest (*Ollier v. Sweetwater High School District*, 2009).

At least two courts have considered the question of whether or not Title IX applies when girls' secondary school sports such as basketball, volleyball, and softball are played during a "nontraditional" season. For example, boys' and girls' basketball are a traditional winter sport and girls' volleyball is a traditional fall sport. The federal district court in Michigan considered this question when the Michigan High School Athletic Association (MHSAA) scheduled several girls' sports in nontraditional seasons (*Communities for Equity v. Michigan High School Athletic Association,* 2001). The court held that this type of scheduling of girls' sports violated the Equal Protection Clause, Title IX, and Michigan state law. Particularly telling in this case was a finding by the court that girls' basketball was originally scheduled in a nontraditional season to "avoid inconveniencing the boys' basketball team." A similar case in New York considered decisions by school districts in a region of the state to schedule certain girls' sports during nontraditional seasons (*McCormick v. the School District of Mamaroneck and the School District of Pelham,* 2004). The Second Circuit Court had little problem affirming a trial court ruling that this practice by local school districts is in violation of Title IX.

Title IX prohibits retaliation for reporting potential violations. This protection now extends to coaches and other adults who work with PK–12 public school athletic programs. The U.S. Supreme Court recently held that Title IX's private right of action encompasses claims of retaliation against an individual (in this case a girls' basketball coach) after he complained about sex discrimination in the school's athletic program (*Roderick Jackson v. Birmingham Board of Education,* 2005). Roderick Jackson, the girls' basketball coach, complained unsuccessfully to his supervisors about discrepancies in equipment and facilities. He then received negative work evaluations and was ultimately removed as the girls' coach. It is important to note that the Court did not hold that Coach Jackson was dismissed from his coaching position in retaliation for his complaints, only that he is entitled to offer evidence to support his claim of retaliation.

Interscholastic athletics are not generally governed by state or federal statute, but rather by a state activity association. The Tennessee Secondary School Athletic Association (TSSAA) serves as a typical illustration. Founded in 1925, TSSAA is a voluntary association composed of member secondary schools in Tennessee. A Board of Control consisting of nine board members elected by the member schools governs the Association. Changes to the TSSAA constitution and bylaws are possible only by a majority vote of member schools. Funding for the association is derived primarily from state tournament revenues and member fees. Activity associations have not traditionally received state funding and have not been considered state actors by the courts. This is an important point. As a state actor, associations would be subject to the U.S. Constitution, and association bylaws would be open to judicial review. In *Brentwood Academy v. TSSAA* (2001), the U.S. Supreme Court considered just such a question. The *Brentwood* case involved the First Amendment rights of private-school (Brentwood Academy) coaches to communicate with and recruit student athletes to their school. The U.S. Supreme Court held that the association is a state actor because of the pervasive entwinement of state school officials in the structure of the association (*Brentwood v. TSSAA*, 2001).

Participation in interscholastic activities has traditionally been considered a privilege, and students have not had the same property and liberty interest in athletics or other extracurricular activities as they do in access to the general curriculum. However, some due process rights could conceivably be afforded to student athletes in light of the *Brentwood* decision. The Eighth Circuit Court implicitly acknowledged a senior softball player's right to due process before being dismissed from the team for missing a game. The coach announced to the team that the offending player was expelled from the team before ascertaining the player's side of the story. However, the court found that because the superintendent, principal, and coach met soon afterward with the player and her parents, the due process requirement of a hearing had been met by the district (*Wooten v. Pleasant Hope R-VI School District*, 2001). At least some school-district attorneys advise against establishing the practice of providing some due process rights before dismissing students from extracurricular activities. However, the rudimentary due process rights outlined in *Goss* do not seem burdensome when applied to extracurricular participation.

Another area of potential litigation includes student athlete eligibility for college sports. In order to be awarded athletic scholarships and compete at the intercollegiate level, student athletes must meet certain guidelines established by the National Collegiate Athletic Association (NCAA). Included in these guidelines are "core curricular" course requirements that students must complete in order to be eligible for scholarships and participation. All high schools are required to submit to the NCAA Clearinghouse a list of courses for approval. The Clearinghouse checks transcripts of potential college athletes to certify eligibility. Several incidents of high school counselors or principals failing to provide accurate lists to the Clearinghouse have resulted in student athletes being declared ineligible. These incidents have naturally resulted in several lawsuits against high school principals or counselors. In general, courts have granted summary judgment for the school district and have not held individual school employees accountable for these oversights (Abbott, 2002).

Linking to PRACTICE

Do:

- Annually evaluate the opportunities for and treatment of boys' and girls' extracurricular activities. For example, examine budgets, travel allotments, schedules, funding for uniforms and equipment, and equity of facility use.
- Both Title IX and the ISLLC standards require an affirmative response to any inequalities.
- Reassignment of coaches should be made for reasons other than in retaliation for complaining about Title IX violations.
- Provide training for athletic directors, coaches, band and choir directors, and other sponsors regarding school extracur-

ricular policy and applicable state association rules.

- If a student is facing dismissal from a state association–sponsored activity, afford reasonable opportunities for *rudimentary* procedural due process (the student is informed of the reasons, has a chance to tell his/her side of the story, and, if denying the allegation, is given an explanation of the evidence) before a final decision is made. This precaution appears not to be common practice. However, an ounce of prevention almost always makes decisions more defensible and should increase the chances of summary judgment should a legal challenge occur. This level of protection is not necessary in cases of reasonable punishments such as extra running, benching, or apologies to the team.

• Encourage or require coaches and sponsors to meet with the parents of students involved in extracurricular activities. Rules for participation should be clearly outlined, should not be vague or overbroad, and should be related to the activity. Explain rules, expectations of participants, and reasons for possible dismissal from the activity.

• Encourage parents to contact coaches or sponsors if there is any question regarding rules, procedures, or punishments.

• Know the NCAA Clearinghouse rules. Clearly mark "approved" courses in student curriculum guides or other documents students and parents use to make curricular decisions.

• Invite parents to meetings with counselors, coaches, and band and choir directors to discuss the Clearinghouse rules and the courses approved by the campus or district.

Title IX and Pregnancy

Title IX prohibits discrimination based on a student's actual or potential parental, family, or marital status that treats students differently on the basis of sex. Section 106.40 of Title IX provides guidance on the treatment of pregnant students. The following guidelines apply to most public K–12 schools.

1. Schools may not discriminate or exclude any student from an educational program or activity, including any class or extracurricular activity, on the basis of pregnancy, childbirth, false pregnancy, termination of pregnancy, or recovery, unless the student requests voluntarily to participate in separate programs.

2. It is permissible (and possibly advisable) to require a student to obtain a certification from a physician that the student is physically and emotionally able to continue participation so long as such a certification is similarly required of all students for other physical or emotional conditions.

3. Schools must treat pregnancy, childbirth, false pregnancy, termination of pregnancy, and recovery in the same manner and under the same policies as any other temporary disability.

4. Schools shall treat these conditions as a justification for a leave of absence for so long a period as is deemed medically necessary by the student's physician. After this time period the student shall be reinstated to the status which she held when the leave began.

Summary

Parents, students, community members, legislators, and educators do seem to agree on at least one thing: Safe and orderly schools are important. School leaders are empowered to achieve this safety and order by a wide variety of laws and policies at the national, state, and local levels. At the other end of the spectrum, students are required to relinquish many of the rights they have as citizens once they cross onto school grounds. In addition, students can be held accountable by school authorities for some acts outside the school that create disruption in the school. However, students do not check all of their rights at the schoolhouse gate. Interestingly, those individuals charged with protecting the limited rights of students are the very people who have the most authority to violate them. Effective school leaders understand the legal and ethical obligation to provide for a safe and orderly school, protect the rights of students, understand the need for a positive school culture based on social cooperation, and engage in honest interactions with students, parents, and others. Finding this balance may well be one of the biggest challenges future school leaders at all levels will face.

CONNECTING STANDARDS TO PRACTICE

BAD BOYS

Riverboat High School Senior Kyle Lacy could be witty, smart, charming, and exasperating—usually all at the same time. In early October, high school principal Tara Hills suspended Kyle for 3 days for being disrespectful to his Senior English teacher, John Mills. While on suspension, a state trooper found 2 ounces of marijuana hidden in the trunk of Kyle's car during a routine traffic stop. Kyle was charged with possession of marijuana and possession of drug paraphernalia.

Riverboat High School students were notified at the beginning of school that they would be held accountable for out-of-school conduct that has "some impact on what happens in school." Sharon Grey had in fact used this rule a few times when students were involved in some out-of-school conduct that created a problem at school. Current high school principal Tara Hills suspended Kyle for an additional 5 days for his drug possession arrest. Now, she was being pressured by several faculty members to make an example of Kyle and recommend that he be expelled for the remainder of the semester and banned from extracurricular activities for the remainder of the school year. Several teachers had approached Tara expressing their concern that failure to expel Kyle would make a sham of school rules. They also cited disruption of the educational process by noting that Kyle's younger brother, a Riverboat sophomore, was in the car at the time of the stop. Tara had overheard several students talking about Kyle's arrest, and the subject had apparently come up in some classes. She had stopped to listen during her scheduled classroom visits, and some of the discussion about the wisdom of legalizing marijuana had become spirited. But she had not noticed a groundswell of support for Kyle or any more classroom banter regarding recent events than usual.

Question

Argue for or against the expulsion of Kyle Lacy for the remainder of the semester. Clarify the legal question. Cite ISLLC standards, legal guidelines (i.e., procedural and substantive due process, off-campus behavior, and school discipline), and the idea of a well-ordered school to justify your answer. Write a letter or memorandum to the superintendent or school board president outlining your response to the problem of Kyle Lacy.

CHAPTER 6

Student Search

INTRODUCTION

The right to be free from unreasonable searches starts with the assumption that any search is an invasion of privacy. However, at school and school-sponsored events, these rights protect students from only unreasonable searches, not from all searches. The problem is defining what search under what circumstances is reasonable. This chapter addresses this question by examining the law related to a variety of student searches. The decision-making process is further guided by the ethical principles of Jeremy Bentham and selected ISLLC standards.

FOCUS QUESTIONS

1. What legal principles define school officials' authority to search students?
2. What ethical guides should school leaders use in making search decisions?
3. When may a student search be unreasonable?
4. When may student lockers, automobiles, and book bags be searched?
5. What are the legal parameters of drug dogs and drug testing?

KEY TERMS

Principle of
   proportionality

Probable cause

Reasonable cause

School resource
   officers

Urinalysis

Utilitarianism

CASE STUDY

Walkabout

Johnson City Middle School (JCMS) assistant principal LaDonna Fields was participating in her favorite administrative duty: walkabout. JCMS had been built in the early 1960s on the edge of the city. By the 1990s, JCMS was surrounded on all sides by homes, in some cases separated from backyards only by dilapidated fencing and hedgerows. Concerns over school safety had resulted in a board policy officially called *territoriality*. Territoriality basically required that an administrator walk around the boundaries of JCMS facilities at least 1 day per week to establish a presence in the neighborhood. The activity quickly became known as *walkabout.*

It was a particularly nice day that LaDonna had chosen for her weekly duty. She was taking her time walking about, looking in parked cars, behind shrubberies, and other potential hiding places for "misplaced" JCMS students. Out of the corner of her eye she glimpsed what looked like a person behind one of the shrubs on a neighboring property. She decided to investigate and to her surprise found eighth-grader Tasha Moore hiding behind the shrub. Dressed in the "school uniform" of skinny denim jeans, a tank top, and an oversized men's oxford shirt, Tasha did not seem to see LaDonna until she spoke. A smile crossed LaDonna's face as she said, "Hi, Tasha. I heard you were missing from math class again."

Tasha was an intelligent and popular student who had been elected class secretary and middle school homecoming queen. Tasha lived with her mother, who worked in a nearby city, and Tasha had many hours of unsupervised time on her hands. Another student had told LaDonna that Tasha often brought "pills" to school and sold them to students during lunch and between classes. LaDonna knew the informant was notoriously unreliable, but she had decided to take a special interest in Tasha and make an example out of her. This was her chance. Or so she thought.

"Well, Tasha, I guess I need to ask you why you are hiding here."

Tasha replied with as much conviction as she could, "Waiting for my mom. I have a dental appointment."

LaDonna replied, "Yeah, right, and I'm the tooth fairy. Now why are you not in math class, and why are you hiding here?" When Tasha did not answer, LaDonna said, "Let me see your purse, please." Tasha hesitated, but did hand the purse to LaDonna, who opened it and immediately found a book of hall passes apparently taken from the administrative offices or a teacher's desk. Hall passes were used by teachers and administrators to admit students who were late to class or late to school, or to give permission to use the restroom from class. After finding the hall passes, LaDonna continued to search the purse. Further digging revealed a couple of condoms in a zippered inner pocket, some rolling papers normally used to smoke marijuana, three $20 bills, and, most interesting to LaDonna, a single pill. "Come with me, please, Tasha."

Once in her office, LaDonna asked Tasha, "What kind of pill is this? Where did you get the money? Do you have any more pills?"

Tasha replied, "My mother gave me the money to buy food. The pill is a prescription ibuprofen for cramps. I don't have any more, and I don't know how it got in my purse."

Her suspicions growing, LaDonna asked Tasha to remove her outer shirt and turn her pockets inside out. Finding nothing of interest in Tasha's pockets, LaDonna asked Tasha to bend over so she could visually examine the contents of Tasha's brassiere. The examination did not reveal any pills. Tasha was obviously embarrassed and asked to call her mother.

LEADERSHIP PERSPECTIVES

The Fourth Amendment to the U.S. Constitution reads, in part, "The right of the people to be secure in their persons, houses, papers, and effects, against unreasonable searches and seizures, shall not be violated . . . but upon probable cause." The Fourth

Amendment, however, does not prohibit all searches, just *unreasonable* searches. In other words, the Fourth Amendment does not protect all privacy interests, just those that society recognizes as legitimate. Thus, reasonableness depends on the circumstances or context of the search. For example, searches of person and property have become commonplace in airports, at federal courthouses, and at most large sporting events. Just as society has accepted certain searches of persons and property in the name of safety, students in school are likewise required to acquiesce to reasonable searches of their persons and property (**ISLLC Standard 3**).

> **ISLLC Standard 3**

The U.S. Supreme Court has held that even a limited search of a person is a substantial invasion of privacy (*Terry v. Ohio,* 1967). However, the U.S. Supreme Court has again carved out a special niche for students on school grounds and at school-sponsored events. Consequently, students do not enjoy the same Fourth Amendment rights inside the schoolhouse gate as they do outside. For example, some random searches have been declared unconstitutional in society (see, for example, *City of Indianapolis v. Edmond,* 2000, holding random drug-detection dog searches of stopped vehicles to be unconstitutional) that might very well pass muster at a school (see, for example, *Horton v. Goose Creek Independent School District,* 1983, finding canine searches of school lockers and automobiles in school parking lots constitutional). However, just as students do not leave all of their First Amendment rights at the schoolhouse gate, they do not lose all of their Fourth Amendment rights to be free of unreasonable searches in schools (*New Jersey v. T. L. O.,* 1985). The problem is defining the term *unreasonable*. Most educators and parents would agree that stealing hall passes and allegations of selling pills to students during lunch, as illustrated in the case study "Walkabout," should be taken seriously by school officials. They would also most likely agree that at some point any search could become unreasonable and detract from the greater good of the school culture (**ISLLC Standard 5**). But, at what point does a student's expectation of privacy outweigh the obligation of school leaders to maintain good order and discipline in the school? In other words, at what point does a *reasonable* search become *unreasonable*?

> **ISLLC Standard 5**

ISLLC Standard 5D calls for school leaders to consider and evaluate the potential moral and legal consequences of their decision making. This is especially true when deciding to search a student's person or property. Searches that are initially justifiable can easily slide onto a slippery slope that leads to an unreasonable search. The case study "Walkabout" is an illustration of this slope. Tasha is certainly guilty of skipping class. She may also be guilty of other things, including meeting a boyfriend in the middle of the day, stealing hubcaps, or numerous other misdeeds. Drug use and/or possession with the intent to distribute on school campuses are serious problems that should be addressed. But, does the evidence support the assumption that Tasha is in possession of illegal contraband? Would the search of Tasha's purse be justified in this situation? Assuming that the search of Tasha's purse is justified, would finding the single pill justify a search of her pockets and shirt? Would finding the single pill justify a search of an eighth-grade student's brassiere?

> **ISLLC Standard 5D**

To illustrate, visualize the reason for a search and the relative intrusiveness of a search on a continuum. One end of the continuum would include relatively minor items such as a small amount of money. The other end of the continuum would include drugs and weapons. The intrusiveness of the search could be visualized on the same continuum starting on one end with a cursory search escalating to a search of pockets or jackets and culminating with an intrusive strip search. The problem occurs when the reason for the search and the relative intrusiveness of the search become out of balance. For example, a search of an eighth-grade student's underwear for a $5 bill seems unreasonable, and a cursory search for drugs or weapons violates school administrators' obligation to keep students safe. The point is this: Starting and stopping a student search at the appropriate point on the continuum is difficult. This is especially true when emotions are high. Consequently, decisions to search a student or her or his property, and the even more difficult decision when to terminate a search, can create considerable legal and ethical dilemmas for school leaders (**ISLLC Standard 5D**). However, the utilitarian ethics of Jeremy Bentham may provide guidance.

ISLLC Standard 5D

UTILITARIANISM: STUDENT SEARCHES AND THE GREATER GOOD

Jeremy Bentham (1748–1832), an influential British philosopher, is considered to be the founder of modern utilitarianism. *Utilitarianism*, or *utility*, views the "greatest happiness of the greatest number" to be the goal of all ethical actions and the primary purpose of a just and fair government: in other words, "the greater good" of all concerned. Bentham uses *utility* to describe the tendency of an action to produce "benefit, advantage, pleasure, good, or happiness" or to prevent the happening of "mischief, pain, evil, or unhappiness" to the affected person or to the community in general. Bentham was concerned about the rights of the individual in society. In fact, he finds it counterproductive to consider society without an understanding of what is in the interest of the individuals within that society. In other words, it is counterproductive to consider the happiness of students within a school without first considering the relative happiness or utility of the individual students in the school. One can assume that individual happiness is promoted by effective strategies that lead to a safe and secure building environment (**ISLLC Standard 3**). It can also be assumed that some strategies designed to promote a safe and secure building environment can be counterproductive and subtract from the relative happiness of students and others. Utility then considers how an action (for example, a student search policy) tends to add or subtract from the sum of the pleasures or pains of each individual in the school. An action thus promotes utility in respect to the school at large when the tendency it has to augment the happiness of the individual students in the school outweighs the potential for individual student unhappiness (Bentham, 1970).

ISLLC Standard 3

To meet this purpose, Bentham viewed the primary aim of law and government as guaranteeing security for citizens (**ISLLC Standard 3**). Security, and especially security of expectation, is the foundation of happiness for society and the primary aim of legislation. These same principles are applied, though to a lesser degree, to students in school. Equity, defined as fairness or evenhandedness, also plays an important role in Bentham's utilitarian philosophy. Although inferior or subservient to security, equity also is a necessary condition for achieving the greater good. Therefore, Bentham's principle of utility does not mean that the greatest number or those with the most influence have the right to oppress the lesser number, or less influential, just because these actions may increase the total amount of happiness (and freedom from pain) of the majority or more influential. Rather, Bentham's utility principle seeks an "equal quantity of happiness" for every member of the community in question.

ISLLC Standard 3

He realized that at times happiness or unhappiness could not be distributed equally. Student searches are a good example. The relative unhappiness of an individual student subjected to a *reasonable* search for illegal drugs or a weapon would be subservient to the overarching need for security of the school at large. However, the relative unhappiness of an individual student subjected to an *unreasonable* search would detract from the greater good and subvert the overarching need for security of expectation.

At first glance, Bentham's principle of utility may seem far removed from efficient and effective strategies for promoting a safe and secure building environment. However, considerations of the principle of utility, or the greatest happiness for the greatest number, serve as the foundation for safe schools and a framework for promoting the types of school cultures called for in **ISLLC Standard 3**.

ISLLC Standard 3

Bentham's thoughts on the purpose of government also included considerable attention to the authority of the government to punish individuals. To this end, he developed several guidelines concerning the legitimacy of punishment and the proportion between punishments and offenses (***principle of proportionality***). These principles are summarized here:

1. The general object of laws (or policy) should be to augment the greater good of the school community. School rules, policies, and punishments governing student searches should be designed to exclude those actions (or, in Bentham's terminology, *mischief*) that subtract from this happiness.

2. However, in Bentham's view all punishment causes harm. Therefore, punishment *should not* occur under the following circumstances:
    a. Where there is no misbehavior to prevent: in other words, where it is *groundless.*
    b. Where the punishment will not *prevent* misbehavior or action.
    c. Where the *harm created by the punishment is greater* than the act it was designed to prevent: in other words, where it is arbitrary and capricious.
    d. Where it is *needless,* or where the mischief may be prevented, or cease of itself, without the punishment (Bentham, 1970, pp. 158–159).

3. If the object of policy is to prevent harm, then there will be times when punishment is required and therefore worthwhile. In other words, there are times when punishment promotes the greater good. Conversely, a lack of punishment or overzealous punishment detracts from the greater good. Bentham developed four subordinate objects of punishment to guide the development of worthwhile punishment to promote security:
    a. The first object is to prevent, insofar as it is possible and worthwhile, all sorts of misconduct.
    b. However, if it is not possible to prevent all rule violations, the next object is to induce the person to commit an offense less serious or disruptive, rather than more serious or disruptive.
    c. When a person has resolved to commit a particular offense, the next object is to dispose the person to cause no more of a violation.

than is necessary to accomplish his or her objective: in other words, to cause as little disruption as possible.

d. The last object is, whatever the mischief is, to prevent it at as low a cost as possible.

4. Subservient to these objects or purposes of punishments are several rules (selected by the author) or canons by which the proportion of punishments to offenses is to be governed.

   a. *Rule One:* The amount of the punishment must be proportional to the offense.

   b. *Rule Two:* The greater the disruption, the more worthwhile it is to expend the energy to administer the punishment.

   c. *Rule Three:* Where two offenses come in competition, the punishment for the greater offense must be sufficient to induce students to prefer the less.

   d. *Rule Four:* The punishment should be adjusted in such a manner to each particular offense in a way that would serve as a deterrent or restraint for committing the offense.

   e. *Rule Five:* The punishment ought in no case to be more than what is necessary to bring it into conformity with Bentham's principles of punishment.

   f. *Rule Six:* Where a particular student's misbehavior is conclusively indicative of a habit, the punishment may be increased to a point that not only deters the individual offense being addressed, but also other similar offenses that are likely to have been committed with impunity by the same offender.

   g. *Rule Seven:* In adjusting the quantum (amount) of punishment, pay attention to the circumstances by which all punishment may be rendered unprofitable.

Source: These principles were selected and adapted by the author from *An Introduction to the Principles of Morals and Legislation* (pp. 165–171), by Jeremy Bentham, edited by J. H. Burns and H. L. A. Hart, 1970. New York: Oxford Press.

Applying Utility to Decision Making

Bentham points out that the primary purpose of policy should be to exclude those acts that substantially threaten security and interfere with a positive learning climate. Every policy, however, creates an *offense* (Bentham, 1970, p. 302). In other words, it is only by making a rule against some act that school leaders can implement a punishment for breaking the rule. Certainly school district policies that regulate and punish the taking of property and the possession of illegal drugs or weapons are necessary to protect the learning climate (**ISLLC Standard 3**). However, as Habermas (1987) and Sergiovanni (2000) point out, it is possible (and according to Sergiovanni, common) for these policies and practices designed to protect the learning climate to, in fact, have a negative impact on school culture.

ISLLC Standard 3

The problem is in finding the right *proportionality* among the need for a policy, the enforcement practice associated with the policy, and the utility of the school community. The case study "Walkabout" illustrates this. Starting with the assumption that any search is an invasion of privacy, Bentham's principles of proportionality apply to the situation facing assistant principal LaDonna Field in "Walkabout." Examine Bentham's four principles governing when a punishment should not occur. Does LaDonna know for sure that Tasha brings pills to school to sell to students, or does she simply suspect that it may be true? It is possible that this search is groundless (Principle 2a). As previously stated, Tasha is more than likely guilty of skipping class. But does skipping class justify the search of a student's purse? Does finding the hall passes in Tasha's purse justify a further search of the purse? Does finding the one pill in a zippered pocket inside the purse justify a search of Tasha's pockets? Her brassiere? Has this search gotten to the point where the harm created by the search is greater than the act (Principle 2c)? Or, as Bentham implies, does the evil created by the search outweigh the good? In this case, it is not difficult to imagine the potential negative consequences for the reputation of LaDonna Field escalating with each step

ISLLC Standard 5D

in the search. Is this an example of what is meant by **ISLLC Standard 5D**: "Consider and evaluate the potential moral and legal consequences of decision-making"?

The last rule concerns the preventability of an act, thus making the search needless. In this case, proper procedures regarding when students may return to the classroom late or use the restroom may be necessary. Bentham's fourth rule regarding when punishment should not be inflicted is particularly germane. In Bentham's view, the object of policy is to prevent "mischief." Thus, policies that are designed to prevent mischief and a need to search students are preferable to policies designed to allow for the search of students.

Even the best policies, however, may not always prevent the need for a search. When this task becomes necessary, Bentham's seven rules presented in this chapter governing the proportionality of punishment to offense provide guidance. For example, Rule Two states that the greater the potential harm to school utility, the greater the worth of the search. Knowing where to start and more importantly at what point to stop a search for contraband, a $20 bill, or any other item can be particularly difficult. However, Rule Five states that the extent of the search should not be any greater than is necessary to accomplish the purpose of the search. The other rules similarly apply and, in different language, have been applied by the U.S. Supreme Court and federal district and appellate courts considering the search of school children.

STUDENTS AND THE FOURTH AMENDMENT

Bentham's principles of proportionality can be viewed as a balance between the reason for a search and the relative intrusiveness of the search. In decidedly different language, but very similar to Bentham's principles of proportionality, the U.S. Supreme Court considered the balance between the need for a search and the relative intrusiveness of the search in *New Jersey v. T. L. O.* (1985). This landmark Supreme Court case began when a New Jersey high school teacher discovered T. L. O. (then a 14-year-old freshman) and another student smoking in the school lavatory. When confronted by the assistant principal, T. L. O. denied that she had been smoking and claimed that she did not smoke at all. The assistant principal demanded to see her purse. He found a pack of cigarettes and a package of cigarette rolling papers commonly associated with the use of marijuana. Searching further, he found some marijuana, a pipe, plastic bags, a substantial amount of money, an index card containing a list of students who owed T. L. O. money, and two letters that implicated her in marijuana dealing. The student was referred to law enforcement. After several appeals, the New Jersey Supreme Court ordered the suppression of the evidence found in T. L. O.'s purse, holding that the search of the purse was unreasonable. The U.S. Supreme Court granted certiorari.

The Court first concluded that the Fourth Amendment's prohibition on unreasonable searches and seizures applies to searches conducted by public school officials. The Court then confronted the question of whether the search in this case was unreasonable. The Court concluded that it was not. After further thought, the Court did consider the question of the proper standard for assessing the legality of searches conducted by school officials and the application of these standards to this case. The Court took notice of the difficulty of maintaining discipline in the public schools, but found the situation not so dire that students could not claim at least some legitimate expectations of privacy. However, maintaining discipline and security in schools requires some degree of flexibility. Consequently, the Court held that school officials need not obtain a warrant before searching a student under their authority. Further, the Court freed school officials from the probable cause standard of law enforcement and instead found that the legality of a search of a student should depend on the *reasonableness under the circumstances* of the search. This is an important point. ***Probable cause*** may be described as when a "fair probability" or a "substantial chance" exists that the search will discover evidence of criminal activity (*Illinois v. Gates*, 1983). *Reasonable suspicion* may be described as a "moderate chance" that the search will reveal evidence of wrongdoing (*Safford v. Redding*, 2009).

In an effort to clarify the parameters of "reasonableness," the Court established the following guidelines:

1. The search should be justified at inception
2. The search should be reasonably related in scope to the reason for the search
3. The search should be reasonably related to the objective of the search
4. The search should not be excessively intrusive in light of the age and sex of the student and the nature of the infraction

These concepts are fluid in that the decision to search does not occur in a vacuum. Therefore, the context in which the search takes place is the determining factor. For example, reasonable suspicion can include a teacher or other school employee witnessing a student violating school rules. In the case of *TLO*, the Court found that the teacher's accusation of smoking justified the hypothesis that TLO, might have cigarettes in her purse. Finding the rolling papers warranted a further search that, ultimately, uncovered the student's possession of marijuana. The discovery of marijuana justified the further examination of a zipped pocket in the purse that revealed the list of names and the money. Think about the case study "Walkabout." Does the fact that Tasha is skipping math class and hiding behind some shrubs in violation of school rules justify the hypothesis that she may have contraband (stolen hall passes, drugs, and so forth) in her purse?

Reasonable suspicion can also be established when school officials receive firsthand information from a student, parent, or other member of the school community regarding individual students. For example, the 11th Circuit Court held that a reliable tip from another student with some collaboration provided reasonable grounds to search a student's coat (*C. B. v. Driscoll,* 1996). A tip from law enforcement also establishes reasonable suspicion. For example, when a school principal was informed by police that a student might have a gun on school property, the tip established reasonable suspicion to detain, question, and search the student (*In re D. E. M.,* 1999). This decision also established that when school officials act independently on tips from law enforcement, they do not act as agents of the police. In short, reasonable suspicion considerably lowers the bar for the justification of a search of a student or her property at school or school activities. However, school officials should weigh the credibility of the information before making a decision to search (see *Fewless v. Board of Education of Wayland Schools,* 2002, as an example of this logic).

Reasonable suspicion can also be justified when a student is the only person (or one of a very few students) present at the time of the rule violation (Stader, 2003). For example, a third-grade teacher discovered that $10 she was holding for a student was missing. There were only three students in the classroom at the time the money disappeared. Therefore, individualized suspicion was not necessary to search the three students (*Watkins v. Millennium School District,* 2003). It can be assumed that at some point the number of students present would make a search for $10 unreasonable, but three is not the number. This case also illustrates how quickly a reasonable search can become unreasonable. The teacher initially asked the three students to empty their pockets. When nothing was found, she instructed the students to "pull out their waistbands." When this search did not yield the missing $10, that would have been a good time for the teacher to stop. However, the teacher took each student into a supply closet where she looked into their underwear. The court found this part of the search intrusive and in violation of school policy.

Students can be disciplined for refusing to submit to a reasonable search. For example, the Fourth Circuit Court upheld the suspension of a student for refusing to allow a search of his backpack. The court found that school officials had developed reasonable individualized suspicion, not by way of any particular information but rather by the process of elimination (*DesRoches v. Caprio,* 1998).

Reasonably related in scope considers the balance between the reason for a search and the intrusiveness of the search. The U.S. Supreme Court recently considered the balance between the reason for a search and the relative intrusiveness of the search in *Safford Unified School District #1 v. April Redding* (2009). As LaDonna Field in the case study "Walkabout" may learn, the balance between the reason for a search and the relative intrusiveness of a search can get quickly out of hand.

The U.S. Supreme Court granted certiorari in *Safford v. Redding* (2009) to consider two questions: (1) Did the search of Savana's bra and undergarments by school officials acting on reasonable suspicion that she had brought forbidden prescription and over-the-counter drugs to school violate the Fourth Amendment? and (2) is the official who ordered the search entitled to qualified immunity?

In an 8–1 decision, with Justice Thomas dissenting, the Court held that the search of Savana Redding's bra and underpants for forbidden prescription and over-the-counter drugs did violate the Constitution. One week before the search of Savana Redding, a fellow student reported to Safford Middle School Principal Kerry Wilson that students were bringing drugs and weapons to school. The student also reported that he had become ill after taking one of the pills offered to him. On the day of the search of Savana, the same student gave Wilson a white pill (later identified as ibu-profen 400 mg, available only by prescription) given to him by Marissa Glines. A search of a binder associated with Marissa revealed illegal contraband including a blue pill, several white pills, and a razor blade. Marissa implicated Savana as the source of the pills. At Wilson's direction, Marissa was then subjected to a search of her bra and underpants by administrative assistant Helen Romero. The search revealed no additional pills.

Wilson summoned Savana Redding to his office. Marissa's implication and sev-eral teachers reporting that Marissa and Savana were friends justified the search of Savana's outer clothing and backpack in the privacy of Wilson's office. As Justice Souter, writing for the majority, explained, "If Wilson's reasonable suspicion did not support a search of Savana's bag and outer clothing, it would not justify any search worth making." No pills were found in her bag or outer clothing.

Wilson then directed administrative assistant Helen Romero to conduct a strip search of Savana. Savana was instructed to remove her outer clothing and pull out her bra and the elastic band on her underpants. No pills or other contraband were found. The Court reasoned that the strip search of Savana violated the second and third prongs of *TLO*. In essence, at least according to the majority, the intrusiveness of the search of Savana's bra and underpants did not match the nature of the infraction that justified the search in the first place. The court held that both "subjective and reason-able societal expectations of personal privacy support the treatment of [a strip search] as categorically distinct, requiring distinct elements of justification . . . for going beyond a search of outer clothing and belongings." A search this extensive of a 13-year-old student's bra and underpants calls for suspicion that it will pay off. In this case the fatal mistake was a lack of specific suspicion that Savana was hiding drugs in her undergarments. In addition, Wilson should have been aware of the limited threat pre-sented by the prescription ibuprofen and over-the-counter painkillers. In other words, assistant principal Wilson violated Bentham's principles of proportionality in that the relative harm created by the search of Savana's bra and underpants was greater than the act it was designed to prevent.

At this point the Court considered the question of qualified immunity. A six-member majority of the Court found enough significant differences among lower court rulings to cast doubt on whether the Court had been sufficiently clear in *T. L. O.* In short, the discrepancy among lower court interpretations of *T. L. O.* when applied to strip searches made it difficult for a reasonable assistant principal to know that the strip search of Savana Redding under the circumstances described clearly violated her established constitutional rights.

It is important to note that Justice Stevens and Justice Ginsburg disagreed. The two justices argued that Savana's right was clearly established at the time of the search of her undergarments. Justice Stevens opined that this was "in essence, a case in which clearly established law meets clearly outrageous conduct." In his view, just because some lower courts had misread the precedents of *T. L. O.* did not miti-gate a well-established right. In short, Justices Stevens and Ginsburg argued that assistant principal Wilson should be held liable for the unconstitutional strip search of Savana Redding. As this case illustrates, an intrusive search, no matter how justi-fied, is an inherent risk to both the person conducting the search and the students they serve.

Linking to PRACTICE

Do:

- Make sure that district and campus policy outline when, where, why, and by whom students may be subjected to search. Policy should describe reasons for and purposes of the policy.
- Provide a copy of all search policies to parents, law enforcement, students, and staff.
- Attend booster club, PTA/PTO, and other parent organization meetings to discuss and clarify school search policies (Stader, 2003).
- Provide training for all staff in the legal requirements of student searches. Training should stress the importance of the relationship between the reason for the search and the scope of the search (Stader, 2001b).
- Superintendents and school district attorneys should discuss with local boards of education whether or not to ban strip searches of students under any circumstances. As the court pointed out in Safford, several school districts around the country have implemented this policy. Some states have passed laws limiting strip searches by public school employees. For example, Missouri law allows a school employee to strip-search a student only when a commissioned law enforcement officer is not available and when weapons, explosives, or substances that pose an imminent threat of physical harm may be involved (RSMo 167.166.1).
- Generally, the most difficult and risky decision school administrators make is

not whether to start a search, but rather when to terminate a search. Therefore, school districts should provide ongoing professional development for principals and assistant principals regarding student searches. The professional development should involve school attorneys and include specific examples of justification, reasonable scope, and reasonable relatedness to the objective of the search (Stader, Greicar, Stevens, & Dowdy, 2010).

- Intrusive searches are most often justifiable when there is reasonable suspicion that the student possesses a weapon or other dangerous item that poses an immediate threat of safety to the student, the student body, or to others (Stader et al., 2010).
- Follow Bentham's proportionality principle. The greater the potential harm (drugs and weapons, for example), the greater the justification for intrusive searches.
- Stop and think before escalating to a more intrusive search.
- Consider: When in doubt, don't.

Do Not:

- Abandon common sense.
- Make search decisions in the heat of the moment.
- Ever conduct or authorize intrusive searches for small amounts of money or items that do not present a danger to others in the school.

NONINTRUSIVE SEARCHES

Most courts recognize the difference between the search of a person or a person's personal property and a search of objects such as book bags, lockers, and automobiles on school property. This section provides examples of nonintrusive searches such as locker searches, use of metal detectors, and searches of items taken on field trips.

Field Trips and Overnight Stays

Students' diminished expectations of privacy apply to field trips and school-sponsored overnight trips. However, a written policy makes search decisions more defensible (Stader, 2003). A New York district court upheld a search of a student's motel room that revealed alcohol and significant quantities of marijuana in a locked motel-room safe. The search was judged to be reasonable based on the facts that students had been asked to sign waivers agreeing not to use or possess illegal substances, that students had been informed that rooms were subject to search (or at least to "room checks"), and, most significantly, that the principal smelled marijuana around a cluster of students outside one of their rooms. The court concluded that "when public school students are acting in a supervised environment, under the control of public school teachers or administrators, the search must merely be reasonable under the circumstances" (*Rhodes v. Guarricino*, 1999).

Student Lockers

A diminished expectation of privacy also applies to student lockers. This is a good thing since locker searches are relatively common. In 2007–2008, 54% of students age 12 to 18 reported locker checks by school personnel (Robers, Zhang, & Truman, 2010). However, several court decisions illustrate the wisdom of having a clear locker search policy consistent with state law before searching individual student lockers. A U.S. district court in Kansas found that a school policy stating that lockers were the property of the school resulted in a lowered expectation of privacy. Consequently, district personnel had sufficient grounds to search a student's locker in light of the probability of finding missing contraband (*Singleton v. Board of Education USD 500*, 1995).

Metal Detectors

Daily metal detector checks are not common in public schools. In fact, in 2007–2008 only about 1% of public schools reported daily metal detector checks and 5% reported at least one random metal detector check for weapons (Robers et al., 2010). The relatively rare use of daily metal detector checks may have more to do with cost of equipment and personnel than legal concerns. Courts have been relatively consistent in considering metal detectors to be minimally intrusive and an effective way to keep weapons out of schools.

RANDOM SWEEPS FOR CONTRABAND In 2007–2008, about 11% of public schools participated in one or more checks, sweeps, or camera checks for drugs or weapons not including dog sniffs (Robers et al., 2010). These practices are generally applicable only to secondary schools, designed to keep weapons and other contraband out of schools, and are designed to be minimally intrusive (see *State of Florida v. J. A.*, 1996). However, the Eighth Circuit Court found a policy of random classroom searches of secondary students and their belongings by the Little Rock School District (LRSD) to be unconstitutional (*Doe v. Little Rock School District*, 2004). LRSD had a policy of randomly selecting classrooms, then instructing students in the selected classroom to empty their pockets, place all items including purses and backpacks on their desks, and exit the room. The court reasoned that students do have a diminished expectation of privacy compared to most people in public situations. However, school children are entitled to expect some degree of privacy in the personal items that they bring to school. The balancing act, according to the court, is finding the point at which the needs of the school to maintain discipline and protect students outweigh students' expectation of privacy. In this particular case, the Eighth Circuit Court held that the LRSD may not deprive students of their Fourth Amendment rights simply by announcing that these rights will no longer be honored. The court concluded by stating, "While the line separating reasonable and unreasonable school searches is sometimes indistinct, we think it plain that the LRSD's search practices cross it."

Drug Dogs

The quest for drug-free schools has included the assistance of drug detection dogs provided by local law enforcement. In 2007–2008 about 22% of public schools had one or more random dog sniffs to check for drugs (Robers et al., 2010). The Fifth Circuit Court clarified the fundamental legal guidelines for canine searches in *Horton v. Goose Creek Independent School District* (1983, cert. denied). Goose Creek school district, in response to a growing drug problem, instituted a policy of randomly taking drug detection dogs to the various campuses in the district where the dogs sniffed students' lockers and cars. The dogs were also taken on leashes into classrooms to sniff the students themselves. The court considered two questions: (1) Is the sniffing of a drug-detection dog a search? (2) To what extent are students protected by the Fourth Amendment from searches by school officials? The court established that dog sniff searches of lockers and cars did not constitute a search and were permissible. Justification to extend the search is obtained when the dog alerts to a particular car or locker. However, the random dog sniffing of persons is not permissible and constitutes a violation of students' Fourth Amendment rights.

Automobile Searches

Reasonable-suspicion searches of student cars in school parking lots are generally treated in the same manner as other reasonable-suspicion searches of students. For example, the Supreme Court of Mississippi upheld the suspension of a student for possession of alcohol found in his truck in the school student parking lot (*Covington County v. G. W.,* 2000). The school principal and security officer responded to a note from a teacher that a particular student was drinking in the parking lot. The note from the teacher provided the reasonable suspicion necessary for the search of the student's truck, and the alcohol found in the truck served as grounds for the suspension. Random sweeps of school parking lots for drugs or weapons are also usually upheld. For example, when the Warminster (Pennsylvania) police swept a high school's premises for drugs, they noticed part of a beer carton in Kristin Ream's car (*Ream v. Centennial School District,* 2001). Summoning Miss Ream, the police obtained her permission to search the car. The search unearthed a ring box with 45 Ecstasy pills. Miss Ream was suspended and recommended for expulsion (she was already on probation for possession of marijuana). The Superior Court of New Jersey, Appellate Division, similarly concluded that vehicle searches conducted by school officials need only satisfy the reasonable suspicion standard (*New Jersey v. Best,* 2008).

Linking to PRACTICE

Do:

- Make random searches of student book bags, backpacks, or other student-carried items part of campus and school district field-trip policy and practice.
- Use campus policy to clarify that lockers are the property of the school and that students have reduced expectations of privacy for personal items such as book bags, backpacks, gym bags, and jackets stored in lockers.
- Make sure that policy clearly states that automobiles in the school parking lot may be subject to search.
- Announce to students, teachers, parents, and visitors that random or mandatory metal-detector searches may be conducted.

- Make sure that the use of drug-sniffing dogs is outlined in policy. The policy should include when dogs will be used and what will be subject to search. The policy should also establish that a dog alert would provide reasonable cause for continued searching.

Do Not:

- Initiate drug dog searches, metal detectors, or random sweeps without considering the importance of such actions on the district or campus "utility." In other words, does the discomfort sometimes caused by the presence of police and drug dogs outweigh the need for such measures?

SCHOOL RESOURCE OFFICER: LAW ENFORCEMENT OR EDUCATOR?

The past few years have seen a fundamental shift in philosophy regarding police officers in schools. Seen at one time to be a liability, police officers, often referred to as *school resource officers* (SROs), are now welcome additions in many schools. In 2007, 69% of students ages 12 to 18 reported the presence of security guards and/or assigned police officers in their school (Robers et al., 2010). Any controversy notwithstanding, there is little doubt that law enforcement should be involved in some school safety concerns with which educators have little if any expertise and experience. For example, searching suspects for weapons and the proper methods of confronting armed suspects are fundamental to law enforcement training. However, the movement to include police officers in an educational setting to enforce school policy may be complicated by some unresolved legal issues. These legal issues are particularly apparent when students are searched. The primary legal question concerns whether or not SROs are bound by the more stringent probable cause standard or by the more lenient *reasonable cause* standard established in *TLO*. The answer seems to depend on by whom and how the search was initiated. Recently, courts have tended to analyze searches conducted by law enforcement in schools based on the circumstances of the search, the reasonableness of the search, and, most importantly, who initiated the search. If school administrators initiate the search, the lower reasonable cause standard seems to hold (*Shade v. City of Farmington*, 2002). However, when a reasonable person could assume that the SRO is acting as a law enforcement officer, then the higher standard is necessary. A Tennessee state court of appeals (*R. D. S. v. State of Tennessee*, 2008) explains the difference this way:

> We hold that the reasonable suspicion standard is the appropriate standard to apply to searches conducted by a law enforcement officer assigned to a school on a regular basis and assigned duties at the school beyond those of

an ordinary law enforcement officer such that he or she may be considered a school official as well as a law enforcement officer, whether labeled an "SRO" or not. However, if a law enforcement officer not associated with the school system searches a student in a school setting, that officer should be held to the probable cause standard.

The fine line between law enforcer and educator is never more pronounced than when police or child protection agencies come to the school to interview a student. The U.S. Supreme Court reviewed two cases during the 2010–2011 terms that address this particular question. The first case considers whether child-abuse investigators violate the Fourth Amendment rights of students by interviewing them at school without a warrant or parental consent about suspected child abuse (*Greene v. Camreta*, 2009). Camreta, a state child protective officer, and several other state officials interviewed a 9-year-old girl at school regarding allegations of parental sexual abuse. The Ninth Circuit Court held that seizing the student without a warrant, court order, parental consent, or exigent circumstances violated the Constitution. The court further held that the officials were entitled to qualified immunity. Camreta and others appealed to the U.S. Supreme Court asserting that the requirement for a warrant, court order, or parental permission would place an undue burden on state protection officers in future cases of alleged child abuse. There are two legal questions involved: (1) May state officials appeal a finding of qualified immunity, and, more importantly to educators, (2) should child protection officers be required to obtain a warrant, court order, or parental permission to interview children who may be victims of parental sexual abuse? The Court answered the first question in the affirmative. Unfortunately, the U.S. Supreme Court sidestepped the most important question by finding the case moot and vacated the Ninth Circuit Court holding. The student in question now lives in Florida, is rapidly approaching her 18th birthday, and no longer needs protection from the challenged practice. It is unfortunate that the Court did not consider the question of whether or not child protection officials need a warrant, court order, or parental permission to interview minor students at school regarding suspected or alleged parental sexual abuse (*Camreta v. Greene*, 2011).

The second case considers a decision by the Florida Supreme Court holding that a juvenile burglary suspect interrogated at school by police officers was not in custody during the school interrogation and need not have been given *Miranda* warnings (*In the Matter of J. D. B.*, 2009). The U.S. Supreme Court disagreed to some extent. Then, 13-year-old special education student J. B. D. was questioned at school by a police officer and school administrator about some neighborhood robberies. He finally admitted to taking part in the robberies. J. B. D. was not informed that he had the right to remain silent or to leave at any time. In addition, his guardian grandmother was not contacted. The Court held that "it is beyond dispute that children will often feel bound to submit to police questioning when an adult in the same circumstances would feel free to leave. Seeing no reason for police officers or courts to blind themselves to that commonsense reality, we hold that a child's age properly informs the *Miranda* custody analysis." A child in school being interviewed by a police officer and a school administrator would feel pressured to conform to the questioning and not have a clear understanding that she or he would be free to leave at anytime. The Court remanded the case back to the state court to determine if J. B. D. was in custody at the time of the questioning (*J. B. D. v. North Carolina*, 2011).

Linking to PRACTICE

Do:

- Initiate discussions and a memorandum of understanding with local law enforcement regarding the role of the school resource officer (SRO).
- Recommend that this agreement become part of board policy.
- Always involve SROs or local law enforcement in searches for weapons, especially when guns may be present.

- It may be advisable for school boards to develop a clear policy regarding police or child protection officials requesting to interview minor children at school.

Do Not:

- Involve the SRO or local law enforcement in minor disciplinary issues or in a search for small amounts of money or inexpensive items such as pens, calculators, or games.

URINALYSIS TESTING

In an effort to combat drug use among students, several school districts have instituted a policy of drug testing via *urinalysis*. Courts have supported reasonable-suspicion drug testing policies. For example, the Seventh Circuit Court upheld a school administrator's ordering of medical assessment of a student based on a supervising teacher's suspicion that he was under the influence of an illegal substance while attending an after-school smoking cessation program (*Bridgman v. New Trier High School District*, 1997).

However, reasonable suspicion does not equate to carte blanche urinalysis testing. The Third Circuit Court overruled a district court decision regarding student urinalysis (*Gruenke v. Seip*, 2000). A high school swim team coach, suspecting a team member to be pregnant, required a pregnancy test of the suspected student before he would allow her to continue on the team. The student and her mother sued the coach, alleging violation of the student's Fourth Amendment rights and interference with privacy regarding personal matters. The suit also included claims under Pennsylvania tort law (see Chapter 10 for a discussion of the law of torts). Policies aimed at various groups or classes of students also require some discretion. The Seventh Circuit Court reversed a lower court decision supporting the suspicionless drug testing of all students suspended for fighting. The court clearly believed that drug testing based on individualized reasonable suspicion was well within administrator prerogatives. However, being disciplined for fighting did not provide the individualized suspicion necessary to negate students' Fourth Amendment rights (*Willis v. Anderson Community School*, 1998).

Random Urinalysis Testing

The issue of random drug testing of student groups was first addressed by the Supreme Court in *Vernonia School District v. Acton* (1995). Faced with a student drug crisis, school administrators in Vernonia School District established that student athletes were the leaders of the drug culture. After several failed attempts to curb the problem by other means, the district resorted to random drug testing via urinalysis of students participating in athletic contests. The *Vernonia* policy involved the testing of athletes at the beginning of the particular sports season. Once each week the names of participants were placed in a pool, from which a student blindly drew the names of 10% of the athletes for random testing. The selected boys produced a sample at a urinal, fully clothed with their backs to a monitor who stood several feet away. Girls produced a sample from a closed bathroom stall. A monitor waited outside and listened for normal sounds of urination. Samples were sent to a lab and checked for cocaine, marijuana, and amphetamines.

A student athlete who tested positive was required to submit to a second test to check the accuracy of the first test. If the second test was positive, the athlete's parents, the student, and the school principal met and chose between participating for 6 weeks in an assistance program that required weekly urinalysis, or suspension from athletics for the remainder of the current season. A second positive test resulted in suspension from participation for the rest of the season, and a third positive test required suspension for the next two athletic seasons.

The court found that a reasonable nexus between the drug testing and the need to maintain order in the school must be established for this type of search to pass constitutional muster. The court found this method to be a legitimate exercise of school administrative authority for several reasons: (1) student athletes have a diminished expectation of privacy; (2) the privacy interest compromised by the process of obtaining urine samples under the policy was negligible; (3) the district had established that student athletes were leaders of the drug culture; (4) the severity of the need was established; and (5) the district established an increase in injuries to competitive athletes.

A few districts took the leeway granted in *Vernonia* to include students in other groups, not just student athletes, for random drug testing policies. However, various lower courts remained at odds over the legality of random testing of student groups other than student athletes. For example, the Seventh Circuit Court upheld a lower court decision supporting the random drug testing of all students involved in extracurricular activities as well as those students driving to school (*Todd v. Rush County Schools,* 1998). The testing included alcohol, illegal drugs, and nicotine. In spite of the district's inability to demonstrate a correlation between these groups of students and drug or alcohol use, the court believed that *Vernonia* had substantially lowered the bar for student privacy. In *Joy v. Penn-Harris-Madison School Corp.* (2000), the Seventh Circuit Court was soon faced with another case involving the random drug and nicotine testing of a wide range of student groups: those students involved in extracurricular activities, all students driving to school, students voluntarily submitting to the random testing, and all students suspended for 3 consecutive days for misconduct. The court reluctantly upheld this policy, except for the nicotine testing of students driving to school, based solely on the precedence established by the Seventh Circuit Court in *Todd*. The justices made it clear that if not for the previous ruling and the strong concept of "let the decision stand" (*stare decisis*), in their view this policy would not pass constitutional muster.

The various lower court interpretations of *Vernonia* continued when the Western District Court of Oklahoma issued a permanent injunction enjoining the district from enforcing the provisions of the policy requiring suspicionless testing of students engaged in nonathletic activities including band, choir, FHA, FFA, and cheerleading (*Earls v. Board of Education of Tecumseh Public Schools,* 2000). Citing a lack of evidence presented by the district to demonstrate some identifiable drug abuse problem among a sufficient number of students in the groups singled out for testing, the 10th Circuit Court supported the lower court decision (*Earls v. Board of Education of Tecumseh Public Schools,* 2001).

On appeal, the U.S. Supreme Court acknowledged that the reasonableness of a search is balanced by the nature of the intrusion against some legitimate governmental interest. However, student constitutional rights are different in public schools, and privacy interests are limited where the state is responsible for maintaining discipline, health, and safety. In this case, the random drug testing policy was undertaken for just such a purpose, which is to protect students from drug use. Further, the policy had been applied only to those groups governed by the Oklahoma Secondary Schools Activities Association (OSSAA). Consequently, the students affected by this policy had agreed to a limited expectation of privacy (*Board of Education of Independent School District No. 92 of Pottawatomie v. Earls*, 2002).

CHALLENGES TO RANDOM TESTING UNDER STATE CONSTITUTIONS The legality of random urinalysis testing has been challenged with some success under state constitutions. For example, the Colorado Supreme Court overturned a trial court decision that upheld a drug testing policy similar to *Todd v. Rush* (*Trinidad School District No. 1 v. Lopez*, 1998). The Colorado Supreme Court gave weight to three factors that distinguished this policy from *Vernonia*: (1) The policy included students enrolled in for-credit classes; (2) the policy included student groups not demonstrated to have contributed to the drug problem; and (3) there was no demonstrated risk of immediate physical harm to members of the marching band. The court rejected the district's argument that members of extracurricular programs were "role models" and consequently had diminished expectations of privacy. The court also rejected the district's argument that random testing of these groups of students was the most efficacious method of addressing a growing drug problem. Similarly, the Pennsylvania Supreme Court (*Theodore v. Delaware Valley School District*, 2003) and the Washington Supreme Court (*York v. Wahkiakum*, 2008) also found the suspicionless urinalysis drug testing of students in extracurricular activities (Pennsylvania) and student athletes (Washington) to violate the respective state constitutions. However, the Indiana Supreme Court (*Linke v. Northwestern*, 2002) and the Wyoming Supreme Court (*Hageman v. Goshen County School District*, 2011) found that the mandatory random testing of students involved in extracurricular activities did not violate their respective state constitutions.

Linking to PRACTICE

Do:

- Have evidence of a drug problem and communicate carefully with parents and community members before adopting random urinalysis policies. This makes these practices more defensible.
- Discuss the efficacy of these policies and efforts to combat the problem by other, less intrusive, means. This strengthens the rationale.
- Make sure the policy will reach the target group. In other words, it makes little

sense to drug test student athletes when the target population (the reason for the policy) is not involved in athletics.
- Follow the urinalysis policies, practices, purposes, collection methods, and treatment options outlined in *Vernonia School District v. Acton* (1995) and *Board of Education of Independent School District No. 92 of Pottawatomie v. Earls* (2002).

Summary

The majority opinion in *T. L. O.* was an attempt to free school officials from the probable-cause standard of law enforcement. However, students do retain a privacy interest while at school, and the "reasonable under the circumstances" standard established by the Court is at best ambiguous. Therefore, a definitive determination of when school officials' interests in maintaining order and enforcing discipline outweigh students' expectations of privacy may not always be possible. Consequently, deciding to search or continue with a search often remains a judgment call that might be open to criticism. However, sound search policies and procedures, based on the ethical principles of Jeremy Bentham and the legal principles established by the courts, make these judgments more defensible. School district written policy should outline the circumstances under which students may be subjected to search and delineate who may conduct student searches. Training for all administrators, faculty, and staff in the legal requirements of student searches is necessary. The training should include examples of minimally intrusive searches and stress the importance of the relationship between the reason for the search and the scope of the search. These policies should be communicated to students, faculty, staff, and parents. Administrators should attend booster club, PTA, and other parent organization meetings to discuss and clarify school search policies.

CONNECTING STANDARDS TO PRACTICE

HELLO, OPERATOR

Eighth-grader Susan Smith, captain of the cheerleading squad and an honor roll student at Jefferson Middle School, was quite popular among her classmates and teachers. Everyone admitted that she could be a little recalcitrant, so it was not a big surprise when world history teacher Wendy Morse sent Susan to Jefferson assistant principal Donner. Apparently, Susan had refused to put her cell phone away in class. Arriving in Mrs. Donner's office, Susan argued that she was text messaging her fellow cheerleaders about a change in bus times to the next game. At first Susan refused to give up her cell phone, but after some thought to the possible consequences, reluctantly relinquished her turned-off phone to Mrs. Donner. Susan was assigned detention the next day and sent on her way. A few class periods later, Susan was again in the office, this time with her mother present. Mrs. Donner had turned Susan's phone on and read her text messages. The first two text messages were to her fellow cheerleaders and her mother about a change in bus times to the next game. Further searching revealed an arrangement to buy Ecstasy from a local community college student. Susan was referred to the Juvenile Office, dismissed from the cheerleading squad, and charged with criminal conduct (attempting to purchase illegal drugs). Susan's attorney called Sharon Grey and argued that the search of her cell phone was illegal.

Question

Argue for or against the legality of the search of Susan's cell phone text messages. Clarify the legal question. Cite ISLLC standards, legal guidelines, and Bentham's principle of proportionality and/or the idea of a well-ordered school to justify your answer. Write a memorandum to the superintendent or school board president outlining your view.

CHAPTER 7

School Safety

INTRODUCTION

Maintaining school safety has emerged as one of the most important roles of campus and district leaders. When speaking of school safety, many educators, parents, and students are referring to weapons and school shooters. Most certainly any weapon in school or any threat of violence is serious business. However, promoting school safety encompasses more than efforts to keep weapons out of school. It also includes efforts to promote a positive school culture based on security and equity. Security and equity require school leaders to take measures to reduce student victimization such as sexual harassment and bullying. This chapter addresses the utilitarian views of security and equity as well as school safety issues such as zero tolerance policies and threat assessment; student-on-student victimization such as sexual harassment, bullying, and date violence; sexting; security cameras; and Internet safety.

FOCUS QUESTIONS

1. What does the term *school safety* mean?
2. Is consistency in the application of zero tolerance policies rational?
3. How important is student-on-student victimization as a school safety issue?
4. Should district policies designed to reduce peer sexual harassment apply to gay and lesbian students?
5. What is dating violence? Is dating violence a school safety issue?
6. What are some of the legal issues associated with security cameras?
7. What is "sexting," and how should schools respond to the problem?

KEY TERMS

Bullying	Deliberate indifference	Student victimization
Cyberbullying	Sexting	Threat assessment
Dating violence	Sexual harassment	Zero tolerance

CASE STUDY

That's Not Fair!

Eighth graders Megan Smith and Aaron Accord had been best friends since they sat next to one another in third grade. Aaron had been taunted and bullied by other boys and girls since sixth grade. Since the beginning of seventh grade, the bullying had taken on a sexual context, and the bullies started calling Aaron "gay," "faggot," and similar words on a daily basis. On a least one occasion, Aaron had been punched and kicked in the boys' restroom by three eighth-grade boys. Aaron tried to stay away from the bullies, but they seemed to find him no matter where he was in the school. Megan had defended Aaron on several occasions and had even been suspended for 2 days for fighting one of the bullies. Starting in November, Aaron began skipping school, his grades fell, and his parents became concerned that he was depressed. Both parents had taken time from their jobs to speak with middle school Principal John Armbruster about the bullying and their concerns about Aaron. Principal Armbruster acknowledged that he had heard some of the taunting and had told the students to "knock it off." He also informed Mr. and Mrs. Armbruster that Aaron needed to "toughen up and knock the socks off of one of the bullies."

The next day Aaron told Megan that he had brought a knife to school, and that the next time he was shoved into the boy's restroom and punched, he was going to use the knife to defend himself. He also told Megan that he was depressed and thinking seriously about suicide so "they will not have me to pick on anymore." Megan persuaded Aaron to give her the knife and promised to stay as close as she could to him all day. Megan planned on going to Aaron's parents that evening to tell them that Aaron was afraid about coming to school and had brought a knife to school for protection. She was also determined to tell them what Aaron had said about suicide.

Megan was summoned to Principal Armbruster's office right before lunch. Principal Armbruster told Megan that a student had told him that she had a knife at school. Megan tried to explain, but Principal Armbruster was not interested. He sent Megan unescorted to her locker to retrieve the knife. Megan went straight to her locker, removed the knife from her gym bag, and returned to the office. By the time she arrived, the school resource officer was in the office. Principal Armbruster informed Megan that she was going to be suspended for 10 days, referred to the police for weapon possession on campus, and recommended for a 1-year expulsion under the district zero tolerance policy. Megan shouted, "That's not fair! If you would do your job, Aaron wouldn't be called those names and be beaten up in the restroom!"

LEADERSHIP PERSPECTIVES

In the not-too-distant past, the issue of Megan taking a knife from her friend might have been viewed much differently than in the introductory case study. However, the Columbine High School shootings in April 1999 changed this mindset, and school safety has become a serious matter. In the *MetLife Survey of the American Teacher* (MetLife, 2003), students, teachers, parents, and principals overwhelmingly reported that school safety is the most important part of the principal's job. As **ISLLC Standard 3C**

ISLLC Standard 3C

states, school leaders must communicate to students, teachers, parents, and community members that the welfare and safety of students and staff is a primary concern and any weapon or school safety issue regardless of circumstances will be taken seriously. Anything less would be a breach of public trust.

Consequently, the need to balance the authority of school leaders with the responsibility to maintain order in a positive and caring school often generates difficult choices for school administrators. Principal Armbruster in the case study "That's Not Fair!" is faced with just such a challenge. Principal Armbruster is required to take school safety seriously. Under state and federal law, it is possible that Megan could be expelled for up to one school year. One of the common themes of this text is that Megan, like all students, has the right to be treated fairly simply because she is a student and a person. Megan may very well have had a good reason for doing what she did. After hearing about Aaron's parents' conversation with Principal Armbruster, she may have believed that school administrators would punish Aaron rather than the bullies. She may have been trying to protect her friend the only way she knew how. After all, she is a young teenager and most likely has little experience with serious issues of sexual-orientation **bullying** and suicide ideation. Whatever decisions are made by school officials should be defensible. They should balance good order and discipline with Megan's basic right to be treated fairly. This balance can be difficult. But, **ISLLC Standard 5** encourages Principal Armbruster to reflect on his decisions and think about how an understanding of ethical behavior impacts his leadership.

ISLLC Standard 3

ISLLC Standard 5

ISLLC Standard 5

ISLLC Standard 5

THE PURPOSE OF POLICY

According to the utilitarian philosopher Jeremy Bentham (1970), the purpose of all governmental action should be to produce benefit, good, or happiness and to prevent evil, mischief, or unhappiness to the individuals whose interest is being considered. One theme throughout this text is that all good schools are reasonably orderly. Bentham uses the term *greatest happiness principle* or *utility* to define or quantify this concept. Utility depends on two basic principles: security and equity (fairness). Security in Bentham's view is a means to the end and a necessary precondition for the maximization of the greater good. **ISLLC Standard 3C** is about security. Another theme throughout this text is the concept of fairness or equity. Fairness, although subservient to security, also serves as a precondition for the maximization of happiness. In the utilitarian view of Jeremy Bentham, the primary purpose of district or campus policy should be to promote the principles of security and equity. In other words, the purpose of all school district policy should be to promote the utility (or the greater good) of the school community.

ISLLC Standard 3.0

ISLLC Standard 3C

ISLLC Standard 5

To Bentham, a community is a fictitious body, composed of the individual persons who are considered as members. For example, the school community is composed of students, teachers, administrators, school board members, parents, and others who are affiliated, even temporarily, with the district or campus. The general happiness of the community can only be considered in terms of the individuals who are members of the community. In other words, the utility of the community cannot be considered without considering the utility of the individual members of which the community in question is composed. This is an important point. Utility is measured not by some vague concept of what is good for the community, but rather by what is in the best interests of the individual members of the community.

Utility is not possible without security. The principle of utility depends on the deliberate creation of policy and practice specifically implemented to provide for security. Security results from policy that averts pain or danger. For Aaron in the opening case study "That's Not Fair," this would mean policy and practice designed to protect him and other students from ongoing bullying. Without this basic principle in place, all other efforts to promote equity and the greater good of the school community will surely fail. Rules against fighting, appropriate supervision of students, and efforts to prevent bullying are examples of policy implemented to promote security and avert pain. For example, Aaron fears for his safety in school and brings a knife for protection. Utility is also not possible without fairness. In Megan's case she believes she is not being treated fairly because she was trying to help her friend. Bentham, and common sense, recognizes that not all pain or danger can be avoided. In fact, the act of making policy to provide security to prevent pain or danger creates conditions that may result in punishment (or pain) for those individuals who violate the policy. However, Bentham clearly recognized the need for proportional punishment for transgressors as a necessary component of policy designed to promote community utility.

SCHOOL SAFETY

Violent deaths—defined as a homicide, suicide, legal intervention (involving a law enforcement officer), or unintentional firearm-related death—in which the fatal injury occurred on the campus of a functioning elementary or secondary school in the United States are rare but tragic events. For example, in the 2007–2008 school year, 1,701 youth ages 5 to 18 were victims of homicide or suicide. Of this number, 21 homicides and 5 suicides occurred at school. This number, although significant, equates to 1 homicide or suicide of a school-age youth at school per 2.1 million students enrolled during the 2008–2009 school year. This statistic has remained virtually unchanged from 1992 to 2009. In fact, youth homicides and suicides are significantly more likely to occur away from school than at school (Robers, Zhang, & Truman, 2010).

In spite of these facts, concerns over weapons and school shooters remain at the forefront. Peterson, Larson, and Skiba (2001) write:

> Whereas school shootings involving multiple victims are still extremely rare . . . these statistics are hardly reassuring as long as the possibility exists that it could happen in our school, to our children. Whatever the absolute level of school violence and disruption, it is clear . . . schools and school districts must do all they can to ensure the safety of students and staff. (p. 346)

ISLLC Standard 3 ▶ As **ISLLC Standard 3** indicates, school safety is indeed serious business, and maintaining safe schools is a significant part of the role of school administrators. Therefore, school districts and school administrators have been empowered by a variety of federal, state, and local laws and policies with the intention of promoting school safety. At the federal level, the most visible school safety law is the Gun-Free Schools Act (GFSA, 1994). The GFSA was reauthorized as part of No Child Left

Behind (NCLB, 2001). GFSA requires that each state have a law that requires all local education agencies (LEAs) to expel from school for at least 1 year any student determined to have brought a firearm to school or to have possessed a firearm at school. GFSA allows local school administrators to modify (for example, shorten) any disciplinary action for a firearm violation on a case-by-case basis. The primary purpose behind this provision is to allow school district administrators or boards of education to take the circumstances of the infraction into account and, if necessary, to ensure that the legal requirements of IDEA are honored. This information must be reported to the U.S. Department of Education and must include the name of the school concerned, the number of students expelled from each school, and the type of firearms involved.

NCLB also includes the following clarifications:

- Students must be expelled for possessing a gun in school, not just for bringing a gun to school.
- Any modifications to expulsions under GFSA must now be in writing.
- NCLB makes exceptions for lawfully stored firearms inside a locked vehicle on school property, and firearms brought to school or possessed in school for activities approved and authorized by the district.
- "Firearm" includes not only guns but also other dangerous devices such as bombs, rockets, and grenades.
- Disciplinary action taken against Individualized Education Program (IEP) students must be consistent with the provisions of IDEA.
- Expelled students *may* be provided with educational services in an alternative setting.

GFSA data indicate that these efforts may be having a positive effect. There has been a general downward trend in the rate of student expulsions for weapon possession per 100,000 students nationwide since the 1998–1999 school year. Recent data indicate an 11% reduction in expulsions per 100,000 students from the 2005–2006 to the 2006–2007 school years. Some of this reduction may be attributable to an increase nationally in modifications to the 1-year expulsion requirement for weapon possession. In school year 1997–1998, just 30% of expulsions for students determined to have brought a firearm to school were modified (e.g., reduced below the 1-year standard). During 2005–2006, 45% of expulsions for students determined to have brought a firearm to school were modified. In 2006–2007, more than half (53%) were modified (U.S. Department of Education, 2010).

State legislatures have also passed numerous school safety measures. Since 2006, virtually every state legislative body has passed some form of school safety legislation (Education Commission of the States, n.d.). For example, Missouri law empowers school districts to expel or deny admission to any student charged or convicted of a list of violent acts committed anywhere (RSMo 167.171.3).

School District Responses

Individual schools and school districts have responded similarly and increased security measures. Students ages 12 to 18 report an increase in security cameras to monitor the school (from 39% in 1999 to 66% in 2007), security guards and other assigned police officers (54% in 1999 to 69% in 2007), and locked entrance or exit doors during the day (from 38% in 1999 to 61% in 2007) (Robers et al., 2010). School districts have also uniformly enacted "zero tolerance" policies in response to GFSA for students possessing a weapon in school. *Zero tolerance* is generally defined as a school district policy that mandates predetermined consequences or punishment for specific offenses, regardless of the circumstances, disciplinary history, or age of the student involved. The stated purpose of zero tolerance policies is to send a clear and consistent message that school officials are still in charge and that certain proscribed acts (weapon possession, threats of violence, drugs or alcohol, fighting, or even tardiness) will not be tolerated (Education Commission of the States, 2002).

Support for zero tolerance, once almost universal, now appears to be waning in many states. However, as long as school administrators follow school district policy and observe all due process rights, courts have been supportive of zero tolerance suspensions even when the expulsion seems, at least on the surface, to defy rationality. For example, the Third Circuit Court recently upheld the 3-day suspension of a kindergarten student for saying, "I'm going to shoot you" while playing "guns" with friends at recess (*A. G. v. Sayreville Board of Education,* 2003). The court reasoned that the student had knowledge of the underlying conduct for which he was sanctioned. The 10th Circuit Court took a similar position when a senior student (Butler) was expelled in spite of a hearing officer's finding that he had unknowingly brought weapons to school when he borrowed his brother's car, concluding that (1) the district has a legitimate interest in providing a safe environment for students; (2) based on this legitimate interest, there is a rational basis for the suspension of Butler when *he should have known he brought a weapon onto school property;* and (3) the district's decision was not arbitrary, nor did it "shock the conscience." Consequently, the decision to expel Butler under the circumstances, even for 1 year, does not violate the substantive due process rights of Butler (*Butler v. Rio Rancho,* 2003).

Generally courts have not held school administrators liable for school shootings or injuries as a result of weapons as long as reasonable action was taken. For example, a federal district court in Colorado has dismissed numerous suits against school and law enforcement officials in the aftermath of the Columbine High School shootings. In another example, John Smith brought a gun to school and fatally shot one of his first-grade classmates (*McQueen v. Beecher Community Schools,* 2006). Certainly, John Smith's parents, teachers, his principal, and the district superintendent have spent countless hours second-guessing the decisions that led to this incident. However, absent any evidence of *deliberate indifference* on the part of the school district, the court could find no reason to hold the teacher, principal, or district superintendent liable for the shooting.

Consistency May Not Always Be Rational

Although there is little ambiguity regarding the expulsion of truly dangerous students, some school district applications of zero tolerance policies cast doubt on the wisdom of school administrators. The case of Benjamin Ratner serves as a classic example (*Ratner v. Loudoun County Public Schools,* 2001). In a case similar to the opening case study "That's Not Fair!" a young friend informed Benjamin that she had inadvertently brought a knife to school in her binder that morning. Benjamin knew the student and was aware of previous suicide attempts. He put the binder in his locker with the intent of telling both his and her parents after school. School officials obtained knowledge of the knife. Benjamin was suspended for 10 days for possessing a knife on school grounds. He was notified 2 days later that he was being suspended indefinitely pending further action by the school board. On judicial appeal, the Fourth Circuit Court refused to consider Benjamin's case, finding he had been given constitutionally sufficient, even if imperfect, due process. In a concurring opinion in *Ratner,* Judge Hamilton questioned the wisdom of the decision: "Each (Benjamin, his family, and common sense) is the victim of good intentions run amuck." It is easy, however, to find fault in Benjamin's choice not to give his friend's binder to a principal, a counselor, or a trusted teacher.

The problem is straightforward: Not expelling a dangerous student carries significant consequences for all concerned. But, are all weapon possessions created equal? Is consistency rational? As the Sixth Circuit Court pointed out, consistency is not a substitute for rationality, and a school board may not absolve itself of its legal and moral obligation to determine whether students intentionally committed the acts for which their expulsions are sought by hiding behind a zero tolerance policy intended to make the student's knowledge a nonissue (*Seal v. Morgan,* 2000).

If consistency is not always rational, how may school leaders meet their legal obligation to keep schools safe? The answer may be a well-established threat assessment policy that is publicly justified and supportive of a fair system of cooperation. In a U.S. Secret Service/Department of Education study of targeted school violence, Fein and colleagues (Fein et al., 2004) present a *threat assessment model* based on an analysis of the facts and evidence of behavior in a given situation. Weapon possession should never be taken lightly. However, the central question of a threat assessment is whether a student poses a threat, not whether the student made a threat. ***Threat assessment*** is composed of two parts: threat *inquiry* and threat *investigation*. Both use fact-based evidence developed and gathered from a variety of sources to justify return to school, disciplinary decisions, or potential criminal charges.

The first step, *threat inquiry*, is carried out by district officials or a school-based threat assessment team. Assume, for example, that an initial inquiry determines that the student, such as Megan Smith in the introductory case study "That's Not Fair" poses little if any threat to others. Evidence gathered can be used to justify an alternative punishment such as short-term suspension, in-school suspension, or short-term referral to an alternative placement. However, if the initial threat inquiry is inconclusive or supportive of a medium or high threat assessment, the more formal *threat investigation* is activated (Fein et al., 2004). Common sense indicates that activation of the threat investigation process should be accompanied by short-term (10 days or less) or emergency expulsion of the student. Threat investigation would include local law enforcement, a more thorough internal review of the factors surrounding the incident, and possibly referral to a local counseling agency for their assessment. It is important to note that threat inquiry should precede threat investigation. The threat assessment model is illustrated in Figure 7–1.

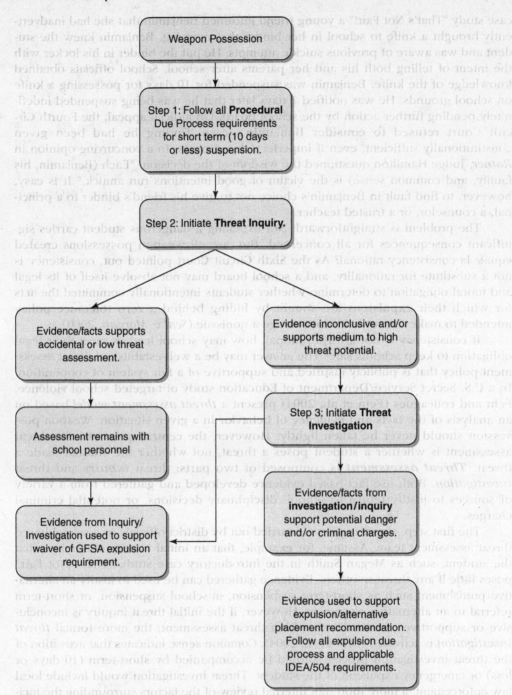

FIGURE 7–1 Threat assessment.

Linking to PRACTICE

Do:

- Have a clear and unambiguous policy regarding threats of violence and weapons in school. Leave no doubt in anyone's mind that weapons in school will be taken seriously and punishments will follow.
- Recommend the adopting of a formal board of education policy authorizing school officials to conduct a threat assessment. Excellent guidelines for policy formulation are presented on pp. 34–35 of *Threat Assessment in Schools* (Fein et al., 2004). This publication is available free of charge from the U.S. Department of Education.

- Develop objective criteria to use in suspension or expulsion decisions. Criteria could include factors surrounding the incident, previous behavior of the student, relative severity or threat of the incident, and evidence of school support.
- Work with students, parents, and community groups to articulate and explain school district policy and practice.

Do Not:

- Abandon common sense. The provision to modify any disciplinary action for a weapon violation in GFSA (and confirmed in NCLB) is there for a reason.

STUDENT VICTIMIZATION

Unfortunately, student victimization in various forms is relatively common in public schools. **Student victimization** may include bullying, intimidation, gender-based sexual harassment, sexual harassment based on real or perceived sexual orientation, dating violence, and sexting. Victimization can occur in the classroom, in school hallways, on school playgrounds, in locker rooms, at school-sponsored events, in cyberspace, in social media, and by cell phone. Student victimization can be perpetrated by peers, older students, and adults in the school. Victims may experience a decline in grades, increased absenteeism, a failure to develop positive self-esteem, withdrawal and depression, and suicide ideation. Therefore, efforts to address student victimization should be part of any comprehensive approach to school safety (Stader, 2011).

SEXUAL HARASSMENT

Sexual harassment is defined as unwanted or unwelcome behavior of a sexual nature. Sexual harassment may include unwelcome sexual advances, request for sexual favors, and other conduct of a sexual nature. Sexual violence (i.e., sexual assault or coerced sex) is also prohibited by Title IX (Dear College, April 4, 2011). Title IX protects students from sexual harassment in all school programs or activities, regardless of who the harasser may be, as long as the school maintains control of the program or activity. For example, schools may be liable for sexually harassing behavior by a teacher, an administrator, a custodian, or another student anywhere on school grounds, at school-sponsored events, or on a school bus. Schools may also be liable for sexual harassment or assault after school hours when the behavior involves teachers and students. For example, a male 11th-grade science teacher in Georgia used a fictitious scholarship program as a scheme to lure students to his home. At least one of the students was sexually assaulted by the teacher. The District Court held that the teacher used his position of authority to give a stamp of legitimacy to the scholarship program (*Hackett v. Fulton County School District,* 2002).

Two types of sexual harassment have been established by law: quid pro quo and hostile environment.

QUID PRO QUO HARASSMENT: Sexual harassment in which the satisfaction of sexual demands is made the condition of some benefit. For example, quid pro quo harassment occurs when a school employee causes a student to believe that he or she must submit to a sexual demand in order to participate in a school program, or in return for a favorable educational decision or a favorable grade in a course. Whether the student submits or not is beside the point. The fact that the demands were made makes the conduct unlawful (Garner, 2006).

HOSTILE ENVIRONMENT HARASSMENT: A hostile environment is created when unwelcome sexually harassing conduct becomes so severe, persistent, or pervasive that it affects a student's ability to participate in or benefit from an educational program or activity or creates an intimidating, threatening, or abusive educational environment. Hostile environment harassment may be created by school employees, other students, school volunteers, cafeteria workers, and so on (Garner, 2006).

Liability under Title IX

The **Office for Civil Rights** (OCR) is responsible for the enforcement of Title IX. OCR prefers that claims be settled in a peaceful manner. OCR does not seek monetary relief for victims of sexual harassment. However, the U.S. Supreme Court has established that a damages remedy is available to students for an action brought to enforce Title IX (*Franklin v. Gwinnett County Public Schools,* 1992). This case involved a high school student who alleged that she was subjected to continual sexual harassment and abuse, including coercive intercourse, by a male teacher at the school. The student also alleged that other teachers and the school principal had knowledge of the sexual abuse but took no action in response to this knowledge.

A few years later the U.S. Supreme Court considered the question of what criteria should be met before monetary damages were available to students subjected to abuse by school employees (*Gebser v. Lago Vista Independent School,* 1998). This case differs from *Franklin* in that a student had sexual relations with one of her teachers but did not report the relationship to school officials. The police encountered the teacher and student having sexual intercourse in the teacher's car and arrested the teacher. The Court held that monetary damages were recoverable for teacher-on-student harassment when:

1. A school district official who at a minimum has authority to institute corrective measures on the district's behalf has actual notice of the allegations, and
2. The school official or officials are *deliberately indifferent* to the teacher's misconduct.

These criteria establish that school districts and campus administrators can be held accountable for *respondeat superior* [Latin for the doctrine holding the "employer liable for the employee's wrongful acts committed within the scope of employment"

(Garner, 2006, p. 619)] of an employee's quid pro quo or hostile environment sexual harassment if the employer had reasonable notice of the harassment and filed to take appropriate corrective action. In essence, the district is not liable as long as an official who has the authority to institute corrective measures takes action as soon as the teacher-on-student sexual harassment becomes known to the official (see *Henderson v. Walled Lake Consolidated School District*, 2006; *P. H. v. The School District of Kansas City, Missouri*, 2001). Officials who have authority to institute corrective measures include campus principals, assistant superintendents, and superintendents.

Once actual notice is established, responding appropriately to allegations of teacher-on-student sexual misconduct is essential. For example, a principal's failure to adequately respond to parental complaints regarding a fourth-grade teacher's sexual abuse of their son resulted in a $400,000 jury verdict against the school district (*Warren v. Reading School District*, 2002). And, not surprisingly, a trial court held that the failure to investigate or confront a female teacher after various school personnel complained to the principal that the teacher was having sex with male students constituted an "unreasonable response" (*Doe v. School Admin. Dist. No. 19*, 1999).

Linking to PRACTICE

Do:

- Ensure that employee training includes warnings that appropriate boundaries with students should be established. These boundaries should be made clear to all students, with particular attention to middle school and high school students.
- Also make sure that employee training includes examples of behaviors that may indicate inappropriate boundary crossing by teachers, students, or others.
- Be sure that school district policy provides clear reporting guidelines and contact

information for faculty, parents, and students to report incidents of suspected boundary crossing or suspected sexual misconduct.

Do Not:

- Ignore warning signs of inappropriate boundary crossing by employees or students. An inquisitive mindset is important. See Investigation of Employee Misconduct in Chapter 11 (Teacher Employment, Supervision, and Collective Bargaining).

Student-on-Student Sexual Harassment

The U.S. Supreme Court next considered the circumstances under which a district could be held monetarily liable for failure to adequately respond to student-on-student sexual harassment (*Davis v. Monroe County Board of Education*, 1999). In a decision similar to *Gebser v. Lago Vista* (1998), the Court found that under certain circumstances districts could be held monetarily liable for student-on-student (peer) sexual harassment. The case before the Court involved a prolonged pattern of alleged sexual harassment of LaShonda Davis by a fifth-grade classmate. During this several-month period, LaShonda and her mother reported incidents to at least two classroom teachers and a physical education teacher on several occasions. The incidents finally ended in mid-May when the male student was charged with, and pleaded guilty to, sexual battery. However, during this time period LaShonda's grades suffered, and at one point her father discovered a suicide note. It was also alleged that the male student was not disciplined during the period of prolonged harassment. In addition, no effort was made to separate the two students, and it was only after several months that LaShonda was allowed to change her seat so as not to be near the male student.

The Court found school districts to be liable for student-on-student sexual harassment under the following conditions:

1. School personnel have actual knowledge of the harassment, and
2. School personnel are *deliberately indifferent* to the sexual harassment, and
3. The harassment is so severe, pervasive, and objectively offensive that it can be said to deprive the victim(s) of access to the educational opportunities or benefits provided by the school.

The Court pointed out that the harassment must take place in a context subject to the school district's control. In the Court's reasoning, this makes sense in that school personnel should not be directly liable for indifference where the authority to take remedial action is nonexistent. This indicates that school personnel would not be responsible for addressing harassing behavior that occurs at, for example, a local mall or a privately sponsored event not under the control of the school. However, school personnel would be responsible for addressing harassing behavior at school dances, during recess, on school buses, or for behavior that may "spill over" into the school context.

In order to prevail in a monetary-damages suit, the student must demonstrate all three prongs established by the Court. First, school officials must have actual notice or knowledge of the alleged harassing behavior. In adult–student harassment, the school authority must be someone who at a minimum has the authority to initiate remedial action. In most cases, this would include the campus principal and most certainly the district superintendent. However, when considering student-on-student harassment, teachers also have the authority to discipline, correct, or refer students to administrative personnel. Regardless, once appropriate school officials have knowledge of the alleged behavior, *Davis* imposes a duty to act.

Next, school officials must demonstrate deliberate indifference or take actions that are "clearly unreasonable." The majority in *Davis* saw no reason why a court could not distinguish a response that is "clearly unreasonable" from one that is "reasonable." In response to some of the concerns of the dissenting justices, the majority attempted to point out that schools are not like the adult workplace, and every immature act of every student in school was not grounds for suspension or expulsion. Children and young adults are still learning appropriate behaviors and during this learning process may interact from time to time in a manner that would be unacceptable to adults. School administrators were to continue to use good judgment and develop age-appropriate and educationally sound approaches to confronting the problem. To further emphasize this point, the Court restated the concept from *New Jersey v. T. L. O.* (1985) that judges should refrain from second-guessing the disciplinary actions taken by school administrators. Consequently, school administrators should continue to enjoy flexibility in disciplinary decisions involving peer harassment as long as their actions are not deemed "deliberately indifferent." In short, all that *Davis* requires is that the response not be *clearly unreasonable* (*Clark v. Bibb County Board of Education*, 2001; *Gabrielle M. v. Park Forest-Chicago Heights*, 2002; *Soper v. Hoben*, 1999).

Although no specific response is required, the school must respond and must do so reasonably in light of the known circumstances. Thus, if a school official has knowledge that the remedial action taken is not effective, then reasonable action in light of these circumstances is required. In other words, if a school official knows that efforts to remediate are ineffective, yet continues to use these same methods to no avail, the official has failed to act reasonably in light of the known circumstances. For example, in repeated incidents of sexually harassing behavior, simply continuing to "talk to" the offending students will not pass as a reasonable response (*Vance v. Spencer County Public School District,* 2000). It would seem from this argument that a flexible policy that takes into consideration the age of the students involved, the severity of the harassment, and previous efforts to remediate should define the term *reasonable response*.

Finally, the harassment must rise to the level of being so severe, pervasive, and objectively offensive that it can be said to deprive the victim(s) of access to the educational opportunities or benefits provided by the school. For example, the Sixth Circuit Court found that when sexually harassing behavior becomes so pervasive that it forces the victim to leave school on several occasions, results in a diagnosis of depression, and ultimately forces the victim's withdrawal from school, the behavior rises to the level of systematically depriving the victim access to an education (*Vance v. Spencer County Public School District,* 2000). Consequently, the Sixth Circuit Court confirmed a $220,000 jury award in this case. Using a similar approach, the 11th Circuit Court (*Hawkins v. Sarasota County School Board,* 2002) ruled that female students were not entitled to damages for student-on-student sexual harassment. The court found that although the harassment was persistent and frequent, none of the students' grades suffered, no observable change in their classroom demeanor occurred, and none of the students reported the harassment to their parents until months had passed.

Linking to PRACTICE

- School districts should develop well-articulated mechanisms for reporting sexual harassment. Each campus should have a Title IX coordinator. Teachers and other adults in the school should be required to report incidents or reports of sexual harassment to the campus Title IX coordinator. The report should be investigated as soon as practical. Evidence of teacher-on-student harassment should be reported to the district Title IX coordinator immediately.
- School officials should flexibly apply response mechanisms to both the victim and perpetrator, taking into account the ages of the students involved and the context of the behavior. For example, a first-grader who kisses another first-grader on the cheek during recess may be guilty of breaking school playground rules but is not guilty of sexual harassment.
- All incidents of suspected harassment and the response to the suspected behavior should be carefully documented.
- District- and campus-based school and community partnerships should be formed to explain reporting and disciplinary policies and prevention efforts and to solicit input and support from the local community.

SEXUAL ORIENTATION HARASSMENT

As of 2005 only nine states (California, Connecticut, Maine, Massachusetts, Minnesota, New Jersey, Vermont, Washington, and Wisconsin) and the District of Columbia have statutes specifically protecting students on the basis of sexual orientation and/or gender identity (Kosciw & Diaz, 2006). Courts in the states with nondiscriminatory laws have found school districts liable for violating state sex discrimination policies or for a failure to protect students from sexual orientation harassment. For example, the Supreme Court of New Jersey upheld the findings by the director of the Division on Civil Rights that Toms River School District violated the state Law Against Discrimination by not protecting L. W. from ongoing peer harassment based on his sexual orientation (*L. W. v. Toms River Regional Schools Board of Education*, 2005). Following similar logic, a Massachusetts appeals court held that a 15-year-old transgender eighth-grader has the right under state law to attend school wearing clothing that expresses his female gender identity (*Doe v. Yunits*, 2000).

It seems logical to assume that cases similar to *Toms River* will increase as more state legislatures pass nondiscrimination laws. However, at present, most student-on-student sexual orientation harassment cases have been heard in federal court. Federal courts generally consider either equal protection or Title IX when deciding student-on-student sexual orientation harassment cases. An equal protection claim requires the student to show that school officials did not abide by antiharassment policies when dealing with sexual orientation harassment, that officials were deliberately indifferent to the harassment, or that the student was treated in a manner that is clearly unreasonable. For example, in *Nabozny v. Podlesny* (1996), the Seventh Circuit Court held that school administrators are not immune from an equal protection claim involving student-on-student sexual orientation harassment. In this case, student Nabozny was repeatedly subjected to verbal and physical abuse because of his sexual orientation. School administrators had a policy of investigating and punishing student-on-student battery and sexual harassment, but allegedly turned a deaf ear to Nabozny's complaints. Despite repeated reporting by both the student and his parents to several school officials including principal Podlesny, little or no action was taken to either discipline the offending students or protect Nabozny (despite promises to the contrary) from the students in question. In fact, evidence suggests that some of the administrators themselves mocked Nabozny's predicament. The harassment (including a mock rape and a physical assault) resulted in Nabozny making two suicide attempts, running away from home, and eventually dropping out of school. On review, the Seventh Circuit Court reversed and remanded Nabozny's equal protection claim, stating, "We are unable to garner any *rational basis* for permitting one student to assault another based on the victim's sexual orientation." In November 1996, the district agreed to a $900,000 settlement with Nabozny (Bochenek & Brown, 2001). Rational basis is the lowest form of scrutiny for an equal protection claim. A district must be particularly negligent under the rational basis test. Therefore, a finding under this standard by the court surely expedited the large settlement with Nabozny.

The Ninth Circuit Court of Appeals followed similar logic and a rational basis standard of review to find ample evidence of deliberate indifference to the ongoing sexual orientation harassment of six high school students (*Flores v. Morgan Hill*, 2003). Without admitting wrongdoing, Morgan Hill School District agreed to a $1.1 million settlement and a promise to create a mandatory training program to promote gay tolerance (American Civil Liberties Union, 2004).

In 2000, two separate federal district courts (California and Minnesota, respectively) decided that schools could be held liable under Title IX for acting with "deliberate indifference" toward students who have reported persistent and severe homophobic harassment at school (*Montgomery v. Independent School District No. 709*, 2000, and *Ray v. Antioch Unified School District*, 2000). As the California Federal District Court stated:

> [There is] no material difference between the instance in which a female student is subject to unwelcome sexual comments and advances due to her harasser's perception that she is a sex object, and the instance in which a male student is insulted and abused due to his harasser's perception that he is a homosexual, and therefore a subject of prey. In both instances, the conduct is a heinous response to the harasser's perception of the victim's sexuality, and is not distinguishable to this court. (*Ray v. Antioch Unified School District*, 2000)

These decisions established important precedents for the application of Title IX sexual harassment standards to several cases that followed (Meyer & Stader, 2009). In fact, students have been remarkably successful in claiming deliberate indifference to sexual orientation harassment under Title IX. For example, school districts have settled for $451,000 (*Henkle v. Gregory*, 2001; Lambda Legal, 2001), $27,000 (*Doe v. Perry Community School District*, 2004), and $440,000 (*Theno v. Tonganoxie*, 2005).

In summary, school districts have been held liable for violating state nondiscrimination laws, for not equitably enforcing their own rules, and/or for their deliberate indifference to the sexual orientation harassment of students (Meyer & Stader, 2009). A common theme among these cases is a failure to take reasonable action once the sexual orientation harassment became known to school officials. Therefore, it is incumbent on school districts to take affirmative steps to provide a positive, supportive, and safer school culture for all students.

Teacher or Other Adult Harassment of LGBT Youth

The value of teacher and other adult support for lesbian, gay, bisexual, and transgender (LGBT) students cannot be underestimated. In a study of LGBT youth, Human Rights Watch found that in virtually every case where these students reported a positive school experience, they attributed that fact to supportive teachers (Bochenek & Brown, 2001). However, this is not always the case. For example, Thomas McLaughlin appealed to a federal district court in Arkansas alleging that his choir teacher at Jacksonville Junior High School (Pulaski County, Arkansas) asked him if he was gay (*McLaughlin v. Pulaski County*, 2003). When he responded yes, she told Thomas that she found homosexuality "sickening," asked Thomas if he knew what the Bible says about homosexuality, and offered him some scriptures. Thomas also alleged that his computer teacher called him "abnormal" and "unnatural." When Thomas protested, he was sent to an assistant principal, who preached religious views about homosexuality. At some point Thomas was suspended for 2 days, allegedly for talking to other students about being made to read the Bible by the assistant principal, and later threatened with 4 more days for complaining about his 2-day suspension. The district agreed to a $25,000 settlement with Thomas and his attorneys (Trotter, 2003). This case illustrates that this district court, at least, views adult-on-student sexual orientation harassment similarly to student-on-student sexual orientation harassment. The case also puts school districts (at least in the Eighth Circuit) on notice that this type of harassment will not be tolerated.

Linking to PRACTICE

Do:

- Review district policy and sexual harassment training practices for district personal. Be sure the training includes student-on-student sexual harassment based on sexual orientation. The training should provide examples of student homophobic behaviors that may rise to the level of hostile environment. Affirm that the reporting procedures for heterosexual harassment apply to harassment based on real or perceived sexual orientation.
- Review school district policy and supervision models to ensure that they prohibit homophobic remarks by school employees. Educate faculty and staff on the potential harmful effects of peer harassment on LGBT students and the importance of support for these students.
- Insist that campus administrators apply the same disciplinary standards to student-on-student harassment based on sexual orientation that are applied to all sexual harassment or sexual assault incidents reported in the school. Affirm that once campus administrators have actual knowledge or notice of student-on-student harassment, district policy imposes a duty to act.
- Collect data to determine the extent of peer harassment based on sexual orientation in district schools. Set annual measurable objectives and research- and literature-based intervention strategies designed to decrease the incidence and severity of peer harassment based on sexual orientation.
- Ensure that students are aware of policies protecting students from peer harassment and that these polices will be enforced.

BULLYING

It is well established that peer bullying, especially when it is ongoing and frequent, is a stressful experience with a negative impact on feelings of emotional safety, regardless of the mental health of the victim (Newman, Holden, & Delville, 2005). A wide variety of negative behaviors fall under the bully label including social exclusion, intentional damage to personal property, and hate-filled language and graffiti (Devine & Cohen, 2007). Unfortunately, peer bullying is a relatively common occurrence in schools. In 2007, about 32% of students ages 12 to 18 reported being bullied at school. Of the students who reported being bullied, 21% reported being made fun of, called names, or insulted, 18% reported they were the subject of rumors, 6% were threatened with harm, 11% reported being pushed, shoved, tripped or spit on, 4% were tried to make do things did not want to do, 5% were excluded from activities on propose, 4% had property destroyed, 2% reported hurtful information on the Internet and another 2% reported unwanted contact on Internet. The majority (79%) reported being bullied inside the school and 23% said that they were bullied outside on school grounds. In addition, 7% reported that they had avoided a school activity or one or more places in the school in the past 6 months because of fear of attack or harm (Robers et al., 2010).

Although somewhat disputed, the link between school bullying and school shooters served as a catalyst for virtually every state legislative body to pass some form of anti-bullying law in the years after 2002. These laws vary considerably in content and scope, in the legal requirements that school districts must meet, in requirements placed on the state board of education, and in defining bullying. Regardless, once appropriate school officials have knowledge or reasonably should have known of alleged bullying, state antibullying laws and school board policies impose a duty to act. Bullying or harassment based on race, color, national origin, sex, or disability may also violate civil rights statues (i.e., Title VI of the Civil Rights Act of 1964; Title IX, Section 504 of the Rehabilitation Act of 1972; and Title II of the Americans with Disabilities Act), enforced by the Office for Civil Rights (Dear Colleague, October 26, 2010). If an investigation into harassment that violates any of these civil rights has occurred, "a school must take prompt and effective steps reasonably calculated to end the harassment, eliminate any hostile environment, and prevent the harassment from recurring" (Dear Colleague, October 26, 2010, pp. 2–3).

Clear legal guidelines regarding school district responsibility for peer bullying are not currently available. However, numerous suits are moving through various federal and state courts. For example, according to the *Courthouse News Service* (www.courthousenews.com), Texas parents blame their 13-year-old son's suicide on their school district's deliberate indifference to the ongoing bullying he was experiencing (Ross, 2011). Bullying creates a hostile environment, and although little case law is available, it seems reasonable to assume that when ruling on these cases, courts will depend on the *Davis* standards of knowledge, deliberate indifference, or failure to take reasonable action, and whether the bullying was severe and pervasive enough to interfere with the victim's education. For example, a federal district court in New York used the hostile environment framework and the deliberate indifference of school personnel to find that ongoing peer bullying denied a disabled student a free and appropriate public education (FAPE) under IDEA (*T. K. v. New York City Department of Education*, 2011).

Cyberbullying

Feinberg and Robey (2008) define *cyberbullying* as follows:

> [It is] sending or posting harmful or cruel text or images using the Internet (e.g., instant messaging, e-mails, chat rooms, and social networking sites) or other digital communication devices, such as cell phones. It can involve stalking, threats, harassment, impersonation, humiliation, trickery, and exclusion. (p. 10)

Several states have added cyberbullying laws to their already existing antibullying laws. These laws, however, do not create firm ground for school leaders to discipline students for cyberbullying that occurs or originates off school grounds. Unfortunately, the U.S. Supreme Court has not explicitly addressed technology-enabled speech originated off-campus, and lower court decisions have been inconsistent regarding a school district's legal rights and/or obligation to address off-campus cyberbullying. This leaves school leaders in a legal quandary (Conn, 2010).

Conn and Brady (2008) report that several school districts have suspended or expelled students for cyberbullying. However, it is well established that student off-campus speech has more protection than on-campus speech. Therefore, school districts generally must demonstrate that student off-campus speech is a true threat or creates substantial disruption on campus, or that substantial disruption to good order and discipline could reasonably be forecast. For example, a high school student sued her school district for suspending her for posting a video clip made off-campus on a website in which students made derogatory, sexual, and potentially defamatory statements about a 13-year-old classmate. A federal district court held that the suspension violated the First Amendment rights of the suspended student, stating that at most, the school had to address the concerns of an upset parent, a student who temporarily refused to go to class, and five students missing some undetermined portion of their classes, and a fear that students would "gossip" or "pass notes" in class did not rise to the level of a substantial disruption (*J. C. ex rel. R. C. v. Beverly Hills*, 2010).

The Office for Civil Rights has indicated that off-campus sexual harassment may also create a hostile environment on-campus in certain situations. It would seem reasonable to assume that similar logic could be applied to off-campus bullying or cyberbullying. Therefore, if evidence indicates that the off-campus conduct has created a hostile learning environment at school, OCR rules create an obligation to act and take steps to protect the student from further bullying or retaliation from the perpetrator (Dear Colleague, 2011, April 4). For example, the Fourth Circuit Court of Appeals upheld the 5-day suspension of a high school student who created a MySpace.com webpage called "S.A.S.H.," which stands for "Students Against Sluts Herpes." The student invited approximately 100 people to her MySpace "friends" list to join the group. The website was largely dedicated to ridiculing a fellow student in the school. The court, citing *Tinker v. Des Moines* (1969) and *Donniger v. Niehoff* (2008), found that the postings were "sufficiently connected to the school environment as to implicate the School District's recognized authority to discipline speech which materially and substantially interferes with the requirements of appropriate discipline and collides with the rights of others" (*Kowalski* v. *Berkeley County Schools*, 2011).

Linking to PRACTICE

Do:
- Educate parents and students on the negative impact of bullying and cyberbullying.
- Develop and enforce clear rules regarding student bullying and cyberbullying. Make policy clear that off-campus behavior that creates a material or substantial disruption on campus or creates a hostile

environment may be subject to school-administered discipline.
- Train faculty to recognize the signs of depression or other mental or physical problems associated with bullying.
- Educate students on proper social networking and cyberetiquette.

SEXTING

Although there is no legal definition, *sexting* generally refers to teens taking sexually explicit photos of themselves or others in their peer group and transmitting those photos by text messaging to their peers. It is generally understood that sexting does not include sexually explicit photos sent by minors to adults or photos sent as a result of blackmail or coercion (National Center for Missing & Exploited Children, 2009). Some surveys indicate that as many as 30% of teens 12 to 17 who own cell phones may have "sexted" by sending sexually suggestive nude or nearly nude images of themselves to someone else via text messaging or have received a nude or nearly nude image on their phone (Lenhart, 2009). Sexting has caught many school leaders by surprise, and until recently few school districts had policies regarding it. Consequently, at least a few school districts have referred students to local prosecutors (Wastler, 2010).

Prosecutors have brought child pornography charges against participants. For example, Jorge Canal sent a sexually explicit picture to a female student he had known for more than a year. Canal was found guilty of disseminating obscene material to a minor under Florida state law. He was sentenced to 1 year of probation and notified that he would be forced to register as a sex offender (*State v. Canal, Jr.*, 2009). Other prosecutors have opted for education. In 2008, school officials in Tukahannock (Pennsylvania) High School discovered saved images of nude or seminude teenage girls on several students' confiscated cell phones. After threatening the students with child pornography charges, the prosecutor notified the parents of 20 students who appeared in or possessed the images that the students would be required to participate in a 6- to 9-month education program or face criminal charges. Several students and their parents, supported by the American Civil Liberties Union, appealed to the district court (*Miller v. Skumanick*, 2009). The district court granted a temporary restraining order prohibiting the prosecutor from initiating criminal charges against the students for two relatively innocuous photographs in question (Wastler, 2010). A unanimous Third Circuit Court of Appeals affirmed the district court ruling (*Miller v. Mitchell*, 2010).

It is generally acknowledged that child pornography charges and registration as a sex offender may not be appropriate for teens sexting between peers. Since 2009, at least 10 states have enacted bills to address teen sexting (National Conference of State Legislatures, 2010). These laws for the most part define sexting as the electronic transmission or possession of sexually explicit images. Some states, such as Arizona, have classified possession or transmission of sexually explicit images as a class 2 misdemeanor. Other states, such as Illinois, have laws that prohibit the transmission of sexual images of another minor. Violators may be adjudicated as a minor in need of supervision and ordered to obtain counseling or community service (National Conference of State Legislatures, 2010).

In addition, sexting may be viewed as a form of cyberbullying and under certain circumstances creates a hostile environment that has a negative impact on the educational opportunities of the victim. In these cases school leaders would seem to have an obligation to act to protect the victim from further harassment and take steps to eliminate the hostile environment.

Linking to PRACTICE

Do:

- Educate parents and students about the dangers of sexting. Once pictures are viral, the sender no longer has control over who sees the images, how they are used, or how they are posted in social networking sites.
- Develop a simple process for students, parents, and others to report incidents of sexting regardless of where the images originate.
- Train faculty to recognize the symptoms associated with peer harassment.

Do Not:

- Hesitate to contact parents when incidents of sexting become known.

DATING VIOLENCE

The Centers for Disease Control and Prevention (CDC) (2008) defines *dating violence* as violence that occurs between two people in a close relationship. Dating violence may include physical violence (pinching, hitting, shoving, or kicking), emotional violence (threatening a partner or harming his or her sense of self-worth), and sexual violence (forcing a partner to engage in a sex act when he or she does not or cannot consent). Dating violence is relatively prevalent and affects the mental health of the victim (CDC, 2008). Studies indicate that at a minimum 10% of high school students are victims of dating violence in one form or another. Among female students who date in high school, some data indicate that as many as 30% are victims of dating violence. The data also indicate that victims of dating violence have an increased risk of drug and/or alcohol use, suicide ideation or attempt, and risky sexual behavior (CDC, 2008). In short, dating violence affects the mental and physical health of the victims and is thus a serious school safety issue (Carlson, 2003).

Several states require school districts to educate students on the issue of dating violence. For example, Georgia law requires the state board of education to develop a rape prevention and personal safety education program, and a program for preventing teen dating violence for grades 8 to 12 (S. B. 346). Texas state law requires each school district to adopt and implement a dating violence policy to be included in the district improvement plan (37.0831 Texas Education Code). The policy must include a definition of dating violence and address safety planning, enforcement of protective orders, training for teachers and administrators, counseling for affected students, and awareness education for students and parents. Except for states that require some form of education concerning the problem, dating violence at high school campuses has been largely ignored (Carlson, 2003). Regardless of the reasons why dating violence has traditionally not been addressed by school districts, Carlson (2003) proposes that dating violence can be viewed as identical to sexual harassment. The only difference is that dating violence occurs between dating partners, whereas sexual harassment is unwanted or unwelcome behavior of a sexual nature regardless of whether the perpetrator and victim are dating. The effects of off-campus dating violence often carry over to the school environment. For example, if a student alleges that she was sexually assaulted, forced to have sex, or physically abused by her boyfriend and is being taunted and harassed by other students or her boyfriend, the school should take into account the off-campus conduct when evaluating whether there is a hostile environment on campus (Dear Colleague, 2011, April 4). Naturally, in cases of alleged sexual assault or coerced sex school districts have an obligation to involve law enforcement as well.

In addition, dating violence can be a form of bullying, and a student could potentially claim that the school or school district was deliberately indifferent to the dating victimization. If some or all of the emotional abuse from a dating partner is conducted electronically by text messaging, social networking, and so forth, a student could claim deliberate indifference to cyberbullying on the part of schools or school districts. Carlson (2003) makes the following recommendations:

- Middle schools and high schools need to educate all students about dating violence. The education should include the signs of an unhealthy relationship.
- Train staff and faculty to recognize, prevent, and stop dating violence. Staff and faculty should follow the same curriculum as students including learning about the dynamics of dating violence and identifying the signs and symptoms of teen abuse.

- School districts should develop policies and procedures for handling student complaints about dating violence. Most school districts already have such policies and practices in place for handling sexual harassment complaints. Adding dating violence to this process makes intuitive sense.
- Schools should educate parents about dating violence.

SECURITY CAMERAS

In 2007, 66% of students ages 12 to 18 reported the use of one or more security cameras to monitor school (Robers et al., 2010). Security cameras and recording devices may not be a panacea, but they are very good at deterring outsiders from coming on campus. They also deter students from committing infractions and can be invaluable to school administrators and law enforcement when dealing with alleged violations of school rules or criminal codes (Stader, 2011). According to Brady (2008), the U.S. Supreme Court has developed two legal tests that provide guidance in analyzing the legality of emerging surveillance technology. In *Katz v. United States* (1967), the Court held that recordings may be unconstitutional when a person has an expectation of privacy that society is prepared to recognize as reasonable. The second case, *Kyllo v. United States* (2001), involved the use of thermal imaging technology. The Court held that when surveillance technology is not in general public use, the surveillance is a search and a warrant is required.

Therefore, it seems reasonable to assume that video surveillance is permissible in areas where an expectation of privacy is minimal, such as hallways, parking lots, or playgrounds. However, video surveillance is not permissible in areas where a reasonable person would have an expectation of privacy. For example, a jury recently awarded $40,000 each to 32 students who were taped by security cameras in a Cookeville, Tennessee, middle school locker room ("Students filmed in locker room win case," 2007). In 2002, the Overton County School Board had approved the installation of video surveillance equipment throughout the middle school building. The cameras transmitted images to a computer terminal in the assistant principal's office. The images were also accessible via remote Internet connection, and they were accessed 98 times through Internet service providers. The Sixth Circuit Court upheld the jury award, stating, "Some personal liberties are so fundamental to human dignity as to need no specific explication in our Constitution.... Surreptitiously videotaping [the girls] in various states of undress is plainly among them" (*Brannum v. Overton County School Board*, 2008).

According to the National Forum on Educational Statistics (NFES) (2006), videotapes or photographs directly related to a specific student created and maintained by the school district are educational records and are subject to FERPA. For example, consider a situation in which a student engages in a fight in a school hallway and the video of the fight is used as evidence to discipline the student. The video would be included in the involved student's education record, and the school would need to obtain consent before publishing or disclosing the contents of the video to unauthorized individuals. However, at least according the NFES, other noninvolved students in the video would be considered "set dressing" (not relevant to the incident) and not covered by FERPA.

One controversial use of security cameras is in classrooms. However, the use of video cameras in the classroom as part of teacher appraisal has been upheld by at least one court. For example, a Texas state court upheld a school board decision to terminate the employment of a teacher based in part on video evidence (*Roberts v. Houston Independent School District*, 1990). The court held that a public school classroom is not a zone where a teacher has a right to privacy. More recently, a California state court upheld the use of a video camera in an office shared by three employees because one of the employees was suspected of unauthorized use of the computer after school hours (*Crist v. Alpine Union School District*, 2005).

INTERNET STATUTORY PROTECTIONS

Parental concerns over protecting children, especially young children, from the potential dangers of the unfettered Internet have not been lost on the political agenda setters of both major political parties. This concern has led to several federal legislative efforts. Among these efforts are the Child Online Privacy Protection Act (COPPA), the Children's Internet Protection Act (CIPA), and most recently the Protection of Pupil Rights Amendment (PPRA).

Child Online Privacy Protection Act

The Child Online Privacy Protection Act (15 USCS 6501, 1998) requires the Federal Trade Commission to enforce rules regarding children's online privacy. COPPA applies to the online collection of personal information of children under 13. Personal information includes such information as full name, home address, e-mail address, telephone number, or any other information such as hobbies that would allow someone to identify or contact the child. The act also applies to information collected via cookies or other types of tracking mechanisms that are tied to individually identifiable information (Federal Trade Commission, www.ftc.gov). The Federal Trade Commission considers any website that includes subject matter, models, language, or advertising marketing to children to be accountable to this act. Websites must contain plain language prominently displayed outlining the types of information collected, parental rights, and how the operator uses the personal information. Release or sharing information to a third party requires parental signature (Conn, 2002).

Children's Internet Protection Act

The Children's Internet Protection Act (2001) requires schools and libraries to enforce a policy of Internet safety that includes the use of filtering or blocking technology in order to qualify for E-rate discounts. CIPA (20 USCS 9134) requires that schools develop and enforce an "Internet safety policy" that protects against Internet access to visual depictions that are obscene, constitute child pornography, or are harmful to minors. Local communities are responsible for determining what constitutes prohibited materials and appropriate school actions under CIPA. At a minimum, however, the district must provide reasonable public notice and hold at least one public hearing that addresses school Internet safety policies and practices.

The American Library Association and others challenged the constitutionality of CIPA. The U.S. District Court for the Eastern District of Pennsylvania, based on First Amendment claims, found the act unconstitutional. The U.S. Supreme Court reversed. Although unable to agree on a rationale for their decision, among the various opinions the Court held that the act does not impose an undue burden on libraries; Internet access in libraries is not a "traditional" or a "designated" public forum; concerns of "overblocking" could be easily resolved; libraries traditionally had censored pornographic literature by choosing not to purchase such material; and the act is a legitimate exercise of congressional spending power. In addition, Justices Kennedy and Breyer expressed the view that CIPA serves a legitimate government interest in protecting young users from material inappropriate to minors (*United States v. American Library Association,* 2003).

Protection of Pupil Rights Amendment

The Protection of Pupil Rights Amendment applies to programs that receive federal funding. PPRA is intended to protect the rights of parents and students by ensuring that schools and contractors make available for inspection by parents any instructional materials used in connection with a survey, analysis, or evaluation funded by the U.S. Department of Education and ensuring that schools and contractors obtain written parental consent before minor students are required to participate in any such survey that reveals information such as political affiliations, mental or psychological problems, sex behavior and attitudes, or illegal, antisocial, or other self-incriminating behaviors. For all practical purposes, filtering software with all its imperfections is the only technology available to meet this requirement (Conn, 2002).

Family Educational Rights and Privacy Act

The Family Educational Rights and Privacy Act (20 USCS 1232g) covers the release of student records to third parties. Release of such data for students under 18 is not permissible without parental permission. FERPA applies to identifiable student personal, academic, and disciplinary records. It requires that parental permission be sought whenever student information, especially photographs or other likenesses, are published on the school website.

Linking to PRACTICE

Do:

- Schedule yearly public meetings to explain campus or district Internet filtering software. Explain how the software works, the kinds of sites blocked by the software, and punishments for bypassing the software.

- Consider making lists of age-appropriate websites for student use. Share this information with teachers, students, parents, and community members.

- Consider restricting student research for term papers, essays, and so on to "approved" search engines such as ERIC.

- Publicize student privacy rights, including directory information, in a wide range of formats including teacher handbooks, as part of acceptable use policies, newsletters to parents, and on the school website. Regardless of this dissemination, it is probably good policy to obtain affirmative parental permission before posting any student data on school websites.

Do Not:

- Refuse parents or other community members access to information regarding the types of sites students and teachers are accessing.

Summary

School safety has evolved into one of the most important tasks associated with campus and district leadership. Security, especially security of expectation, is a prerequisite for learning. Security is not possible without equity. Security and equity are the foundations for meeting **ISLLC Standard 3**. Security and equity come in many forms, including policies and practices to keep weapons out of school. Security of expectation also includes policy and practices that address teacher-on-student and student-on-student victimization. Student victimization includes sexual harassment, bullying, dating violence, and sexting. Once knowledge of safety or victimization issues are know, the ISLLC standards and federal and state law place an affirmative duty on school leaders to effectively respond to eliminate the victimization.

ISLLC Standard 3

CONNECTING STANDARDS TO PRACTICE

THE LADY IN RED

Without preamble, Riverboat High School principal Tara Hills said, "Sharon, I may have a Homecoming problem." Assistant Superintendent Sharon Grey was well aware of the tradition and importance of Homecoming to the Riverboat School District and community. Homecoming consisted of a week full of spirit days, hall decorating, float building, bonfires, pep assemblies, the Friday afternoon parade, the all-important Homecoming game, and the equally important Homecoming dance. Parents and alumni played a large role in the festivities. By tradition, the Homecoming dance capped the weeklong activities, and large numbers of community members came to watch the final dances, view the Homecoming attire, and witness the all-important crowning of the Homecoming Queen.

It was also tradition at RHS to allow students to invite outside guests to the Homecoming dance, provided that the guest was properly registered in the office before the dance. Such was the case on the first day students were allowed to register outside dates as Andrew Wade, a 18-year-old senior, signed up his date, Lindsay Lewis, a 19-year-old freshman at the local community college. Andrew was notably excited and did not hesitate to show Lindsay's picture to everyone who would take the time to look. Andrew

cornered Tara in the office, Lindsay's picture in hand. "This is the dress she is wearing to the dance. We simply shopped for hours, but finally found this wonderful red one. Isn't she simply gorgeous?"

Reaching across the desk, Tara handed Lindsay's picture to Sharon. Lindsay definitely made an impression. Tall and svelte, she posed on a stool wearing a radiant smile, her long brown hair flowing over a very short electric red dress that revealed several inches of muscular leg. "That's some dress, all right," was all Sharon could muster. "Does this meet the Homecoming dress code requirements?"

Smiling, Tara replied "You changed that policy, remember?"

"Oh yeah, right. Maybe not one of my smarter ideas. So, what's the problem?"

"Well, I don't know how to say this: Andrew's date is transsexed. I have already heard from several parents who are concerned about this situation. I just sent two boys to assistant principal Tommy Thompson for pushing Andrew in the hallway. Andrew told me they were calling him names. As you know, this community is very traditional, and I don't think this is going to go over very well."

Sharon returned to her office. Some telephone messages waited on the desk. She scanned them. Several were typical calls, but a few caught her eye: The superintendent wanted to speak to her about the Homecoming dance, the chairman of the local ministerial alliance would appreciate an explanation of how outside Homecoming dates were screened, and Andrew Wade's father wished to speak to Sharon regarding the assault on his son that morning.

Question

Argue for or against allowing Andrew Wade to attend the Homecoming dance with Lindsay as his date. What legal protections, if any, does Andrew Wade have? Cite ISLLC standards, case law, Dear Colleague letters from OCR, and ethical principles to support your answer. Write a memorandum to the superintendent or school board president outlining your view.

CHAPTER 8

Equal Protection, English Language Learners, and Desegregation

INTRODUCTION

The ISLLC standards call for educational leaders who "safeguard the values of democracy, equity, and diversity." The legal requirement that reflects this standard is called equal protection. *Equal protection* means that the law applies equally to everyone regardless of race, ethnicity, religion, sex, and so forth. This chapter presents several aspects of equal protection as the concept applies to student access to a public education, placement, discipline, English language learners, and school desegregation. John Rawls's "justice as fairness" concept is expanded to include discussions of social justice and social capital.

FOCUS QUESTIONS

1. What are social justice and social capital, and how are these concepts related to equal protection?

2. Should race, ethnicity, or sex ever be considered to achieve a diverse student body?

3. Should students be required to document U.S. citizenship before enrolling in public education?

4. What information should public school districts be able to obtain from families before allowing their children to enroll in public schools?

5. How are civil rights laws enforced?

KEY TERMS

De facto segregation   English language learners   Social justice
De jure segregation   Equality of opportunity   Unitary status
Disparate impact   Office for Civil Rights

CASE STUDY
In All Fairness

Lucinda Chavez sat silently as Father Michael Lewis approached the microphone to address the Centerville Board of Education. Lucinda had been superintendent for only a few months, but she already knew much of the history of Centerville School District (CSD). Until the 1960s, Centerville had been a dual school system composed of the Lincoln Schools for African American children and the Centerville Schools for White children. After considerable encouragement from the state government, the schools were consolidated in 1968. Since that time, CSD had been officially integrated. Lucinda knew that Father Lewis planned to use anecdotes to support his claim that racial inequalities in educational opportunities and discipline practices remained commonplace at CSD. Unfortunately, from what Lucinda could ascertain, Father Lewis had a legitimate concern.

Father Lewis spoke eloquently as he told the story of 12-year-old Alejandro. Alejandro's parents had come to Father Lewis's church for help. They finally admitted that they were in the country illegally and told of the hardships they had endured to finally reach Centerville. Now broke, hungry, and desperate for work, the parents had tried to enroll Alejandro in school. According to Alejandro's parents, Centerville Middle School counselors and administrators had requested proof of citizenship, which of course they did not have. Administrators were reportedly rude and threatened to call the police. Afraid of deportation, Alejandro and his parents fled the school and into Father Lewis's church.

Father Lewis told the story of Michael. Michael was a bright African American youth whom Father Lewis knew well. By the time Michael was in the ninth grade, he was being watched closely by several college basketball recruiters. Unfortunately, Michael was not always teacher friendly and, in spite of his repeated request for placement in college prep courses, he was placed by his high school counselors in lower-track courses and study hall. As graduation approached, it was obvious even to Michael that his dreams of playing college basketball had ended when his course work did not meet NCAA Clearinghouse requirements. By age 22, Michael was wealthy, feared, and dead. His mother and Father Lewis blamed the Centerville High School faculty for denying Michael the opportunity to take college courses. Father Lewis than spoke of the number of African American and Latino children in "dumbed-down" classes, the lack of access to advanced placement courses, the harsh discipline of any child of color who happened to cross the line, and the discrimination in numbers and value of scholarship awards to children of color.

Father Lewis ended his speech: "Ladies and gentlemen of the board, these are our children, and with them go all of our hopes and dreams. In all fairness, the insidious discrimination in Centerville School District must end." As Father Lewis sat down to thunderous applause, the board chairperson thanked him and moved to appoint a committee to study the problem. Lucinda knew it would be a difficult challenge to lead the board to a reasoned discussion of Father Lewis's claims.

LEADERSHIP PERSPECTIVES

According to Frances Fowler (2009), the values of equality and fraternity are fundamental to educational policy in the United States. Equality as a policy value is also often referred to as *social justice*. *Equality* is defined in the U.S. Constitution ("All men are created equal") and in the Fourteenth Amendment ("No State shall . . . deny to any person within its jurisdiction the equal protection of the laws"). This does not mean that all citizens have equal ability or the right to an equal share of property. Rather, it means that all citizens are of equal status, and the law is going to apply equally to everyone. For example, Title IX was designed at least in part to provide equal protection for female athletes, desegregation law is based on equal protection for minority children, and Title VI of the Civil Rights Act of 1964 prohibits discrimination based on race, color, or natural origin by recipients of federal funds.

   Fraternity (or *social capital*) can be defined as the "ability to perceive other members of one's society as brothers and sisters, to have a sense of responsibility for them, and to feel that in difficult times one can turn to them for help" (Fowler, 2009, p. 112). The importance of the development of social capital within the larger school

ISLLC Standard 6E community is reflected in **ISLLC Standard 6E**. Social capital is derived from the various resources, social support systems, and organizations that shape the normative environment in which a school functions. Two valuable sources of social capital are schools and families. The practice of racial integration, the integration of English language learners into the public school culture, and the inclusion or mainstreaming of special education children in the regular classroom are examples of policies designed to promote equality and social capital among diverse groups of students (Fowler, 2009).

ISLLC Standards 4 and 5 **ISLLC Standards 4 and 5** call for school leaders to embrace the values of social justice and to understand and promote the development of social capital within the larger school community. These standards promote the understanding

ISLLC Standard 4B and appreciation of a community's diverse resources, the promotion of positive relationships with families and caregivers, the safeguarding of democracy, equity,

ISLLC Standard 4C and diversity, and the promotion of social justice. In the case study "In All Fairness," Father Lewis is asking the school district to examine these normative prac-

ISLLC Standard 5C tices that in the opinion of Father Lewis have undermined the values of social

ISLLC Standard 5E justice and social capital in the Centerville community. However, the values of social justice and social capital sometimes conflict with the deeply held values that define not only individual persons, but the larger school culture as well. Lucinda Chavez may indeed face a difficult challenge in confronting long-held normative practices that fracture feelings of equality and brotherhood in the Centerville School District.

JUSTICE AS FAIRNESS: PROMOTING EQUALITY AND FRATERNITY

The ethical concepts of a well-ordered school based on John Rawls's ideas of social cooperation and public justification were discussed in Chapter 5. This concept was derived from Rawls's (2001) first principle of "justice as fairness," which states:

> **Principle One:** Each person has the same indefeasible claim to a fully adequate scheme of equal basic liberties, which scheme is compatible with the same scheme of liberties for all. (p. 42)

The justice as fairness concept will be further extended to the ethical considerations of equality (social justice) and fraternity (social capital) embedded in the ISLLC standards. The concepts of equality and fraternity are considered in the second of Rawls's Principles of Justice:

> **Principle Two:** Social and economic inequities are to satisfy two conditions: first, they are to be attached to offices and positions open to all under conditions of fair equality of opportunity; and second, they are to be to the greatest benefit of the least-advantaged members of society (the difference principle). (pp. 42–43)

Rawls's second principle consists of two conditions under which inequalities may exist. The first condition of the second principle considers *fair equality of opportunity*. The second condition of the second principle considers when *inequalities are justified*.

Fair Equality of Opportunity

Fundamental to Rawls's first condition is the idea of a school community where all participants have a fair **equality of opportunity**. Fair equality of opportunity requires conditions that do not permit some to have unfair bargaining advantages over others in the school community. Fair equality means not only that opportunities (such as advanced courses, the best teachers, access to technology, honors, scholarships, and preferred offices) should be open in the formal sense, but that *all members should have a fair chance to attain and benefit from these opportunities*. That is, all students, regardless of sex, ethnicity, socioeconomic status, or race, should have an equal opportunity for the best basket of goods and services available to any other student in the school community. In the opening case study "In All Fairness," both Alejandro and Michael were seemingly denied equality of opportunity. Alejandro was denied access to school, and Michael was denied the *opportunity* to enroll in college prep courses.

Rawls uses a hypothetical "veil of ignorance" to illustrate the concept of fair equality of opportunity. Under a veil of ignorance, parties do not know or consider race, ethnicity, sex, or native endowments such as strength or intelligence as they strive for fair equality of opportunity. This hypothetical construct provides a world view free of past behaviors, political power, or birth rights of the participants. It leads to terms of cooperation that are fair and supportable by public discourse. This concept is hypothetical because it is of course impossible to attain. However, the basic idea of a veil of ignorance to create a system of cooperation that is fair and supportable is the driving force behind the ethical obligation of fundamental fairness demanded by the ISLLC standards.

The Justification of Inequalities

The second condition of the second principle views inequalities to be justifiable as long as these inequalities are to the greatest benefit of the least advantaged members of the school community (*difference principle*). The difference principle is subordinate both to the first principle of justice (guaranteeing the equal basic liberties) and to the first condition of the second principle (fair equality of opportunity). The difference principle is designed to apply within the background of the school community in which these prior conditions are already satisfied.

Inequalities may or may not be defined in terms of race, ethnicity, sex, or socioeconomic status. For example, a student may be advantaged in one area (musical talent, for instance) and disadvantaged in another area (mathematical talent, for instance), with little relationship to sex or race. However, sometimes race, ethnicity, and sex serve as the background to the practice of "silent tracking" that results in lesser opportunities for some students such as Michael in the case study "In All Fairness." This type of discrimination is the most insidious and most difficult form of inequality to confront. However, it may be these conditions that Father Lewis is asking the Centerville School District to address, not all inequalities in the basket of goods and services available to all students. For example, providing a student with extra tutoring, use of technology to better communicate, or English as a second language classes is justifiable as long as all the other conditions are met in the school. In other words, equality of opportunity (social justice) based on fair and equal treatment and justifiable inequalities provides the basis for a school culture from which social capital (fraternity) can emerge. Table 8–1 illustrates the interrelationships of these concepts.

TABLE 8–1	Equality of opportunity matrix	
	Low social capital	**High social capital**
Low social justice	*Quadrant 1* ■ Stratified classes characterized by discrepancies based on sex, race, and/or ethnicity. ■ Benefits of the full basket of goods and services available to only a few. ■ Perceived inequality permeates the school community. ■ Student conflict defined by differences in race, ethnicity, and/or sex.	*Quadrant 2* ■ Stratified classes characterized by discrepancies based on sex, race, or ethnicity. ■ Benefits of the full basket of goods and services available to a few students. ■ Perceptions of inequalities not apparent in the school community. ■ Student groups get along for the most part, and conflict is rare.
High social justice	*Quadrant 3* ■ Stratified classes not generally distinguishable by race, sex, and ethnicity. ■ Full basket of goods and services available to most students. ■ Perceptions of inequalities remain in the school community. ■ Student conflict sometimes defined by race, ethnicity, and/or sex.	*Quadrant 4* ■ Classes not stratified by race, ethnicity, and/or sex. ■ Full basket of goods and services available to all students. ■ Privileges available to all students based on need. ■ Community perception that equal treatment is commonplace. ■ Student conflict rare.

Table 8–1 may be used to estimate the relative levels of social justice and social capital embedded in the school culture. For example, a Quadrant 1 school would represent a campus culture that has both low social justice and low social capital. Some of the indicators of this type of culture may include stratified classes, perceived inequality permeating the school and community, and student conflict often defined by race, ethnicity, socioeconomic status, or sex. Centerville School District in the case study "In All Fairness" may represent a Quadrant 1 or a Quadrant 3 school culture. A Quadrant 3 school would present many of the same inequalities as a Quadrant 1 school. However, the school and community do not perceive these inequalities, or else those affected by them feel powerless to confront those who may have the power to institute change. A Quadrant 4 school represents a healthy school where social justice and social capital are embedded in the culture. Indicators of this type of school culture include little if any stratification of classes based on race, sex, or socioeconomic status; the justification of inequalities; and community perceptions of equal treatment. It is important to note that few schools would always fall into a particular quadrant. Rather, what is important to consider is where a particular campus culture generally falls in the social justice–social capital continuum.

From a practical standpoint, placing a school within a particular quadrant provides a starting point for discussion. For example, in the case study "In All Fairness," it would be important for Lucinda Chavez to determine if the schools in the Centerville School District are predominately in Quadrant 1 or Quadrant 3. If, for example, some campuses in the district are Quadrant 1, then Father Lewis is correct and the ISLLC standards require an affirmative response. If, on the other hand, most campuses are in Quadrant 2, then efforts at public justification may be the appropriate response.

Linking to PRACTICE

Do:
- Collect and analyze student data in areas such as class assignments, special education, and office referrals or disciplinary actions. Any disproportion requires an affirmative response to address the underlying causes.
- Analyze data to determine if any inequalities are to the greatest benefit of the least advantaged.
- Gather community and student data to determine perceptions of inequalities.

EQUAL PROTECTION: A LEGAL THEORY TO PROMOTE BASIC FAIRNESS

A civil right is the right of an individual to personal liberty guaranteed by the Bill of Rights and the Thirteenth, Fourteenth, Fifteenth, and Nineteenth Amendments to the Constitution. These rights specifically address voting, due process, and equal protection under the law (Garner, 2006). **ISLLC Standard 5** illustrates the importance placed on equal protection for all students. This chapter focuses on the concept of equal protection as it applies to student discrimination in access, placement, and discipline, English language learners, and desegregation. Understanding and appropriately responding to these legal concepts are part of **ISLLC Standards 2, 3, 4, and 5.**

ISLLC Standard 5

ISLLC Standards 2, 3, 4, and 5

DISCRIMINATION

Student discriminatory complaints based on race, color, or national origin may be filed with the ***Office for Civil Rights*** (OCR) of the U.S. Department of Education. OCR enforces several federal laws that prohibit discrimination, including Title IV and Title VI of the Civil Rights Act of 1964. Title IV prohibits discrimination based on race, color, or national origin by public school districts. Title VI prohibits discrimination based on race, color, or national origin by recipients of federal funds. Title VI also prohibits districts from unjustly utilizing school structures, defined as admission requirements, placement in classes or grades, assignment to special education classes, disciplinary practices, suspension/expulsion policies, and so forth, that have a discriminatory effect on students based on race, color, or national origin (Dear Colleague, 2011, May 6). Complaints may be filed by the victim(s) of alleged discrimination or by other persons or groups on behalf of the alleged victim(s).

In addition to disciplinary and placement practices, OCR under Title VI also considers issues of racially hostile environments. A racially hostile environment occurs when race-based harassment is "sufficiently severe, pervasive, or persistent so as to interfere with or limit a student's ability to participate in or benefit from the services, activities, or opportunities offered by the school" (Dear Colleague, 2010, October 26, p. 1). School leaders are responsible for addressing harassment incidents when they know or reasonably should have known about the harassing behavior. Once an investigation reveals that discriminatory harassment has occurred, school leaders have an affirmative duty to take reasonable and prompt steps to end the harassment and prevent it from recurring.

OCR's primary objective is complaint resolution by facilitating voluntary resolutions or negotiated agreements for voluntary compliance. If negotiations fail, the OCR will resort to the referral of cases to the U.S. Department of Justice (Office for Civil Rights, 2000, *Annual Report to Congress*). In other words, compliance with a voluntary OCR agreement may be the better part of valor for most school districts found to be in violation of any federal discrimination law. The following Linking to Practice is based on the OCR's Oct 26, 2010, Dear Colleague Letter.

Linking to PRACTICE

- School districts should have well-publicized policies prohibiting student-on-student or employee harassment based on race, color, natural origin, or sex.
- School districts should have well-publicized procedures for students, parents, or others to report harassment.
- Policies should prohibit retaliation for reporting incidents of harassment.
- Districts should have ongoing staff development designed to recognize harassment in any form.

- School board policy should require faculty and staff to report harassment to proper building-level administrators.
- School board policy should require building administrators to investigate any allegations of harassment and report their findings to selected central office personnel.
- Be aware of any signs of a racially hostile environment and take immediate and reasonable action once it is known to school officials.

Legal Remedies to Title VI Claims

Two legal frameworks regarding discriminatory conduct are available under Title VI of the Civil Rights Act of 1964 (a) disparate impact and (b) adverse impact claims. **Disparate impact** considers whether or not a policy or practice unfairly treats a particular group in a school. Examples of disparate impact may involve unfair treatment of students based on race, color, national origin, sex, or handicapping condition. Unfair treatment may include such things as policies and practices that cause disproportionate numbers of students of color to be referred for disciplinary action; higher suspension and expulsion rates for various groups of students; and significant numbers of students in lower track courses identifiable by race, color, or national origin. Disparate treatment claims require demonstration of both disparate treatment and intentional discrimination. Because school officials rarely publicly admit to intentional discrimination in policy or practice, this claim is particularly difficult to sustain.

The adverse impact theory considers policies that result in an adverse impact on a disparate number of students based on race, color, or ethnicity. Although neutral on the face, these policies result in a disproportionate number of students of a particular race, color, or national origin suffering maximum punishment for a particular offense or disproportionately placed in remedial classes or special education. The difficulty of demonstrating adverse impact claims on a legal level may be challenging, especially when the policies apply to school safety. For example, disparate and adverse impact were among the claims of students in *Fuller v. Decatur* (2000). In this particular case, several high school students were expelled for their involvement in a fight at a football game. The students alleged that school district policy resulted in a practice of arbitrary expulsions with regard to African American students. The trial court ordered Decatur administrators to produce expulsion records for the past 2 years disaggregated by race. African American students comprise 46% to 48% of the student body in the Decatur District. The summary data provided by district administrators indicated that 82% of the students expelled during this period were African American. The remaining 18% were White.

The court noted that the statistical data would lead a reasonable person to speculate that the expulsion decisions were affected by the race of the student. However, the court noted that indications of the race of the student being considered for expulsion were never presented to the school board. The court also noted that White students had been expelled for similar types of offenses. Therefore, the court found that the students failed to demonstrate that "any similarly situated Caucasian students were treated less harshly; they failed to establish that race played any role in the School Board's expulsion decision."

The difficulty of demonstrating adverse impact claims on a legal level may be challenging, especially when the policies apply to school safety. However, an examination of disproportionate impact can be sobering. In a nationwide study of racial discrimination in public education, Gordon, Piana, and Keleher (2000) concluded:

• African American students especially, along with Latinos and Native American students, are suspended or expelled in much greater numbers than their White peers. For example, in Austin, Texas, 18% of the student population is African American, 43% Latino, and 37% White. African American students accounted for 36% of the suspensions and expulsions, Latino students 45%, and White students

18%. A similar pattern is apparent in the other 10 cities for which disaggregate data were available for the study.

- Students of color are more likely to drop out—or be pushed out—of school and less likely to graduate than are White students.
- Students of color have less access to advanced classes or programs for gifted students.

These findings led the researchers to conclude: "What concerns the nation's almost 17 million students of color and their communities is that, regardless of anyone's intent, they receive an inferior education" (p. 3). Regardless of intent or the difficulty of successful legal challenges to school policy, **ISLLC Standards 4 and 5** require school leaders to examine and address inequalities in the educational system at all levels. This is what Father Lewis in the case study "In All Fairness" is asking.

ISLLC Standards 4 and 5

Linking to Practice

Do:

- Collect, analyze, and disaggregate student discipline data to determine if there is evidence of disparate impact of policy and practice. If the data show disproportionate impact, school leaders are obligated to constructively address the situation.
- Analyze student demographics in various honors courses, reading groups, and so on for disproportionate representation.

Do Not:

- Allow teachers or other adults to create, tacitly approve, or ignore racial hostility in any form in the classroom, hallways, or at after-school activities.
- Ignore evidence of disproportionate representation based on race, sex, or national origin in office referrals, suspension and expulsion data, advanced or honors courses, advanced reading groups, gifted and talented programs, and so on.

ENGLISH LANGUAGE LEARNERS

The education of **English language learners** (ELLs) is inexorably intertwined with the political and philosophical debate over illegal immigration, tax dollars, and citizenship. Public PK–12 schools are not immune from this debate. The legal history surrounding ELL students started in San Francisco in 1971. A class action suit was brought against the San Francisco public school system by non–English-speaking Chinese students alleging that they were not provided with an equal educational opportunity and were being denied equal protection as provided by the Fourteenth Amendment (*Lau v. Nichols*, 1974). The U.S. Supreme Court did not validate the students' equal protection claim, but rather relied on Title VI of the Civil Rights Act of 1964, which prohibits discrimination based on race, color, or national origin by any recipient of federal funds.

Also in 1974, the U.S. Congress passed the Equal Education Opportunities Act (20 USC Sec. 1703), which prohibits, among other things, any state from denying equal educational opportunity to an individual on account of his or her race, color, sex, or national origin, by failing to take appropriate action to overcome language barriers that impede equal participation in the instructional program.

Two other landmark cases regarding ELL students soon followed. In 1981, the Fifth Circuit Court of Appeals developed a three-pronged test to determine whether a school district was in compliance with the Equal Educational Opportunities Act (*Castaneda v. Pickard*, 1981). The three-part test included the following: (1) The school is pursuing a program informed by an educational theory recognized as sound by some experts in the field or, at least, deemed legitimate experimental strategy; (2) the program and practices actually used by the school system are reasonably calculated to implement effectively the educational theory adopted by the school; and (3) the school's program succeeds, after a legitimate trial, in producing results indicating that the language barriers confronting students are actually being overcome. The Fifth Circuit also concluded that segregation of ELL students is permissible only when the benefits outweigh the adverse effects of the segregation.

In 1982, the U.S. Supreme Court held that the Fourteenth Amendment prohibits states from denying access to a free public education to any child residing in the state, whether present in the United States legally or otherwise (*Plyler v. Doe*, 1982). *Plyler* establishes that ELL students are entitled to the same basket of goods and services provided by public schools to all children who reside within the district boundaries. *Plyler* makes clear that the undocumented or noncitizen status of the child or her or his parent(s) is irrelevant to the child's entitlement to a public education (Dear Colleague, 2011, May 6). As the Court stated in *Plyler*, "Obviously, no child is responsible for his (or her) birth and penalizing the . . . child is an ineffectual—as well as unjust— way of deterring the parent."

According to the Office for Civil Rights (Dear Colleague, 2011, May 6) **school districts may:**

- Require students or their parents to provide proof of residency within the district. For example, districts may require copies of phone and water bills or lease agreements to establish residency. However, a school district's requirements to establish residency must be applied in the same way for all children.
- A school district may require a birth certificate to ensure that a student falls within the district-mandated minimum and maximum age requirements. However, a district may not deny enrollment based on a foreign birth certificate.
- Request a student's social security number during enrollment in order to use it as a student identification number. The district must inform the student and parent that providing a social security number is voluntary and explain how the number will be used.
- A district may request race or ethnicity data.

A district may not:

- Ask about citizenship or immigration status to establish residency within the district, nor may a district deny admission to a homeless child because he or she cannot provide the required documents to establish residency.
- A district may not prevent enrollment because the child has a foreign birth certificate.
- A district may not prevent enrollment because parents refuse to provide a social security number.

A BRIEF HISTORY OF DESEGREGATION

At the turn of the 20th century, several states in both the North and South had laws that either required or allowed school districts to establish and maintain *segregated* schools for White and African American students (see *Brown v. Board of Education,* 1954). Segregation is the unconstitutional policy of separating people and their children on the basis of color, race, or national origin. Courts define two types of segregation applicable to education law: (1) *De jure segregation* is defined as state or school board policy or practice that separates children by color, race, or national origin. In other words, *de jure* segregation is the intentional separation of students of color and White students. The end result of *de jure* segregation is a dual school system. Historically, schools for students of color have been inferior to schools for White students. *De jure* segregation was found constitutional in an 1896 case that grew out of a Louisiana state law requiring equal but separate railroad cars for "colored" and White passengers (*Plessy v. Ferguson,* 1896). The *Equal Educational Opportunities Act* (EEOA) of 1974 (20 USC Sec. 1703) makes illegal the deliberate segregation of students by school districts on the basis of race, color, or national origin or the transfer of a student from one school to another if the purpose and effect of such transfers increases the segregation of students based on race, color, or national origin. In other words, the EEOA bars *de jure* segregation. (2) *De facto segregation* occurs without the direct intent of a state or school board, but usually because of socioeconomic factors that result in housing patterns that create enclaves of children (both children of color and White children, for example) of the same color or race (Garner, 2006).

The battle over separate but equal schools started 20 long years before the EEOA was passed, when the concept of "separate but equal" as it applies to schools was challenged in 1954 (*Brown v. Board of Education*).

1954 Brown v. Board of Education of Topeka, Kansas (Brown I)

The U.S. Supreme Court considered a Kansas state law that permitted cities of more than 15,000 to maintain separate school facilities for African American and White students. The Court, finding that "education is perhaps the most important function of state and local governments," applied the Equal Protection Clause of the Fourteenth Amendment to education and declared such state laws to be unconstitutional. In unanimously reversing *Plessy,* the Court found that because segregated public schools are not equal and cannot be made equal, the "separate but equal" doctrine of *Plessy* has no place in education. Consequently, school districts should proceed to **unitary status**, meaning that the school system is desegregated to the "greatest extent practical." However, this landmark ruling was just the beginning of a long, arduous, and often contentious legal and political journey that simultaneously united and divided American society. The following summary of court cases captures just a small portion of this journey.

1955: *Brown v. Board of Education* (Brown II)

- Reiterated that racial discrimination in public education is unconstitutional, and all provisions of federal, state, or local law must yield to this principle.

- Required that all vestiges of segregation be eliminated with "all deliberate speed."
- Primary responsibility for desegregation lies with school districts. Local districts must demonstrate "good faith" efforts in the areas of facilities; transportation; administrative, faculty, and staff assignments; and student assignments.
- Federal district courts determined the definition of "good faith efforts."
- Local courts would retain jurisdiction of these cases during any periods of transition.
- Recognized revisions of school districts and attendance areas as one option to remedy *de jure* segregation.

1968: *Green v. County School Board of New Kent County* (Virginia)

The Court was asked to consider whether a "freedom of choice" plan where not a single child regardless of race had changed schools was acceptable. The Court answered that a desegregation plan that is ineffective must be discontinued and an effective plan established.

- School boards operating a dual system are charged with the affirmative duty to take whatever steps deemed necessary to convert to a unitary system.
- Federal district courts were charged with determining "good faith" efforts and that any proposed plan should have a real prospect for success.
- The Court ordered segregation eliminated "root and branch" in a number of different areas including facilities, teaching staff, transportation, and extracurricular activities.

1969: *Alexander v. Holmes County Board of Education* (Mississippi)

The Fifth Circuit Court granted the state of Mississippi a delay in submitting desegregation plans because time was too short to accomplish a complete and orderly implementation of the plans for the next school year. On appeal, the U.S. Supreme Court found that the court of appeals should have denied all motions for additional time.

- Continued operation of segregated schools under a standard of allowing "all deliberate speed" for desegregation is no longer constitutionally permissible.

1971: *Swann v. Charlotte-Mecklenburg Board of Education* (North Carolina)

The Court considered the methods and latitude of federal district courts in enforcing desegregation decrees when school authorities default on their obligation to put forward acceptable remedies.

- Under the principle that *de jure* segregation is unconstitutional, school authorities are clearly charged with eliminating from the public schools all vestiges of state-imposed segregation.
- If school authorities fail in their affirmative obligations, judicial authority may be invoked, and the scope of a district court's powers is broad.
- The extent of the violation determines the scope of the remedy.

- The Court recognized "de facto segregation." The mere existence of single-race schools is not necessarily prima facie evidence of segregation. However, courts have considerable authority to address instances of segregation brought about by discriminatory action of state authorities.

1973: *Keyes v. Denver*

Colorado state law had never required or allowed racially segregated schools as did laws in Kansas, Mississippi, Virginia, or Louisiana (see previous cases). The Court was asked to consider whether, if a school board used various techniques such as student attendance zones, school site selection, or a neighborhood school policy that created or maintained racially or ethnically segregated schools in at least part of the district, a decree was justified directing desegregation of the entire district. The Court answered in the affirmative.

- The Court ruled that if a "substantial portion" of the district is unlawfully segregated by law or systematic action, the entire district must be involved in the remedy.
- The Court recognized that "de facto" segregation does occur, resulting in isolated pockets of segregated schools. However, such cases should be rare.

1974: *Milliken v. Bradley* (Detroit)

A U.S. district court ruled, among other things, that in order to effectively desegregate Detroit schools, it would be necessary to look beyond school district lines.

- Absent interdistrict constitutional violations, racial segregation existing in one district could not be remedied by a multidistrict solution absent evidence that the proposed neighboring districts participated in the segregation process.

1977: *Milliken v. Bradley* (Milliken II)

The Court granted certiorari to consider two questions: May a district court (a) order compensatory or remedial educational programs for school children subjected to past acts of *de jure* segregation, and (b) order state officials to bear part of the costs of those programs? The Court answered yes to both questions. Because it could be shown that both the Detroit Board of Education and the state of Michigan participated in acts of *de jure* segregation, these remedies were within the powers of a district court.

1986: *Riddick v. School Board of Norfolk* (Virginia)

The Fourth Circuit Court affirmed a district court ruling that the School Board of the City of Norfolk had satisfied its affirmative duty to desegregate. This is the first such dissolution of a desegregation order in the United States.

1991: *Oklahoma City Schools v. Dowell*

The Court considered the question of what factors a district court should address in determining whether or not a particular board of education had demonstrated a sufficient "good faith effort" before releasing the district from judicial control.

- Desegregation orders are not meant for perpetuity.
- The Court reinforced the concept that a district must demonstrate that vestiges of past discrimination be eliminated to "the greatest extent practicable."
- A school board is not responsible for racial imbalance that is not traceable to prior violations.
- The district court must examine criteria established in *Green v. County School Board* (1968) more than 20 years earlier plus the *Swann* factor (*Swann v. Charlotte-Mecklenburg Board of Education,* 1973) of equitable resource allocation. The factors a district court should consider include:
  a. Student assignment
  b. Faculty
  c. Staff
  d. Transportation
  e. Extracurricular activities
  f. Facilities
  g. Resources (from *Swann*)

1992: *Freeman v. Pitts* (DeKalb County, Georgia)

The primary legal question in this case considered whether or not a district court may relinquish judicial oversight and control over those aspects (*Green* and *Swann* factors) of a school system in which there has been compliance with a desegregation decree while some of the factors remain not in compliance.

- Desegregation orders can be incrementally dissolved.
- Federal judges have the power to relinquish control of desegregation efforts.
- The district must demonstrate "good faith commitment" to the federal desegregation order as a primary condition of being declared "unitary."
- School boards are not responsible for de facto segregation that occurs after "good faith commitment" to unitary status.
- The Court values local control. Federal supervision is a temporary remedy for past discrimination.

1990: *Missouri v. Jenkins* (Kansas City, Missouri)

- The district court improperly ordered an increase in local property taxes to offset the cost of desegregation order. The Court considered several aspects of the Missouri school funding formula as well as taxing limits and authority of the state.
- The Supreme Court was reluctant to link school segregation and residential segregation to a desegregation order.
- The Court directed the federal trial court to restore control of school systems to local and state authorities as soon as possible.

The End of an Era

In order to be released from judicial oversight (declared "unitary"), a district is required to demonstrate a "good faith effort" over a period of time to comply with the factors established by the U.S. Supreme Court in *Green v. County School Board of New Kent*

County (1968). After more than 50 years of litigation, it appears that the era of court-ordered and court-supervised desegregation of America's schools is coming rapidly to a close. For example, in 2001 the 11th Circuit Court upheld a district court ruling determining that the desegregation litigation involving Duval County (Florida) public schools should end (*NAACP, Jacksonville Branch v. Duval County Schools,* 2001), and it also upheld the dissolution of judicial oversight for Hillsborough County, Florida (*Manning v. School Board,* 2001). More recently, the desegregation order involving Little Rock (Arkansas) Public Schools was settled in five of six areas (*Little Rock School District v. Pulaski County,* 2003); the desegregation order involving the City of Dallas, Texas, was dissolved by the Northern District Court of Texas (*Tasby v. Moses,* 2003); and the longest-running desegregation order in America, involving East Baton Rouge (Louisiana) Parish, was finally resolved after 47 years (*Clifford Eugene Davis Jr., et al. v. East Baton Rouge Parish School Board,* 2003).

A *Compelling* State Interest

As the trend toward the dissolving of desegregation orders continues, concerns regarding the resegregation of America's schools have been expressed. For example, Orfield, Frankenberg, and Lee (2003) pointed out from their research at Harvard University that an unraveling of integration and a return to segregated schools had occurred in the previous decade. The authors found that U.S. public schools were more segregated in 2003 than they had been before busing, magnet schools, and redistricting occurred in the early 1970s. As a result, Latino and African American students were becoming more racially segregated while the average White student attended a school that was 80% White. In response, the authors called for a multiracial vision of school integration that more closely fits our society rather than an approach that moves children of color into largely White schools.

The goal of actively promoting and creating multiracial schools may be politically volatile because it requires considerations of race or ethnicity in student school assignment. The legal question is simple. Is the practice of selecting or placing students in a particular school on the basis of race or ethnicity with the purpose of integrating schools within a district constitutionally permissible? The answer is, rarely. Race and ethnicity are suspect classes. Therefore, the U.S. Supreme Court applies *strict scrutiny* to these cases. Strict scrutiny is the most rigorous standard to meet. In order to prevail, the state must demonstrate that the policy is necessary to achieve a *compelling state interest.* Then the state would have the burden of demonstrating that the method used by the district is *narrowly tailored* to achieve the goal of integrated schools. These are very difficult hurdles to overcome.

The U.S. Supreme Court considered the question of using race as part of the selection criteria in two 2003 cases involving higher education. The first case, *Gratz v. Bollinger* (2003), considered a University of Michigan undergraduate freshman admissions practice that awarded "points" to students in an "underrepresented" race or ethnic minority group. The Court found this practice to violate the Equal Protection Clause for a variety of reasons. The second case, *Grutter v. Bollinger* (2003), considered a University of Michigan Law School admissions policy designed to enroll a "critical mass" of underrepresented students. In this practice, the school considered each qualified applicant individually and through this individualized process actively sought to admit some critical mass of underrepresented minorities for the purpose of attaining a diverse student body. The Court found that the law school has a *compelling state interest* in attaining a diverse student body, and the admissions policy's race-conscious program bore the hallmarks of a *narrowly tailored* plan to achieve such an interest. In essence the law school plan was not focused on race alone but considered all selection factors that may contribute to a diverse student body.

The fact that the Court found a diverse student body to be a compelling state interest in *Grutter* may seem to bode well for considerations of race or ethnicity in school district efforts to create and maintain culturally diverse schools. This is not the case. In *Parents Involved in Community Schools v. Seattle School District No. 1* (2007), decided together with *Meredith v. Jefferson County Board of Education*, the U.S. Supreme Court held that the practice of assigning students to public schools solely for the purpose of achieving racially balanced schools is unconstitutional. The Seattle School District allowed students to apply to any high school in the district. Some high schools are naturally more attractive to students than others. When these high schools became oversubscribed (i.e., received more student applications than space allowed), the district used a system of tiebreakers to decide which of the oversubscribed students would be admitted. The second most important tiebreaker in the Seattle plan was a racial factor intended to maintain racial diversity. The Jefferson County School District, on the other hand, assigned students to a particular school based on the racial makeup of each school. Race was defined by the district as Black and "Other." Asian, Hispanic, and White students were classified as "Other."

The Court held that the student assignment plans of Seattle Public Schools and Jefferson County Public Schools did not meet the narrowly tailored and compelling interest requirements for a race-based assignment plan because they were used only to achieve "racial balance." In short, public schools may not use race as the sole determining factor for assigning students to schools. Justice Roberts concluded his majority opinion by stating, "The way to stop discrimination on the basis of race is to stop discriminating on the basis of race."

Summary

The concepts of social justice and equal protection are embedded throughout the ISLLC standards addressed in this text. Social justice means that all students have an equal opportunity for the best basket of goods and services available to all other students in the school. Equal opportunity does not necessarily mean that students may not be treated differently. In fact, students may be treated differently as long as the differences are designed to benefit the least advantaged. John Rawls's concepts of a school or district based on social cooperation and public justification (First Principle) and equal opportunity and justifiable differences (Second Principle) provides ethical guidance in creating a school community where social justice and social capital may flourish.

Equal protection means that the law should apply to everyone regardless of sex, race, color, or ethnicity. These concepts are codified in Title VI of the Civil Rights Act, which prohibits discrimination on the basis of race, color, or national origin. Violations of Title VI seem difficult to demonstrate, especially when school safety is at issue. However, social justice requires that school policy and practice be examined to determine if these policies disparately affect certain groups in the school. If this determination is made, the ISLLC standards create an affirmative duty to respond.

CONNECTING STANDARDS TO PRACTICE

DISCRIMINATION OR BACKGROUND KNOWLEDGE PART II

Assistant Superintendent Sharon Grey's review of district enrollment in pre–advanced placement and advanced placement (AP) courses indicated that a disproportionate underrepresentation of students of color was apparent at Pocono and Jefferson Middle School (see Discrimination or Background Knowledge Part I, Chapter 1). She also knew from her experience as principal of Riverboat High that most AP courses had a disproportionate under-representation of African American and Hispanic students compared to the overall high school pop-ulation would suggest. When she asked the high school counselors why this was happening, she was told the main reason was the students had not completed pre–AP courses in middle school, thus making them ineligible for AP courses in the high school.

Sharon was concerned about the problem and had met on several occasions with the princi-pals of Pocono and Jefferson Middle Schools and the principal of Riverboat High School to address the concerns. The principals were also concerned and explored their options. One promising option seemed to be a program called Advancement via Individual Determination (AVID). AVID had dem-onstrated success in promoting traditionally un-derrepresented populations in AP and dual-credit courses in several states, including Texas and California. However, the AVID program required

that a coordinator be hired and that teachers pro-vide opportunities for tutoring of students in the program. Sharon had asked the three principals to use the discourse ethics model (Chapter 3) and to meet with faculty who would be affected by the AVID programs to build support.

Unfortunately, the majority of the affected faculty argued that the district could not afford an additional teacher in each of the buildings and that it would take too much of their time to tutor these students. They also would feel pressured to lower their standards. Sharon was disappointed in the response. The superintendent was support-ive of the AVID program and felt that the district could not afford not to address the problem. The superintendent asked Sharon to provide a written recommendation.

Question

Argue for or against the addition of the AVID program in two middle schools and the high school in the district. Cite the applicable ISLLC standards; the Dear Colleague letters of October 26, 2010, and May 6, 2011; affected faculty con-cerns; legal remedies to Title VI claims and the justice as fairness concept to support your an-swer. Write a memo to the superintendent out-lining your conclusions.

CHAPTER 9

Children with Disabilities (IDEIA)

INTRODUCTION

The Individuals with Disabilities Education Improvement Act of 2004 (IDEIA, P.L. 108–446, 2004) is premised on the assumption that "disability is a natural part of the human experience and in no way diminishes the right of individuals to participate in or contribute to society" [IDEIA 2004 § 601 (c) (1)]. According to Congressional findings before the enactment of special education law in 1975, more than half of disabled children were not receiving an appropriate education, and more than 1 million children with disabilities were excluded entirely from public schools across the nation [§ 601(B) (C)]. Special education law is a laudable attempt to rectify the inequalities suffered by children with disabilities. Unfortunately, disputes between parents and school districts concerning special education make it one of the most litigated educational law issues school leaders face. However, school leaders are mandated by federal and state law and the ISLLC Standards to understand and equitably apply the legal rights of disabled children and their parents. This chapter is an attempt to communicate a basic understanding of IDEIA 04.

FOCUS QUESTIONS

1. Under what circumstances is it "fair" to treat similar students differently?
2. When may it be justifiable for some students to receive benefits denied to other students?
3. What are the major principles of IDEIA?
4. How is the balance maintained between the need for orderly schools and the rights of children with disabilities?

KEY TERMS

Behavioral intervention plan (BIP)

Child find

Free and appropriate public education (FAPE)

Functional behavioral assessment (FBA)

IEP team

Individualized Education Program (IEP)

Least restrictive environment (LRE)

Manifestation determination

Mediation

Positive behavioral
support (PBS)

Procedural safeguards

Supplemental (related)
services

Zero reject

CASE STUDY
When Good Parents Go Bad

Justin Jones sat quietly in the chair, a smug look on his face. Justin was an eighth-grade student at Montclair Middle School (MMS). As MMS principal, Marina Marshall had assumed the lead role in the Justin Jones case for several reasons. First, it was only October, and Justin had proven himself to be a real challenge. Second, Justin's parents had become more confrontational over the past year. Last, but not least, Justin was an IEP student.

Justin had apparently pushed Mr. Slaton, the industrial arts teacher, to the breaking point again on Friday. Marina's assistant principal, Johnny Sambothe, had suspended Justin for the remainder of Friday. When Marina heard the news, she had immediately called Justin's parents to schedule this meeting.

As Marina looked at Justin and his parents, she tried to recall all that she had learned about Justin over the past 2 years. Justin had started school at a district elementary school and, by all accounts, had done quite well. In fact, there was little question that he was a very bright young man. Before his fourth-grade year, his parents had requested that Justin be reassigned from one fourth-grade teacher to one more familiar to his parents. As was his practice, the elementary principal had refused to move Justin. In response, Justin's parents had removed him from public school and paid tuition for him to attend a local private school. From what Marina could ascertain, things had gone well for Justin until he was allegedly sexually abused by his male fifth-grade teacher. It had taken some time for his parents to determine the cause of his change in behavior, but as soon as Justin disclosed his secret, they had removed him from the private school and placed him back in the public school program.

Unfortunately, Justin's challenging behavior continued. After extensive testing and evaluation, Justin was determined to be emotionally disturbed. An IEP was developed in cooperation with Justin's parents, and he had easily progressed to the middle school. From this point on, Justin had become an even bigger problem, especially with male teachers. Mr. Slaton was no exception. In fact, Justin seemed to take particular pleasure in causing Mr. Slaton to "self-destruct."

Mr. Slaton was an industrial arts teacher who still conformed to the "dirty shop" philosophy. Marina had grown to appreciate the hands-on practical approach that Mr. Slaton brought to the school, and she had insisted that as many students as possible be scheduled into Mr. Slaton's classes. Mr. Slaton had informed Marina that Justin had passed all of his safety exams. But, he "could not trust Justin not to misuse the power tools." Consequently, Mr. Slaton and Justin were continually at odds over one thing or another in the class. Mr. Slaton believed that Justin presented a danger to others in the class and that he should be removed. Justin's parents believed that he should remain in the class and that it was Mr. Slaton who had the problem, not Justin. In fact, his parents made their point very clear when Mrs. Jones, tears streaming down her face, said, "We're tired of Justin being singled out by your teachers. This is not Justin's fault. If that elementary principal had been more receptive, none of this would have happened. We've cooperated with this school district, and what has it gotten us? We want Justin included in regular classes and to lead a normal life. If Mr. Slaton has a problem, that's just too bad. If Justin is removed from the class, you'll hear from our attorney!"

LEADERSHIP PERSPECTIVE

Conflict over children with disabilities is particularly challenging for school leaders. On one side, children with disabilities have well-defined legal rights outlined in the Individuals with Disabilities Education Improvement Act (IDEIA, 2004). At the same time, the 2004 reauthorization of IDEIA emphasizes parental involvement in the decision-making process and the inclusion of children with disabilities in the regular curriculum. School leaders are charged by law and **ISLLC Standard 2A** to protect these rights. Unfortunately, as the case study "When Good Parents Go Bad" illustrates, disputes do occur. According to the United States General Accounting Office (USGAO, 2003), disagreements between school districts and parents generally occur because parents believe the school has not implemented the Individualized Education Program (IEP) as agreed, over the choice of instructional strategies, or over placement. Failure to adequately address these disputes can be costly. In fact, IDEIA 04 specifically abrogates state immunity (Eleventh Amendment) for violating the act [Sec. 604 (a)].

◄ ISLLC Standard 2A

On the other side, school leaders are challenged to promote and protect the welfare and safety of students and staff. These two interests sometimes collide as in the case study "When Good Parents Go Bad." The problem, of course, is that the enforcement of one requirement sometimes seems to violate the other. For example, in the case study, Marina is faced with the rights of Justin Jones to an "appropriate education" in the "least restrictive environment," parental insistence that Justin be included in the regular industrial arts program, and the needs of Mr. Slaton to provide order and safety in the classroom.

◄ ISLLC Standard 3C

It is understood that Marina cannot unilaterally make changes in Justin's *Individualized Education Program (IEP)*. Rather, she must work with Justin's IEP team and, of equal importance, with Justin, Justin's parents, and Mr. Slaton to reach an equitable solution to the conflict. The importance of this leadership role is reflected in **ISLLC Standards 2, 3C, and 4C**. Standard 2 emphasizes a culture of collaboration and trust, the supervision of instruction, and the maximization of time spent on quality instruction. Standard 3C calls for school leaders to promote and protect the welfare and safety of students and staff. Standard 4C calls for the development of positive relationships with families and caregivers. Marina is modeling these standards in her efforts to proactively communicate with Justin's parents, collaborate with Mr. Slaton's efforts to maximize time spent on quality instruction, and promote a safe environment for Justin and Mr. Slaton. Before making these efforts, however, Marina should be familiar with the mandatory requirements of IDEIA, the rights of Justin's parents, and the options available to her. In addition, her decisions should reflect an understanding of the moral and legal consequences of her decision. But what are Justin's rights?

◄ ISLLC Standards 2, 3C and 4C

◄ ISLLC Standard 5D

What ethical concepts should guide Marina's decision making? This chapter attempts to answer these questions.

CHILDREN WITH DISABILITIES AND EQUITY

Equity can be defined as basic fairness. Fairness, of course, is like beauty: always in the eyes of the beholder. When is it "fair" to treat similar students the same? When is it "fair" to treat similar students differently? When is it justifiable that some students receive benefits denied to other students? These questions are difficult. Some parents, teachers, and school leaders seemingly resent the fact that some children with disabilities take disproportionate time and financial resources and receive more supplemental services than other, "regular" children. It must be remembered however, that before the P.L. 94–142 legislation in 1975, millions of children with disabilities were not receiving a quality education. In fact, many of these students were systematically excluded from the public education system. Many more were isolated from the mainstream of school life and were not educated with their peers [IDEIA 04 § 601 (c) (2)]. Consequently, the laudable goal of special education legislation over the past 40 years has been to ensure that all children with disabilities have available to them a *free and appropriate public education (FAPE)* that emphasizes special education services designed to meet their unique needs and prepare them for further education [§ 601 (d) (1) (A)]. Central to the FAPE provision is the concept that, to the "maximum extent possible," children with disabilities should be educated with children who are not disabled, in the *least restrictive environment (LRE)*.

At its core, IDEIA is about equality and fraternity. As illustrated in the previous chapter, these concepts are considered in the second of Rawls's principles of justice:

> ***Principle Two:*** Social and economic inequities are to satisfy two conditions: first, they are to be attached to offices and positions open to all under conditions of fair equality of opportunity; and second, they are to be to the greatest benefit of the least-advantaged members of society (the difference principle). (pp. 42–43)

Rawls's second principle consists of two conditions under which inequalities may exist. The first condition of the second principle considers *fair equality of opportunity*. The second condition of the second principle considers when *inequalities are justified*.

Fundamental to Rawls's first condition is the idea of a school community where all participants have a fair equality of opportunity. Fair equality means not only that opportunities such as access to the regular curriculum should be open in the formal sense, but that *all members should have a fair chance to attain and benefit from these opportunities*. That is, all students, regardless of disability, should have an equal opportunity for a free and appropriate public education available to any other student in the school community. The second condition of the second principle views *inequalities to be justifiable as long as these inequalities are to the greatest benefit of the least advantaged members of the school community (difference principle)*. The difference principle is subordinate both to the first principle of justice (guaranteeing the equal basic liberties) and to the first condition of the second principle (fair equality of opportunity). The difference principle is designed to apply within the background of the school community in which these prior conditions are already satisfied.

The Individuals with Disabilities Education Act (IDEA) was first enacted in 1975 as P.L. 94–142 (Education for All Handicapped Children Act) and amended by Congress in 1978, 1986, 1990, and 1997 (P.L. 105–17) as the Individuals with Disabilities Education Act. Most recently, IDEA has been amended as the Individuals with Disabilities Education Improvement Act of 2004 (P.L. 108–446). IDEIA outlines six major principles to achieve the goals of equality of opportunity and the justification of inequalities for all children with disabilities (Boyle & Weishaar, 2001; Turnbull, Wilcox, Turnbull, Sailor, & Wickham, 2001). These six principles include (1) zero reject/child find, (2) nondiscriminatory evaluation, (3) appropriate education (IEP), (4) least restrictive environment, (5) procedural due process, and (6) parent and student participation. These principles of IDEIA are interwoven throughout the law and serve as a framework for a review of basic legal principles of IDEIA.

IDEIA AND CHILDREN WITH DISABILITIES

IDEIA defines *child with a disability* as a child with mental retardation, hearing impairments (including deafness), speech or language impairments, visual impairments (including blindness), serious emotional disturbances, orthopedic impairments, autism, traumatic brain injury, other health impairments, or specific learning disabilities [§ 602 (A) (i)]. A *specific learning disability* is defined as

> a disorder in 1 or more of the basic psychological processes involved in understanding or in using language, spoken or written, which disorder may manifest itself in the imperfect ability to listen, think, speak, read, write, spell, or do mathematical calculations. [§ 601 (30) (A)]

IDEIA 04 recognizes that the goals of education for children with disabilities can be made more effective by the inclusion of several factors. Some of these factors (selected by the author; for a full review, see Sec. 601 of IDEIA 04) include:

- Having high expectations for the children and ensuring their *access to the general curriculum in the regular classroom to the maximum extent possible*
- Strengthening the role and responsibility of parents and family by *ensuring meaningful opportunities to participate in the education of their child*
- The use of *scientifically based instructional* practices
- Whole-school approaches for scientifically based early reading programs, *positive behavioral interventions and supports,* and early intervention services
- The use of technology including assistive technology devices and assistive technology services to *maximize accessibility to the general curriculum*
- Parents and schools need expanded opportunities *to resolve disagreements in a positive and constructive way*
- The federal government (and presumably state agencies and local school districts) must *recognize the growing needs of an increasingly diverse society* [§ 601(5-10) (A)-(F)] [Italics added]

ZERO REJECT/CHILD FIND

Zero reject is a rule against exclusion of special education students regardless of the nature or degree of their disabilities. *Child find* requires state education agencies (SEAs) and local education agencies (LEAs) to initiate procedures to locate qualified children who are not being served and notify parents of available services [§ 612 (3)]. IDEIA 04 expands the concept of zero reject further to include children who are homeless or are wards of the state. The child find provisions related to children with disabilities placed by their parents in private schools include several new provisions, including "(a) the child find process shall ensure the equitable participation of privately placed children, and (b) the cost of carrying out this task shall not be considered in determining compliance with the child find provisions" [§ 601 (A) (ii) (II) (IV)]. In short, IDEIA 04 places an affirmative duty on the part of SEAs and LEAs to find, identify, and provide services to qualifying children within the state or district regardless of placement or cost.

NONDISCRIMINATORY EVALUATION

A *nondiscriminatory evaluation* is a fair evaluation to determine whether or not a student has a disability, and, if so, the placement and services required to meet the needs of the student. This principle provides for the inclusion of parents in the evaluation process and the rights of parents to require and obtain evaluations by qualified professionals not employed by the school district. This process is often referred to as the "eligibility determination" stage (Boyle & Weishaar, 2001). Specific procedures for eligibility, summarized from § 614 of IDEIA 04, include:

1. *Request for evaluation.* This may be initiated by the parent, SEA, or LEA.
2. *Parental consent.* Before beginning evaluation, the school or district must obtain written consent to proceed from the child's parents. Evaluation must be completed within 60 days of consent unless the parent repeatedly fails to produce the child for the evaluation. It is possible to pursue evaluation consent through mediation or a due-process hearing if the parent refuses to consent to the evaluation.
3. *Parental involvement.* Parents or guardian and a team of "qualified professionals" make the eligibility determination together. Parents must receive a copy of the evaluation report, as well as any documentation used to determine eligibility.
4. *Assessment discrimination.* IDEIA 04 requires the use of a variety of assessment tools validated for the specific purpose. The use of a single assessment as the sole criterion for eligibility is forbidden. Assessment instruments must not be culturally or racially biased. Attempts must be made to assess non–English-speaking students in their native language. Assessments must be reliable and administered by trained professionals and must identify all educational needs, including social and emotional needs. To avoid misidentification, the evaluation team should consider factors other than a disability that may be affecting performance.
5. *Reevaluation.* Each child with a disability must be reevaluated at least once every 3 years unless the child and the LEA agree that a reevaluation is not necessary. The IEP team determines the extent of the reevaluation and determines what additional data are needed. However, informed parental consent and

parental participation in the reevaluation are required. Parents may provide evaluations and information in the reevaluation process. Further evaluations are required if requested by parents or one of the child's teachers.

6. ***Assessment.*** A statement of any modifications in general state or district assessments is needed. If the IEP team determines that the child will not participate, a statement of why the state or district assessment is not appropriate and how the child will be assessed must be included.

APPROPRIATE EDUCATION (INDIVIDUALIZED EDUCATION PROGRAM)

The provisions of an appropriate education are outlined in the Individualized Education Program (IEP). The IEP is a document that (1) outlines the educational and supplemental services, (2) provides a plan for an appropriate education, (3) offers a way for parents to participate (and acknowledge agreement or disagreement), (4) serves as a guide for teachers, and (5) proves compliance for the district. The IEP consist of two parts: a meeting and a document (Boyle & Weishaar, 2001). The ***IEP team*** is the group of individuals responsible for developing and writing the IEP. At a minimum, the IEP committee must be composed of (1) the child's parents; (2) at least one general education teacher; (3) at least one special education teacher; (4) an LEA representative qualified to provide—or supervise—special education services and who is knowledgeable about the general curriculum and the availability of resources; (5) an individual who can interpret the instructional implications of the evaluation results; (6) the child, where appropriate; and (7) other individuals as requested by the district or parents [§ 614 (d) (B)].

IDEIA 04 has added language outlining LEA requirements for children with disabilities, who either transfer into or out of the district, including services comparable to those described in the previously held IEP. When children with disabilities transfer, the LEAs involved must take responsible steps to promptly obtain and promptly respond to requests for the child's records [§ 613 (D)(i)(I,II)(ii)(I,II)]. States may require that schools include in the records of a child with a disability a statement of any current or previous disciplinary action that has been taken against the child and transmit such statements to the same extent that such disciplinary information is included in, and transmitted with, the student records of nondisabled children [§ 613 (5) (i)].

The IEP is the written document generated by the IEP committee. IDEIA 04 requires that the IEP be individualized and specific enough to meet the needs of the child. In general, IEPs are composed of the following components [§ 614 (d) (i) (A)]:

1. Present level of academic achievement, including how the child's disability affects involvement and progress in the general curriculum.
2. Measurable annual goals, including academic and functional goals designed to help the child make progress in the general curriculum and meet the child's other educational needs. Annual goals should emphasize an ever-increasing inclusion and success in the general curriculum. The IEP should include annual measurable goals and benchmarks to allow parents and the IEP team to assess progress or lack of progress toward meeting the goals of the IEP. This section should also include how the goals and objectives will be measured and how parents will be regularly informed of progress toward the goals and objectives.

3. A statement of special educational services based on peer-reviewed research to the extent practicable should be provided to the child.
4. The IEP must explain the extent to which the child will *not* participate in the general curriculum with nondisabled students.
5. Commencement, frequency, location, and duration of services and modifications.
6. Transition planning out of secondary education beginning not later than the first IEP to be in effect when the child is 16, and updated annually thereafter, including:
   (a) Appropriate measurable postsecondary goals.
   (b) Details of transition services, including courses of study needed to assist the child.
   (c) One year prior to age of majority: IEP must include a statement that the LEA has informed the child that parent rights will transfer to him or her when the age of majority is reached.
7. Modifications in administration of state or district assessments.

In addition, IEPs must be accessible to teachers and others responsible for the implementation of services. The IEP should include the strengths of the child, parent input, results of the most recent evaluations, and results of state assessments. If the child's behavior interferes with learning, the IEP should include a **behavioral intervention plan (BIP)** and strategies and supports to address the behavior [§ 614 (B) (i)]. The IEP should also address necessary language needs, visual needs, hearing needs, and assistive technology needs of the child [§ 614 (B) (ii-v)].

Linking to PRACTICE

Campus leadership is particularly important in the IEP meeting and development process. Cindy Bradford (2001) provides the following suggestions for principals:

- Review the student's file before the meeting.
- Do not determine or make placement judgments before the meeting.
- Promises made at the meeting must be fulfilled. Be aware of available resources before making a commitment.

- Think before speaking.
- Avoid acronyms.
- Record meetings and make sure everyone present knows the meeting is recorded.
- Encourage parents to be active participants, but remember that the FAPE belongs to the child, not the parents.

Providing a Free and Appropriate Education (FAPE)

The legal question of what is a FAPE was addressed by the U.S. Supreme Court in *Board of Education of Hendrick Hudson Central School District v. Rowley* (1982). The parents of a deaf student in a regular New York public school claimed that the denial of a qualified sign-language interpreter in all of the student's academic classes violated the FAPE guaranteed by the Education for All Handicapped Children Act (P.L. 94–142). The basic question before the Court was, "What qualifies as a free appropriate education?" The Court held that the intent of the law was not to provide services to maximize each child's potential to achieve a strict equality of opportunity of services. Rather, the intent of Congress was to identify and evaluate handicapped children and to provide them with access to a free public education. The basic floor of opportunity provided by the law consists of access to individualized specialized instruction and related services designed to provide an educational benefit to the handicapped child. Consequently, a FAPE is defined in two ways: (1) Has the LEA complied with the procedures and requirements of the act, and (2) is the IEP reasonably calculated to enable the child to receive educational benefits? An appropriate free public education must meet both prongs of the definition. However, the Court cautioned judges to be careful to avoid imposing their view of preferable educational methods on a school district.

Rowley requires that IEPs pass a two-pronged test: (1) Was the IEP developed in accordance with the procedures mandated by law, and (2) will the IEP enable the child to receive an educational benefit? Although the educational benefit prong may be open for debate, the procedural prong is not. Failure to follow procedures can result in the invalidation of the IEP. For example, in *M. L. et al. v. Federal Way School District* (2003), the Ninth Circuit Court found an IEP to be invalid because the IEP team meeting did not include attendance by a regular classroom teacher as required by law.

Linking to PRACTICE

Do:

- Understand that the definition of a FAPE includes the education of disabled students with regular students to the maximum extent practical.
- Develop a schoolwide plan for inclusion, including professional development for teachers and time for special education and regular teachers to collaborate (Bradford, 2001).

- Make addressing the needs of individual learners part of the formal and informal district teacher evaluation procedures.
- Insist that IEPs be developed "backwards." That is, start with the maximum inclusion, rather than the minimum.
- Always follow the procedural requirements of IEP development and reevaluation as outlined in federal and state law and school board policy.

Related and Supplemental Services

Supplemental (related) services include transportation and other supportive services such as speech–language pathology and audiology services, counseling services, and medical services required for a child with a disability to benefit from special education [§ 601 (26) (A)]. The U.S. Supreme Court considered the definition of medical services in *Irving Independent School District v. Tatro* (1984). Amber Tatro was born with spina bifida and required clean intermittent catheterization (CIC) every 3 to 4 hours. CIC is a simple procedure that can be performed in a few minutes by a layperson with an hour's training. The legal question before the Court most germane to this text is: "Does the Education of the Handicapped Act (P.L. 94–142) require the school district to provide CIC services to Amber?" The Court answered the question in the affirmative. In doing so, the Court created a "bright line test" for the obligation to provide for medical services to children: (1) The procedure must be necessary to enable the handicapped child to remain at school during the day, and (2) services that can be provided only by a physician (except diagnostic or evaluation services) are excluded, but services that can be provided by a school nurse or trained layperson are not.

Related medical services can be expensive, and school districts are naturally concerned about the cost for providing continual care during the school day. The U.S. Supreme Court addressed this concern in *Cedar Rapids v. Garret F.* (1999). When Garret F. was 4 years old, his spinal cord was severed in a motorcycle accident. He was paralyzed from the neck down. In order to attend school, Garret required constant one-on-one monitoring and several related services. All could be provided by a nurse. The district basically argued that the expense of this service was more than required by law. Although recognizing legitimate financial concerns, the Court held:

> It is undisputed that the services at issue must be provided if Garret is to remain in school. Under the statute . . . and the purposes of IDEA, the district must fund such "related services" in order to help guarantee that students like Garret are integrated in the public schools.

Medication

Medication for children with disabilities is also controversial. This is especially true concerning attention deficit hyperactivity disorder (ADHD) and Ritalin, the most commonly prescribed medication for ADHD (Demmitt, Russo, & Hunley, 2003). Ritalin has been demonstrated to increase the ability of some children to pay attention and decrease classroom disruptions surrounding typical ADHD behaviors. The salubrious effects of Ritalin are undeniably beneficial to teachers and administrators. However, some parents may balk at medicating their children. This may be especially true now that the safety of this class of drugs has been questioned. A disconnect between what school personnel want and parental wishes has led to numerous disagreements. According to IDEIA 04, state and local educational agencies *may not require* a child to obtain and presumably take a prescription medication as a condition of attending school, receiving an evaluation, or receiving special education services [§ 612 (25) (A)].

Linking to PRACTICE

Demmitt, Russo, and Hunley (2003) make the following recommendations regarding ADHD children and Ritalin:

Do:

- Even when parents and the IEP team agree, consider Ritalin as only one element in a broader intervention plan for ADHD children.
- Utilize educational or medical practitioners familiar with ADHD in the diagnosis, classification, and IEP development of ADHD children.
- Develop written policies and practices for the distribution of prescription medica-

tion. Ritalin is one of the more abused prescription drugs. Consequently, careful policies protect not only students, but the district as well.

- Provide ongoing professional development and training for teachers who have ADHD children in their classrooms.

Do Not:

- Insist on medication as a prerequisite for the formulation of an IEP.
- Exclude children from school whose parents refuse to medicate their child.

State Tests and Graduation

Public and political criticism of education has served as the catalyst for the federal government and a majority of state governments to implement increased school accountability standards. Along with school accountability legislation, most states have also increased high school graduation requirements for students. Central to the increased accountability is the implementation of standardized state tests designed to measure student knowledge and skills at various grade levels, and in some cases to classify or rate individual districts and schools in the state. At the federal level, the No Child Left Behind Act (2002) is a school accountability law that requires the inclusion of all students in state accountability testing. NCLB does not require passing a state test as part of graduation requirements, but does use the number of students graduating in 4 years (cohort persistence to graduation) as one accountability indicator. Under this legislation, schools and school districts must demonstrate that all students are making "adequate yearly progress" as defined by the state. Inclusion of children with disabilities in statewide assessments and accountability standards is required by IDEIA 04 [§ 612 (15), (16)]. The language of this section brings IDEIA into compliance with the language of NCLB. IDEIA 04 does address alternative assessments of children with disabilities [see § 612 (C) (ii) (I), (II) for full requirements]. Alternative assessments must be aligned with the state's challenging academic content standards and with the requirements of NCLB.

A significant part of the debate over state and federal accountability laws such as NCLB, graduation requirements, and adequate yearly progress is what to do about disabled students. This discussion is particularly germane when states require passing a high-stakes test as part of promotion or graduation requirements. High-stakes tests can be defined as the passing of a state test as a prerequisite to be promoted to a higher grade or graduation from high school. Graduation from high school is viewed as a milestone and significant accomplishment by many people. A high school diploma is also viewed as the minimum requirement for employment in many areas. Consequently, several judicial challenges to high-stakes testing have been brought by parents of children with a disability.

The U.S. Supreme Court has not ruled on a high-stakes test requirement. However, lower courts have been relatively consistent in their support of state efforts to require that students with a disability pass such test as part of graduation requirements under certain conditions. In a landmark decision concerning racial bias and high-stakes testing in Florida, the Fifth Circuit Court held that the high-stakes examination in question may cover matters not taught through the curriculum and that the test's implementation schedule provided insufficient notice. Consequently, the state could not deprive public school students of a diploma on the basis of the test (*Debra P. v. Turlington*, 1981). The injunction issued by the court was lifted once the state demonstrated that adequate notice had been given (*Debra P. v. Turlington*, 1984). In *Brookhart v. Illinois* (1983), the Seventh Circuit Court established that states could require a high-stakes test as a factor in obtaining a diploma as long as a school district could demonstrate (1) that adequate notice had been given to students, (2) that students were sufficiently exposed to most of the curriculum tested, and (3) that parents and teachers had made a reasonable and well-informed decision regarding the best options for the student. In this case however, a 1½-year notice was inadequate, and because it is unrealistic to assume that several of the students would be able to return to school without undue hardship, the school district could not require them to pass the high-stakes test as a prerequisite for a diploma. This line of reasoning was continued by an Indiana court of appeals (*Rene v. Reed,* 2001).

Linking to PRACTICE

Do:

- Make sure that students with a disability have ample notice of state or district requirements and opportunities to learn the material they will be tested on in state or district assessments (Johnson & Thurlow, 2003).
- Initiate multiple discussions of state and local promotion and graduation standards with parents of children with a disability. Lay out all options available, including, but not limited to, diploma options and alternatives to retention in grade if available.

- Continually update parents on their child's progress toward meeting local or state standards.
- Be sure that parents and the child are never surprised about the requirements for or lack of progress toward graduation or promotion.
- Make any diploma options part of the transition plans for students 14 and older. Remember, it is the parent's and child's responsibility to choose among the options. It is the school's responsibility to provide the appropriate educational opportunities and supports to allow the child to successfully fulfill the requirements.

LEAST RESTRICTIVE ENVIRONMENT (LRE)

The LRE is, by definition, inclusion in the general curriculum with students who do not have a disability to the maximum extent appropriate for the student with the disability [§ 612 (5) (A)]. The general curriculum is defined as academic, extracurricular, and other school activities that make up the curriculum offered to nondisabled students. Disabled students may not be denied access unless the nature or severity of the disability is such that education in regular classes cannot be provided with supports and aids. The IEP outlines the supplemental services and aids and justifies the exclusion of the student from various parts of the general curriculum based on the severity and nature of the disability.

Parents must be involved in all placement decisions. IDEIA does not allow for placement decisions after the development of the IEP. Rather, placement decisions must be made as part of the IEP development process, which includes parents. Naturally, it is the definition of *maximum extent appropriate* that holds the greatest potential for disagreement among school officials and parents. IDEIA contains a preference for the inclusion of disabled children in the regular classroom. However, Congress recognized that the regular classroom may not be appropriate for all disabled children under all circumstances. Attempting to maintain this balance has created considerable ambiguity over the definition of LRE. Unfortunately, a consensus definition or test for determining LRE has not emerged from the Circuit Courts.

Private School Placement

IDEIA 04 provides that special education services may be provided to children with disabilities on the premises of private schools, including parochial or religious schools to the extent consistent with the law. Services provided to parentally placed private school children with disabilities, including materials and equipment, are to be secular, neutral, and nonideological [§ 612 (10) (vi) II]. The rights of children with disabilities parentally placed in private schools have been further defined and expanded in IDEIA 04 [§ 611 (10) (A) (i)-(iii)]. For example, IDEIA 04 provides specific language regarding the following:

- The child find process must be designed to ensure the equitable participation of parentally placed children.
- The cost of the identification and participation may not be considered in determining LEA compliance with this requirement.
- LEAs are required to consult with private school representatives and parent representatives of children with disabilities enrolled in the private school in the design and delivery of special education services.
- Private school officials have the right to submit a complaint to the SEA if some disagreement surfaces as to the LEA's compliance with the requirement of IDEIA.

However, school districts may not always be required to provide services at private school locations. For example, the Eighth Circuit Court affirmed a hearing officer's decision that the Special School District of St. Louis was not required to provide special education services at a private school because the Missouri constitution and state IDEA Plan prohibited the providing of services in a sectarian school, and the Special School District had afforded the student "equitable participation" in its special education programs at public expense (*Foley v. Special School District*, 1998).

LEAs are required to pay for private schools if disabled children are placed in or referred to a private school as a means of carrying out the provisions of the IEP or if the LEA cannot or will not provide a FAPE [§ 611 (10) (B) (i)]. However, school districts are not generally liable for private school tuition if the district can demonstrate that a FAPE was made available and the parents unilaterally placed the child in a private school setting [§ 612 (C) (i) (ii)]. A hearing officer may require a district to reimburse parents for private school tuition if the parents can demonstrate that the district did not make a FAPE available to their child in a timely manner (see *School Community of Burlington v. Department of Education*, 1996, and *Florence v. Carter*, 1993). LEAs may not be required to reimburse parents for private placement if:

(a) The LEA followed all parental notification requirements of the intent to evaluate and the parents chose not to make the child available, or

(b) A judge or hearing officer rejects parent claims for reimbursement upon a finding of unreasonableness on the part of the parent [§ 612 (C) (iii) (II, III)].

PROCEDURAL SAFEGUARDS

Procedural due process provides the safeguards necessary to ensure a cooperative process in which children with disabilities benefit from school and in which the school is providing the appropriate services and placements [§ 615 (a)]. A significant part of this process is notice. Once per year, parents must receive written notice of ***procedural safeguards***. A copy of procedural safeguards must also be provided upon initial referral or parental request for evaluation, upon the filing of a complaint, and upon request of the parent [§ 615 (d) (1) (A) (i–iii)]. The notice must contain the legal rights of parents and the obligations of the school district in plain, easy-to-understand language. The notice should be in the parental native language if possible [§ 615 (d) (2)]. IDEIA 04 continues the trend toward giving parents greater access to records and greater rights to participate in decisions and obtain independent evaluations [§ 615 (b) (1)]. This increased parental participation may be a worthy goal. However, it is inevitable that disagreements between school districts and parents over the placement, services, and evaluation of disabled children will occur. The principle of due process is designed so that either party (LEA or parent) may challenge the other's position. The U.S. Supreme Court has held that the burden of proof lies on the party seeking relief (*Schaffer v. Weast,* 2005). Regardless of which party holds the burden of proof, it is clear that IDEIA language assumes inclusion to the greatest extent practical (Howard, 2004).

To further encourage cooperation, IDEIA 04 requires parents (or their attorney) to file a notice of complaint to both the LEA and the SEA that includes the name, address, and attendant school, a description of the nature of the problem, and a proposed resolution of the problem [§ 615 (7) (A) (i) (ii)]. States are required to develop and provide to parents a sample complaint model. The same requirements apply if the LEA is the complaining party. Regardless, the complaining party may not have a due-process hearing until all notification requirements are met.

LEAs must respond to parent complaints within 10 days of receiving the complaint. The response must include (1) an explanation of the reasons for the LEA's proposed action or refusal to take action that caused the complaint, (2) a description of the other options considered by the IEP team, (3) a description of the evaluations used to support the proposed action or refusal to act, and (4) a description of the factors relevant to the agency's proposal or refusal.

Parents must exhaust all administrative remedies before seeking judicial review. In addition, IDEIA 04 has set definitive timelines for mediation and due-process hearings as well as a statute of limitation of 2 years on IDEA claims. District and campus leaders should become aware of these timelines and assiduously follow them.

Mediation

States must provide ***mediation services*** as part of the funding requirements of IDEIA [§ 615 (e)]. Mediation is voluntary, and the state must bear all costs. An impartial third party assists the parents and school district in reaching a mutually acceptable agreement. In an effort to encourage cooperation between the parties, attorney participation is discouraged and attorney fees are not allowable. Mediation may occur as the sole source of dispute resolution or may occur concomitantly with due process. Mediation focuses on communication and creative problem solving, and it does not assign blame. It is designed to produce a mutually acceptable agreement that is in the best interest of the child (Boyle & Weishaar, 2001). However, districts may not use the mediation process to deny or delay any right under IDEIA, including due process.

A trained and impartial mediator presides over all mediation services. *Impartial* means that the mediator is not an employee of the district and does not have a personal or professional interest in the outcome of the process. Mediators should be mutually agreeable to both the district and the parent. Agreements reached must be put into writing and remain confidential. If the mediation process fails, neither party may use information obtained during the mediation process either at a due-process hearing or in a judicial setting.

Hearing Officer

Due process is a formal adversarial process in which an impartial hearing officer listens to evidence presented by both sides. Due process is different from mediation in that there is usually a winner and a loser, and blame is often attached to the losing party (Boyle & Weishaar, 2001). Both sides may be represented by legal counsel. However, the LEA may not have an attorney present unless the parent is accompanied by an attorney. Parties to due process have certain rights:

- The right to have legal counsel or individuals with special knowledge, skills, or expertise applicable to the disability.
- The right to present evidence.
- The right to confront, cross-examine, and compel the attendance of witnesses.
- The right to a written record of the findings and decisions. This record must be made available to the public, consistent with confidentiality provisions.
- Hearing officer decisions are final. However, either party has the right to appeal either to the state educational agency or to the judicial system depending on the circumstances [§ 615 (f)].
- Decisions are public record and are usually available from the website of the state department of education.

Judicial Review and Attorneys' Fees

Either party may appeal a due-process finding to any state court with the power to hear such cases or to any federal district court. The court receives the documentation from the due-process hearing and may accept additional evidence. The court makes a decision on the preponderance of the evidence. Courts have the power to grant "appropriate relief," including changes in placement, additional services, and reimbursement for expenses including parent attorneys' fees, as long as the parents are the prevailing party. Interestingly, an LEA can now recover attorneys' fees from parents when the attorney of a parent files a complaint that is "frivolous, unreasonable, or without foundation" or if the complaint was presented to harass, to cause unnecessary delay, or to needlessly increase the cost of litigation [615 (B) (i) (I-III)]. During the pendency of either mediation or due-process hearings, the child in question remains in the then-current educational placement unless the parent and the LEA agree to a change in placement for the child.

STUDENT DISCIPLINE

IDEIA 04 is an attempt to balance the rights of disabled children with the need for good order and safety in the school. Part of this balance is the use of the relatively new concepts of ***functional behavioral assessment (FBA)*** and ***positive behavioral support (PBS)*** to address students with behavioral issues. Campus and district leadership must pay close attention to these concepts and the procedural safeguards outlined in IDEIA. Knowing how (and when) to implement short-term suspensions or longer-term change in placement is vital to protecting both the student and the district (Bradford, 2001).

In general, IDEIA 04 outlines the following disciplinary provisions [§ 615 (k) (1) (A-D)]:

1. School personnel may consider any unique or special circumstances on a case-by-case basis in making change in placement (defined as alternative educational placement, another setting, or suspension) of children with disabilities;
2. School personnel may remove a child from their current placement to an alternative placement or suspension for up to 10 school days at a time for any violation of school rules to the extent applied to children without disabilities;
3. The relevant disciplinary codes applicable to children without disabilities may be applied to a child with a disability *if it is determined that the behavior is not a manifestation* of the child's disability;
4. Services must continue for children removed from their current placement (suspended, expelled, assigned to an alternative educational placement) for more than 10 school days. This provision is *applied regardless of the outcome* of the manifestation determination proceedings.
5. Children removed from their current placement for more than 10 school days must receive, as appropriate, a functional behavioral assessment and behavioral intervention services and modifications designed to address the behavior violation so that it does not recur.
6. Expands authority to remove a disabled student who brings a gun to school to apply to all dangerous weapons, the knowing possession of illegal drugs and/or the sale/solicitation of the sale of controlled substances, and/or the infliction of serious bodily injury on another person while at school, on school premises, or at a school function regardless of the outcome of the manifestation determination proceedings [§ 615 (k) (1) (G)]; and
7. Added the ability to request a hearing officer to remove a child for up to 45 days if keeping the child in the current placement is substantially likely to result in injury to the child or others [§ 615 (k) (3) (A)].

Advocate concerns regarding the unfair suspension and expulsion of children with disabilities have been addressed in SEA compliance standards. The state educational agency must examine data, including data disaggregated by race and ethnicity, to determine if significant discrepancies are occurring in the rate of long-term suspensions and expulsions of children with disabilities [§ 612 (22) (A) (B)].

Manifestation Determination Reviews

A *manifestation determination* is required when a disciplinary action results in a change in placement [§ 615 (k) (E)]. The manifestation determination is a review and assessment by the IEP team of the relationship between the behavior and the child's disability (Figure 9–1). This relationship is determined by two questions: (1) Is the behavior in question caused by, or does it have a direct and substantial

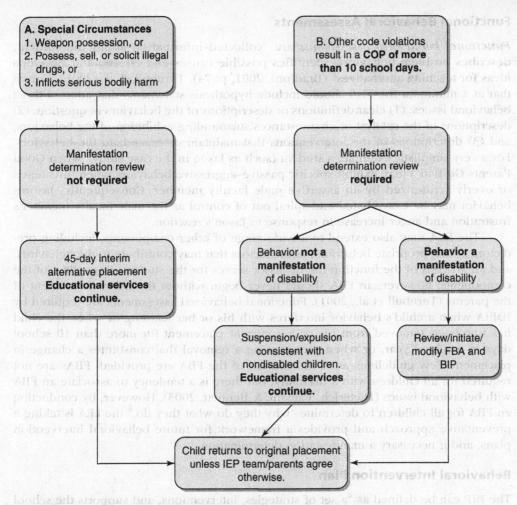

A. Special Circumstances
1. Weapon possession, or
2. Possess, sell, or solicit illegal drugs, or
3. Inflicts serious bodily harm

B. Other code violations result in a **COP of more than 10 school days.**

Manifestation determination review **not required**

Manifestation determination review **required**

45-day interim alternative placement **Educational services continue.**

Behavior **not a manifestation** of disability

Behavior a manifestation of disability

Suspension/expulsion consistent with nondisabled children. **Educational services continue.**

Review/initiate/ modify FBA and BIP

Child returns to original placement unless IEP team/parents agree otherwise.

FIGURE 9–1   Manifestation determination illustrated.

relationship to, the child's disability? and (2) is the conduct in question a direct result of a failure to implement the IEP? If the IEP team and parents determine that the answer to either question 1 or 2 is yes, the *conduct is a manifestation of the child's disability*.

If the behavior is a manifestation of the child's disability, the IEP team:

(a) Conducts a functional behavioral assessment (FBA) and implements a behavioral intervention plan (BIP) for the child;

(b) if a BIP has already been developed, reviews the plan and makes necessary modification to address the behavior; and

(c) returns the child to the placement from which the child was removed, unless the LEA and the parent agree to a change of placement as part of the modifications to the BIP [§ 615 (k) (F) (i) (ii) (iii)].

Functional Behavioral Assessments

Functional behavioral assessments are "collected information about the student, describes problem behaviors, identifies possible causes and effects, and develops ideas for teaching alternatives" (Bradford, 2001, p. 74). Turnbull et al. (2001) suggest that at a minimum the FBA should include hypothesis statements that address three behavioral issues: (1) clear definitions or descriptions of the behaviors in question, (2) descriptions of the catalyst or circumstances surrounding exhibition of the behaviors, and (3) descriptions of the interventions that maintain or exacerbate the behaviors. For a very simplistic example, a student (such as Jason in the case study "When Good Parents Go Bad") may exhibit specific passive–aggressive behaviors when threatened or overly scrutinized by an assertive male faculty member. Consequently, Jason's behavior may be exacerbated and spiral out of control as the male faculty member's frustration and anger increase in response to Jason's reaction.

The FBA may also extend to a wide range of other components, including predictors of inappropriate behaviors, home factors that may contribute to the behaviors, and an analysis of the function the behavior serves for the student. Regardless of the components, however, an FBA should never begin without the informed consent of the parents (Turnbull et al., 2001). Functional behavioral assessments are required by IDEIA when a child's behavior interferes with his or her learning or when the child has first been removed from his or her current placement for more than 10 school days in a school year, or when commencing a removal that constitutes a change in placement. Few guidelines as to the content of the FBA are provided. FBAs are not required for all children with a disability, but there is a tendency to associate an FBA with behavioral issues (Dieterich, Vaillani, & Bennett, 2003). However, by conducting an FBA for all children to determine "why they do what they do," the LEA is taking a preventative approach and provides a framework for future behavioral intervention plans, and if necessary a manifestation determination.

Behavioral Intervention Plan

The BIP can be defined as "a set of strategies, interventions, and supports the school will provide for the student" (Bradford, 2001, p. 74). IDEIA 04 requires a BIP for any student whose behavior impedes their learning or the learning of others [§ 614 (B) (5)]. Turnbull et al. (2001) define "impeding behavior" in the following manner:

> Behaviors that a) interfere with the learning of the student or of others and are externalizing, are internalized, are manifestations of biological or neurological conditions, or are disruptive, b) could cause the student to be disciplined (under state or federal regulations) that could cause any consideration of a change of the student's educational placement, and c) are consistently recurring and therefore require functional behavioral assessment and the . . . application of positive behavioral interventions and supports.

IDEIA 04 does not define the level of impediment that would trigger an FBA, nor does it specially outline how a BIP is to be developed. However, it is clear that the BIP should be based on the FBA and result in *positive behavioral supports* that are tailored to the particular needs of a student with challenging behaviors. In other words, positive behavioral supports should be developed before student behaviors reach the point that disciplinary action is considered (Turnbull et al., 2001). For example, an Iowa administrative law judge (ALJ) overturned the expulsion for drug-related behavior of a 17-year-old learning-disabled/attention-deficit-disordered student. The ALJ concluded that the student's IEP should have been based on a functional behavioral assessment that resulted in a behavioral intervention plan to address the child's drug behaviors that significantly affected his education program and likelihood of disciplinary action (*Lewis Center School District*, 2005). The BIP is particularly important when changes in placement are considered. The IEP team must convene a meeting (11-day IEP) to review and revise the BIP. If the student did not have an FBA or a BIP, the team must complete or review the FBA, then devise appropriate behavioral interventions. It is important to develop appropriate, well-documented, and reasonable BIPs that emphasize positive behavioral interventions rather than punitive approaches.

Hearing Officer Authority

The parent of a child with a disability who disagrees with any decision regarding placement, or the manifestation determination, or an LEA that believes that maintaining the current placement of the child is substantially likely to result in injury to the child or others, may request a hearing [§ 615 (3) (A) (B)]. The hearing officer will hear and make a determination regarding the appeal. The hearing officer may (a) return the child with a disability to the placement from which he or she was removed, or (b) order a change in placement to an appropriate interim alternative educational setting for not more than 45 school days if the hearing officer determines that maintaining the current placement of the child is substantially likely to result in injury to the child or others. During the appeal, *the child remains in the interim alternative educational setting pending the hearing officer decision* unless the parent and LEA agree otherwise. (Note: This is new to IDEIA 04.) However, the LEA must arrange for an expedited hearing. An expedited hearing occurs within 20 school days of the date the hearing is requested. The hearing officer decision must come within 10 school days after the hearing [§ 615 (4) (A)-(B)].

School Safety

Well-publicized acts of school violence and the resultant concerns over school safety have served as the genesis for several laws regarding weapons in school (see, for example, the Gun-Free Schools Act). This concern has extended to students with disabilities. IDEIA 04 allows school districts to move a disabled student to an alternative setting for up to 45 days if the child carries a weapon to school or a school function, or knowingly possesses, uses, sells, or solicits the sale of illegal drugs or other controlled substances. IDEIA has expanded the definition of *weapon* to include a variety of devices that may cause injury or death, but not a pocket knife of less than 2½ inches in length. However, if the student does not have a FBA and BIP in place, IDEIA imposes a duty to complete both procedures either before or not later than 10 days after the student is removed from school (Turnbull et al., 2001). IDEIA also imposes an affirmative duty to conduct a manifestation determination. If the behavior is a manifestation of the child's disability, then the district is generally limited to the 45-day change in placement outlined by the act. However, if the behavior is not a manifestation of the disability, the district may impose further discipline on the student (an extended suspension of longer than 45 days if appropriate under general school board policy, for example). For example, a district court in Maine upheld a hearing officer's determination that the selling of drugs on campus by a learning-disabled student was not a manifestation of his disability. Consequently, the hearing officer was correct in not enforcing the "stay put" provision of IDEIA after the first 45 days of the student's expulsion (*Farrin v. Maine,* 2001). School safety cuts both ways. Not only do school officials have a duty to enforce safe school rules, they also have an affirmative duty to protect disabled students from peer harassment (see, for example, *Shore v. P. S.,* 2004).

Children Not Identified

The disciplinary requirements of IDEIA 04 may also apply to students not yet identified as disabled if school district personnel had knowledge before the behavior precipitated the disciplinary action that the child might have a disability. Factors that may indicate knowledge of a possible disability include:

1. The parent notifies a supervisory or administrative person of the district, or a teacher of the child, that their child is in need of special education services
2. The parent requests an evaluation
3. The child's teacher or other school personnel express specific concerns about a pattern of behavior directly to the director of special education of the LEA or to other supervisory personnel [§ 615 (5) (A) (B)]

Referral to Law Enforcement

IDEIA 04 clearly authorizes school officials to report crimes committed by a child with a disability to appropriate authorities. In addition, copies of the special education and disciplinary records of the child must be shared with the law enforcement agency. The act also states that a juvenile court petition is not a change in placement [§ 615 (9)].

PARENT AND STUDENT PARTICIPATION

To prevent unilateral decision making, parent and student participation in the process from start to finish is part of the safeguards outlined in IDEIA. The concept of parent and child participation is embedded throughout the law. Parents must give informed consent, must be involved in the development of the IEP, and have the right to challenge the decisions of the school district through a variety of means. For example, a consistent failure to inform parents of their rights to a due-process hearing is adequate grounds for holding that an LEA failed to provide an appropriate education and is liable for the tuition cost of a unilateral placement in a private educational program (*Jaynes v. Newport News,* 2001).

SECTION 504 OF THE REHABILITATION ACT OF 1973

Section 504 is a federal civil rights law that prohibits discrimination against individuals with disabilities in programs and activities that receive federal funds, including public K–12 schools and universities (Office for Civil Rights, n.d.). Unlike IDEIA, federal funding is not included in the legislation. Section 504 requires a school district to provide a FAPE to all qualifying students in the district regardless of the nature or severity of the disability. Like IDEIA, 504 defines a FAPE as regular or special education and related aids and services designed to meet the qualifying student's needs. In order to qualify for services, a student must be determined to have a physical or mental impairment that substantially limits one or more major life activities. Temporary physical disability does not qualify for 504 services. Section 504 excludes any student who is currently engaged in illegal drug use. However, Section 504 does allow for disciplinary action for drug or alcohol use to the same extent as nondisabled children in the district.

The Office for Civil Rights (OCR) enforces Section 504. When receiving complaints, OCR provides technical assistance to school districts or parents to ensure compliance with the law and regulations. OCR does not engage in formal mediation services. Rather, OCR offers to facilitate mediation, referred to as "Resolution Between the Parties," to resolve complaints. Both parties must agree to this approach. If all efforts at dispute resolution fail, OCR is empowered to initiate administrative proceedings to terminate federal funding or refer the case to the Department of Justice for judicial proceedings.

Section 504 requires a committee of persons knowledgeable about the student, the meaning of the evaluation data, and placement options to determine eligibility and related aids and services for qualifying individuals. As in IDEIA, the committee must use a variety of evaluative data, and all significant factors related to the student's learning process must be considered. It is unacceptable to use culturally biased evaluations or to depend on stereotypes in decision making.

Districts are required to obtain parental permission for initial evaluations. Section 504 requires periodic reevaluations. Reevaluations are also required before a significant change of placement. OCR considers a suspension or expulsion from the educational program of more than 10 school days a significant change of placement. Transferring a student from one type of program to another (to an alternative school, for example), or significantly reducing services, is also considered a change in placement by OCR.

Summary

Children with disabilities present special challenges to parents, teachers, and school leaders. This challenge, however, in "no way diminishes the right of individuals to participate in or contribute to society." In addition, these challenges should in no way diminish the legal and ethical obligation to make a quality education available for each and every child entrusted to our care. Unfortunately, disputes regarding the definition of an *appropriate education* are common. Special education is the most heavily litigated area of school law. Parents and their children with disabilities have well-defined legal rights and clearly articulated procedural due-process rights. Consequently, the legal rights of children with disabilities should never be ignored out of expediency, personal bias, or ignorance.

CONNECTING STANDARDS TO PRACTICE

THE CASE OF THE RIVERBOAT HIGH SCHOOL CAT BURGLAR

Samantha Stone was a delightful and talented blue-eyed, raven-haired senior who had parlayed her skill as an actress, dancer, and writer into a scholarship to an Ivy League college. By all accounts, by age 8 Samantha had been able to read and comprehend at a 12th-grade level. Her math skills, however, were very poor. Samantha reversed numbers and had great difficulty with even the simplest math problem. By her parents' request, she was tested by the district. Her first IEP called for resource math and inclusion in all other areas.

Samantha's split personality became evident at age 10 when her mother and father divorced. Samantha was Dr. Jekyll: witty, smart, engaging, and irresistible to anyone she met. Her alter ego, dubbed Elvira by her teachers, was Ms. Hyde. Elvira was crude, profane, and flaunted her sexuality to both male and female students and young teachers. During grade school and middle school, her split personality created a continual problem with her teachers, and she was unmercifully teased by her peers. She was often sent to the office and spent countless hours in detention for her behavior. Her middle school principal believed she was faking her illness for attention. However, her troubles brought her mother and father together in a common cause to protect their daughter from the teasing, uncaring teachers and unfair treatment by the principal. Samantha's father exhausted what assets he had on psychiatrists and counselors for Samantha. Eventually she was diagnosed as emotionally disturbed in addition to learning disabled in math. Her IEP now contained a behavioral intervention plan for ignoring and isolating Elvira until Samantha returned. As Samantha progressed through high school, her split personality became much more controllable and Elvira, no longer the center of attention, rarely emerged.

The reports of missing items had started slowly. At first, the items reported missing were pens, calculators, library books, and similar things that assistant principal Tommy Thompson naturally believed were simply lost by inattentive students. However, as the reports escalated, Tommy began to suspect a larger problem. His fears were confirmed when more expensive items including leather jackets, cell phones, jewelry, and MP3 players were reported missing. Parents were calling almost daily to complain about the lack of discipline in the high school. Principal Tara Hills and Tommy spent large amounts of time in the hallways, locker rooms, and parking lots and reviewing surveillance tapes in an attempt to either catch or discourage the perpetrator. All of their efforts were fruitless, and the thievery continued to escalate. In

exasperation, Tommy had dubbed the culprit the Riverboat Cat Burglar. Tara failed to see the humor in his remark, but the sobriquet stuck.

After several weeks of fruitless efforts, Sharon Grey received a call from Tara Hills. "Could you come by Tommy Thompson's office? I think you need to hear this."

When Sharon entered Tommy's office, Samantha was sitting in a chair, crying. "I told her not to do it," sobbed Samantha.

A look of recognition came across Sharon's face. Looking at Tommy she said, "Uh oh."

Almost immediately, Elvira appeared, her blue eyes blazing with anger. In profane and earthy language, Elvira said, "She's lying! Miss Goody Two-Shoes is always trying to get me into trouble! I hate her!"

After several more profanity-laced outbursts heard throughout much of the school, Samantha returned and directed them to her car in the school parking lot. A quick search of the car revealed numerous stolen items. Tara Hills called Samantha's father and suspended her for 10 days pending a manifestation review. After the first 3 days of her suspension, Samantha's father called Sharon Grey at the central office. Samantha's father had been direct. "Ms. Grey, I have contacted Samantha's mother and my attorney. We contend that Samantha's offense was a manifestation of her disability. We also contend that an alternative placement that does not include access to college English, AP American history, and creative writing will not provide her with an appropriate education under the law. We acknowledge your right to change Samantha's placement for 10 days. Any further change of placement will force us to seek a due-process hearing and potential appeal to the federal district court."

Question

Argue for or against an alternative placement for Samantha (and Elvira). Clarify the legal question. Use the ISLLC standards, the manifestation determination review procedures outlined in this text or other sources, the behavior intervention plan in place, the concept of FAPE, and ethical principles to justify your answer. Write a memorandum to the superintendent or school board president supporting your recommendation.

CHAPTER 10

Tort Liability and Risk Management

THOMAS J. GRACA*

INTRODUCTION

This chapter addresses tort liability and risk management in the public school context. Although the particular context of public education creates particular challenges and issues, tort law in the education context is much like tort law in any other context. The concern of tort law is redressing injuries caused by another—either intentionally or merely negligently. The central principles of tort law are not controversial, or really even in any dispute. When a person injures another, the injured person should be compensated. When someone damages the property of another, the owner of the property should be compensated. The only controversies are the measure of compensation, and the types of injuries or damages that should be compensable.

This chapter is different from many of the other chapters in this text in that this chapter has less of an emphasis on seminal cases. In many of the other areas of education law, there are particular influential cases with which a knowledgeable educator should be familiar. For example, *Brown v. Board*, *Tinker v. Des Moines*, or *Lemon v. Kurtzman* are part of the foundation of most school law courses. Of course, there are many significant cases in the law of torts and even in the law of torts as it relates to schools in particular. However, the significance of these cases is that they represent (usually slight) shifts in the law. The focus of this chapter is not on these slight shifts, but instead on introducing tort law in the education context as a foundation for further study. If you desire deeper study after reading this chapter, you should next consult a text that focuses on your state in particular.

FOCUS QUESTIONS

1. Is tort liability in educational settings a blessing or a curse?
2. How can school leaders better manage the risk of tort liability in their schools?

*Thomas J. Graca (J.D., Southern Methodist University; Ed.D., Texas A&M University at Commerce) is Vice President, Planning and Development, Eastfield College, Dallas County Community College District, Mesquite, TX

3. How can school leaders better educate teachers and other education professionals about issues of tort liability and risk management?

4. In what ways do a school's ongoing relationships with parents affect tort liability?

KEY TERMS

Assumption of risk	Duty of care	Risk management
Breach of duty	Foreseeability	Sovereign immunity
Cause-in-fact	Liability waivers	Statutory immunity
Comparative negligence	Negligence	Tort
Contributory negligence	Proximate causation	

CASE STUDY

Girl Fight

Russellville Middle School Principal Paige Littleton was well aware of the ongoing feud between eighth-graders Buffy McGuire and Kathy Harris. Kathy and her group of friends consistently ostracized Buffy, excluded her from conversations, and, as one teacher said, "did their best to make life miserable for Buffy." Buffy's mother had complained numerous times to Principal Littleton about Kathy's bullying and mistreatment of her daughter. Paige had spoken with both girls, referred them to the counselor, and made every effort to keep peace between the girls. However, three days before spring break, Buffy and Kathy began fighting between third and fourth period in a hidden alcove out of sight from teachers in the hallway. At some point in the fight Kathy used a 5-inch pocketknife, and Buffy was seriously injured. Buffy was hospitalized for her injuries and "trauma." Principal Littleton learned later the same day that Buffy's parents had retained legal counsel.

LEADERSHIP PERSPECTIVES

School safety has evolved into one of the most important duties facing campus and district leaders regardless of grade level, school size, or location. This duty is reflected

ISLLC Standard 3C

in **ISLLC Standard 3C**, which calls for school leaders who promote and protect the welfare and safety of students and staff. However, it is simply impossible to protect students and teachers from all potential harm. Why would the fight between two eighth-grade girls at Russellville Middle School be different? Principal Littleton and at least a few teachers were aware of the conflict between Buffy and Kathy and that several "blind spots" existed that made hallway supervision difficult. However, Principal Littleton did not *know* that Buffy and Kathy were going to fight that day, or that Kathy had a small knife. Because Buffy was hospitalized, one can assume a police report was filed. Tomorrow's headline in the Russellville Tattler may read "Student Knifed at Russellville Middle School. Principal says she 'Didn't Know of Danger.'" Yet Principal

Littleton did know of the ongoing feud. She had been informed by Buffy's mother of bullying by Kathy and her friends, and at least one teacher had knowledge of the ongoing ostracism and exclusion of Buffy. So, can Buffy sue the school district? Certainly—anyone can sue at just about any time.

Kathy has likely committed the intentional tort of battery (and possibly a crime). It is conceivable that Buffy and her parents could sue Kathy and her parents. It is also conceivable that Buffy could win a judgment against Kathy. Kathy's parents may have few assets, and winning a lawsuit means nothing if you can get no money from the defendants. So, Buffy most likely will not waste her time suing Kathy. Buffy and her parents, however, definitely want to get some money out of someone to pay for her medical bills, pain, suffering, perhaps lost wages, and likely some other losses as well. Who else is there to sue? The district, of course.

Can Buffy recover from the school or district? Do schools and districts have any liability for injuries suffered by one student at the hands of another? If school districts do have liability for student-on-student violence, the relevant tort would likely be negligence. There is an array of state and federal district court decisions regarding this very question. And the decisions are not consistent. Moreover, student-on-student violence invokes a variety of legal theories of recovery against school systems—many outside of the law of tort. However, we limit our discussion here to the negligence theory.

The concept of tort liability is one way society ensures that local school boards affirmatively meet their responsibility to provide policy designed to promote security within the school community. For example, in the case study "Girl Fight," Principal Littleton met with the two girls, referred them to the school counselor, and was presumably aware of the difficulty in supervising students posed by the school facility. On a larger scale, Principal Littleton and the Russellville Board of Education would need to consider not only the hallways and alcoves of Russellville Middle School, but other areas of the school facilities such as the parking lot, playgrounds, and classrooms when making policy to promote utility of the school community. One way to meet this responsibility is risk management. This chapter attempts to present tort liability and risk management within the utilitarian concepts of security and equity.

> ISLLC Standard 3C

THE LAW OF TORTS

A *tort* is a civil wrong that results in personal injury or property damage, the compensation for which serves sound social policy. The word *tort* is derived from a French word meaning "twisted" or simply "wrong." A tort is "twisted" because one person or institution has upset ("twisted") social equity by causing personal injury to another or damaging the economic interests of another. Tort law in the United States is generally a matter of state common law, though it must be noted that there are exceptions. There are state statutes, federal statutes, and federal common law related to torts. However, most tort law is derived and defined as a matter of state common law. Nonetheless, because nearly every American jurisdiction bases its tort laws on the common law of England, most U.S. jurisdictions apply very similar analyses to similar tort cases. School administrators should take special care in consulting the law of their own state in analyzing a tort or would-be tort case.

As common law, tort law is generally court-made law, rather than legislature-made (statutory) law. Whereas statutory law evolves when legislatures pass bills into law (bills that are usually signed by the chief executive), common law evolves as courts and judges are confronted with (1) new issues legally distinguishable from existing law, (2) changes in culture (e.g., those created by emerging technologies), or (3) evolving social policy considerations. The common law tradition, unique to the United Kingdom and the former British colonies (such as the United States), recognizes that no system of prewritten "rules" can be justly applied to every potential situation. Therefore, as new or unique tort cases come along, judges write opinions that compare and contrast the facts with similar previously decided cases. The judge must then decide which existing law is most appropriate to the case. This decision is added to the common law. Reported judicial decisions are law. As illustrated in Chapter 2, the common law evolves with every reported court case. As each case is decided, it sets a precedent for future cases in future courts in the jurisdiction.

Schools, school systems, individual teachers, and individual administrators could all be either plaintiffs or defendants in tort cases. It is, however, more common for educational institutions and educators to be defendants—the party accused of committing a tort (a would-be "tortfeasor")—in tort cases. Educators and educational institutions are more likely to be defendants for two reasons. First, higher expectations ("standards of care") are applied to educators and educational institutions than are applied to students, parents, and other educational stakeholders. As individual professionals and professional systems, educators and educational systems have more expected of them. Second, educators and educational systems are more likely than the general public to have financial resources. A plaintiff might be happy to win a tort case, but the win is made far less satisfying if the defendant has no assets that a court might seize to satisfy the judgment.

NEGLIGENCE

By far, the most common tort is the tort of *negligence*. In common law, definitions are less significant than in statutory, administrative, or constitutional law. Nonetheless, the definition or description posited by renowned Supreme Court Justice Oliver Wendell Holmes in *Schlemmer v. Buffalo R. & P. R. Co.* (1907) is instructive:

> Negligence consists in conduct which common experience or the special knowledge of the actor shows to be so likely to produce the result complained of, under the circumstances known to the actor, that he is held answerable for that result.

More significant than any definition or description of negligence are the elements of negligence. Although the specific language used to describe the elements and the specific application of the elements varies among American jurisdictions, there is definitely a common pattern. It can be said that generally there are five elements to the tort of negligence: (1) existence of a duty, (2) breach of the duty, (3) cause-in-fact causation, (4) proximate causation, and (5) damages. The elements of negligence are *conjunctive,* meaning that all five must be satisfied to have the tort of negligence. In explaining the five elements, we will refer to the opening case study "Girl Fight."

Duty

The first element of negligence is duty. Humans generally have very few affirmative duties to others. Most of our duties to other human beings are negative duties. The most common are the duties not to engage in behaviors that would cause bodily harm to others or damage to the economic interests (e.g., property) of others. We generally do not have duties to take actions to prevent injuries to others or to prevent damage to others' economic interests. If one is walking down a street and sees that a piano is about to fall out of a window on someone standing beneath, one does not have a legal duty to warn the person standing beneath. Of course, right-thinking people would likely contend that someone who sees the piano has a social or ethical duty to warn, but there would not be negative legal consequences under the common law of tort for failing to do so.

However, there are many examples of "special relationships" that give rise to special (usually affirmative) duties. The relationship between educators or educational institutions and their students is one such special relationship. Educators and educational systems stand *in loco parentis* (from the Latin for "in the place of the parent") in relation to the unemancipated minors in their charge. Teachers and administrators owe a great many legal duties to their students. Among these duties is the duty to maintain a reasonably safe environment in which learning can take place. Whether such a duty exists is a matter of state law, but it is very likely that in many states would find such a duty. Regardless, the affirmative duty to provide and maintain a reasonably safe and efficient learning environment is reflected in **ISLLC Standard 3C**. In the case study "Girl Fight," there is no question that Principal Littleton had an affirmative **duty of care**, because the fight between Buffy and Kathy happened during the school day.

> **ISLLC Standard 3C**

Although educators and educational systems do not have a duty to "shelter a growing child from every possible danger" (*Gathwright v. Lincoln Insurance Co.*, 1985), they do have a duty to take reasonable steps to protect the children in their charge. This duty arises commonly when a child–student suffers an illness or injury, or is in danger of suffering an illness or injury during the school day. Educational professionals have a duty to aid children–students who are injured or in danger of suffering an illness or injury.

Breach

The second element of the tort of negligence is *breach*. The element of **breach of duty** can be satisfied when the would-be tortfeasor fails to live up to her identified duty. The fact of the matter is that when someone or some property is damaged, it is not always someone else's (or even anyone's) fault. In most tort cases, the breach is an action, though it could possibly be an omission.

In order to be held liable for a tort, a defendant must have taken some action or failed to fulfill some obligation related to the complained-of injury. A teacher/administrator very likely has a duty to provide aid to a student who is in danger of being injured. Imagine that a teacher becomes aware of a student in danger, and that the teacher *does*, in fact, provide aid to the best of his ability. Say, for example, that teacher directs a student to call the local emergency number, directs another student to go get the school nurse, and then personally intervenes and comes to the aid of the student.

The teacher has likely not breached a duty. If the teacher has not breached a duty, he may not be held liable for the tort of negligence. Even if the child is injured or, in the worst case, dies, the teacher who fulfilled his duty to aid the student is not liable—assuming he did not breach some other duty—because he did not fail to fulfill duty.

It is only when the teacher fails to fulfill a duty that the breach element is satisfied. The breach occurs when the teacher fails to exercise the care that a "reasonably prudent" teacher in the same situation would exercise. The breach could be either malicious or merely negligent. Examples of malicious breaches might be if the teacher sees Buffy and Kathy fighting, but simply decides that he doesn't want to get involved, or decides that he doesn't really like Buffy (doesn't care if she is injured by Kathy). But most breaches are not malicious; they are merely negligent. Imagine that a student who sees the fight start seeks the aid of a teacher by calling for help and the teacher thinks that the student is "crying wolf," so he fails to aid the student. Would this be a breach? Maybe. What if the teacher thinks the student is just playing around? Would this be a breach? Maybe. What if, rather than coming to the aid of Buffy, the teacher only tells the students to "knock it off," returns to his classroom, and calls for an administrator. Would this be a breach? Maybe.

You probably find those "maybe" answers less than satisfying. Those actions are breaches if it is determined that a "reasonably prudent" teacher would have exercised better care. Who decides what a reasonably prudent teacher would do? Finders-of-fact (usually juries) get to decide—if the case gets to court. The inquiry into whether particular actions or omissions amount to breach is profoundly fact-intensive. It depends on the specific facts of each particular situation. But the standard is usually the same—the reasonably prudent person, the reasonably prudent teacher, the reasonably prudent principal, the reasonably prudent counselor, the reasonably prudent superintendent, and so forth.

Whether the duty was breached—in other words, whether the school violated the requisite standard of care—is a deeply fact-intensive inquiry. Of course, teachers cannot possibly protect students from every possible danger. So, does this would-be "breach" violate the standard of care expected of a reasonably prudent teacher? Given the many peculiarities of this situation, this will likely be a difficult question for a jury to answer. Anyone who has ever worked in a school knows that even if administrators and teachers do everything correctly, fights still happen. So, the fact that there was a fight does not necessarily mean that the standard of care was violated. Whether the duty was breached here will depend on a number of factors. Was the hallway well supervised? Did the administration have any reason to believe that a fight would happen? What did faculty and administrators do when they learned of the fight?

Cause-in-Fact Causation

The third element of the tort of negligence is *cause-in-fact* causation. This is also sometimes called "but-for" causation. In order to be liable for the tort of negligence, the action or omission determined to amount to a breach of a duty must be a cause-in-fact of the injury suffered. In other words, the injured person would not have suffered the injury *but for* the breach. The breach must have been in the chain of events that led directly to the injury. This is a very low standard. The breach must be such that, if it did not happen, the injury complained of would not have happened.

Assuming for the sake of argument that the teacher did breach a duty, the next issue is whether that breach was a cause-in-fact of the complained-of injuries. Our hypothetical fight in the hallway provides some examples. Imagine that a jury determines that our teacher—a male coach—breached a duty to Buffy when he merely told the girls to "knock it off" and did not try to stop the fight. The jury determines that if the coach had intervened, Buffy likely would not have been seriously injured. They have determined that "but for the teacher's breach, Buffy would not have been seriously injured."

But what if the jury decides that Buffy would have been injured even if the teacher breached his duty to make a reasonable effort to separate the girls? Then it cannot be said that "but for the teacher's breach, the student would not have been injured." If the jury decides that Buffy would have been injured either way—regardless of the teacher's breach—then the breach is not a cause-in-fact of her injuries.

Even breaches that are very minor or in the distant past could potentially be causes-in-fact of an injury. The principal limitation is chronology. A breach that occurs *after* the injury is complete can never be a cause-in-fact of the injury. Go back to our teacher who disliked Buffy and gave her no help. Imagine if, when the teacher learned of the incident, Buffy was already seriously injured. The teacher's breach would then not be a cause-in-fact of Buffy's injuries, and the teacher could not be held liable for negligence. (I hope the school or school district would take employment action, but the teacher was not negligent—as a *matter of law*—in her injury.) Although a breach that comes after an injury is complete can *never* be a cause-in-fact of the injury, not all breaches that come before the injury are necessarily causes-in-fact. Remember the logical fallacy *post hoc, ergo propter hoc*. Simply because A precedes B, A is not necessarily a cause of B. Even serious breaches of significant duties that precede an injury are not necessarily causes-in-fact of the injury.

Proximate Causation

It is because the standard for cause-in-fact causation is so low that ***proximate causation*** is an additional element to the tort of negligence. If cause-in-fact causation is "but-for" causation (a relatively simple matter of logic), then proximate causation is "legal" causation (a very complex matter of social mores and public policy). Historically, there has been great diversity among the American jurisdictions about proximate causation. For the most part, this diversity has evaporated over the past half century. Proximate causation has been reduced to a single idea—***foreseeability***.

For most American jurisdictions, the test of proximate causation is little more or less than whether the injury should have been foreseeable to the breacher at the time of the breach. Note that the language of that previous sentence again seeks (to the extent possible) an objective answer—"should have been." It does not ask whether the injury was actually foreseen by the would-be tortfeasor. It asks whether a reasonable person, teacher, or principal would have foreseen the injury. This is another fact-intensive inquiry—the determination of which will be made by the finder-of-fact in a tort case (usually a jury).

So, let us continue to assume *arguendo* that our teacher had a duty to attempt to separate the fighting girls, that the teacher breached the duty, and that the breach was a cause-in-fact of the injuries suffered by Buffy. Would a reasonably prudent teacher have foreseen the injuries? Probably. A reasonably prudent teacher would very likely have foreseen that two students fighting would be likely to sustain injuries without some intervention. Right? Or would a reasonably prudent teacher believe that two young healthy girls would not be able to seriously injure one another? It is probably safe to say that most juries would find the injuries foreseeable—but probably not every jury. This is both the genius of the jury system and a challenge facing those who attempt to predict the outcomes of negligence cases.

One can argue that injuries are easily foreseeable when schools fail to fulfill their duty to maintain a safe environment. One can also argue that holding school districts responsible for the malicious actions of students is not sound social policy. If, for example, Buffy and Kathy had no previous history of violence and school officials were unaware of any problems between the young women, then courts would tend to assume that Kathy's actions were not foreseeable (see *Dadich v. Syosset High School,* 2000, and *Kennedy v. Seaford,* 1998, for example). In this particular case, however, Principal Littleton knew of the animosity between the two girls, teachers had remarked that Kathy made every effort to make life miserable for Buffy, and Buffy's parents had complained to the principal. So, was the fight foreseeable? Probably. But, was it foreseeable that Kathy would seriously injure Buffy with a weapon? Maybe not.

Damages

The fifth and final element of the tort of negligence is damages. *Damages* are the physical or property injuries complained of. Even if the first four elements are met, there is no negligence unless there is a cognizable injury. The goal in calculating damages is to compensate victims for their losses. Damages associated with physical injuries tend to be things such as medical bills, pain and suffering, and lost wages (if the victim is employed). When the physical injuries are especially serious (e.g., in the case of death), damages can increase very rapidly, including things such as loss of future wages, loss of companionship, emotional distress, and even funeral expenses—over and above the damages already described. In exceptional cases, additional "special" damages could be appropriate as well. In the case of property damages, damages tend to be cost of repairing, refurbishing, or replacing the property damaged. Of course, in exceptional cases, additional "special" damages could be appropriate.

This fifth element is both a prerequisite to judgment and the measure that will be used to determine the amount of a judgment. If there are not any cognizable damages, there is no negligence. As we consider our case study, damages are obvious here. Physical injury, suffering, pain, lost wages, and so forth are all reasonable and measurable damages. Buffy has a couple of types of damages. Buffy experienced physical injury. She certainly incurred medical expenses and might also have experienced pain and suffering. Whereas the medical expenses will be easily calculable, a jury will potentially have greater difficulty in calculating the monetary value of Buffy's pain and suffering.

If there are cognizable damages (and the first four elements are met), the calculation of the damages will also serve as the basis for the amount of a judgment that a court will enter. In terms of recovery, the damages are almost always exclusively monetary. Many tort victims desire to recover damages other than money—often orders requiring the tortfeasor to remedy the cause of the injury. These types of

TABLE 10–1	Elements of the Tort of Negligence
Duty	Educators have an affirmative duty to take reasonable steps to protect children in their charge while at school or at school-sponsored events regardless of location. The legal question is: Was there a *duty of care?*
Breach	A failure to exercise the affirmative duty of care that a reasonably prudent teacher, counselor, or principal in the same situation would exercise. Would a similarly placed reasonably prudent teacher (for example) have acted in the same way?
Cause-in-fact	The injury would not have occurred *but for* the breach. Would the student not have been injured but for the failure to act in a "reasonably prudent" manner?
Proximate cause	The injury or danger "should have been" *foreseeable* by a reasonably prudent teacher, counselor, or principal.
Damages	An injury must result from the breach for the tort of negligence to be considered. For example, even if a principal had a duty of care, breached the duty of care, did not act in a "reasonably prudent" manner, and should have foreseen that the situation was fraught with danger, if no injury occurs there is no tort of negligence.

damages are nearly always denied. However, it is worth noting that most negligence cases will not even get this far—or even as far as the courthouse steps. Most negligence cases are settled between the parties, and actual litigation is merely a threat that plaintiffs use to spur settlement. At the settlement stage, using the "extramonetary" damages just described is an excellent strategy for both educational professionals and school systems. This is usually the biggest question mark in a negligence case. How will the jury calculate damages? The minimum amount a jury may determine in any negligence case is $1. Historically, the sky has been the upper limit. Multimillion-dollar judgments in death actions—especially those where the victim is a child—are not uncommon. In the past decade, so-called tort reform (discussed again later in this chapter) has attempted to place statutory upper limits (usually called *caps*) on the amount of negligence damages. The future has yet to write itself in regard to statutory caps.

These five elements of the tort of negligence are summarized in Table 10–1.

Linking to PRACTICE

Do:

- Educate teachers and others responsible for the supervision and safety of students on the five elements of negligence.
- Know state law and school district policy regarding supervision, transportation, and monitoring of students. Educate teachers, coaches, and others on these laws and policies.
- Develop affirmative policies for supervision of students during the school day and at extracurricular events. Educate teachers, coaches, and others on the rationale for these policies.

DEFENSES TO NEGLIGENCE

Even if a plaintiff is successful in proving all of the five negligence elements, the plaintiff will still have to overcome any of the (so-called "affirmative") defenses to the tort of negligence. In the educational context, four defenses arise more often than any others: contributory or comparative negligence, assumption of risk, sovereign immunity, and statutory immunity. In other words, even if a court finds that a defendant has committed negligence, the defendant will not be held to answer for negligence if the defendant successfully establishes the applicability of the defense.

Contributory or Comparative Negligence

The first defense is contributory or comparative negligence. *Contributory negligence* and *comparative negligence* are mutually exclusive defenses—the applicability of either is dependent on the laws of the particular jurisdiction. The rationale and purpose for each is the same—to limit the ability of a plaintiff to collect from a defendant for negligence in situations where the plaintiff himself was also negligent. So, if the plaintiff shares the blame, then the plaintiff's ability to recover will be limited.

The contributory negligence theory is not widely available. Where it is available, the contributory negligence approach requires that if a plaintiff is at all negligent, the plaintiff will take nothing. Contributory negligence is an absolute defense. If the defendant is 99% responsible for the injury and the plaintiff is only 1% responsible, the plaintiff still takes nothing. Any negligence at all on the part of the plaintiff is a bar to her recovery. This defense is not available in most cases in most jurisdictions.

The defense that is more likely to be available in your jurisdiction is the defense of comparative negligence. Comparative negligence seeks to proportion financial responsibility based on the percentage of the damages attributable to each party's negligence. If the plaintiff proves that the defendant had been negligent (duty, breach, cause-in-fact, proximate cause, and damages) and the defendant proves that some conduct on the plaintiff's part had contributed (cause-in-fact and proximate cause) to the damages, a jury would need to determine the percentages of responsibility. Imagine that a jury had determined that the plaintiff sustained $10,000 of damages, that the defendant was 65% responsible, and that the plaintiff was 35% responsible. In such a case, the judgment a court would likely enter in the plaintiff's favor would be only $6,500—even though the damages were $10,000. The percentage of the damages attributable to the plaintiff's conduct is subtracted from the total damages the plaintiff incurred. The exact application of the principle of comparative negligence varies greatly from state to state.

It is not uncommon for a state to use a comparative negligence theory with a contributory negligence wrinkle. They add the wrinkle as the plaintiff's responsibility reaches 50%. In many jurisdictions, when the plaintiff is either "at least 50%" responsible or "more than 50%" responsible, the contributory negligence wrinkle kicks in, and the plaintiff is completely barred from any recovery. If we reexamine our $10,000 damage finding with this wrinkle, we can see the following. If the defendant is 65% responsible and the plaintiff is 35% responsible, then the plaintiff recovers $6,500. But if the defendant is 35% responsible and the plaintiff is 65% responsible, then the plaintiff recovers $0. If the defendant is 51% responsible, the plaintiff takes $5,100; but if the defendant is only 49% responsible (a difference of only 2%), the plaintiff takes nothing.

In education contexts, recall that schools and education professionals are more likely defendants than plaintiffs. And students and parents are more likely plaintiffs. When defendant schools and defendant educators seek to utilize the contributory or comparative negligence against a plaintiff student, another issue arises. It is more difficult to prove that a child has been negligent than an adult. The proximate causation element (defined primarily as foreseeability) is more difficult to prove against a child. Children are held to a lower standard of care than their adult counterparts. In fact, most jurisdictions prohibit children under the age of 7 (the "age of accountability") from ever being found negligent. Teachers and administrators in early childhood education, therefore, will almost never be able to assert contributory or comparative negligence against a child–plaintiff. Children between the ages of 7 and 14 are presumed to be incapable of negligence. However, the courts recognize that particular 7- to 14-year-old children are capable of negligent behavior. That is, particular 7- to 14-year-old children do have the cognitive and psychological intelligence to foresee the legal consequences of particular actions. Therefore, it is possible for a plaintiff to overcome the presumption of incapacity with a defense of contributory or comparative negligence against a 7- to 14-year-old child's negligence case. Adults and children over the age of 14 are presumed capable of negligence. Therefore, most high school teachers and administrators will have the defense of contributory or comparative negligence available to them when a student alleges negligence.

Assumption of Risk

The second common defense to negligence is the defense of *assumption of risk*. Even if a defendant is liable for the damages associated with negligent behavior, the defendant may assert that the plaintiff assumed the risk of the defendant's negligence. The defendant will either assert that the plaintiff expressly assumed the risk or that the plaintiff made a conscious choice to assume the risk. Much as in contributory negligence, the context of the schoolhouse creates particular challenges for defendant schools and defendant educators who wish to assert the defense of assumption of risk.

Schools and educators frequently seek to obtain express assumptions of risk from both students and their parents prior to potentially dangerous activities—for example, athletic competitions, travel by motor vehicle, activities off the premises of the school, and other situations that could potentially pose a risk beyond what would commonly be expected in an educational setting. They seek the express assumption of risk through documents called variously *liability waivers*, *hold harmless*, *consent*, *indemnity*, and other labels. (Each of these labels has a distinct legal effect varying somewhat by jurisdiction—indemnification is a profoundly distinct concept from waiver of liability—but the effect that schools and educators desire with each is the same.) So, do these documents have any legal effect? It depends. No doubt more than one educator has been told that his liability waiver isn't worth the paper it's printed on. That's probably not true. But it's also not true that simply because one signs a waiver he cannot recover.

It's probably more likely to be true that a liability waiver signed only by a minor child truly is worthless. A liability waiver is roughly analogous to a contract. In the United States, minors are not liable in the law of contract. Depending on your state, the age of majority is either 17 or 18. A minor cannot enter into a binding contract.

Because these liability waivers are either contracts or very closely analogous to contracts, a minor cannot be a party to one.

However, a minor's parents certainly can be. So, if the child's parents agree to the waiver, does it have effect? Presumably, yes. However, if the agreement is contrary to public policy, it will have no effect. Because contract (like tort) is primarily a matter of state law, the policy desires of various branches of the state governments—including the courts themselves—come into play. The primary policy consideration is how much responsibility schools and educators should have for protecting the children in their charge. To what extent should schools be responsible for protecting children from themselves and their parents? If a parent signs a particular liability waiver that is not in his child's best interests, should schools and educators still not be responsible for their actions—because of the special relationship among schools, educators, and children? It is a deeply complex question of social values and competing political theories. School counsels, for the most part, continue to encourage the use of these waivers—and it probably is good advice, regardless of the legal effect the waivers will actually have.

In the case of an implied assumption of risk, the analysis is almost exactly the same. Defendant schools and educators will likely have a very difficult time attempting to assert as a defense that a child herself assumed the risk. Because of children's minority, they simply cannot assume a risk. It is more likely that their parents can implicitly assume a risk on a child's behalf. However, in the grand scheme of things, it is still not very likely—because of both the policy considerations discussed earlier and the difficulty in obtaining evidence of a parent's implied consent.

Sovereign Immunity

For most of human history, each government has had but one sovereign—a monarch under any of dozens of potential titles. The ones most common to western Europe and the United Kingdom (our legal forbear), of course, were queen and king. In the United States, our sovereign is not a queen or king—or any one person for that matter. We—"the people," as they say—are sovereign. The president of the United States is not our sovereign. The people of the United States collectively are sovereign. Such is the defining characteristic of any form of republicanism or democracy.

Sovereigns are immune to lawsuits in their own courts. There are a number of potential ways of justifying *sovereign immunity*. The first is simply a matter of practicality: Why would someone with the power of creating law allow you to sue her in her own courts—why would a queen create a system of law that allowed herself to be sued? It is simply a matter of political power. In the United States, we do not have a queen. The United States itself—as established by the people—is the sovereign. The United States has the power of law. Why would it create laws in such a way that we could be sued? Another potential explanation is the utilization of resources and economic policy. If the United States could be sued for any of its negligence, the potential exists for an untoward number of negligence actions (founded or not) to be pending against the United States in the federal courts. This would create an unreasonable burden on the government to fund courts, U.S. attorneys, and the like. A third potential explanation is monetary policy. If the United States prints its own money (which it does), then the judgments against it could unreasonably affect the amount of U.S. dollars in existence, which could have a definite effect on currency valuation. The doctrine has a long history in the United States—going back at least as far as Alexander Hamilton's *The Federalist 81:* "It is inherent in the nature of sovereignty not to be amenable to the suit of an individual without its consent." There are many other potential explanations and justifications for the immunity of the sovereign (see, for example, Giuttari, 1970).

Our federal system has complicated matters even further. Not only is our nation sovereign, each of the states is also sovereign. That is, the people of each state are collectively sovereign of their state. The United States is a "big sovereign" made up of many "little sovereigns." In a similar way, each state—as a sovereign—is immune. The governor of Idaho is not sovereign, but Idaho is.

Sovereign immunity is a relevant defense for schools: Most schools are in some way a part of state government, and each state is sovereign. The exact system of organization that a particular state has chosen will determine the exact applicability of the doctrine. However, the doctrine has applicability in all 50 states (though to a profoundly lesser extent in California, Illinois, and Pennsylvania). It protects school systems (districts, boards of education, county school boards, and the like) and individual schools from tort liability. It does not protect individuals (teachers, principals, and superintendents are not sovereigns). Even if a school is negligent, it can generally be said that the school is not responsible for compensating the victims of its negligence. However, the doctrine is not absolute.

The principal limitations on the defense of sovereign immunity are state tort claims acts and public policy considerations. Tort claims acts are statutes enacted in all 50 states that allow the state to be sued. (There is also a Federal Tort Claims Act.) Essentially the tort claims acts define certain situations in which the state consents to being sued in its own courts. These situations generally involve situations where the state is acting like a private citizen or private business—rather than acting like a sovereign.

The most obvious situation in which a school or district is acting like any other business is in reference to its land and buildings. Owning land is not the kind of activity that is reserved nearly exclusively to government. Private citizens own land, and companies own land. Owning land creates duties on the part of land owners to those individuals who are visitors on that land. So, schools and school districts will be less likely to be protected by the doctrine of sovereign immunity in "premises liability" actions. For example, land owners have a duty to properly maintain their premises, a duty to warn visitors of potentially dangerous situations, and the like. Because public school children spend the vast majority of the school day on land and in buildings owned by the school district, this is a significant exception to the doctrine of sovereign immunity.

Public policy considerations are the other significant exception. Even though the doctrine of sovereign immunity might technically apply as a legitimate defense to a district's or school's negligence, there could be a countervailing interest that trumps the immunity. Such policy considerations are particularly likely to come into play in the school setting. Because children are among the most vulnerable of our citizens, the state's policy of desiring safe environments in which children can learn might prevail over the state's desire to remain immune from lawsuits. This part of the law—where significant, independent policies come into conflict with one another—is one of the places where judges have the most power in our system. There are few bright lines in policy. This is definitely one of the gray areas where educational, social, and political value systems will come into conflict.

Statutory Immunity

You will recall from earlier in this text that statutes are one of the principal sources of American law. Statutes are those points of law created by elected legislatures and approved by elected executives. Many states have enacted statutes that grant (various levels of) immunity from tort lawsuits to educators. There is not any consistent historical or legal ideology based on which these states have granted this immunity to teachers. The grant of *statutory immunity* is simply a policy decision made by the legislatures of many states. For example, in some states educators are shielded from liability when acting within the scope of their duties, exercising judgment or discretion, not using excessive force to discipline a student, or operating a motor vehicle.

Why would these states grant immunity to educators? The explanations are diverse. Some include the desire to attract and maintain highly qualified teachers, to give teachers greater authority over their classrooms, to minimize the costs of litigation, to reform the tort system one step at a time, and to simply insulate teachers from the consequences of their own negligence. All of these explanations (as well as most others not listed) are policy decisions. The immunity need not exist at all, and where it does exist, it could be taken away. The grant of immunity is a conscious choice that a state may take or not take. The immunity could be absolute, or it could cover only certain actions. It could be very narrow, very broad, or anywhere in between. It could be total immunity, immunity beyond a certain dollar amount, or immunity only up to a certain dollar amount.

THE PAUL D. COVERDELL TEACHER PROTECTION ACT OF 2001   The Paul D. Coverdell Teacher Protection Act of 2001 (named after the late Democratic senator from Georgia who had introduced the act in a prior Congress) was included in the "No Child Left Behind" education bill. The Teacher Protection Act states that if teachers and principals follow school rules and act within the scope of employment responsibilities, they will not be subject to liability. The act does not protect teachers or principals when operating a motor vehicle or when engaged in criminal misconduct, gross negligence, reckless misconduct, or a flagrant indifference to the safety of the individual harmed. It also states that tough standards should be applied before punitive damages are allowed, and that teachers and principals should be liable only for their "fair share" of fault for harm and not for injuries caused by others.

TORT REFORM   Tort reform is similar in some ways to statutory immunity in the sense that it is intended to reduce the amount of tort litigation. Tort reform involves legislation that restricts remedies to negligence or that caps damages awards, especially punitive damages, typically to $100,000. Advocates of tort reform argue that it lowers liability insurance premiums and prevents plaintiffs from receiving windfall judgments. Opponents contend that tort reform denies plaintiffs the recovery they deserve for their injuries (Garner, 2006).

TABLE 10–2	A Summary of Defenses to the Tort of Negligence
Contributory–comparative negligence	The plaintiff (student, parent, etc.) contributed to or shares in the blame for the injury. Sometimes not applicable if the child is 7–14 years old.
Assumption of risk	The student made a conscious choice to assume the risk inherent in the activity. Particularly appropriate for competitive athletic participation.
Sovereign immunity	A state is sovereign and immune from suit. As an agent of the state, sovereign immunity may protect the school district, but not individuals (teachers, counselors, principals, etc.). Generally does not protect school districts from failure to remediate faulty equipment, inherently dangerous situations (ice on the sidewalk, for example), or failure (for example) to properly maintain a gymnasium ceiling and roof.
Statutory immunity	Some state laws grant immunity to individuals (teachers, counselors, principals) from suit. Varies widely by state. The federal Paul Coverdell Act also provides for statutory immunity.

Even with absolute immunity, a teacher, principal, or superintendent can be sued. The immunity is simply a defense that the educator will assert. Moreover, asserting the defense does not necessarily mean the defense will be successful. The immunity can be challenged on any number of policy or other grounds. Having immunity does not mean that educators should cease exercising an appropriate duty of care. The immunity simply creates another hurdle over which a student–plaintiff must jump in order to be successful in a negligence action. The immunity is an attempt to lessen the likelihood of a teacher being sued, and if he is sued, to make it more difficult for him to be found liable.

The four affirmative defenses to the tort of negligence are summarized in Table 10–2.

INTENTIONAL TORTS

Intentional torts are another class of torts. There are principally four intentional torts that could be confronted in the educational context: (1) battery, (2) assault, (3) false imprisonment, and (4) intentional infliction of emotional distress. What distinguishes the intentional torts from the tort of negligence is the requirement of a particular state of mind on the part of the tortfeasor—intentionality. It is not possible to accidentally assault someone, or unintentionally commit a battery.

Battery

A *battery* is "an intentional act that causes harmful or offensive bodily contact" (e.g., *Etheredge v. District of Columbia*, 1993). The first part of a battery is the commission of an intentional act. The batterer must commit the act intentionally—however, the batterer need not intend the outcome, or even intend the particular victim. Intent can be transferred from an intended victim to the actual victim. The second part of the intentional tort of battery is harmful or offensive bodily contact. The batterer must either actually touch the victim's person (punch, hit, shove) or cause someone or something else to touch the victim's person (pushing someone else or tossing an object). One's person is usually extended beyond one's physical body to include clothing, things one is carrying, etc.

The batterer need not have intended the harm or offense; she need only have intended the touch. It is relatively easy to determine if a contact is harmful. Physical injury is usually what is required. Offensive contact might be a little bit more difficult to predict or recognize. Juries have found many seemingly innocuous touches to have been offensive. When the touches are directed at children, juries tend to be even more likely to find the touch to have been offensive. Again, a "reasonable person" standard is applied. Would a reasonable person have taken offense at the touch? Educators should be careful whenever touching another person in the school context—especially touching children. Of course, there are plenty of other potentials for battery in the schoolhouse. Whenever any object gets thrown—even if not "at" anyone—the potential for a battery exists if someone finds his way into the path of the thrown object. So long as the act was intentional, the intent follows the act.

Assault

The most common law definition of assault is:

> An actor is subject to liability to another for assault if (a) he acts intending to cause a harmful or offensive contact with the person of the other or a third person, or an imminent apprehension of such contact, and (b) the other is thereby put in such imminent apprehension. (*Restatement Second of Torts,* 1974, § 21)

In other words, assault is like an attempted battery or a threat of a battery. As a sort of attempted battery, an assault would be when one tries to make harmful or offensive bodily contact, fails to do so, but does create an imminent apprehension of harmful or offensive contact. As a threat of a battery, an assault would occur whenever one threatens to make harmful or offensive bodily contact and puts the victim in imminent apprehension of the contact.

How do we know whether the victim was in "imminent apprehension" of harmful or offensive bodily contact? Well, we have to ask whether a reasonable person in the same situation would have been in imminent apprehension. And a jury will decide. Does the issue of assault occur often in educational settings? It depends on whom you ask. Some say that at any large school there are numerous assaults every day—among students, between teachers and students, and even among assistant principals and students and teachers. Whether this assertion is true or not, it is rather rare that one of these would-be assault victims brings the matter to the courthouse. It would be much more likely that the school's internal disciplinary procedures (discussed elsewhere in this text) would remedy the situation to the victim's satisfaction. Nonetheless, educational leaders should be aware of the potential for liability under the assault theory.

False Imprisonment

The third of the intentional torts relevant to the educational setting is false imprisonment. Admittedly, the intentional tort of false imprisonment is only a very rare issue in public school law. Because the issue does arise on occasion, it is worthy of a brief introduction. False imprisonment is a situation where one person intentionally confines another in a fixed space for an unreasonable period of time without legal justification. Do schools and educators imprison students? Yes—all the time. However, not every confinement is "false." Schools and educators are legally justified—in fact, often obliged—to confine students. We confine students to particular plots of land, buildings, and even particular rooms within buildings. During the school day, this confinement is justified. It is one of the jobs of school systems to keep students in the place they are supposed to be—so that children can learn. We even use confinement as a disciplinary tool—with "timeout" areas (and in the recent past with "timeout boxes"). This is not false imprisonment.

The most likely situation in which a school district or educator might be accused of false imprisonment is outside of the school day. In early childhood and elementary school settings, this might be in a situation where an unauthorized person has come to pick up a child after the school day, and the school refuses to release the child. In middle and high schools, it would more likely occur in situations where educators confine student movements at football games, dances, and the like. In general, so long as the educator is acting in an "educator" role—that is, *in loco parentis*—the educator is legally justified in confining the child in reasonable spaces for reasonable periods of time. Would it be reasonable for an early childhood teacher to confine a 5-year-old child in the school building until it could be determined if "Uncle Walt" is really authorized to take the child home? Of course. It would be derelict for the teacher to do anything else. Would it be reasonable for a middle school principal to keep her students locked up in an inner room of the school building—maybe even against their parents' wishes—after school hours but during a severe tornado warning? Probably. Would it be reasonable for a high school assistant principal to contain a group of students in the grandstand at a football game as a fight is breaking out in the parking lot? Sure. In all three situations, the educator is acting in the interests of safety and security. The educator is acting just as a reasonable parent would in the same situation.

Schools and educators would have to act in an extremely unreasonable way in order to be liable for the intentional tort of false imprisonment. So long as educators and schools are acting reasonably and in the best interests of the children, it is very unlikely that their confinements would be found to be anything other than legally justified.

Intentional Infliction of Emotional Distress

In tort law generally, emotional or psychological injury is not compensable unless it accompanies physical injury. Intentional infliction of emotional distress is an exception to this general rule. The tort is reserved for situations in which a defendant has behaved so maliciously that the "extreme outrageousness" of the conduct leads us to believe that the defendant intended nothing other than intentionally interfering with the plaintiff's peace of mind. The bar to proving intentional infliction of emotional distress is very high. This intentional tort is reserved only for the most extreme situations.

Linking to PRACTICE

Do:

- Caution teachers about pushing, shoving, or throwing objects at students. This seems like common sense, but in the sometimes emotionally charged school day, a recalcitrant child can provoke even the most patient of adults.
- Be very careful in administering corporal or physical punishment (see Chapter 5). Never administer physical punishment that is specifically forbidden by state law or school board policy.

- Think carefully about the situation, the age and sex of the student(s), and the rationale before holding students against their will.

Do Not:

- Hesitate to investigate questionable behavior (see Chapter 11).
- Ignore or tolerate verbally abusive teachers, coaches, or others associated with the school. This also seems like common sense, but unfortunately such behavior is sometimes tolerated.

MANAGING THE RISK OF TORT LIABILITY

The financial risks associated with tort liability are significant. Central to the roles of school leaders is the task of managing these risks. This does not mean that school leaders are (or should be) expected to eliminate all potentially risky situations from the schoolhouse. Eliminating all tort risk would be impossible, and even if it were possible, it would likely not be desirable. Education is a risky business. Think about it—we put upwards of 2,500 adolescents in some high school buildings. This fact alone—even if there is expert supervision in the safest buildings on the planet with the best-intentioned of children—is a dangerous situation. Although the sheer numbers may not be as large in middle and elementary schools, the danger is no less great. This dangerous situation is made worse by increasing child–adult ratios, deferred maintenance on buildings, and children whose intentions are sometimes less than pure. Moreover, the educational outcomes that we desire require that we infuse even more danger. We put scissors into the hands of children and corrosive chemicals into the hands of adolescents—all in between transporting them on increasingly busy and dangerous roads in aging school buses.

The task of *risk management* in such a situation is daunting. And the stakes are no less great. Nonetheless, school leaders are charged with managing these risks. These risks are managed through (1) insurance policies, (2) social control polices, and (3) facility inspection and maintenance.

Insurance

Insurance is a very highly regulated industry in all U.S. jurisdictions. The regulation of the expenditure of public funds on insurance is likely even more highly regulated in your state. In most school districts, insurance—if it is a part of the district's risk management plan at all—is purchased at the district level. It is most unlikely—probably unheard-of—that individual campuses within a system would purchase their own insurance policies.

One area where school districts are most likely to purchase insurance is for transportation. Motor vehicle insurance is likely a necessity for most school districts.

In terms of managing tort risks, so-called liability insurance is almost always advisable and is usually required by state statutes. It is not uncommon for districts to also purchase policies that protect the district's investment in its own vehicles (*collision* or *comprehensive*).

In addition to insurance that school districts might purchase, it is becoming increasingly common for individual educators to purchase various types of liability policies. In addition to liability policies that might be available directly from insurance companies or through professional insurance brokers or agents, teacher unions, professional associations, and even school systems and districts could (and do) offer liability protection to teachers, administrators, and even school board members. These individual policies often will provide for both the amount of a settlement or judgment against the individual and the costs of legal representation. If one is considering purchasing an individual liability policy, she should be advised to read the policy carefully to ascertain exactly the protections that she is purchasing.

Social Control and Strategic Supervision

Social control policies are the rules, regulations, and practices that have been designed to control the movement, behaviors, and actions of students. These policies are usually compiled into a code of student conduct. A code of student conduct usually contains a list of rules for student behavior and the punishments or sanctions for failure to follow these rules. In 2007, over 95% of public schools reported that codes of student conduct were in place (Robers, Zhang, & Truman, 2010). Social control policies can also include so-called target-hardening practices such as metal detectors, security guards, security cameras, and locked doors.

Strategic supervision plans are designed to provide consistent and effective supervision of students, especially in areas of the school where the potential for injury is increased. Examples may include hidden alcoves as in our case study, playgrounds, dressing rooms, and laboratories. Territoriality considers control over the surrounding area by the use of physical attributes that delineate space and express ownership. School administrators cannot be expected to provide security in surrounding neighborhoods, but it is important to establish control in a rational way that seems to make sense to most people. Social control policies, strategic supervision, and territoriality are absolutely necessary not only for effective teaching and learning, but also to decrease the risk of the tort of negligence.

Facility Inspection and Management

Campus leaders are responsible for inspecting and maintaining their campus buildings. Even if these tasks have been delegated to a professional maintenance person or engineer, the responsibility is still the principal's. Although it would not be appropriate for most principals to check the gauges on the boiler every hour or tighten every gas valve in the chemistry lab, principals should be personally involved in inspection and maintenance. The role of the principal in facility maintenance and inspection is an executive role. In addition to the regular management of staff who coordinate the daily inspection and maintenance, the principal should plan and supervise major infrastructure updates, should walk through the facilities daily, and should personally coordinate the master facility plan.

The past two decades have seen a great deal of deferred maintenance in public buildings. School buildings are no exception. Thus, the next few years will likely see an increasing number of large facility enhancement projects—both as a result of the deferred maintenance and as a result of the increasing role of technology. When these major facility projects are undertaken, it must be the job of the school principal to coordinate them. Invariably—even if undertaken during the summer—these projects temporarily displace people and services. Likewise, the projects likely create seriously dangerous conditions during construction. Unfortunately, the "do not enter" and "danger" signs that are usually more than sufficient in office buildings usually do not deter children and adolescents in the least. Generally, temporary barriers need to be constructed to keep curious students out. Even if the construction foreperson says that the signs are enough, you know the work being done and you know your students— the call is yours.

Summary

Tort law is not a fun topic. Nobody likes talking about getting sued. However, the lack of joy in the topic makes it no less important. A single serious avoidable injury on a campus has the potential of ending a principal's career. So, although it is certainly true that no one wants to see a child or adolescent injured, you also want to keep your job. If you have not yet been motivated to take tort liability and risk management seriously, knowing that your job is on the line should do the trick. Managing the risk of negligence is hard,

intellectually taxing work. Your efforts will likely not be valued too terribly highly by the teachers in your building. Here's what they'll say after you leave the room: "Oh, she's just afraid of getting sued; if she wasn't such a scaredy-cat, maybe we'd be able to get something done here instead of wasting all this time on goofy safety garbage." It's not a compliment. But it is your job. A principal who can create a "culture of safety" on her campus will go a long way toward becoming a successful long-term principal.

CONNECTING STANDARDS TO PRACTICE

INTO THE DANGER ZONE

Sharon Grey had arranged a meeting with Riverboat High School athletic director Blanche Barnhart, Principal Tara Hills, and school district attorney Roger Garcia. All the participants knew that the purpose of the meeting was to consider the injury to Lucy Overstreet. Coach Barnhart started the meeting with a brief background summary. Riverboat High School has a deep swimming pool used for interscholastic diving competition. The high school also has a racing pool used by the swim team for competitive racing. The racing pool is three and a half feet deep at each end. On the deck in front of each of the six swimming lanes in this pool is a starting block standing 18 inches

above the water level. In competitive meets, participants in the various races typically stand on the starting block and, when the starter horn sounds, dive into the water. In some specific races, however, participants start the race already in the water.

With this background, Principal Tara Hills added her knowledge regarding Lucy Overstreet. Lucy had demonstrated excellent swimming skills and as a 14-year-old freshman had tried out for the swim team. Unlike many of the freshman trying out for the team, Lucy had never swum competitively and was at a disadvantage from the moment she stepped into the pool area. But her natural ability presented a great upside, and she was placed on the JV team by head coach Ron McKay. Soon after being selected for the team, Lucy and her parents informed Coach McKay that she had little if any experience diving from the starting blocks and that she had a deep-seated fear of injury from diving into the shallow water.

Coach McKay instructed two veteran swimmers to help her practice diving off the deck of the diving pool into deep water. Assistant Coach Tracy observed her dives and stated that Lucy needed more practice. Her teammates also remarked that Lucy had gone in too deep. Coach McKay apparently heeded this advice and scheduled Lucy to participate in two relay events. In these events the first swimmer starts in the pool, swims two or four laps of the pool and "touches" the second swimmer, who dives into the pool from the starting blocks. At the third meet of the year with archrival North High School, Coach McKay advised Lucy that she could help the relay team be more competitive if she swam third rather than first. Lucy informed Coach McKay that she was afraid of diving off the blocks, did not know how to dive off the blocks, and begged him to allow her to continue to swim first. Coach McKay refused and told Lucy that if she did not move to the third position, she would be off the swim team (Lucy's view) or would be off the relay team (Coach McKay's view). She was also not given the opportunity to start her leg of the race from the pool deck rather than the starting blocks, which is permissible by state activity association rules. Two relay members were instructed to help her practice. During Lucy's second practice dive, she hit her head on the bottom of the pool, was knocked unconscious, sustained a severe concussion, and fractured two vertebrae in her neck. If not for the quick thinking of one of her teammates, Lucy would most likely have drowned. Fortunately, Lucy's prognosis appears good but she will need several months of physical therapy, suffers short-term memory loss from the concussion, and will miss most if not all of her freshman year because of her injuries.

School attorney Garcia spoke. "As you know, Lucy's parents have sued the district and Coach McKay for negligent training, supervision, and control of the swim team members to protect them adequately against diving accidents. The suit claims that Coach McKay breached his duty of care to adequately protect members of the team against diving accidents. The breach was cause-in-fact of the injury, and because it was foreseeable, the breach is a proximate cause of Lucy's injuries. The suit asks for the district to cover all of Lucy's medical bills including physical therapy, provide her with homebound instruction, and pay Lucy $500,000 for pain and suffering."

Attorney Garcia stated, "My first reaction was that Lucy had assumed a risk when she went out for the swim team. In fact, her parents did sign the activity association model assumption of risk form. However," he continued, "the activity association has an addendum to the bylaws that specifically addresses diving from starting blocks into shallow water. The addendum notes that diving into water less than 5 feet deep is dangerous and that 95% of swimming injuries occur in water 5 feet deep or less. The manual states: 'Even an experienced diver can be seriously injured by diving improperly ... or diving from starting blocks without proper training and supervision.'" Attorney Garcia continued, "The addendum than provides specific instructions on how swimmers are to be certified to dive from starting blocks. I have some concerns that these procedures were not followed." He looked at each of the administrators. "I would like for you to draft a recommendation to the superintendent on whether or not to settle with Lucy's parents."

Question

Argue for or against a settlement with Lucy's parents. Clarify the legal question. Cite applicable ISLLC standards, the elements of the tort of negligence, and ethical principles to support your answer. Are all of the elements of the tort of negligence present? There is an inherent risk in any sport, and students are frequently injured. Not every injury is severe, and the vast majority of injuries do not require missed playing time, much less hospitalization and physical therapy. It is also true that not every injury is foreseeable. But, was Lucy's injury foreseeable? If you assume Coach McKay breached his duty (and I am not saying he did), was the breach cause-in-fact of Lucy's injury? Besides assumption of risk, are there other defenses to the tort of negligence in this case? Write a memorandum to the superintendent or school board president with your response.

CHAPTER 11

Teacher Employment, Supervision, and Collective Bargaining

INTRODUCTION

Schools are a people-intensive business, and school districts regardless of size allocate the majority of available funding (sometimes as much as 85–90%) to salaries and benefits for employees. Parents and other stakeholders expect the best teachers for their children. They also demand sound stewardship of this public trust. Consequently, recruiting, selecting, and supervising employees is an important, some might say the most important, role for school leaders. At the same time, teachers and other school employees are protected by a variety of employment laws. Sound stewardship requires an awareness, understanding, and acceptance of these laws and policies. Effective school leadership also requires that they be fairly applied in order to create cooperative environments.

The basic ethical and legal principles concerning employment, teacher supervision, and collective bargaining that apply to most states are emphasized in this chapter. These laws vary, sometimes substantially, from state to state. Therefore, leadership candidates and instructors are encouraged to obtain and use state law to guide discussions in this chapter.

FOCUS QUESTIONS

1. How can employment policy and practice be evaluated to determine its impact on school culture?

2. What protections from capricious or arbitrary employment decisions should public school teachers enjoy? Are these protections too little or too much?

3. How and when should the performance and behaviors of teachers be documented?

4. Should teachers be allowed to bargain collectively with a school district? What should they bargain for?

KEY TERMS

Adverse employment
   decision

Affirmative action

Bona fide occupational
   qualification (BFOQ)

Collective bargaining

Continuing contracts

Disparate impact

Disparate treatment

Equal Employment
   Opportunity
   Commission (EEOC)

Immorality

Incompetence

Insubordination

Just cause

Nexus principle

Performance appraisals

Probationary contract

Remediation plan

Title VII

Union

CASE STUDY

Discrimination?

Jason Whitehead glanced across the table at the face of Corinne Lodge, the board chairperson. Corinne was obviously unhappy. He looked around the table. The other six board members seemed in varying degrees to share Corinne's displeasure. This was Jason's first year as superintendent of Pine Valley School District (PVSD), a relatively small school district in Johnson County. Easy access to interstate highways and a major metropolitan complex made Pine Valley a thriving community. Pine Valley, unlike many neighboring districts, faced continuing increases in enrollment. Over the years, the population had grown, and in that time the teaching staff had almost doubled. Corinne said, "I'm concerned about some of the allegations in this letter. Mr. Whitehead, I would like to see this investigated." Several other board members nodded in agreement with Corinne's statement.

Two days before the regular October school board meeting, Jason, the board president, and each of the board members had received identical letters signed by a majority of the members of the Pine Valley Teachers Organization. The letter read, in part, "For the past several years the PVTO has remained silent as the superintendent and his administrative team consistently demonstrated favoritism and discrimination in employment decisions. Administrators routinely ignored the recommendations of faculty search committees and hired friends, friends of friends, and relatives to teaching positions in the district. Teachers and others who were considered friends of the administration were given preferential treatment, greater access to the more desirable teaching assignments, and access to steps on the career ladder. Administrators routinely ignored reports of misconduct, including at least three reports of sexual misconduct and several reports of teachers using school property for personal use when the reports involved their friends. At the same time teachers who were critical of administrative decisions, reported suspected misconduct, or protested student disciplinary decisions were routinely placed in undesirable teaching assignments, received low performance reviews, and suffered adverse employment decisions including termination. While PVTO will remain dedicated to the children in our classrooms and schools, we will no longer stand quietly by while unfair labor practices, questionable decisions regarding hiring/firing/demoting teachers, and favoritism are common practice."

Jason was fairly sure that board policy was in compliance with state and federal law. But, he had to admit to himself that he had heard many of the same concerns from community members and a couple of area superintendents he had met. Jason agreed with the board. A good review of employment practices was required.

LEADERSHIP PERSPECTIVES

Education is a people-intensive business. Consequently, considerable portions of public funds generated for public education are allocated to teacher, staff, and administrator salary and benefits. In fact, it is difficult to imagine a school district where a majority of the total expenditures of the district are not encumbered by salaries and benefits. **ISLLC Standard 3B** requires school leaders to obtain, allocate, align, and efficiently utilize human, fiscal, and technological resources. In the case study "Discrimination?" it is this standard about which the teachers' organization is expressing their concern. In addition, Jason is legally required to ensure that Pine Valley employment policy is in compliance with federal and state law. Consequently, Jason Whitehead's concerns about past employment practices at Pine Valley may be well founded.

Human resources managers and those responsible for recruiting, selecting, and supervising employees have a particular duty to treat all current and potential employees fairly, in an ethical manner, and without bias (Rebore, 2011). The responsibility to treat employees fairly is embedded in **ISLLC Standards 2A, 3A, 3B, 3E, 5A, and 5C**. In the case study "Discrimination?" it is the part of school district practices concerned with acting with integrity, with fairness, and in an ethical manner that the PVTO is apparently challenging. In other words, a significant portion of the teacher organization, or at least the most influential members, do not believe that teachers are being treated fairly at Pine Valley School District. Jason Whitehead has been challenged by the PVTO and the board of education to evaluate these practices to ensure that the employment practices at PVSD meet the legal requirements outlined in **ISLLC Standard 5**. In addition, Jason is being challenged to evaluate district policy and practice to ensure these policies meet the ethical requirements outlined in **ISLLC Standard 5B**.

Ethical considerations are particularly important in human resources management (Rebore, 2011). People, regardless of job description, often face difficult decisions where the lines between right and wrong, ethical and unethical are blurred. Individuals with supervisory roles in public schools are particularly vulnerable because their decisions (or failure to decide) affect everyone, including students, parents, and employees. This is the essence of **ISLLC Standard 5B**, which calls for school leaders to model self-awareness, reflective practice, transparency, and ethical behavior. To meet this standard, Ronald Rebore (2011) provides three foundations for the importance of ethical considerations in human resource management:

1. People are in a constant state of becoming either a better person and professional or a person who gradually loses his or her integrity. Rebore believes that it is often the culmination of small judgments and decisions over time that determines the sort of person and human resources manager one becomes.

2. Those responsible for human resource management (including principals and associate or assistant principals) have a definitive and lasting impact on the school district as an institution.
3. Any action that shows preferential (or prejudicial) treatment to certain people is contrary to the development of personal integrity and to the proper operation of the school district.

If the allegations made by the Pine Valley Teachers Organization are true, past and possibly current administrators have violated all of Rebore's ethical foundations of human resource management. They may have also violated several federal laws as well as the basic concept that teachers should be treated fairly simply because they are human beings. Jason Whitehead may be faced with a difficult task. Past practice can at times be difficult to challenge, especially if this practice is deeply ingrained in the school culture. The utilitarian principles of John Stuart Mill, however, may provide guidance in such an undertaking.

UTILITARIANISM AND EMPLOYMENT PRACTICES

J. S. Mill, a student of Jeremy Bentham, first published his concepts of *utilitarian ethics* in 1861 as a series of three essays. In Mill's view, all action should be taken for the sake of some end (Mill, 1998). More importantly, this action should be taken with a clear and precise concept of the purpose of the action. In other words, policy and the reasons for the policy should be designed with a specific purpose in mind before implementation. The question is, of course, what should this purpose be? According to Mill, the purpose of actions should be to diminish pain and create the most happiness. Mill adopted the word *utility* from his mentor Jeremy Bentham to describe this concept. Mill defines utilitarianism (or the *greatest happiness principle*) as follows: "Actions are right in proportion as they tend to promote happiness, wrong as they tend to produce the reverse of happiness" (p. 55). In Mill's view of utilitarianism, the rightness or wrongness of actions should depend on the foreseeable, or expected, outcomes of the action. In short, all action should be taken with the expected intent to promote happiness. For this discussion of J. S. Mill's utilitarian ethics, the greatest happiness principle can also be viewed as "the greater good." In other words, the purpose of action should be to promote the greater good.

It is important to point out that in this view of utilitarianism, the standard for greatest happiness is not the policy maker's own happiness, but rather the greatest amount of overall happiness. This is the *directive rule* of Mill's utilitarian ethics. In this view, employment policies (all policy that affects employees, including leave policy, work rules, salaries and benefits, supervision models, and investigations of misconduct) should not be designed to produce happiness for a board member, an administrator, a search committee, or the teachers' union. Rather, the policy should be designed to promote the greater good among all concerned. This is an important point. Utility is not about what continually makes some group of people happy. Rather, it is about policy and practice that is designed to find a balance between the needs of the organization for efficiency and order and the needs of the employees for satisfaction in their work (a sense of community and individual importance). Thus, utilitarian ethics does not require that actions produce happiness for everyone, but rather the greatest happiness for all concerned. In fact, Mill recognized and articulated the need for negative consequences in his writing as an important factor in the utility of a society. For example, the use of a professional growth plan to improve a teacher's deficiency or the proper investigation of allegations of employee misconduct may be viewed as negative by the affected individual, but promote the greater good of the school community. Part of the utilitarian concept, however, is how these negative consequences should be applied (see Bentham's views of the role of government outlined in Chapter 6).

School cultures that encourage collaborative efforts as outlined in **ISLLC Standard 2A** require that all involved view the school, or school district, as a society of equals. A society of equals may "only exist on the understanding that the interests of all are to be regarded equally" (Mill, 1998, p. 78). In fact, cooperative school cultures are characterized by feelings that the best interests of others are also in one's own best interest. These feelings not only improve social ties; they also serve as a catalyst for continued healthy growth in school culture. In other words, cooperative school cultures cannot exist where the interests of all concerned are not the primary foreseeable outcome of all action.

For example, in the case study "Discrimination?" Jason Whitehead and the board of education would ideally view employment policy and practice as contributing to the greater good of students and teachers in PVSD. Jason Whitehead has been charged by the board of education and challenged by the teachers' organization to fairly evaluate employment policy and practice. It is easy to argue that the purpose of employment policy should be to promote the greater good. How, though, can the greater good be determined?

Mill identifies legal rights, moral rights, desert (what is deserved), contracts, impartiality, and equality as six concepts of justice congruent with utilitarianism or the greater good. A short description of each of these concepts and an evaluation model follows:

- *Legal rights:* It is thought unjust to deprive anyone of any legal right that they possess.
- *Moral rights:* It is possible for some law or policy to violate the moral rights of individuals. These laws or policies are unjust.
- *Desert:* It is thought unjust for someone to receive something that they do not deserve. This concept works for both good (receiving an award or acknowledgment, for example) and a bad (a reprimand, for example) that are not deserved.
- *Contracts:* It is unjust to break voluntary agreements with others.
- *Impartiality:* It is thought unjust to be inappropriately partial.
- *Equality:* Justice requires equality, except when inequality is more beneficial overall.

These concepts of justice can be organized into a table to assess the relative utility of school district or campus culture (Table 11–1).

For example, in the case study "Discrimination?" Jason Whitehead has been challenged to objectively evaluate the employment policy and practices at PVSD. Part of this evaluation and nonjudgmental data collection could include an analysis of the relative utility of employment policy and practice. In this example, each of the six concepts of justice consistent with utility could be given a score. This rough total

TABLE 11–1	An Assessment of School Utility		
	High Utility (3 Points)	**Medium Utility (2 Points)**	**Low Utility (1 Point)**
Legal rights	• All employment policy meets established legal rights. • Legal rights are honored and consistently enforced. • Employment decisions are clearly nondiscriminatory.	• All employment policy meets established legal rights. • Legal rights are usually honored and enforced. • Some employment decisions seem discriminatory.	• Policy meets established legal requirements. • Legal rights are generally ignored or applied only when convenient. • Overt discrimination in employment.
Moral rights	• Employment policy respects the moral rights of all individuals. • Discrimination based on race, sex, national origin eliminated.	• Employment policy respects most of the moral rights of individuals. • Some discrimination based on race, sex, national origin apparent.	• Employment policy is applied inequitably. Moral rights are respected only when necessary. • Discrimination "hidden" within employment decisions.
Deserts	• Employment decisions based on objective criteria. • All awards and punishments are objectively applied in all cases.	• Most employment decisions are based on objective criteria. • Awards and punishments are generally deserved.	• Employment decisions are usually based more on whom one knows or personal contacts. • Awards and punishments preferential.
Contracts	• All contracts, written and verbal, are honored.	• Written contracts are generally honored. Verbal contracts are sometimes broken.	• Written or verbal contracts have little or no meaning.
Impartiality	• Employment decisions are impartial. • Benefits and rewards are distributed with impartiality.	• Most employment decisions are impartial. • Benefits and rewards are generally distributed with impartiality.	• Partiality is not only common but accepted practice. • Partiality is apparent in distribution of benefits and rewards.
Equality	• Employment policy is equitable, except where inequalities are beneficial to the greater good.	• Employment policy is generally equitable. • Some inequalities are not for the greater good.	• Employment policy is not equitable. • Inequalities serve self-interest rather than the greater good.

Scoring guide: 15–18 points, high-utility school culture; 11–14 points, medium-utility school culture; less than 10 points, low-utility school culture.

could then be used to rate the relative overall utility of the district. If problem areas exist, then the data can be used as justification for changes in policy and practice. The matrix and the data collected could also be used to justify current practices. If this is the case, other deeper issues—ones that are not really related to employment policy—may exist between the union membership and the board of education. Consequently,

Jason could use a communication model such as "Resolving Issues of Conflicting Interest," outlined in Chapter 3 and Chapter 12, to develop a better understanding of the apparent underlying issues.

It is important to note that a similar utility model could be adapted to a variety of policy analysis questions. Examples could include student discipline practices, the allocation of funding for instructional supplies, or equal access to extracurricular activities for boys and girls.

LEGAL ISSUES IN EMPLOYMENT

In decidedly different language, Mill's six concepts of justice congruent with utilitarianism guide much of the employment law in the United States. To this end, the U.S. Congress has passed a variety of laws to address discrimination in employment practices. The most significant of these laws is Civil Rights Act of 1964, particularly Title VII, 42 U.S.C. § 2000e (P.L. 88-352). *Title VII prohibits discrimination* in employment practices on the basis of *race, color, religion, gender, or national origin under any federally assisted educational program*. The act places an affirmative duty on school districts to discover and eliminate discriminatory practices. The **Equal Employment Opportunity Commission (EEOC)** was created by this act. The EEOC enforces most employment discrimination laws. Teachers and other school district employees must first pursue EEOC remedies before they may file suit under Title VII. The EEOC has an excellent website at www.eeoc.gov. The Office for Civil Rights (OCR) also enforces employment discrimination laws, including all civil rights laws and the Americans with Disabilities Act. OCR also has an excellent website at www.ocr.gov.

Basically, two types of discrimination are defined by Title VII: disparate treatment and disparate impact. **Disparate treatment** applies when an individual claims that he or she was demoted, fired, passed over for a promotion, or not hired because of race, color, sex, religion, or national origin. In order to prevail under Title VII, the teacher would need to demonstrate (1) that she is a member of a protected class and (2) that she was terminated from her employment because of her protected class. If the teacher is a member of a protected class, the burden of proof shifts to the school board to demonstrate a valid reason for their decision. For example, a black, female Missouri teacher with 10 years of experience was dismissed by her school board (*Shanklin v. Fitzgerald,* 2005). In this case, the board was able to demonstrate that the teacher was dismissed for legitimate reasons (failure to improve in specific areas) and not because of her race. In another example, an experienced female high school basketball coach applied for the head boys' basketball coaching position when the head coach resigned (*Fuhr v. School District,* 2001). A selection committee recommended a less qualified male applicant. The case involved the denial of a promotion (assuming of course that moving from head girls' coach to head boys' coach is a promotion, which may or may not be true) to a member of a protected class. The burden of proof shifts to the board to demonstrate that the female coach was denied the promotion because of a valid reason, not because of her sex. Do you see why?

Disparate impact occurs when a facially neutral policy has an unequal effect on minority groups. The parameters of disparate impact as the term relates to employment practices were defined by the U.S. Supreme Court in *Griggs v. Duke Power Co.* (1971). In this case, an employer required a high school diploma or passing an IQ test as a precondition of employment. However, the company could not show that the requirement was reasonably related to job performance. The Court held that Title VII does not prohibit an employer (a school district, for example) from using objective criteria. In fact, objective criteria may well be the best defense against discrimination. Please see *Ricci v. DeStefano* (2009) and *Lewis v. City of Chicago* (2010) for examples of disparate treatment and disparate impact in employment.

Key Federal Discrimination Legislation

In addition to Title VII, the U.S. Congress has passed a variety of laws designed to specifically address different kinds of discrimination. These laws protect a wider group of individuals (protected class) and make it easier for these individuals to demonstrate discrimination. Table 11–2 includes a summary of the key federal legislation that affects educator employment.

Several issues germane to educational leadership, which include sexual harassment, hostile work environment, ethnic or religious discrimination, drug/alcohol use, and the Americans with Disabilities Act Amendments, are discussed in more detail.

Sexual Harassment

Harassment on the basis of sex in the workplace is a violation of § 703 of Title VII. Sexual harassment is defined under two legal theories: quid pro quo and hostile environment.

Quid pro quo occurs when submission to sexual conduct is used as a basis for employment or refusal to submit to sexual conduct results in an ***adverse employment decision*** (EEOC, 1999, 2002). The acquiescence to the request or refusing the request is not the point. The fact that the demand was made rises to the level of sexual harassment.

A *hostile environment* occurs when unwelcome sexual advances, requests for sexual favors, and other verbal or physical conduct of a sexual nature have the purpose or effect of unreasonably interfering with work performance or create an intimidating, hostile, or offensive working environment (EEOC, 1999, 2002).

Title VII does not prohibit all conduct of a sexual nature in the workplace, which of course would be impossible; only *unwelcome sexual conduct* that rises to the level of a hostile environment or quid pro quo harassment is illegal (EEOC, 1999). The law also prohibits retaliatory actions for reporting or refusing to submit further to the harassment. For example, a retaliatory claim could include discharge, demotion, transfer to a less desirable position or location, or denial of a promotion that could be traced to the reporting of unwelcome sexual conduct or a refusal to submit to sexual conduct (EEOC, 2002).

An employer is responsible for acts of sexual harassment between employees where the employer (or supervisory personnel) knows or *should have known* of the conduct unless immediate and corrective action was taken (EEOC, 2002). The unwelcome component of sexual harassment is defined by the recipient. What may start as welcome sexual attention may quickly become unwelcome. To overcome the difficulty sometimes inherent in defining *unwelcome* (or when actions become unwelcome), courts use the "reasonable person" standard. In other words, if sexual conduct looks unwelcome, sounds unwelcome, and the reaction of the recipient appears to mean that it is unwelcome, then it is unwelcome. Isolated incidents of offensive sexual

TABLE 11–2	Key Federal Legislation Affecting Educator Employment
Federal Legislation	**Significance**
Civil Rights Act of 1871, 42 U.S.C. § 1983	Allows suits for injunctive relief and compensatory damages against public school districts that through policy or practice deprive individuals of U.S. Constitutional and federal statutory rights. Public employees are also subject to suit under this statute. This law is very important in the enforcement of federal rights under the Fourteenth Amendment, because it provides the mechanism by which an individual may bring a cause of action against a state actor (includes school boards) for a deprivation of a constitutional right or a right guaranteed by laws of the United States.
Equal Pay Act of 1963, 29 U.S.C. § 206 (d)	Requires all employers subject to the Fair Labor Standards Act (school districts are included) to provide *equal pay for men and women performing similar work.*
Section 701 of the Civil Rights Act of 1964	Ensures *equal treatment of women experiencing pregnancy*, childbirth, or related medical conditions. Includes how fringe benefits are applied.
Civil Rights Act of 1964, Title VI	Prohibits exclusion or discrimination under federally funded or assisted programs because of race, color, or natural origin.
Civil Rights Act of 1964, Title VII	Prohibits discrimination in employment due to race, color, religion, sex, or natural origin.
Executive Order 11246 (1965, amended 1967)	Required government contractors to take affirmative action to assure equal treatment.
Age Discrimination in Employment Act (ADEA) of 1967	Prohibits discrimination against individuals 40 years of age or older unless age is a bona fide qualification reasonably necessary to carry out job responsibilities. *Eliminates mandatory retirement age policies. Makes it illegal to adopt a policy or practice of hiring only beginning teachers.*
Equal Employment Opportunity Act of 1972 (Title VII), 42 U.S.C. § 2000e	Amended the Civil Rights Act of 1964 and greatly strengthened the powers and jurisdiction of the Equal Employment Opportunity Commission (EEOC) *in the enforcement of the law* and extended coverage of the law to include (a) all private employers with 15 or more persons; (b) all educational institutions, public and private; (c) state and local governments; (d) public and private employment agencies; (e) labor unions with 15 or more members; and (f) joint labor–management committees for apprenticeship training.
Title IX of the 1972 Education Amendments, Discrimination Based on Sex, 20 U.S.C. § 1681	Prohibits exclusion of participation in or denial of benefits or *discrimination against persons on the basis of gender* in any program receiving federal financial assistance.
Rehabilitation Act of 1973 (P.L. 93-112)	Ordered federal contractors not to discriminate against handicapped persons in employment decisions. Section 504 prohibits discrimination against "otherwise-qualified" individuals (those individuals who can perform the job requirements) because of handicapping condition.
The Vietnam Era Veterans Readjustment Act of 1974	Encouraged the employment of Vietnam-era veterans.
The Pregnancy Discrimination Act of 1979	Amends Title VII to prohibit discrimination on the basis of pregnancy, childbirth, or medical condition related to pregnancy or childbirth. *Pregnancy must be treated the same as any other disabling illness for purposes of health benefits.*

TABLE 11–2   (Continued)

Federal Legislation	Significance
Immigration Reform and Control Act of 1986	Requires employers to verify eligibility to work in the United States. It is *unlawful to knowingly hire or continue to employ an unauthorized alien.*
Drug-Free Workplace Act of 1989	*Requires school districts to maintain a drug-free work environment.* Districts may choose either to offer rehabilitation services or to dismiss staff members who are convicted of drug abuse offenses in the workplace. Districts must inform employees of the dangers of drug abuse and the penalties for drug use. Employees must report criminal drug convictions to the district and must disclose to future employers any workplace drug convictions.
Civil Rights Act of 1991	Designed to strengthen and improve federal civil rights laws prohibiting discrimination because of race, color, or natural origin. *Provides for damages in cases of deliberate violation of civil rights laws.*
Omnibus Transportation Employee Testing Act of 1991	Requires school bus drivers (among others) to submit to controlled-substance testing. Includes preemployment, postaccident, and random testing; reasonable suspicion testing; and return-to-duty testing. Board policy should outline procedures and consequences for failing a drug test.
The Health Insurance Portability and Accountability Act of 1996 (HIPAA)	Protects the privacy of individually identifiable health information.
Family and Medical Leave Act of 1993	Eligible employees are entitled to a total of 12 work weeks of leave during any 12-month period for birth of a child; adoption or foster care of a child; to care for the spouse, child, or parent of the employee for a serious health condition; or because of a serious health condition that makes the employee unable to perform the functions of the position.
Uniform Services Employment and Reemployment Rights Act (USERRA, 1994)	Prohibits discrimination because of past, present, or future service in the uniformed services. Includes hiring, promotion, reemployment, retention in employment, and benefits.
The Genetic Information Non-discrimination Act of 2008 (GINA)	Makes it unlawful to fail or refuse to hire, or to discharge, any employee, or otherwise to discriminate against any employee with respect to the compensation, terms, conditions, or privileges of employment of the employee, because of genetic information with respect to the employee.
Americans with Disabilities Act Amendments Act of 2008	The act emphasizes that the definition of *disability* should be construed in favor of broad coverage of individuals to the maximum extent permitted by the terms of the ADA.
Fair Labor Standards Act of 1938 (Amended 2010)	Hourly employees are limited to 40-hour workweek unless the employee receives overtime compensation at a rate not less than one and a half times regular rate.

conduct or remarks generally do not create an abusive or hostile environment. However, a single incident that is especially egregious or shocks the conscience (i.e., a sexual assault or fondling) may rise to the level of sexual harassment (EEOC, 1999).

Same-Sex Sexual Harassment

Sexual orientation harassment in the workplace was not the "principal evil" Congress intended to address in Title VII. Nevertheless, in *Oncale v. Sundowner* (1998), the U.S. Supreme Court extended Title VII to include same-sex sexual harassment by stating, "Sexual harassment must extend to sexual harassment of any kind that meets the statutory requirements." *Oncale* has been applied by several courts to same-sex harassment (see *Mota v. University of Texas*, 2001, as an example). Sexual stereotyping has also been found to be illegal (*Price Waterhouse v. Hopkins,* 1998). *Price Waterhouse* would, for example, prevent the discharge of a male teacher for effeminate characteristics or of a female employee for being overly masculine. In mixed-motive cases with both good and bad reasons (gender stereotyping, for example) intertwined, the burden of proof shifts to the school board. The board must demonstrate that it would have made the decision anyway, based on the good reason, even if it had not allowed the bad reason (sexual stereotyping) to play a role—and so no violation has occurred (*Desert Palace v. Costa,* 2003).

Hostile Work Environment

In addition to sexual harassment that results in a hostile work environment, Title VII prohibits verbal and written conduct based on race, ethnic origin, or religion that creates a hostile work environment. The U.S. Supreme Court in *Burlington Industries v. Ellerth* (1998) makes it clear that supervisors are legally responsible for a failure to prevent and remediate a hostile work environment if the supervisor had reasonable notice of the harassment and failed to take adequate corrective measures (see *Henderson v. Walled Lake*, 2006, as an example). As Rebore (2011) points out, the harassing conduct does not have to occur in person. Technology such as text messaging, e-mail, Twitter, and social media make it possible for harassing conduct to occur at anytime or anyplace. Thus, abusive e-mails, text messages, Twitter posts, or social media messages that create a hostile work environment are a violation of Title VII. School officials should be aware of their responsibility to prevent abusive or hostile language or messages in any medium. A well-written employee policy that clearly states that the district will not tolerate abusive or hostile language or messages at school or in electronic formats at anytime may be the better part of valor.

Ethnic or Religious Discrimination or Harassment

Title VII prohibits workplace discrimination based on the real or perceived religious or ethnic background of employees (EEOC, 2005b). Employers (school boards) may be liable for harassment or discrimination by supervisors, teachers, other school personnel, or nonemployees. School districts are required to make *reasonable accommodations* for religious practices unless doing so would create an undue hardship for the district. Reasonable accommodations may include leave for religious observances, time or place to pray, and ability to wear religious garb (a hijab, for example).

DRUG-FREE WORKPLACE The federal Drug-Free Workplace Act of 1990 (41 USC Chapter 10) requires public school districts to certify that the district will provide a drug-free workplace by establishing a drug-free awareness program to inform employees about (1) the dangers of drug abuse in the workplace; (2) the district's policy of maintaining a drug-free workplace; (3) any available drug counseling, rehabilitation, and employee assistance programs; and (4) the penalties that may be imposed on employees for drug abuse violations. It is important to note that the Drug-Free Workplace Act does not require termination for an employee who tests positive for drugs or alcohol at school. In fact, the act specifically mentions drug and/or alcohol counseling as an option. But, the act does support a school board decision to terminate an employee who does test positive.

Americans with Disabilities Act

It is illegal to discriminate against a qualified individual on the basis of disability. School districts are required to make *reasonable* accommodations for individuals with disabilities. The Americans with Disabilities Act is enforced by the federal Office for Civil Rights.

The Americans with Disabilities Amendments of 2008 (42 U. S. C. 12102, Section 3, effective January 1, 2009) significantly expanded the definition of disability to mean "(A) a physical or mental impairment that substantially limits one or more major life activities of such individual; (B) a record of such an impairment; or (C) being regarded as having such an impairment. Major life activities include, but are not limited to, caring for oneself, performing manual tasks, seeing, hearing, eating, sleeping, walking, standing, lifting, bending, speaking, breathing, learning, reading, concentrating, thinking, communicating, and working. A major life activity also includes the operation of a major bodily function, including but not limited to, functions of the immune system, normal cell growth, digestive, bowel, bladder, neurological, brain, respiratory, circulatory, endocrine, and reproductive functions."

An individual meets the requirement of being regarded as having such an impairment if the individual establishes that he or she has been subjected to an action prohibited under the act because of an actual or perceived physical or mental impairment, whether or not the impairment limits or is perceived to limit a major life activity. The burden of proof shifts to school districts in cases where an employee faces an adverse employment decision and claims a disability. The determination of whether an impairment substantially limits a major life activity must be made without regard to the ameliorative effects of mitigating measures such as (1) medication, medical supplies, equipment, or appliances, low-vision devices (which do not include ordinary eyeglasses or contact lenses), prosthetics including limbs and devices, hearing aids and cochlear implants or other implantable hearing devices, mobility devices, or oxygen therapy equipment and supplies; (2) use of assistive technology; (3) reasonable accommodations or auxiliary aids or services; or (4) learned behavioral or adaptive neurological modifications.

AFFIRMATIVE ACTION AND OCCUPATIONAL QUALIFICATIONS

Affirmative Action

Title VII, along with other employment laws, attempts to make hiring practices neutral and does not require that school districts favor one person over another. However, a voluntary *affirmative action* plan to remediate past discrimination in employment may not be unlawful reverse discrimination if a district can demonstrate that (1) a statistical disparity exists between race or sex for a particular job category, (2) the district was (or is) guilty of past discrimination, (3) efforts do not unnecessarily penalize the rights of nonminority applicants, and (4) efforts are designed to terminate when the goals of the plan have been achieved (Alexander & Alexander, 2012). Because affirmative action is based on race or sex, courts apply a strict scrutiny standard. Strict scrutiny requires that the district would need to show that the affirmative action plan is necessary to achieve a *compelling state interest*. The plan would also need to be narrowly tailored to achieve this goal. These standards have become very difficult to meet.

BFOQ

Compliance with federal nondiscrimination laws requires an understanding of the term *bona fide occupational qualification (BFOQ)*. A BFOQ is a requirement essential or necessary for performing a particular job. Whether a bona fide occupational qualification is allowed depends on whether the job qualification is reasonably necessary and narrowly fashioned in the job description. For example, a job qualification for a bilingual English-/Spanish-speaking third-grade teacher in an elementary school with a population of English language learners may be reasonable and narrowly fashioned. However, a job description calling for only teachers of Hispanic origin may not be reasonable. Similarly, it seems reasonable to specify a female for a position that requires the supervision of a girls' locker room (Rebore, 2011). Race, marital status, religious affiliation, and family plans are never BFOQs. The only exception is that a private religious school may require that applicants profess a particular faith. Requesting preemployment information that discloses or tends to disclose an applicant's sex, race, ethnic origin, or religion likely constitutes evidence of discrimination (EEOC, 2005a).

LICENSURE AND CONTRACTS

The criteria for teacher and administrator certification and licensure are set by state law and regulations. Currently all states have enacted laws establishing the certification or licensure requirements of professional public school employees, including the approval of the content of teacher education programs. Each state may establish any number of requirements for teacher and administrator licensure that presumptively qualifies a person to teach, including educational requirements, test scores, United States citizenship, good moral character, or any other conditions considered important. Courts are supportive of these requirements as long as the requirements for licensure are not arbitrary. State certification test have been upheld by the courts when the state can demonstrate a reasonable connection between the knowledge and skills measured on the test and the duties of the teacher (see, for example, *Association of Mexican-American Educators v. State of California*, 2000). All states empower the licensure issuing agency (usually the state board of education) to revoke teaching license for a variety of reasons. Courts are reluctant to overrule state mechanisms for the revocation of teaching licenses. For example, a Florida appellate court refused to substitute its judgment for a decision by the Florida Practice Commissions to revoke the certificate of a teacher for sending sexually oriented e-mail to seventh-grade students (*Wax v. Horne,* 2003).

The terms and conditions of teacher and administrator contracts are established by state law and regulation. Public school employees must agree to the legal conditions and abide by whatever requirements and stipulations are set forth by the state legislature or state board of education. In general, the legal authority to issue contracts to individuals to serve the needs of the school district is delegated to local boards of education. This is an important point. In most cases only boards of education have the authority to enter into valid employment contracts, discipline employees, or terminate contracts.

A contract is binding on both parties. Contracts can be changed or voided with the agreement of both parties. A *breach* occurs when one party fails to meet the terms of the contract. When one party breaches a contract, the other party is entitled to damages (money) in proportion to the damage done by the breach. Most, if not all, states allow boards to legally breach teaching contracts because of declining enrollment or financial needs. This type of breach, usually called reduction in force, is designed to allow boards of education to meet changing financial or enrollment situations. Reduction in force requires a nondiscriminatory policy. Courts usually do not second-guess these decisions as long as the board does not discriminate, uses some objective criteria, and follows state law, any negotiated agreements, and board policy. For example, a school district would be hard pressed to justify a policy that allowed for the layoff of veteran or tenured nonminority teachers before nontenured minority teachers (*Wygant v. Jackson Board of Education*, 1986).

Types of Contracts

There are four general types of public school employment contracts: (1) at-will, (2) probationary, (3) term, and (4) continuing. *At-will* employment is usually reserved for noncertified personnel such as custodians, maintenance workers, cafeteria workers, clerks, or secretaries. Teachers are sometimes employed on an at-will basis for supplemental duty assignments such as junior class sponsor. At-will employees generally have an expectation of continued employment for the duration of the pay period. Termination during the pay period (e.g., monthly for custodians, or for the school year for a chess club sponsor) may require sufficient evidence to support the decision. However, if the district waits until the end of the pay period, few if any due process requirements are necessary (Kemerer & Crain, 2010). It would seem that little if any documentation would be necessary to terminate a term contract. This may not be the case. As Kemerer and Crain (2010) point out, a term employee who is terminated may elect to challenge the nonrenewal and could, for example, file a complaint with the EEOC claiming that refusals of sexual favors factored into the decision. In these cases, the supervisor should have documentation related to poor job performance or some other reason unrelated to the allegation of quid pro quo sexual harassment.

A ***probationary contract*** is normally issued to inexperienced teachers or teachers new to a school district. Probationary contracts are for 1 year. A probationary contract can be terminated at the end of the contract year if the district believes it is in the best interest of the district. According to Kemerer and Crain (2010), the nonrenewal of a probationary teaching contract is generally the easiest negative employment decision to defend. Again, probationary contracts can be terminated at the end of the term for any good reason (but never for a bad reason). The district only has to comply with state statutes regarding notice that the contract will be terminated at the end of the contract period. For example, in Texas probationary teachers must be notified no later than 45 days before the last day of instruction under the contract (TEA 21.103). In Missouri, probationary teachers must be notified of nonrenewal on or before April 15 (RSMo 168.126). If challenged, administrators should be prepared to defend their nonrenewal recommendations. However, the burden is clearly on the teacher to establish that the district had an impermissible motive (bad reason), not on the district to demonstrate a valid (good) reason (Kemerer & Crain, 2010).

Termination of probationary contracts *during the term of the contract* requires formal due process requirements. Districts must generally give the probationary employee an explicit directive to improve or change his or her conduct and an opportunity to comply with the directive (Kemerer & Crain, 2010). For example, Missouri state law outlines the following due process requirements for probationary teachers during the term of the contract: The board of education through its authorized administrative representative, must (1) provide the teacher with a written statement clearly identifying areas of deficiency or incompetence, (2) furnish the teacher an opportunity to correct the problem and (3) give the teacher 90 days to demonstrate improvement. If improvement satisfactory to the board of education has not been made within 90 days of the receipt of the notification, the board of education may terminate the employment of the probationary teacher immediately or at the end of the school year (RSMo 168.126).

Term contracts are for specified lengths of time. Term contracts are usually reserved for superintendents and experienced principals. Some states, such as Texas, allow term contracts for up to 5 years; other states, such as Missouri, allow term contracts for up to 3 years. Like probationary contracts, term contracts can be nonrenewed with sufficient notice at the end of the term of the contract. Termination during the term of the contract naturally requires more careful attention (Kemerer & Crain, 2010).

Continuing contracts (called *tenure contracts* in some states) were initially created by state legislatures as a job security device to protecting against arbitrary termination by local school boards. Currently 19 states continue to use the term *tenure*, whereas a number of states use *continuing contract* terminology (Frey, 2010). A continuing contract bestows a property right to continual employment in the district until the employee retires, resigns, dies, is terminated, or agrees to a change in contract status (Kemerer & Crain, 2010). Most states require a probationary period of 2 to 5 years' continuous service in a district. School boards have wide latitude in deciding whether to grant initial tenure as long as decisions are not discriminatory (Frey, 2010). Employees must meet all the requirements of the job to maintain the position. For example, failure to complete certification requirements, failure to renew a certificate, or failure to obtain an adequate number of continuing education credits would be reason to terminate the employment of a teacher in a district. The U.S. Supreme Court has upheld the termination of a continuing contract teacher because of a willful failure to earn continuing education credits as required by board policy (*Harrah Independent School District v. Martin,* 1979).

Teachers who have earned a continuing contract cannot be dismissed except by good cause as set forth by state law. It is a common misunderstanding that continuing contract teachers cannot be terminated for instructional inadequacies. This is not necessarily true. But, the burden of proof shifts from the teacher to the board of education to demonstrate a valid reason, rather than the teacher being required to demonstrate that the board used a "bad" or discriminatory reason for the decision. Consequently, extensive documentation is often required in defending decisions to terminate (or recommend termination of) a continuing contract teacher (Kemerer & Crain, 2010). Tenured or continuing contract teachers do not have a right to a particular teaching assignment, to a choice of schools within a district, or to indefinite employment.

Teacher tenure has long been a hot-button issue, and it should not be surprising that the concept of continuing contracts is being reexamined in several state legislatures around the county. In 2010, for example, 11 states modified at least some part of their tenure laws (Frey, 2010). The use of 1- to 3-year term contracts for teachers in the place of continuing contracts is an emerging trend in some states, including Texas. In general, it is most likely safe to assume that the decision of nonrenewal of a term contract should be supported by documentation of deficiency or incompetency on the part of the teacher in question (Kemerer & Crain, 2010). The importance of documentation is considered in the next section.

TEACHER SUPERVISION

State law (and school board policy) requires the evaluation of teaching performance. **ISLLC Standards 2D, 2F, and 2I** reflect this requirement by calling for school leaders to supervise instruction, develop the instructional capacity of staff, and monitor and evaluate the impact of the instructional program. Teacher evaluation instruments typically contain job-related criteria such as instructional methodology, lesson planning, meeting the needs of varied learners, alignment of instruction and student assessments with state tests, and positive classroom management skills. Areas other than teaching may also be included. These areas, called interpersonal and organizational relationships, may include criteria such as relationships with fellow teachers and administrators, following board policy and campus rules, and cooperative relationships with parents. However, criteria used in the evaluation of teaching performance should be rationally related to the job of teaching. What is important is that the behavior be validly related to the requirements of the job and that it can be observed. In short, only observable behaviors related to the job are fair game for evaluation (Rossow & Tate, 2003).

Documentation of Performance

Proper documentation is essential in the justification of employment decisions. Kemerer and Crain (2010) list several types of documentation: (1) oral directives, (2) notes to file, (3) performance appraisals, (4) specific incident memoranda, and

(5) summary memoranda. *Oral directives* are simple verbal directions. Oral directives may be appropriate for minor transgressions and for first-time offenders. The downside is that the lack of documentation limits their usefulness later in a nonrenewal or termination defense. *Notes to file*, the second form of documentation, can help alleviate this drawback. Notes to file that accompany oral directives can assist in recalling specific times, dates, and conversations regarding certain behaviors. These notes can help establish a pattern of noncompliance or misbehavior that can later be used in a more formal memorandum or reprimand. Notes to file, however, should stick to the facts and nothing but the facts.

Performance appraisals include the documentation required by state law and school board policy. There are generally two forms of teacher performance appraisal: formative and summative. Formative evaluations usually consist of classroom observations, analysis of lesson plans, and observations of teacher interactions with students, parents, colleagues, and others. Summative evaluations consist of the summaries and conclusions from formative evaluations and are used to justify continued employment or termination/nonrenewal of employment. Performance appraisals are often standardized formats mandated by state law or school board policy by which the performance of all teachers is periodically evaluated. The frequency is determined by the type of contract and school board policy or state law.

A *specific incident memorandum* applies to a specific incident or a pattern of incidents that is sufficiently serious that a written record should be made. Regardless of the circumstances, these memoranda should contain several essential elements. Kemerer and Crain (2010, pp. 2–4) explain these elements as follows:

1. Use district or campus letterhead to emphasize the importance of the correspondence.
2. Do not forget the date.
3. Describe the nature of the allegation, the nature of the administrator's investigation if one was required, dates and times of specific incidents, and the dates on which the supervisor has spoken with the employee regarding the allegations.
4. Set forth a findings of fact.
5. State conclusions regarding what happened and which laws, policies, administrative directives, or ethical provisions were violated by the actions of the employee.
6. Issue specific directives regarding future conduct.
7. Offer the employee an opportunity to respond within a specified time period.
8. Require the dated signature of the employee. If the employee refuses to sign, have a third party witness that the employee has received the document.

The final type of document outlined by Kemerer and Crain (2010) is the *summary memorandum* or *last chance memorandum*. This document pulls together and summarizes the record of observations, notes, and conversations from a particular period of time. The summary or last chance memorandum may include data from prior years if relevant to establishing a continuing pattern of deficiency. However, some caution is required when using prior year data. Regardless of the type, a careful documentation system is essential to effective personnel decisions.

Linking to PRACTICE

Do:

- At the district level, train campus principals to develop an organized documentation process. Principals should train assistant principals and other supervisory personnel (department heads, mentor teachers, or instructional specialists, for example, if these individuals serve as evaluators) in proper documentation of teaching and interpersonal skills of teachers. Kemerer and Crain (2010) provide excellent examples of documentation that can be adapted to any state or local requirements.
- Clarify the types of behaviors that may result in some form of written record. Insist that all supervisory personal comply.
- Use evidence generated from the teacher's formative and summative performance assessments to justify renewal or nonrenewal of a probationary contract teacher. There is no excuse for personal bias or unprofessional conduct when making these kinds of recommendations.

Do Not:

- Document every incident of noncompliance. For example, a single incident of being a few minutes late to lunch duty may not rate a specific incident memorandum or a remediation plan.
- Show up at a school board meeting with plans to recommend the termination of a continuing contract without good documentation that demonstrates a pattern of failure to meet the criteria established for teachers in the district and documentation of efforts to remediate the behavior (if applicable). Remember, the burden of proof is on the administrator in nonrenewal of continuing contract teachers. Never try to bluff your way through a termination hearing before your local board of education.
- Use a documentation system as a method to bully employees or make life miserable in an effort to force a resignation or transfer.
- Use e-mail as a documentation system.

Grounds for Dismissal of Continuing Contract Teachers

There are basically two types of teacher behavior that are grounds for termination: remediable and nonremediable (Kemerer & Crain, 2010). *Nonremediable* behaviors are grounds for nonrenewal or immediate termination. Examples of nonremediable behavior may include violent behavior that puts students at risk of harm or injury, felony conviction, or inappropriate sexual or interpersonal relationships with students. *Remediable* behaviors require a chance for the teacher to improve or remediate the behavior. Examples may include a lack of lesson planning, failure to follow directed changes in teaching methodology, incidents of insubordination, or difficulties in classroom management. The *remediation plan* (*professional growth plan*) is a document that advises an employee of deficiencies, outlines a plan to improve, assists the employee in meeting the plan, and gives a reasonable time to comply (usually 30 to 90 days as defined by state law). Opportunities for remediation (changes in teacher behavior) are generally required before mid-year termination of probationary teachers and almost always for continuing contract teachers for these types of deficiencies. It is not always required, but sound practice, to provide remediation opportunities for probationary teachers before a decision to terminate at the end of the contract period is made (Kemerer & Crain, 2010).

Almost every state (Kansas is the only exception) has statutes that outline reasons for the termination of a teacher's contract (Frey, 2010). Terms such as *insubordination*, *neglect of duty*, *immorality*, *incompetence*, and *just cause* are common threads in many state statutes (Frey, 2010). For example, Missouri state law empowers local boards of education to terminate the employment of continuing contract teachers for incompetence, inefficiency, insubordination, excessive absence, or conviction of a felony (RSMo 168.144). This section discusses these criteria in more detail.

INSUBORDINATION *Insubordination* can be defined as the willful and deliberate defiance of reasonable school rules or the reasonable directions of a person in a supervisory capacity. Insubordination may be the easiest of the grounds for dismissal to define and document. The teacher or subordinate either obeyed a rule or order or disobeyed it (Rossow & Tate, 2003). However, employees can be insubordinate if they refuse to comply with a directive that relates to their job description. For example, a third-grade teacher who refused to supervise recess would be insubordinate, whereas a custodian who refused the same directive would not be refusing a directive related to her job description (Rebore, 2011). Naturally, employees would not be expected to follow a directive that may be illegal, is discriminatory, puts students in danger, or violates the constitutional or statutory rights of others.

NEGLECT OF DUTY Excessive or unreasonable absence from work can be substantiated only by a board policy that defines what is meant by *excessive absence*. A documented pattern of absences from work over a period of time will most likely suffice as long as the employee does not suffer from a disability covered by the Americans with Disabilities Act as Amended (Rebore, 2011).

INCOMPETENCE *Incompetence* requires that the teacher demonstrate an inability to perform the duties required by the teaching contract. This may be the most difficult cause to document (Rebore, 2011). A charge of incompetence usually requires more than one incident of ineffective or substandard performance. However, a properly documented number of bad days or lessons can serve as the basis of a charge of incompetence. In other words, repeated documentation of incidents that clearly show deficiencies in the teacher's job-related performance is usually necessary to justify incompetence. In addition, incompetence is usually considered a remediable offense. Consequently, many (if not all) states require that a remediation plan and an opportunity for the teacher to rectify any deficiencies be implemented before the recommendation for termination. One area that is frequently included in a charge of incompetence is failure to properly maintain classroom discipline (Rossow & Tate, 2003). A deficiency in classroom management may be the easiest to document. However, it is important to note that having an occasionally disruptive class may not qualify as incompetence.

In a review of recent litigation involving challenges to incompetence, Rossow and Tate (2003, p. 26) conclude that (1) incompetence is whatever the board of education says it is, as long as an objective measurement can be demonstrated; (2) a period of remediation with the administration providing resources to help the teacher is necessary; (3) once a teacher has established himself or herself as an effective teacher with a record of positive evaluations, it may be more difficult to demonstrate incompetence; and (4) a pattern and reasonable forecast that the teacher will not improve is often necessary when teachers have established a positive evaluation record. In short, the dismissal of a continuing contract teacher for incompetence can be difficult.

IMMORAL CONDUCT It is difficult to dispute the right of a public school district to regulate the job performance of public school teachers. It is also difficult to argue that teachers are not role models. In fact, teachers have great potential to influence, either positively or negatively, the lives of the students entrusted to their care. Typically, moral fitness or *immorality* is a judgment call by the board of education (Rossow & Tate, 2003). A Missouri Court of Appeals advanced a good working definition of immorality as follows:

> Immoral conduct (is) contemplated behavior sufficiently contrary to justice, honesty, modesty or good morals, or involving baseness, vileness or depravity so as to support the inference that the teacher understands the conduct to be wrong. (*Youngman v. Doerhoff,* 1994)

Certainly, some forms of behavior, such as the commitment of felonious acts, sexual relationships with students, or possession of child pornography, should justify termination from public school employment. The problem, of course, is in defining *immoral conduct* in less clear-cut situations. However, the nexus principle provides some legal guidelines. The *nexus principle* can be defined as demonstrating a relationship between the behavior in question and the teacher's professional responsibilities and teaching effectiveness. The nexus principle was first outlined by the California Supreme Court (*Morrison v. Board of Education,* 1969). A California public school teacher was terminated because of an alleged single homosexual incident. As part of this decision, the court pointed out that no evidence had been presented that the single incident in question had negatively affected the teacher's ability to teach or interfered with the efficient operation of the school. Although not every jurisdiction requires a nexus as outlined in *Morrison,* the concept of a relationship between the behavior and fitness to teach has gained considerable support among most courts attempting to find the balance between the rights of teachers and boards of education. The term *fitness to teach,* although broad, generally refers to a teacher's ability to maintain classroom discipline, the potential impact on students, and the impact on parental attitudes (Fulmer, 2002).

In an analysis of court decisions related to teacher termination for immorality or similar reason, Fischer (1999) found that many courts consider intent, foreseeability, and knowledge in determining a nexus between the behavior and fitness to teach. *Intent* refers to whether or not the act in question was deliberate. *Foreseeability* considers whether or not harm to students was a predictable result of the conduct in question. *Knowledge* refers to whether or not the teacher knew or should have known that the conduct would negatively affect his or her fitness to teach. In cases where the conduct meets all or some of these criteria, courts are more likely to support termination (see *Lehto v. Board,* 2008, and *Youngman v. Doerhoff,* 1994, as examples).

For example, providing alcoholic beverages to students would certainly qualify as an *intentional act.* Most school district policies may not have a specific rule that states, "Providing alcoholic beverages to students may result in termination of employment." However, the act of providing the beverages would have a *foreseeable* impact on a teacher's ability to maintain good order and discipline and would affect parental perceptions of the teacher. In addition, it should not take a legal scholar to understand that providing alcoholic beverages to underage students is against the law and could negatively affect almost anyone's definition of fitness to teach. Other behaviors, such as possession of illegal drugs or inappropriate sexual contact with a student, would clearly establish a nexus between the behavior and fitness to teach.

A misdemeanor arrest for prostitution or the solicitation of prostitution can be considered so morally offensive that it may be reasonable to terminate a continuing contract teacher. However, private gay, lesbian, bisexual or transsexual lifestyles are not cause for employee dismissal (Rebore, 2011). Rebore argues that although this lifestyle may be unacceptable to many in the community, these practices are displayed publicly on television and other media to such an extent that the impact on students has been nullified. However, advocating nonconventional lifestyles at school may put the employee at risk of termination.

JUST CAUSE, OR CONDUCT UNBECOMING A TEACHER These terms are catchall phrases in some state statutes. For example, some states (such as Arizona, Hawaii, Indiana, Maine, Massachusetts, New Jersey, New Mexico, and Virginia) use terms such as *good cause* or *good and just cause* as reasons for terminating teaching contracts. A few states (such as Iowa, Michigan, Montana, Ohio, Rhode Island, and Texas) have distilled reasons for termination of continuing contracts to such terms as reasonable and *just cause*, good cause, or good and just cause (selected from Frey, 2010). These terms are not without ambiguity. Texas, for example, defines *good cause* as follows: "For good cause as determined by the local school board, good cause being the failure of a teacher to meet the accepted standards of conduct for the profession as generally recognized and applied in similarly situated school districts throughout Texas." Other, less common reasons, such as cruelty (Illinois), dishonesty (Louisiana and Nevada), and brutal treatment of a pupil (Mississippi), are included in some state statutes (selected from Frey, 2010).

Appeals Process

Every state provides continuing contract teachers alleging wrongful termination with the right to request a hearing before an impartial tribunal. In some states (Arizona, Connecticut, Idaho, Iowa, Louisiana, Maryland, Mississippi, Missouri, Nebraska, and New Mexico, for example) the hearing is conducted by the local school board. In a few states the appeal may be presented to a hearing officer (Alabama, Colorado, Illinois, Kansas, New York, Oregon, and Washington, for example). Some states allow for the initial appeal to be determined by collective bargaining negotiations (selected from Frey, 2010). All states allow teachers to appeal a termination decision from the impartial tribunal or hearing officer to a state court with jurisdiction to hear their case.

Linking to PRACTICE

Do:

- Follow state law and school board policy.
- Know the difference between a remediable and a nonremediable behavior.
- Document, document, document.
- Consider failure to follow or meet the behavioral changes outlined in a remediation plan as the primary reason for termination recommendations (Kemerer & Crain, 2005). For example, the Eighth Circuit Court recently upheld the termination of a continuing contract teacher because of her failure to improve in certain areas in which she was repeatedly provided assistance by the district. In other words, she repeatedly did not meet the requirements of the remediation plan (*Shanklin v. Fitzgerald*, 2005).

Do Not:

- Undertake the dismissal of a continuing contract teacher lightly or for personal reasons.
- Jump to conclusions. There is a difference between poor judgment and immoral behavior.

INVESTIGATIONS OF EMPLOYEE MISCONDUCT

Respondeat superior is the doctrine that holds employers liable for employees' wrongful acts committed within the scope of employment (Garner, 2006). In the context of school leadership, this concept means that the failure to adequately supervise employees and investigate alleged misconduct can result in a charge of negligent supervision or retention. Consequently, allegations of employee misconduct should be thoroughly investigated. Investigating allegations of employee misconduct is not easy. But, a careful investigation serves as the foundation for effective documentation and justification for any action taken. It also demonstrates that the administrator has not been careless, negligent, or deliberately indifferent to potential employee misconduct.

The procedural due process rights (and other Constitutional rights) of the teacher or other school employee being investigated should always be honored. The U.S. Supreme Court has established that public school employees facing disciplinary action have the following due process rights: (1) oral or written notice of the charges, (2) an explanation of the evidence on which the charge is based, and (3) an opportunity for the employee to present his or her side of the story (*Loudermill v. Cleveland Board of Education*, 1985). In addition, some school boards may have a negotiated working conditions agreement. This agreement becomes board policy when accepted by the board. Consequently, a careful examination of the agreement further ensures that the investigator does not violate board policy. Further procedural due process varies somewhat from state to state and is generally outlined in state law and school board policy.

Some fundamental guidelines do exist regardless of state law or negotiated agreements. First and foremost is the importance of not delaying beginning an investigation. Do not assume guilt. However, failing to investigate after becoming aware of allegations or rumors of sexual misconduct, teacher-on-student sexual harassment, or other serious allegations may place the administrator and district at risk of liability for a failure to adequately supervise employees (Kemerer & Crain, 2010).

The importance of a fact-based approach that protects the due process and privacy rights of the possible student–victim and the employee cannot be underestimated. A failure to protect both the student and the employee may also place the administrator and the school district at risk of liability. Kemerer and Crain (2010, pp. 2–7) recommend involving the parents or guardians of potential student victims as much as possible in the investigation of employee misconduct. This may seem somewhat risky, but it is probably better to have parents as partners than to have them find out later that their child was the victim of employee misconduct.

Most states allow for the suspension with pay of employees accused of serious misconduct pending the outcome of an investigation. Evidence of employee sexual misconduct is almost always grounds for immediate termination of employment. Less severe misconduct may result in suspension with or without pay, a reprimand, and/or a remediation plan. Once the investigation has been concluded warn the employee of retaliation. Retain all documentation. These documents should not be inserted in the employee's file because (1) there is a possibility of reprisal by the employee, (2) it is difficult to excise personally identifiable information under FERPA, and (3) some of the information gathered may be misleading or false (Kemerer & Crain, 2010).

Resignation, Nondisclosure Agreements, and Defamation

"The answer to every school administrator's prayer in making difficult personnel decisions is a voluntary resignation" (Kemerer & Crain, 2010, p. 1–22). The authors may be correct. Resignations work to everyone's benefit. However, it is important to avoid bullying, coercion, or duress in an attempt to force a resignation. Do not attempt to make an employee's time at school so unpleasant that she or he will have no choice but to resign. Although anyone may file a grievance, these actions may spell trouble for the administrator. For example, an employee could claim that the supervisor's behavior created a hostile work environment and seek redress from EEOC. If the employee is a member of a protected class, than an appeal to OCR is possible. It is also possible for a court to find bullying, coercion, or duress in an effort to force a resignation or more seriously the fabrication of a reason or animus toward the employee a form of intentional tort. An intentional tort generally requires that the supervisor intends the consequences of the act (*Staub v. Proctor Hospital*, 2010). In other words, intentionally bullying or making life miserable for an employee may be a form of intentional tort.

Some simple recommendations from Kemerer and Crain (2010) include:

1. Consider having a witness present when discussing the option of resigning with an employee.
2. Allow the employee to have an attorney or union representative with her or him. However, make it clear that the representative is there only to advise and represent the employee. The representative should not be allowed to question the administrator's findings or take over the meeting.
3. Advise the employee of applicable school district grievance and due-process procedures.
4. If the evidence indicates that the employee has been involved in sexual misconduct, committed a felony, or other serious misconduct defined by state law, inform the employee that action against her or his teaching certificate may be undertaken.
5. Require the employee to submit the resignation to a person authorized to receive it and to acknowledge its receipt.

In an effort to expedite the exit of an employee accused of serious misconduct with as little negative publicity and political fallout as possible, some districts may be tempted to enter into a *nondisclosure* agreement in exchange for the resignation of the accused (or guilty) employee (Mawdsley & Permuth, 2003). A nondisclosure agreement generally includes a neutral letter of recommendation and a restriction on the part of the district on the disclosure of the charges that led to the resignation in the first place. However, nondisclosure agreements create several problems including potential liability on the part of the district for violating the nondisclosure agreement (see *Pierce v. St. Urain Valley School District*, 1999). More importantly, school districts where the employee is applying for job may face a difficult task obtaining accurate data when another school district enters into a nondisclosure agreement with an employee (see *Shrum v. Kluck*, 2001).

In a recent study of 15 cases in 11 states of individuals with present or past histories of sexual misconduct, the U.S. Government Accounting Office (GAO) (2010) found that several factors contributed to the hiring or retention of individuals with histories of sexual misconduct:

1. ***Resignation:*** In four of the cases investigated by the GAO, school officials allowed teachers who would have been subjected to disciplinary action for sexual misconduct to resign. These teachers were able to truthfully inform other school districts that they had never been fired from a teaching position. In three of these cases, the district provided positive recommendations for the individuals.

2. ***Nonexistent preemployment criminal history checks:*** In 10 of the 15 cases, school officials did not perform preemployment criminal history checks.

3. ***Inadequate criminal history checks:*** Many criminal history checks may not be adequate because they are not national fingerprint-based checks.

4. ***Ignoring red flags on employment applications:*** Several districts failed to follow up on missing or troubling responses to questions on the employment application.

Employees who engage in sexual misconduct are likely to engage in similar conduct in the future. School districts should take care not to enter into non-disclosure agreements, provide false positive letters of recommendation, fail to check references, fail to adequately complete background checks, or ignore missing information on employment applications.

Virtually every state has laws requiring school district employees to report signs of sexual abuse to state child protective services. Several state legislatures have attempted to outlaw nondisclosure agreements. The Missouri state legislature was the first to pass legislation with the intent of breaking the code of silence on nondisclosure agreements. A recently passed law requires school districts to disclose allegations of sexual misconduct to other school districts when responding to a potential employer's request for information regarding the employee (RSMo 162.068). The law requires the disclosure of whether or not the employee was terminated or chose to resign. A failure to disclose allegations of sexual misconduct may result in liability for damages caused by that failure. This type of law effectively bans nondisclosure agreements.

Defamation

Administrators are often concerned that a frank reply to inquiries about former employees from other school districts might subject them to a *defamation* lawsuit. In this context, defamation is defined as the "act of harming the reputation of another by making a false statement to a third person" (Garner, 2006, p. 188). The terms *libel* and *slander* are different forms of defamation that are often used interchangeably. *Libel* is commonly used to describe written defamation. Defamation that is spoken is *slander*. For some reason, defamation that is broadcast through the media is referred to as libel rather than slander. According to Taylor (2002), in order to meet the definition of *defamation* (either libel or slander), the action or words must be demonstrated to (1) be false, (2) be published, and (3) damage or injure a person's reputation, business, or profession.

In a legal sense, any statement that is true is not defamatory. Therefore, courts have granted *qualified immunity* to school leaders when these individuals are acting in good faith. Good faith requires that the communication be done without malice, with reasonable grounds, in answer to inquiry, and with regard to assisting or protecting the interests of either party or as a duty to society (Alexander & Alexander, 2012). A supervisor's negative comments about a teacher's job performance as part of a board of education consideration of employment would be protected as long as the statements are objective, within the scope of employment, tied to performance standards, communicated without malice, and made in response to inquiries by board members. This speech may not be protected, however, if negative comments about a teacher are shared gratuitously and indiscriminately among anyone who will listen. The same criteria can be applied to reference letters or telephone inquiries from other school districts. The best protection, however, is to stick to the truth and obtain the employee's permission to release information to potential employers before the employee leaves the district (Kemerer & Crain, 2010).

Linking to PRACTICE

Do:

- Always base comments regarding the professional competency of teachers and other staff members on factual information.
- Use data and written reports such as formative and summative evaluations and remediation plans to document information shared with superiors regarding the professional competency of teachers and other professional staff.
- Consult a school attorney *before* entering into a nondisclosure agreement.
- Properly investigate and document alleged misconduct to eliminate the need for nondisclosure agreements by providing justification for contract termination or other adverse employee actions.
- When entering into a nondisclosure agreement, take measures to ensure that individuals with a need to know understand and abide by the agreement. Insist that all inquiries from the media or local

citizenry be referred to school district legal counsel.
- Always check references before making a final decision on potential employees. Short cuts in reference checking of potential employees are a recipe for disaster.

Do Not:

- Indiscriminately share negative personal feelings or evaluations of teachers and other professional staff.
- Allow personal feelings (either positive or negative) to interfere with professional judgment regarding teachers and other professional staff.
- Ignore warning signs such as unwillingness to elaborate, a similar nondescript reference from multiple contacts in the same district, or general letters of reference when checking references. Warning signs of past misconduct are usually present. *Ignore these signs at your own risk!*

COLLECTIVE BARGAINING AND NEGOTIATIONS

A 1960 New York City teacher strike led to the first collective bargaining agreement between a teacher association and a school board. Many states eventually passed public sector collective bargaining legislation that outlined the negotiation requirements and, in most cases, the impasse procedures to regulate negotiations between school boards and teacher groups. Currently, 35 states have collective bargaining laws (Colasanti, 2008b). *Collective bargaining* (or collective negotiations) occurs when employee representatives and employers (representatives of boards of education) formally discuss (and in some cases negotiate) terms of employment such as working conditions, salaries, and fringe benefits. The terms *collective negotiations* and *collective bargaining* are often used interchangeably. For clarity, this text will use *collective bargaining*. Regardless of terminology, whenever employees negotiate collectively with the school district, the employee group is essentially functioning as a labor *union* (Rebore, 2011).

Public school employee collective bargaining rights are controlled by state law and conducted at the school district level (Colasanti, 2008b). Some states, particularly in the South, have "right to work" laws. Right to work laws prevent collective bargaining agreements from requiring workers to join the union, pay dues, and otherwise support the union. These laws do not prohibit collective bargaining. For example, Florida, Idaho, Indiana, and Iowa have both a right-to-work law and a collective bargaining law for all public employees, including teachers. However, most states (Alabama, Texas, Georgia, Louisiana, and Mississippi are examples) that have right-to-work laws do not have public school collective bargaining laws. Most states (California, Idaho, Indiana, Kansas, and Maryland are examples) exclude superintendents and other managerial or supervisory employees from collective bargaining laws. In addition to the types of public school employees covered or excluded, all state collective bargaining laws detail scope of bargaining, impasse procedures, and the legality of strikes (Colasanti, 2008b).

SCOPE OF BARGAINING   Scope of bargaining (scope of negotiations) details which issues are negotiable under state law. The majority of state collective bargaining laws limit the scope of bargaining to wages, salaries, and working conditions. However, some collective bargaining laws allow teachers to bargain over curriculum development, teaching methods, textbook selection, class size, student discipline and budget appropriations (Indiana), grievance and disciplinary procedures (Kansas), fringe benefits (Minnesota), teacher preparation time and materials and supplies for classrooms (Nevada), and labor-management relations (North Dakota) (Colasanti, 2008b).

IMPASSE PROCEDURES   Impasse procedures outline the steps to be taken when a teacher union and a school district cannot agree on a resolution (Colasanti, 2008b). There are four basic types of impasse procedures: mediation, fact finding, arbitration, and strikes. *Mediation* is similar to the discourse ethics model presented in this text. A trained mediator meets with district and union representatives, seeks to understand the perspectives of both groups, and attempts to broker an agreement acceptable to both sides. Currently, 34 states make mediation available to districts and unions (Colasanti, 2008b). The only difference between mediation and *fact finding* is that in fact finding, an impartial panel attempts to broker an agreement between the district and the union. Fact finding is available in 29 states (Colasanti, 2008b). Mediation and fact finding are also similar in that a brokered agreement is not necessarily binding on the parties. *Arbitration* is a more formal process. A trained arbitrator meets with the two sides, collects information, and makes a decision. The arbitrator's decision is usually considered final. Arbitration is available in 21 states (Colasanti, 2008b). Strikes are the least common method of resolution and are prohibited in 22 states. Thirteen states (Alaska, Hawaii, Illinois, Minnesota, Montana, Nebraska, Ohio, Oregon, Pennsylvania, Rhode Island, Vermont, Utah, and Wisconsin) allow strikes (Colasanti, 2008b).

The Negotiation Process

A complete overview of the negotiation process is beyond the scope of this text. Interested readers or those preparing for district leadership are urged to contact their state school boards association (an affiliate of the National School Boards Association, www.nsba.org), their state administrator association (an affiliate of the American Association of School Administrators, www.aasa.org), and the state department of education for complete information. However, this section presents a general overview applicable to most negotiations between teacher unions and school districts.

The essential question in the negotiation process is, who bargains with whom, and for what? The first part of this question (who bargains with whom) concerns *recognition*. Rebore (2011, p. 298) defines recognition as "the acceptance by an employer (board of education) of some group or organization as the authorized representative (of teachers)." Exclusive recognition is the most common form of recognition in education and occurs when a single union represents all teachers. When two or more groups (AFT and NEA, for example) have members in the same school district, then the union that can demonstrate a majority of members becomes the *bargaining unit* (Rebore, 2011). The bargaining unit assumes the responsibility to represent all teachers regardless of union affiliation. The teacher union negotiation team is composed, of course, of teachers. The bargaining unit normally has bylaws or past practice that determines how the representatives are selected to bargain with the school district. In some cases, the state affiliate provides expert advice to the teacher team.

The board of education determines membership for the district team. Experience finds that in smaller school districts, the board of education usually selects two or three board members and the superintendent to represent the district. Larger districts may employ an assistant superintendent or director of personnel who leads the district bargaining team. Rebore (2011) recommends that the district team have at least one building principal elected by the other principals in the district to represent first-line administrators. It is Rebore's contention (and the author's experience) that many principals are critical of school boards (or their bargaining representatives) for "negotiating away" their authority. This is particularly true in today's environment where principals are held accountable for school performance scores.

The answer to the second part of the question, for what do people bargain, is the most difficult. All collective bargaining laws list the scope of negotiations. Salaries and fringe benefits (insurance, personal or sick leave policy, etc.) are relatively simple to define. The union naturally (and legitimately) attempts to bargain for the highest pay and greatest benefits. The school district attempts to maintain fiscal sanity and a balanced budget. At least, one would hope. However, there is little doubt that these divergent views can create considerable disagreement and sometimes long-simmering anger among the parties.

Some states use the term *working conditions* as part of the scope of negotiations. Working conditions are generally defined as "conditions that pertain to the quality of employment" (Rebore, 2011, p. 301). Examples listed by Rebore (2011) include class size and duty-free lunch. Working conditions may also create considerable animosity among the participants. For example, it is difficult to argue against a duty-free lunch for teachers. However, someone has to supervise the cafeteria and playground areas. The question then becomes, "Who should this person be?" The answer to this question is not the union's problem. There is little doubt that board members or members of the district negotiating team are not going to supervise playgrounds. Consequently, building administrators are the ones most likely required to develop a solution. It is at this point that principals in the district need representation on the district negotiation team. In short, even working conditions that seem on the surface to elicit general agreement are subject to considerable divergence of views.

A major concern of both teacher unions and boards of education centers around educational policy. Make no mistake, educational policy is about power. For the vast majority of states it is understood that educational policy is not subject to negotiations (Rebore, 2011). In fact, for all practical purposes, only boards of education are empowered to enact and enforce policy. However, it is virtually impossible to separate policy from working conditions. For example, assume a teacher union negotiates for reduced class size in middle school language arts, math, and science classes. On the surface this is a reasonable request. However, reducing class sizes requires sometimes considerable reallocation of resources, which of course is a policy function (Rebore, 2011).

Linking to PRACTICE

Do:

- The homework necessary for understanding the current contract, needed changes, and, if possible, the rationale behind the union's proposals. Seeking to understand the perspectives of the union can never be underestimated.
- Think long term. Similar to buying a house today with an interest-only loan, depleting the district reserve fund to reduce class sizes for this year with hopes of increased state funding or property taxes next year may not be a good idea.

- Explain your economic situation and bargaining goals simply and directly.
- Support your positions with research and facts.
- Remain positive. Never attack union representatives personally, engage in negative campaigning, or become discouraged. Focus on the solution, not the personalities.
- Think utilitarian ethics. The teacher union represents teachers and should legitimately attempt to obtain the best agreement for teachers. The district team, however, should pursue the greater good of all stakeholders in the district.

Summary

Selecting, supervising, and collectively negotiating with teachers and other employees are difficult but essential tasks. Knowledge of the legal rights of the school district, current employees, and potential employees is paramount in protecting all concerned. There are no excuses for short cuts, personal expediency, or personal biases in this important role of school leadership. In fact, it can be argued that proper employment procedures, supervision, and fair treatment of employees may be the most important undertaking of school leadership. This chapter has outlined basic principles of utilitarian ethics relative to employment practices, contract law, supervision and documentation, employment practices, and collective negotiations applicable to most situations. However, readers are urged to consult state law and local school board policy for a complete understanding of employment responsibilities in a particular state or district.

CONNECTING STANDARDS TO PRACTICE

SEALED WITH A KISS

Assistant superintendent Sharon Grey, Riverboat High School principal Tara Hills, and state school board member Patricia Wu were meeting to discuss the case of Michael Washington. Michael Washington, 22 and a graduate of RHS, was in his first year of teaching social studies at Riverboat High School. Sharon remembered Michael. He had not been a model student at Riverboat, but he had earned an academic scholarship to State University, where he was an excellent student. Tara found Michael to be a natural teacher and to have a friendly relationship with many students. Several veteran teachers had complained that Michael was a little too friendly and seemed more like a student than a teacher. Tara believed that some of the veteran teachers had a difficult time viewing Michael as a young adult and not as the sometimes recalcitrant high school student.

From what Tara and Sharon had gathered, Michael had met 18-year-old North High School senior Shelia Armstrong at a local gym where they shared a personal trainer. Michael and Shelia had immediately connected and had started to casually meet at the gym. They sometimes went together to the city mall. In late October, the relationship between Michael and Shelia escalated and resulted in consensual sex. Michael and Shelia did not make an effort to hide their relationship, but spent most of their time together in Capital City or at Michael's apartment. All was well until the day before the winter break. It was tradition in Riverboat School District for all schools to close at 1 p.m. on this day. Michael

usually stayed in his classroom and worked, but today he had a special date with Shelia, and he left immediately. As Michael walked to his car in the school parking lot that afternoon, Shelia was waiting with a large package. Shelia and Michael shared a kiss in the parking lot. Several veteran teachers and a number of students witnessed the parking-lot kiss.

Soon after the second semester started, the story of Michael and Shelia had taken on a life of its own. The relationship became the topic of conversation in the teachers' lounge, and several of Michael's students asked him about the relationship. One of the teachers in the district contacted the state education department. The state department turned the investigation over to a hearing officer. On May 1st, the hearing officer recommended the revocation of Michael's teaching certificate in spite of the facts that Shelia attended school in a different district, was an adult, and acknowledged instigating the initial sexual encounters. State school board member Wu was conflicted about the recommendation. She came to ask Sharon and Tara their opinion.

Question

Argue for or against the revocation of Michael's teaching certificate. Use the ISLLC standards, legal principles (the nexus principle, for example), and J. S. Mill's ethical principles of the greater good to justify your answer. Write a letter to state board member Patricia Wu explaining your viewpoint.

CHAPTER 12

Teacher Constitutional Law

INTRODUCTION

Once inside the schoolhouse door, public school teachers, like students, do not have the same rights they enjoy as citizens outside the school. At the same time, teachers are often expected to effectively communicate with a wide variety of publics. Finding the balance among encouraging teacher communication and interaction within the school and community, protecting the rights of teachers, and the legal obligation to provide an orderly and efficient school can be difficult. This chapter considers the ethical foundations for effective and efficient communication called for in the ISLLC standards and provides an overview of the legal rights and responsibilities of both teachers and school leaders.

FOCUS QUESTIONS

1. How can cooperative school cultures be developed?
2. Should school boards control the First Amendment rights of employees?
3. How much control over curriculum, instructional methodology, and classroom assessments should school boards have?
4. Should teachers and other professional school employees be required to submit to mandatory drug testing? To the search of their school district–issued cell phones?
5. Should school boards have the right to regulate or discipline teachers for their private associations?

KEY TERMS

Academic freedom

Matters of public concern

Mt. Healthy retaliation test

Safety-sensitive position

CASE STUDY

Good Teacher or Royal Pain?

Assistant Superintendent Danni Skyy was not looking forward to giving testimony in the case of former Rivendell elementary teacher Johnna Long. Two years ago, Rivendell Elementary principal Bill Sears had requested an additional special education teacher to accommodate the increased number of IEP students in his school. Johnna Long had applied for the position and seemed to be a perfect fit for Bill and the Rivendell staff. Johnna quickly gained the reputation of being a real advocate of special needs students at Rivendell. Unfortunately, she also chose to voice her complaints about Bill's leadership, the lack of clear objectives on IEPs, safety concerns for IEP students, and the lack of adequate facilities for IEP students to anyone who would listen, including parents.

Bill Sears had worked several years modeling a culture of cooperation and collaborative decision making at Rivendell. Consequently, he listened to Johnna's concerns. He had personally assessed the facility for safety concerns, reviewed the campus safety plan, and assessed the particular safety needs of special needs students. He asked the district special education coordinator to evaluate several IEPs and implemented her suggestions. Bill had dutifully communicated his review and conclusions to the faculty and had written a letter home to parents explaining the reason for the changes he was making. These efforts did not seem to placate Johnna, and during the last week of school she presented Bill Sears with a revised facilities plan complete with room changes to accommodate special needs children at Rivendell, the moving of several teachers' room assignments, and a revised lunch schedule. Johnna told Bill that several teachers had been involved in the revision and that she had the support of most of the staff. Bill had no knowledge of these discussions, and he told Johnna that he was not going to make changes this late in the school year.

Bill's response did not meet with Johnna's approval. At the end of her first year at Rivendell Elementary, she sent a 10-page letter to Assistant Superintendent Danni Skyy outlining her concerns and criticizing Bill Sears. Johnna's performance-based teaching evaluation during her first year was satisfactory. However, during the second year, Bill Sears begin describing Johnna Long as a "real pain." He also became more critical of her teaching performance. At the April school board meeting, Bill Sears and Danni Skyy recommended that Johnna's probationary contract not be renewed for the next school year. Johnna immediately contacted her union representative and the union attorney. Johnna complained that she had been retaliated against by Principal Sears and Assistant Superintendent Skyy for her efforts to protect and advocate for special needs students at Rivendell. The union attorney claimed that the district had violated Johnna's First Amendment rights and had unlawfully retaliated against her for her protected speech. Danni wondered how much of this was true.

LEADERSHIP PERSPECTIVES

ISLLC Standards 2A, 3D, 4B, 4C, and 4D

The importance of understanding and creating cooperative environments cannot be underestimated, as illustrated by **ISLLC Standards 2A, 3D, 4B, 4C, and 4D**. These standards stress the importance of nurturing and sustaining a culture of collaboration and trust, promoting an understanding and appreciation of the community's diverse cultural resources, and effectively communicating with families and caregivers. Consequently, efforts to include teachers and parents in the decision-making and school improvement processes at the campus and sometimes the district levels are becoming more common. **ISLLC Standard 3** stresses the importance of the efficient and effective management of school operations and facilities. As illustrated by the case study "Good Teacher or Royal Pain?" the question, of course, is at what point efforts to engage teachers and others in productive conversations become counterproductive to good order and efficiency.

> ISLLC Standard 3

The problem Bill Sears is facing in the case study is that not all communication from Rivendell teachers is positive. Bill Sears believes he is making a legitimate attempt to create a cooperative school environment by giving teachers more voice in the decision-making process. Most certainly, concerns about safety and problems with IEPs are to be taken seriously. **ISLLC Standards 2B, 2C, and 3C** require that he recognize that some of Johnna Long's concerns may be legitimate. Bill Sears has an obligation to "monitor and evaluate the management of operational systems." He has, at least on the surface, met these standards by investigating safety planning for special needs students and seeking help from the district special education director in evaluating the IEP process. As noted in Chapter 11, school boards may elect not to renew a probationary teaching contract for any reason as long as it does not violate the legal rights of the employee. At the same time, one of the basic tenets of ethical behavior (as well as due process) is fundamental fairness. The U.S. Supreme Court has recognized that teachers have a special insight into the problems facing schools and that the legitimate expression of these concerns should be protected speech (*Pickering v. Board of Education,* 1968). The Court has also found that an interest in maintaining good order and discipline outweighs some teacher rights (*Connick v. Myers,* 1983; *Garcetti v. Ceballos,* 2006).

> ISLLC Standards 2B, 2C, and 3C

> ISLLC Standard 3A

The problem is, as the case study illustrates, at what point does the speech or behavior cross the line from protected speech to speech that is not protected? How can school leaders facilitate the positive internal and external communication necessary to promote the development of positive family and community relationships while maintaining good order and efficiency? How can school leaders consider and evaluate the potential moral and legal consequences of their decision-making? The discourse ethics of Jürgen Habermas (1990) provides guidance in balancing these responsibilities.

> ISLLC Standard 5D

DISCOURSE ETHICS: PROMOTING A COOPERATIVE SCHOOL CULTURE

Common sense suggests that school leaders are required to understand, address, and solve problems they will encounter on the job. A significant part of the context of problem solving is the fact that the way problems are presented to school leaders frequently reflects a predefined solution from the frame of reference of the problem presenter (Copland, 2000). For example, in the case study "Good Teacher or Royal Pain?" Johnna Long has presented Principal Bill Sears with a predefined solution to what she considers a problem with the particular safety needs of special needs students. As Copland (2000) points out, the problem framing of Johnna Long in the preceding example may be absolutely correct. The fatal mistake occurs in rejecting or embracing the predefined solution before the problem has been clearly defined. **ISLLC Standard 2** calls for school leaders to recognize the conflict inherent in these types of problems and, rather than rejecting or embracing a predefined solution, to reframe the problem in solution-free terms.

In his book *Moral Consciousness and Communicative Action* (1990), the contemporary philosopher Jurgen Habermas proposes several rules of discourse as a *procedure* for reframing problems in solution-free terms and testing the soundness of actions or decisions that are being proposed for adoption. These rules are not rules in the traditional sense. Rather, they are designed to provide a framework or set of guidelines for the negotiation of conflicts in a fair and non-defensive manner (Rebore, 2001, 2003). Rebore (2001, 2003) makes a distinction between mediation and arbitration that provides guidance in the development of a conceptual framework that promotes the types of communicative action necessary for the reframing required of ill-structured problems.

The practical use of discourse ethics considers the difference between mediation and arbitration (Figure 12–1).

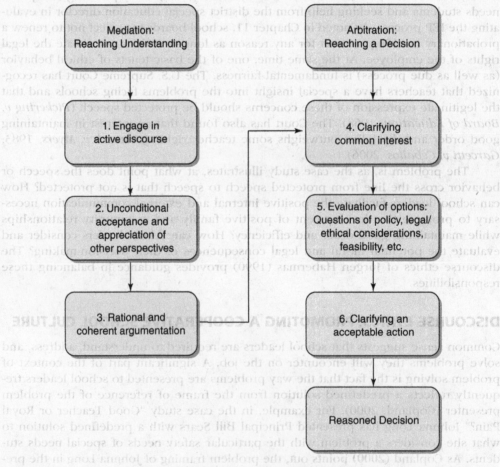

FIGURE 12–1   Discourse ethics: Resolving questions of conflicting interests.

In this model, the concepts of mediation and arbitration are combined to outline a communication model. Mediation is the process of seeking to understand the perspectives of others (Rebore, 2001). Understanding the perspectives of others requires an element of unconditional acceptance, meaning that all views presented as part of the discursive efforts must be accepted as valid. Acceptance in this sense does not necessarily mean agreement (even though agreement is entirely possible), but rather the unconditional acceptance of these views as valid interpretations of the values, needs, and wants of the speaker. Thus, mediation is particularly important because it is by nature designed to facilitate the introduction of empathy into the process of coming to a decision (Habermas, 1990). The value of seeking to understand the perspectives of others as a leadership skill cannot be underestimated. These efforts are particularly important in conversations involving teachers, school leaders, and parents.

Arbitration is the process of selecting from alternatives to reach an acceptable compromise (Rebore, 2001). Whereas mediation is designed to lead participants to clarify a common interest, arbitration may be viewed as negotiating a compromise by striking a balance between competing interests. Of course, if all participants in the conversation are in agreement, the process of forging a compromise may not be necessary. However, this may not always be the case, and several **ISLLC standards, most notably 2A**, call for school leaders who are skilled at creating collaborative environments.

ISLLC standards, most notably 2A

School Cultures and Levels of Cooperation

In schools where cooperation among school leaders, teachers, parents, and others is the norm, participants generally accept the perspectives of others and work collaboratively to solve common problems. Conversely, in schools where collaboration is not the norm, individuals often seek to exert their influence through force or manipulation (Habermas, 1990). The case study "Good Teacher or Royal Pain?" is an example. Rather than continuing to work collaboratively with Bill Sears, Johnna Long is using her community connections and critical letter to the assistant superintendent to influence and possibly force Bill Sears into a decision he may not wish to make. Table 12–1 describes these dimensions of cooperation and serves as a method of analysis of levels of cooperation in the school culture.

Table 12–1 can be used to assess current levels of cooperation in a school or district. For example, a Quadrant 1 school or district is characterized by a strong administrative hierarchy. In these schools and districts, policy decisions are made at the appropriate bureaucratic level and passed down, usually in written form, to subordinates with little explanation. With little stakeholder input or understanding of the rationale behind the decision, compliance by coercion is often necessary. A Quadrant 4 school or district is characterized by continuous efforts to reach understanding and consensus before a final decision is made at the appropriate level. In contrast to a Quadrant 1 school, policies developed in this manner are characterized by general understanding of the rationale, and little if any coercion is required for compliance.

Rivendell Elementary in the case study "Good Teacher or Royal Pain?" may represent a Quadrant 3 school. It is apparent that as principal, Bill Sears is making an effort to improve communication. However, at least in this particular incident, Bill's efforts at open communication have failed to satisfy Johnna Long. Consequently,

TABLE 12–1	School Culture and Levels of Cooperation			
		Low Cooperation		**High Cooperation**
Culture of authoritarian leadership	**QUADRANT 1**	• System design with little thought to lifeworlds • Decisions made from administrative hierarchy • Little or no effort to create consensus for decisions • Imbalance of power particularly evident • Little understanding built into the decision-making process • Parents and others viewed as adversaries	**QUADRANT 3**	• Fragmented lifeworlds evident • Occasional attempts at forging consensus • Sense of "going through the motions" to validate administrative initiatives common among stakeholders • Imbalance of power evident. Expectations that subordinates "toe the party line" common • Parents and others not usually considered
Culture of cooperative leadership	**QUADRANT 2**	• Systems fragment school lifeworlds • Various subgroups or cliques evident (may include administrative subgroups) • Cooperation within subgroups high; low between subgroups • Efforts to forge consensus ineffectual • Subgroups often work at cross purposes or strategically to influence decisions	**QUADRANT 4**	• Systems designed to facilitate meaningful lifeworlds • Collective efforts to build understanding and empathy as precursor to consensus common • High level of teacher/parent and leader/parent conversations • Teachers, parents, and others viewed as full partners

Johnna is working strategically with other school and community subgroups to undermine Bill's authority.

Linking to PRACTICE

Do:

- Train faculty and staff in the use of a cooperative school culture development model such as the one presented in this chapter.
- Start each meeting with a quick review and clarify what stage of the process will

serve as the focus for the meeting (Compton & Nance, 2002).
- Clearly define the roles, parameters of decision making, and any restriction on communication with others outside the committee meeting.

THE CONSTITUTIONAL RIGHTS OF TEACHERS

ISLLC Standard 2 ▸ School leaders are required by law and **ISLLC Standard 2** to promote efficient practices in the management of students and teachers to maintain a facility conducive to teaching and learning. The ISLLC standards also call for school leaders to model and promote effective communication. The problem is that meeting one standard may at times seem to violate the other. Regardless of this difficulty, understanding of personal managerial and leadership responsibilities is part of being an effective school leader.

There is little question that to maintain good order and efficiency, school districts need some leeway to regulate the conduct of employees. Consequently, boards of education have traditionally been given wide latitude to regulate teacher speech, choices of curriculum, and behavior while at school. There is also little debate that teachers serve as role models and, fairly or not, are often held to a higher standard in their personal lives than members of some occupations. Consequently, balancing the rights of teachers with the interests of the larger society, usually represented by parents, boards of education, and state legislative bodies, is a difficult but necessary responsibility. This chapter considers the responsibility to maintain good order and efficiency and employee First and Fourth Amendment rights.

FIRST AMENDMENT RIGHTS

Three general categories of public employee First Amendment rights are discussed here, including academic freedom, freedom of expression, and freedom of association.

Academic Freedom

The concept of *academic freedom* as a First Amendment right was established by the U.S. Supreme Court in *Keyishian v. Board of Regents* (1967). This case involved a New York state loyalty oath with a genesis in the McCarthy Red Scare era that limited teachers' freedom of association. The law allowed the dismissal of state public school employees who spoke "treasonable" or "seditious" words. In overturning this law, the Supreme Court spoke eloquently of the classroom as a "marketplace of ideas," of not "casting a pall of orthodoxy over the classroom," and of the importance of the vigilant protection of constitutional freedoms in America's classrooms. During the 1960s and '70s, courts continued the *Keyishian* trend toward protecting teachers from many restrictions and requirements imposed by school board authority. For example, the First Circuit Court recognized and supported a teacher's right to assign an article from the *Atlantic Monthly* magazine that discussed protest and radical thinking of the day (*Keefe v. Geankos,* 1969).

Since the 1980s, however, this trend has changed, and the elegant rhetoric of *Keyishian* does not reflect reality. In fact, since *Keyishian*, the U.S. Supreme Court has been relatively silent on what level of protection, if any, should be accorded teachers' expression in the classroom (Daly, 2001). Two student cases, *Bethel School District v. Fraser* (1986) and *Hazelwood v. Kuhlmeier* (1988), however, have been regularly applied to teacher classroom speech. The application of these two cases to teacher instructional decisions balances toward school district control. For example, academic freedom does not protect teachers from discipline or termination for showing R-rated films (see, for example, *Fowler v. Board of Education of Lincoln County Kentucky,* 1987; *Krizek v. Cicero-Stickley Tp. High School,* 1989; and *Borger v. Bisciglia,* 1995). Similarly, the selection of plays or choice of music for student performances is not protected by the First Amendment. For example, the U.S. Fourth Circuit Court of Appeals, citing *Hazelwood v. Kuhlmeier* (1988), found that school administrators, not individual teachers, may decide curricular matters, including the selection of a school play (*Boring v. Buncombe County Board of Education,* 1998). The Eighth Circuit Court, citing *Bethel v. Fraser* (1986), overturned a jury verdict and held that a "school district does not violate the First Amendment when it disciplines a teacher for allowing students to use profanity repetitiously and egregiously in their written work" (*Lacks v. Ferguson Reorganized School District R-2,* 1998, cert. denied).

District control may extend beyond the classroom and into the hallway. For example, the Western District Court of West Virginia upheld an administrator's directive to remove a list of banned books from a high school English teacher's classroom door (*Newton v. Slye,* 2000). For several years the teacher posted without incident a list of banned books on the outside of his classroom door. The teacher was informed that at least one of the books (*The Joy of Gay Sex*) on the 1997–1998 list of banned books was objectionable, and Newton was directed to remove the list from his door. Newton would be allowed to post the list in his classroom and continue his habit of discussing the list with his students. The district court, citing *Hazelwood* (1998), rationalized that the posting of the list was part of the curriculum and under the control of the school district. Teacher speech that runs counter to the educational mission of the school or curricular directives may also be subject to censorship. For example, a Los Angeles high school teacher, objecting to a district policy recognizing Gay and Lesbian Awareness Month, created a competing hallway bulletin board containing several antigay statements. The Ninth Circuit Court of Appeals reasoned that school bulletin boards are vehicles for conveying a message from the school district (*Downs v. Los Angeles Unified School District,* 2000).

The cases presented here are similar in that the selection of a curricular topic, instructional technique, or choice of words resulted in controversy and, in most cases, parental complaints. Current court decisions generally make it clear that curriculum and instruction decisions belong to the school district, not to individual teachers. This is particularly the case in those circuits that consistently apply *Hazelwood School District v. Kuhlmeier* (1988) to these questions and illustrates that teachers can be disciplined or terminated for violating district curriculum and instructional guidelines in the classroom and the hallway (Stader & Francis, 2003).

Freedom of Expression

The First Amendment comes into play when an employee contends that she or he has suffered adverse employment action (nonrenewal, firing, suspension, demotion, etc.) because of speech or expressive conduct that the school district claims to be disruptive to the workplace or has suffered retaliation for protected speech (Hudson, 2002). Respect for the rights of teachers to freely express their opinions about a large range of topics is inherent in the effective implementation of **ISLLC Standard 2A**. At the same time, authority to regulate teacher or employee speech that is disruptive to the learning environment or takes away from quality instruction and student learning must be in place. The balance between the rights of a teacher to express her or his opinion and the interest of the board of education in promoting harmony and efficiency to support quality instruction and student learning is often a matter of perspective. The U.S. Supreme Court has attempted to provide guidance in achieving this balance with the following cases: *Pickering v. Board of Education* (1968), *Mt. Healthy*

ISLLC Standard 2A

ISLLC Standard 3E

City School District Board of Education v. Doyle (1977), *Connick v. Myers* (1983), and most recently, *Garcetti v. Ceballos* (2006).

PICKERING V. BOARD OF EDUCATION (1968) In 1961, Marvin Pickering was dismissed by the Board of Education of the Township High School District 205 (Illinois) for sending a letter to a local newspaper regarding a recent tax increase initiative. In the letter, Pickering was critical of the manner in which the superintendent and board had handled past tax proposals. The Court held that *matters of public concern are protected speech*. The court reasoned that teachers as a class are the members of the community most likely to have information and opinions as to how funds are allocated and spent. Accordingly, it is essential that teachers be empowered to speak as citizens on matters of public concern without fear of retaliation. In a later case, protected speech was extended to include speech of public concern that is communicated privately to supervisors rather than spread publicly (*Givhan v. Western Line Consolidated School District,* 1979).

In *Pickering*, the Court also recognized the necessity of maintaining workplace efficiency and harmony. In an attempt to balance the protected interest as a citizen in making public comments and a school district's interest in promoting harmonious working relationships and efficiency in operation, the Court established the following three-pronged test, known as the *Pickering* balance:

1. Protected speech cannot interfere with maintaining either discipline by immediate superiors or harmony among coworkers.
2. Protected speech cannot interfere with the personal loyalty and confidence necessary to proper school functioning.
3. Protected speech cannot damage professional reputations.

MT. HEALTHY CITY SCHOOL DISTRICT BOARD OF EDUCATION V. DOYLE (1977) Doyle was a probationary teacher first employed by the Mt. Healthy district in 1966. In 1969, Doyle was elected president of the Teachers' Association. During his tenure as president, tensions between the association and the board escalated. Doyle also had several questionable incidents during his teaching career at Mt. Healthy, including making an obscene gesture at two girls who refused to follow his instructions in his capacity as cafeteria supervisor and the release of a school memo on teacher dress to a local radio station. Doyle was terminated by the board for "a notable lack of tact in handling professional matters." The statement was followed by references to the obscene-gesture incident and to the memo released to the radio station. After being terminated by the board, Doyle claimed that the release of the memo to the radio station was protected speech and his termination was a violation of his constitutional rights. The U.S. Supreme Court agreed with Doyle that the release of the memo was protected speech. The Court held, however, that if the district can demonstrate that a *teacher would have been terminated for reasons other than protected speech*, no violation of constitutional rights has occurred.

The *Mt. Healthy* **retaliation test** considers whether the protected speech was a motivating factor in an adverse employment decision or if the decision would (or could) have been reached for other legitimate reasons. For example, in *Mt. Healthy,* the school board cited both Doyle's protected speech and his questionable professional decisions as reasons for his termination. It is interesting to note that Doyle prevailed at the trial and circuit court. The U.S. Supreme Court reversed primarily because the circuit court failed to determine by a preponderance of the evidence that the board would, or could, have reached the same conclusions without considering the protected speech. This ruling not only has been beneficial to employees, but also has allowed school districts to claim the "*Mt. Healthy* defense." In short, the board of education claims they would have reached the same conclusion regardless of the fact that the protected speech may have pushed them over the edge. For examples of the *Mt. Healthy* retaliation test, see *Cockrel v. Shelby County School District,* 2001, and *Settlegoode v. Portland Public Schools,* 2004.

CONNICK V. MYERS (1983)   The U.S. Supreme Court further defined protected speech by holding that *matters of personal interest are not protected speech.* New Orleans assistant district attorney Sheila Myers was informed that she would be transferred to another area of responsibility. Myers refused to be transferred and she distributed a survey to coworkers addressing office policies. When Myers's boss found out about the survey, he fired her. The Court held that when an employee speaks on matters of personal interest rather than matters of public interest, a federal court is not the proper forum in which to review the wisdom of a personnel decision. In addition, it is not necessary for a state agency, such as a school district, to "clearly demonstrate" that the speech in question "substantially interfered" with efficiency and good order. Rather, the limited First Amendment interests of employees to address matters of personal concern do not require state agencies to tolerate action that can reasonably be related to disruption, undermining of authority, and/or destruction of close personal relationships necessary for the efficient operation of the campus or district. The Court held that state agencies (schools included) do not necessarily have to tolerate insubordinate or disruptive behavior, or behavior that undermines authority.

When considering an adverse employment decision for protected speech, courts often consider the *Pickering-Connick* balance. The *Pickering-Connick* balance requires a two-pronged test. The first prong considers two questions:

1. Does the speech address matters of public concern?
2. Can the teacher demonstrate that his or her free-speech interests outweigh the efficiency and harmony needs of the campus or district leadership?

The second prong of the *Pickering-Connick* test also considers two questions:

1. Does the speech impair discipline or harmony among coworkers?
2. Has the speech impaired close working relationships where personal loyalty and confidence are necessary?

Part of the problem is defining *matters of public concern.* Curriculum, school safety, negotiated contractual issues, and alleged malfeasance are usually considered matters of public concern (Stader & Francis, 2003). School districts can argue, however, that the employee is speaking about matters of personal concern rather than as a citizen on matters of public concern (Hudson, 2002). The questions facing school leaders and courts are, of course, (1) the definition of *matters of public concern,* (2) *how much disruption is necessary* before an employee's protected right to speak out on matters of public concern, either privately or publicly, impairs discipline or harmony among coworkers, and (3) at what point protected speech affects personal loyalty to the extent that it *interferes with close working relationships* between teachers and school leaders. For example, in *Pickering* the Court pointed out that Pickering's letter was received with a certain amount of boredom by almost everyone except the members of the board of education. In addition, the board was too far removed to assume any working relationship with Pickering, and his relationship with his immediate supervisors did not suffer. The case before the Court in *Connick* presented another situation. Myers's survey and her refusal to be transferred affected her working relationship with her *immediate* supervisors. *Fales v. Garst* (2001) and *Thompson v. Mt. Diablo Unified School District* (2003) are two examples of the application of the *Pickering-Connick* test to public school employees.

Personal loyalty and harmony between campus principals and district leadership has received special consideration by the courts when considering the *Pickering-Connick* balance. Consequently, courts generally side with the school district when disagreements between campus and district leaders result in an adverse employment decision, even when the speech can be viewed as protected speech. For example, the Seventh Circuit Court, in applying the *Pickering-Connick* test, found that as "a policy maker in the School District, [an elementary principal] owed her superiors a duty of loyalty" (*Vargas-Harrison v. Racine Unified School District,* 2001). The Sixth Circuit Court responded similarly by concluding that the interest of a "tension-free superintendent/principal relationship outweighed [principal]'s interest in trying to make himself look good at the expense of [superintendent]" (*Sharp v. Lindsey,* 2002).

GARCETTI V. CEBALLOS (2006) As part of his job as a deputy district attorney, Richard Ceballos was asked by a defense attorney to review a search warrant affidavit. After visiting the site and examining the affidavit, Ceballos expressed concerns about the affidavit to his superiors as well as members of the sheriff's department responsible for the warrant. Ceballos's concerns resulted in a heated meeting between members of the district attorney's office and sheriff's deputies. At trial, the defense attorney challenged the warrant affidavit. Ceballos testified about his concerns regarding the affidavit. In the aftermath of the trial, Ceballos claimed he was subjected to a series of retaliatory employment actions. Using the *Pickering* balance, the Ninth Circuit Court held that Ceballos's speech was protect. The U.S. Supreme Court chose to address the question of "whether the First Amendment protects a government employee from discipline based on speech made pursuant to the employee's official duties." In a fractured 5–4 decision, the court held that *speech made pursuant to the employee's duties is not protected by the First Amendment.* The court stated, "When public employees make statements pursuant to their official duties, the employees are not speaking as citizens for First Amendment purposes, and the Constitution does not insulate their communications from employer discipline. Ceballos wrote his disposition memo because that is part of what he, as a calendar deputy, was employed to do." The court reasoned that if Ceballos's supervisors thought his memo and testimony to be inflammatory or misguided, they had the authority to take corrective action.

The majority did recognize that "exposing governmental inefficiency and misconduct is a matter of considerable significance" and that public employers should "as a matter of good judgment be receptive to constructive criticism offered by their employees." The court went on to hold that this concept is reinforced by the powerful network of legislative enactments—such as whistle-blower protection laws and labor codes—available to those who seek to expose wrongdoing. Garner (2006, p. 777) defines a whistle-blower act as "a federal or state law protecting employees from retaliation for properly reporting employer wrongdoing such as violation a law or board policy, malfeasance, or endangering public health or safety."

Pickering, Mt. Healthy, Connick, and *Garcetti* Applied

In the introductory case study "Good Teacher or Royal Pain?" special education teacher Johnna Long has expressed concerns about a lack of clear objectives on IEPs, safety concerns for several special needs students, and the lack of adequate facilities for special needs students. Applying the *Pickering* balance, we can assume that the concerns expressed by Johnna Long are matters of public concern. A reading of the case study also does not indicate that her public expression of protected speech significantly interfered with Bill Sears's ability to manage the school or with good order or efficiency. The district could claim the *Mt. Healthy* defense and argue that Johnna Long was not a very good teacher. Because her deficiencies were documented by the school principal's formative and summative performance-based teacher evaluation, her contract would not have been renewed anyway. At this time, however, it seems that discussion of *Pickering* and *Mt. Healthy* may be moot.

Although *Garcetti* did not involve K–12 schools, an analysis of 11 recent court cases by Kallio and Geisel (2010) found overwhelming evidence that courts around the nation are applying *Garcetti* to teacher and administrator retaliation cases. Applying the *Garcetti* rationale to Johnna Long's speech would significantly shift the balance in favor of the school district. It would be reasonable to assume that her concerns about safety and a lack of adequate facilities were part of her job as a special education teacher. When teachers or administrators are speaking as a part of their job and not as private citizens, there seems to be little if any protection from retaliation by supervisors. Several examples of this logic include *Casey v. West Las Vegas Independent School District* (2007), *Almontaser v. New York City Department of Education* (2008), and *Williams v. Dallas Independent School District* (2010).

Social Media

Employee use of social media such as Facebook, MySpace, Xanga, Friendster, and so forth has become commonplace. It is clear that employees have some freedom to express themselves in social media. However, because the Internet provides a communication medium for content to travel inside the schoolhouse gate as well as into the homes of parents and students, the use of social media by school employees has created significant ambiguity and controversy (Nidiffer, 2010). Problems arise when postings affect the district. Public school employees are protected by the U.S. Constitution and do not lose all of their rights to freedom of expression. Consequently, balancing the First Amendment rights of employees to express themselves in social networking sites and the needs of the school district for efficiency, harmony, and good working relationships can be difficult. Generally, questionable use of social media by school employees may be analyzed along four lines of reasoning: (1) First Amendment, (2) the nature of the offending conduct, (3) the nexus between the conduct and job performance, and (4) school board policy and any collective bargaining agreements (Todd, DiJohn, & Aldridge, 2008).

FIRST AMENDMENT CONSIDERATIONS Courts generally apply the *Garcetti-Connick-Pickering* test to determine whether or not a teacher's speech posted on the Internet is protected by the First Amendment (Todd et al., 2008). If the speech is made pursuant to the employee's job description, it is most likely not protected under *Garcetti*, and the district may be free to discipline the employee without much problem. If the speech is not related to the employee's job description and is of personal concern, the speech falls under *Connick* and is not protected. If it can be established that the speech is not pursuant to the employee's job description and is a matter of public concern, courts should apply the *Pickering* balance. If the speech has no impact on good working conditions or personal loyalty or if the speech is of such importance that the need for good working conditions becomes secondary, it may be protected.

THE NATURE OF THE OFFENDING CONDUCT Postings that portray illegal activity or inappropriate conduct, such as communication of a sexual nature with a student, are not protected. These behaviors are not remediable (see Chapter 11), and immediate suspension while investigating the conduct and eventual termination are possible.

THE NEXUS BETWEEN THE POSTINGS AND JOB PERFORMANCE Most controversial postings do not portray illegal activity or inappropriate contact with students or others. In these cases, most courts would apply the nexus principle, usually defined as fitness to teach (see Chapter 11). It is possible that some controversial postings are remediable behaviors in that the employee may not realize that other employees, parents, and possibly students are reading the post. A simple directive to remove the postings and to refrain from similar activity may be in the best interest of the employee and the school district. However, other controversial posting may create such disruption to good order and discipline, harmony among the faculty, and personal loyalty and confidence that the behaviors are not remediable and termination is the only option.

For example, Jeffery Spanierman's employment was terminated for his MySpace conduct that was disruptive to the school environment (*Spanierman v. Hughes*, 2008). Specifically, his communication with students was similar to that of a peer rather than his position as a teacher and demonstrated an unprofessional rapport with students. In another example, Stacey Snyder was removed from her student teaching assignment for her unprofessional postings on MySpace (*Snyder v. Millersville University*, 2008). These two cases illustrate that teachers or other school employees can be terminated or disciplined for disruptive or inappropriate social networking speech even if the postings are created off-campus with personally owned computers.

SCHOOL BOARD POLICY, NEGOTIATED AGREEMENTS Postings that violate school board policy are grounds for termination. In addition, it is important to follow all due process rights and negotiated agreements while investigating employee misconduct.

Private Association

The U.S. Supreme Court has held that teachers' rights to association are protected (*Keyishian v. Board of Regents*, 1967). But what if the association might be at odds with the educational mission of the school or interferes with good order and efficiency in the school? A case involving a New York City science teacher illustrates this balance (*Melzer v. Board of Education,* 2003). Melzer had been a long-standing and active member of the North American Man/Boy Love Association (NAMBLA). Melzer's NAMBLA membership became an issue when a local television station aired a news story naming him as an association member. The school parents' association expressed outrage, and many parents threatened to remove their children from school and mount a protest if Melzer was allowed to return to work. In addition, a majority of the students in school spoke in opposition to Melzer's return. The board of education proceeded to terminate Melzer's employment. On appeal, the Second Circuit Court found that Melzer's right to associate with NAMBLA may be protected. The disruption to the mission of the school caused by his association, however, justified his termination.

Employees have private association rights. These rights are controversial only when students, parents, or community groups object. The problem is deciding when the association rights of the teacher outweigh the need to maintain good order and efficiency. Some decisions are easy. For example, it should not take a legal scholar to understand that membership in NAMBLA would interfere with good order and discipline. Not all decisions, however, are this simple. School leaders are often faced with substantive questions such as how much control they (or the school district) want in teachers' choices of private associations, who should decide, and how much disruption they (or the school district) can tolerate. For example, sexual minority teachers do not qualify as either a suspect or quasisuspect class, but are generally entitled to the same protections as any other identifiable group (*Romer v. Evans,* 1996; *Beall v. London City School District,* 2006; *Glover v. Williamsburg,* 1998, as examples).

FOURTH AMENDMENT RIGHTS

The Fourth Amendment ("The right of the people to be secure in their persons . . . papers, and effects, against unreasonable searches and seizures, shall not be violated . . . but upon probable cause") protects citizens from unreasonable search and seizure. Employees do not forfeit all of their Fourth Amendment rights when entering the schoolhouse gate. As in all other aspects of public schools and constitutional law, however, the courts have been asked to balance the rights of teachers and others in school with the needs of the school district to maintain order, safety, and efficiency. Consequently, courts have again carved out a compromise between the strict probable cause standard of the Fourth Amendment and the perceived needs of school officials to be held to a lesser standard to conduct reasonable searches of teachers and other school employees. The definition of *reasonable,* however, is open to debate.

The U.S. Supreme Court has not ruled on school employees' Fourth Amendment rights, and there are surprisingly few court cases involving a search by public employers of employees' offices, desks, computers, and so forth. As Nathan Roberts (2003) suggests, public school employees' Fourth Amendment rights may have best been outlined in *O'Connor v. Ortega* (1987). In *Ortega,* the U.S. Supreme Court established that the legality of public employee workplace searches would depend on the *reasonableness* of the search both at inception and in scope. In *Ortega,* the court held that

> ordinarily, a search of an employee's office by a supervisor will be "justified at its inception" when there are reasonable grounds for suspecting that the

search will turn up evidence that the employee is guilty of work-related misconduct, or that the search is necessary for a noninvestigatory work-related purpose such as to retrieve a needed file.

In other words, school officials should have at least a moderate chance that a search will reveal violations of school policy or criminal conduct before undertaking a search of employee property.

A Court of Appeals of Georgia decision concerning a principal's search of an employee's computer illustrates this point (*Joines v. State,* 2003). While a teacher at Fort Valley (Georgia) Middle School, Joines was convicted of three counts of child molestation. On appeal after his conviction, Joines claimed that the evidence found on his school computer by school personnel should not have been admissible in court. The court upheld the use of the evidence, reasoning that (1) the school principal received information from another teacher that prompted her to examine Joines's computer, (2) this information served as justification for her search in the first place, (3) after accessing Joines's computer, she found what she described as a Playboy-type Internet site, (4) this discovery justified contacting the school technology expert to investigate what was on the computer's hard drive, and (5) this investigation led to more incriminating evidence. Consequently, the search was justified at inception, it was reasonable in scope, and the principal was acting in her proper capacity. It would also seem logical to assume that evidence gathered in this manner could be used in school district discharge or disciplinary proceedings.

The U.S. Supreme Court recently applied similar logic to a SWAT police officer's pager owned by the city police department (*City of Ontario v. Quon,* 2010). The Court held that the search of the officer's text messages was reasonable at inception and in scope. The officer habitually went over the prescribed text message limit. A review of the text messages revealed several inappropriate text messages. The officer was terminated from his job.

Roberts (2003) concluded from his review of workplace searches that teachers and others should be put on notice that desks, computers, educational materials, school district-owned cell phones, and so forth are the property of the school district. This declaration creates a diminished expectation of privacy in those areas. Many, if not most, school districts require that employees (and students) sign an acceptable use policy (AUP) form before given access to district owned computers and networking. An AUP creates a diminished expectation of privacy, and searches of district-owned computers and cell phones would normally require only reasonable suspicion. Roberts concludes, however, that searches involving potential criminal activity or personal items such as wallets, purses, or briefcases should be held to the higher "probable cause" standard.

Linking to PRACTICE

Do:
- Include in school district policy and in AUP agreements information regarding district ownership of school computers and cell phones if applicable and the fact that these devices are subject to search.

- When making a decision to search a district computer or cell phone, follow the guidelines established in *O'Connor v. Ortega* (1987) or *City of Ontario v. Quon* (2010).
- Be sure that the scope of the search does not exceed the parameters established by the reason for the search in the first place.

Drug Testing

Courts have consistently recognized a board's authority to order drug testing of employees when reasonable suspicion of drug or alcohol use is present. *Hearn v. Board of Public Education* (1999) illustrates judicial support for reasonable-suspicion drug testing. Sherry Hearn was a veteran teacher. She was also very vocal in her opposition to the school's "zero-tolerance" drug, alcohol, and weapons policy. In April 1996, school administrators ordered a lockdown, and the campus security officer escorted the county law enforcement officer and a drug dog on a sweep of school property. During the search, the dog alerted on Hearn's unlocked car in the school parking lot. A search turned up a small amount of marijuana in her ashtray. Under school policy, Hearn had 2 hours to take a urinalysis test for drug use. She declined to do so without first consulting her attorney and was subsequently terminated for insubordination. A urinalysis test conducted the next day was negative, but the board refused to alter their position. The 11th Circuit Court was not impressed with Hearn's arguments for reinstatement. The court found that Hearn's car search was reasonable based on the probable cause generated by the dog sniff. Consequently, her refusal to submit to a drug test within the 2-hour time frame violated board policy and put her at risk of termination (Stader & Francis, 2003). Other courts have also supported reasonable-suspicion drug testing (see *Knox County Education Association v. Knox County Board of Education*, 1998, and *Young v. Board of Education*, 2003, as examples).

Random Drug Testing

The U.S. Supreme Court has established that random drug or alcohol testing by urinalysis may pass constitutional muster when an overriding state interest outweighs individual privacy rights. The catalyst for upholding suspicionless drug testing is typically a history or evidence of drug or alcohol use by the target population. Employment in a *safety-sensitive position*, however, substantially lowers the bar for determining the legality of suspicionless testing. *Safety-sensitive* basically means that the potential for harm caused by illicit drug or alcohol use is of such magnitude as to justify a compelling state interest in suspicionless testing. The test for *safety-sensitive* involves two questions: (1) Are the duties performed by the employee so fraught with risks of injury to others that even a momentary lapse of attention may have disastrous consequences, and (2) does a clear nexus between the nature of the employee's duty and the risk of injury exist (*Skinner v. Railway Labor Executives Assn.*, 1989)?

In 1989, the Knox County (Tennessee) Board of Education (KCBE) established a drug-free workplace policy that provided for the suspicionless drug testing of all individuals applying for a position in the district and all current employees transferred or promoted within the district. In 1991, the Knox County Education Association (KCEA) challenged the policy in district court. The United States District Court for the Eastern District of Tennessee struck down the policy, primarily on privacy and methodology issues.

The court, however, chose to answer the question of whether or not teaching qualifies as a safety-sensitive position. Considering the nature of teaching and the obligation to maintain a safe environment for students, the court answered the safety-sensitive question in the affirmative and included principals, teachers, traveling teachers, teacher aides, and school secretaries in its ruling. In addition, teachers were found to have diminished expectations of privacy because educators work in a highly regulated industry (state licensure requirements, mandated curriculums, etc.) and the care and safety of students is an inherent part of the job requirements. Consequently, the interest of the state in random or suspicionless drug or alcohol testing outweighs the privacy interest of the individual educator.

In 1994, because of the ruling establishing teaching as a safety-sensitive employment position, the Knox County Board of Education adopted a revised policy. The KCEA once again challenged the policy. The Sixth Circuit Court let the policy stand in its entirety. This finding was made in spite of the fact that there was no evidence of a history of substance abuse among teachers and other employees in the Knox County School District. In addition, the district could not produce any evidence that inattentiveness or negligence had contributed to safety concerns. It is difficult to argue, however, that teachers do not hold safety-sensitive positions, and the court had little problem justifying the constitutionality of the revised Knox County testing policies.

There would seem to be little if any societal and legal ambiguity regarding the rights of a school district to require the drug testing of any employee who demonstrates symptoms or characteristics of alcohol or illegal drug use that affect teaching performance or student safety. Random testing policies, however, may be more debatable. Courts for the most part seem to agree that the special needs test is satisfied in a school setting. This finding substantially lowers the bar for random testing. Therefore, if a random drug testing policy is well written, is minimally intrusive, and is handled with discretion, the policy may well stand in most circuit courts.

Linking to PRACTICE

Do:

- Have clear policies and procedures for reasonable-suspicion drug testing of teachers and other professional staff. The policy can be part of a negotiated agreement or adopted by the board of education.

- Use evidence to support random drug testing of school employees.
- Consider the impact on employee morale or general "utility" (see Chapter 6) before enacting random drug testing policies.

Summary

Finding the balance between the constitutional rights of public school teachers and the need for order, efficiency, and harmonious working relationships is sometimes difficult. Finding this balance requires an understanding of fundamental legal principles established by the various courts and the ethical obligations of fairness embedded in the ISLLC standards

addressed in this text. The courts have granted a wide range of authority to school leaders to regulate the speech, instructional options, and associations of public school teachers. The ISLLC standards, however, call for school leaders who are proficient at creating the types of cooperative school cultures where the voices of all stakeholders are heard.

CONNECTING STANDARDS TO PRACTICE

GOOD SPORT?

Sharon Grey looked at the superintendent as the board chairperson said, "I would like to hear what Ms. Grey thinks." Sharon paused to gather her thoughts. The April special session of the Riverboat School District Board of Education had only one agenda item, the case of Athletic Director Barnhart. As principal of Riverboat High School, Tara Hills had recommended that girls' volleyball coach Blanche Barnhart be promoted to the position of athletic director on the retirement of long-time AD Franklyn Smith. Coach Barnhart's appointment as athletic director was not without controversy among central office personnel. Business manager Fred Jones was the most vocal critic. In addition to the district budget, Fred was in charge of transportation, facilities management, and purchase orders. With the reluctant support of the superintendent, by a vote of 5–2 the board had approved Coach Barnhart as athletic director the previous May.

During the summer, Coach Barnhart revised the athletic budget to more equally distribute funds among the major boys' and girls' sports and had insisted that the boys' and girls' basketball teams equally share the varsity gym for practice times. There was some grumbling, but most coaches understood Coach Barnhart's reasons for the change. It had been traditional at Riverboat that the football team was allowed to leave far away Friday night games at 1 p.m. and travel by charter bus. Players were fed before the game at local restaurants at district expense. This practice created considerable animosity among the coaches of other sports and many teachers.

Starting in the fall, Coach Barnhart directed that the football team would now leave far away games at 3:00 p.m. in regular district-sponsored buses. The booster club would be responsible for feeding players at restaurants if that was their wish. It was at this point that Fred Jones began to routinely reject purchase requests for girls' athletics. As facility manager, he also arranged the bas-ketball practice schedule so that the boys' teams had access to the varsity gym immediately after school. Coach Barnhart arranged a meeting with Fred Jones, the superintendent, and Sharon Grey in early October. The meeting did not go well and ended in an argument.

In December, a local newspaper reporter presented to the superintendent and Fred Jones an open records request for all budget information broken down by sport that included anticipated revenue from the district, anticipated expenditures, purchase requests, actual expenditures, and projected balances at the end of the fiscal year. The reporter also requested documentation of practice schedules for all sports, transportation expenditures by sport, and other expenditures by sport. She had specifically asked for expenditures by sport for food and other "benefits."

Fred Jones and the superintendent were not happy. They believed that Coach Barnhart had contacted the reporter and told her exactly what documents to request. The superintendent had requested the special board meeting to discipline Coach Barnhart by removing her as athletic director and head volleyball coach at the high school and assigning her to teach middle school social studies. Coach Barnhart claimed (without acknowledging that she had contacted the reporter) retaliation for her protected speech.

Question

First, argue for or against the legality of the adverse employment decision affecting Coach Barnhart. Clarify the legal question. Cite ISLLC standards and legal principles of teacher First Amendment rights to support your argument. *Second*, argue for or against the recommendation based on ethical principles presented in this text. Write a memo to Assistant Superintendent Sharon Grey outlining your position.

CHAPTER 13

Law, Ethics, and Educational Leadership

Making the Connection

INTRODUCTION

This chapter presents examples from the ISLLC standards of the relationship between law and ethics. The chapter also provides examples of how knowledge of law and the application of ethical principles to decision making helps guide school leaders through the sometimes treacherous waters of educational leadership.

FOCUS QUESTIONS

1. How may ethical considerations and legal knowledge guide school leader decision making?
2. Why is it important to consider a balance between these two sometimes competing concepts?

CASE STUDY

So Many Detentions, So Little Time

Jefferson Middle School (JMS) was the most racially and culturally diverse of the three middle schools in Riverboat School District, a relatively affluent bedroom community within commuter distance of Capital City. Unfortunately, the culture of Jefferson Middle School was not going well. Over the past 5 years, assistant superintendent Sharon Grey had seen JMS become a school divided by an underlying animosity along racial and socioeconomic lines. This animosity was characterized by numerous clashes between student groups, between teachers and students, between campus administrators and teachers, and between teachers and parents. Sharon finally concluded that JMS was a "mess."

After much thought and a few sleepless nights, Sharon as part of her job description made the recommendation to the Riverboat school board to not reemploy Jeremy Smith as principal of JMS. Immediately after the board decision, Sharon organized a search committee of teachers, parents, and campus administrators and began the process of finding the right principal for JMS. The committee finally agreed on Charleston Jones. Charleston was a relatively inexperienced campus administrator but had impressed the committee with his instructional leadership knowledge, intelligence, and youthful energy. However, the job of stabilizing JMS was proving to be more of a challenge than anyone had anticipated.

Charleston had instituted a schoolwide discipline plan and had insisted that teachers and school administrators not deviate from the plan. However, he could sense that things were still not right. Animosity among student and parent groups remained just below the surface, ready to erupt at the slightest provocation. Clashes between teachers and students were still relatively frequent. Teachers still blamed one another, school administrators, and the school resource officer for a lack of order in the school. Change was not coming quickly to RMS, and Charleston understood that although school management had improved, several aspects of school culture were less than desirable. Student suspension rates remained high, and parental support was waning. As one of the assistant principals remarked after the umpteenth student referral, "So many detentions, so little time!"

Charleston felt the need to talk. He reached for the phone and made an appointment with assistant superintendent Sharon Grey. Charleston, surprised at Sharon's willingness to meet with him on short notice, confessed his concerns. "I'm not sure I'm cut out for this," he said. "Sure, discipline is better, but the suspension rates are still too high, administrators are spending way too much time on what I view as trivial problems, and we haven't made the progress on test scores that we should be making. It doesn't take much to create a crisis where students are bickering, parents are calling, and board members are questioning the superintendent. Teachers are still not happy and send too many students for administrative punishment. When this happens, teachers think we don't do enough, parents think we are too harsh with their children, and students complain that we never listen and always take the teacher's side. It seems like someone is always challenging some decision or another. I am here at 6:00 a.m. and often don't leave until later that night. I even spend some Saturday mornings here at school. The harder I work, the further behind I get. Well, you know the story."

Sharon simply replied with a laugh, "You haven't found the balance."

Sharon's simple response puzzled Charleston, and he hurriedly ended the conversation. Reflecting later that evening, Charleston muttered, "What in the world does she mean by 'finding the balance'? I don't get it. I guess I need to call back."

LEADERSHIP PERSPECTIVES

The role of campus or school district leader is not an easy job. Charleston Jones, Sharon Grey, and the other school leaders presented in the case studies throughout this text face difficult challenges that would test the abilities of even the most experienced and capable. Sharon Grey's answer to Charleston Jones, "Find the balance," is deceptively simple. Paul Begley (2004) defines *balance* as finding "an appropriate equilibrium between competing forces." Finding equilibrium, according to Begley, is particularly difficult in the environment in which today's school leaders function. A significant part of the problem, according to Begley, is that school leaders are constantly bombarded with multiple agendas. Policies and politics at the national, state, and local level, parent concerns, an increasingly diverse student population, accountability demands, and community views are just a few examples. The fact that many of these agendas have competing interests complicates matters even more. For example, as illustrated in Chapter 3, federal court rulings regarding religious expression in school can conflict with student and community values. And, as Chapters 4, 7, and 11 illustrate, the First Amendment speech rights of teachers and students sometimes create considerable conflict within a campus and community.

The legal system at the federal, state, and local level often provides guidance and should influence decision making. In fact, the legal system is in many ways designed to guide school leaders in finding the appropriate balance between the interests of the individual and the interest of the state in providing an efficient and safe school for children. Knowing federal, state, and local laws, policies, and regulations is an important part of effective school leadership. However, as this text has illustrated, knowledge of law does not always provide an exact or fixed answer to many of the dilemmas faced by school leaders (Sperry, 1999). This text is full of examples of choices made by teachers, principals, superintendents, and school boards that resulted in legal challenges. Although the vast majority of court decisions related to public PK–12 education are made in favor of the district, some of these decisions seem questionable at best. Consequently, adding ethical considerations to legal principles can give a deeper understanding of the implications of decision making on the greater school community (Rebore, 2001). This idea of adding ethical principles to knowledge of law is conceptualized in **ISLLC Standard 5D**. `ISLLC Standard 5D`

In Chapter 1, ethics was defined by three questions: (1) What does it mean to be a school leader? (2) How should the human beings in schools treat one another? (3) How should the educational institutions that we call *school* be organized? These questions, like Sharon Grey's answer to Charleston Jones, may seem simple. However, it is how these questions are answered that to a large extent determines and perpetuates the choices school leaders make when confronted with questions of competing interests. In other words, ethical principles force a consideration of why some action should (or should not) be taken (Rebore, 2001).

Finding the appropriate equilibrium between competing interests is particularly important when applying legal and ethical principles to decision making. The following concepts demonstrate a few of the competing interests illustrated in this text.

What's Legal and What's Right (or Wrong)

ISLLC Standard 5 calls for an understanding of how to promote educational fairness `ISLLC Standard 5` and apply legal principles to provide a safe, effective, and efficient facility. School leaders are required to promote school safety and organize the systems of the school to create an efficient organization. However, they must do so in a fair way that respects the rights of others. This dual role of guardian of fairness and overseer of safety and efficiency may be the most difficult of the balancing acts school leaders must face.

For example, school leaders are empowered by a variety of federal and state laws and school board policies to promote safety and efficiency. Courts are reluctant to overrule local administrative and school board decisions that promote safe schools (see *Wood v. Strickland*, 1975, for example). However, the understandable reluctance to substitute the views of federal and state judges for a local board of education's interpretation of policies places school leaders in a role that is unique in our society. For all practical purposes, school leaders and boards of education are the "law." There is little doubt that this unique situation facilitates the interests of the state in promoting efficiency and order in public schools. However, as a consequence, school leaders (especially campus leaders) must simultaneously serve the roles of chief investigator, prosecutor, judge, jury, and executioner (Sperry, 1999). In other words, the very individuals most responsible for protecting the rights of students, teachers, parents, and others are also the ones with the greatest opportunity to violate these rights. There is no substitute for a firm knowledge and understanding of legal principles, state law, and local school board policy in decision making to promote school efficiency and safety. There is also no substitute for fairness in the application of this authority granted to school leaders.

Policy and People

Fundamental to fairness is an understanding and appreciation for the balance between policy and people. According to Jürgen Habermas (1987), all social systems are composed of two worlds: a systemsworld (policy) and a lifeworld (people). The systemsworld consists of the management designs that provide for an effective and efficient facility. For example, the school schedule, rules against fighting and bullying, curriculum articulation, and school board procedures for grievance resolution are just a few of the policies necessary for a safe, effective and efficient educational program. School boards and school leaders are empowered by a variety of national, state, and local policies and laws to support systemsworld efforts to promote good order and school safety. For example, school leaders may suspend or expel unruly students, institute drug testing policies for participants in cocurricular activities, search student lockers, suppress speech by teachers and students on campus that is counter to the educational mission of the school, and terminate the employment of inefficient or ineffective teachers.

The lifeworld is represented by the normative behaviors and practices that define school culture. A positive culture reflects the type of cooperative environment articulated in **ISLLC Standard 4**. This text presents several ways of measuring the relative degree of cooperativeness of school culture. Regardless of the measure, a positive school culture provides students, teachers, and others with a sense of community and personal importance.

Both the lifeworld and the systemsworld are important. **ISLLC Standard 3C** is an example of this balance between people and the necessity for effective and efficient campus or district policies. However, the lifeworld and the systemsworld are in constant competition for dominance. A dominant lifeworld or systemsworld creates a dysfunctional culture that inhibits and stymies cooperative efforts to address the needs of all stakeholders. A dominant systemsworld creates a campus or district culture characterized by fractured relationships, anonymity, and loneliness. In a systems-dominated culture, policy is more important than people, creativity is marginalized, and most students and teachers do only the minimum required to stay out of trouble. Conversely, a lifeworld-dominated school culture is characterized by an undermining of control, an overattachment to the organization, and the ignoring of achievement goals and objectives (Habermas, 1987).

The point is this: Neither a systemsworld-dominant nor a lifeworld-dominant culture is conducive to the success of all stakeholders. The leadership challenge is to find a balance between policies and people to create a school culture that is not only effective and efficient, but designed to support positive interactions where fairness and a sense of acceptance, belonging, and importance are a normative part of school culture (Sergiovanni, 2000). This is a particularly difficult but necessary balance.

Order and Freedom

ISLLC Standard 3C calls for a "safe, efficient and effective learning environment"—in other words, order. **ISLLC Standards 5C and 5E** require school leaders to honor the rights of others by promoting equity, democracy, and social justice—in other words, freedom and equality. These values of order and equality are ingrained in American culture. They also often conflict, particularly in public schools. In fact, the conflict between freedom and order is at the base of many legal disputes between school districts and teachers, students, and parents. Student speech (especially student off-campus speech), the political speech of teachers, religious expression, and the rights of parents to control the education of their children are examples of the conflict between order and freedom common in schools across the nation. In an effort to balance the sometimes competing values of freedom and order, courts have consistently carved out a special niche for schools. The freedom-of-speech cases for students and teachers presented in this text exemplify this attempt to balance the freedom rights of students and teachers with the equally compelling needs of school leaders to maintain effective, efficient, and orderly schools.

The guidelines established in these cases, however, are often ambiguous. The challenge for school leadership is to find the proper balance in the individual and sometimes unique cases that arise. Some applications of these legal principles are relatively easy. For example, a teacher advocating illegal drug use or a student's profane tirade in a school hallway or classroom would clearly create disorder and run counter to the educational mission of any school. However, what about teacher or student speech that raises issues of racial inequality or the rights of sexual minority students? These issues can certainly create controversy. But, at what point, if any, should the speech be suppressed because of the controversy? At what point does student or teacher speech become a "substantial disruption"? Just exactly whose rights should student speech be required to collide with, and at what point does a teacher's right to speak on matters of public concern become disruptive of efficiency and order? In other words, when should the hecklers make policy? This is the challenge of finding the balance between order and freedom.

Privacy and Safety

School leaders have a legal responsibility and ethical obligation to keep schools safe. Public support for safe schools initiatives is strong. For example, a 2004 survey of adult parents of public school students in grades 5–12 found that 88% supported the establishment and enforcement of zero-tolerance suspension policies for serious violations (Public Agenda Foundation, 2004). At the same time, school leaders are expected to demonstrate a respect for the rights of students and teachers.

Balancing privacy and safety can be particularly difficult when making student or teacher search decisions. Again, the U.S. Supreme Court has created special rules governing searches of students and public employees. Recognizing the need for safety as a compelling state interest, these rulings substantially lower the bar for the legality of searches of persons and property on school grounds. However, American society and legal jurisprudence consider any search an invasion of privacy. The challenge is in finding the right proportionality among the need for a search, the rights of the individual, and safety. In other words, the balance between privacy and safety is not always as easy as it appears.

Equality and Inequality

Equality means fairness, impartiality, and evenhanded dealing (Garner, 2006). The concept of equality is addressed throughout the ISLLC standards. For example, all of the ISLLC standards include the phrase "An educational leader promotes the success of every student by. . .," **ISLLC Standard 5C** refers to "educational equity," and **ISLLC Standard 5E** uses the term "social justice." Regardless of the terminology, educational equity or fairness means a school community where all participants have a fair opportunity to the best basket of goods and services available to all others (Rawls, 2001). Examples of educational equity include ensuring that all participants have equal opportunity to benefit from technology resources, advanced courses, cocurricular activities, the best teachers, student support services, and learning resources.

Sometimes, advocating for the success of all students or for that of students with special and exceptional needs requires inequalities. According to John Rawls (2001), inequalities can be justified as long as any inequalities are to the greatest benefit of the least advantaged of the school community. For example, extra tutoring to allow a traditionally underrepresented subgroup of the school community to be successful in advanced courses is justifiable as long as an equal opportunity to enroll in the courses has been integrated into the school culture. This is an important point. The justification of inequalities is subservient to fair equality of opportunity. In other words, providing extra help for students who do not have a realistic chance of enrolling in advanced courses in the first place violates the basic principle of equality.

It is rare for teachers, parents, and school leaders to openly advocate excluding certain individuals from educational opportunities. Consequently, the conflict generated by equality and inequality comes in a variety of disguises. Sometimes better-educated and affluent parents have opportunities to influence policy that place their child (and similar children) in an advantageous situation compared to the exclusion of other children. In other situations, the demand for "fairness" creates pressure to treat all participants "the same" even when circumstances are different. Some zero-tolerance policies are an example of treating everyone the same regardless of circumstances in the name of fairness.

Finally, inequalities can be costly. Competition for time and money sometimes creates competing needs for limited resources. Advocating for more resources to the greatest benefit of the least advantaged can create considerable controversy. Finding the balance between the needs (or wants) of the many or most influential and the needs of the few or disenfranchised can be challenging. However, providing equality of opportunity for all participants and justifying inequalities is part of the definition of educational equity.

Facilitator and Decision Maker

The ISLLC standards call for school leaders to "nurture and sustain a culture of collaboration, trust, learning, and high expectations" and "Build and sustain positive relationships with families and caregivers." In other words, school leaders are expected to be skillful communicators who respect the diverse views of students, parents, and teachers. These diverse views often present issues of conflicting interests. School leaders must develop the skills to acknowledge and respect competing interests, clarify common interests, and reach an acceptable decision. These efforts can be particularly challenging when participants feel that their integrity or their deeply held beliefs have been challenged. These efforts can also be challenging when collaborative efforts result in decisions that are not in the best interests of all students or that promote the opportunities of some students over others. In other words, it is possible that some members of the school community may act strategically to get their way rather than work for the greater good of all concerned. It is these situations that challenge even the most skillful campus and district leaders. The case studies presented in this text illustrate the difficulty of balancing the need for effective communication skills with the need for a conscious choice rather than acquiescence to demands. The importance given to effective communication and consensus building may well be one of the most significant changes in expectations for school leaders. These skills, however, represent one of the characteristics that separate school leaders from school managers.

ISLLC Standard 3A

ISLLC Standard 4C

RESPONDING TO CONFLICT

Conflict is inherent in the professional lives of school leaders. Conflict results whenever school leaders face a choice, especially when they are trying to find equilibrium between competing interests. Even decisions that are dictated by school policy or state law can generate conflict. However, the conditions of a school or district are not the result of outside forces. Rather, as a significant part of the school, the school leader must assume some responsibility for creating the conditions of the school. Ronald Rebore (2001) explains this concept in this manner:

> The decisions (school leaders) make are free choices, even though they [may] flow from policies of the board of education. . . . They are free choices because the [school leader] is not extraneous to the leadership of a given building [or district]. [Any] decision carries a personal consequence for that [person]. *He or she personally changes with every decision.* [italics added] (p. 42)

Rebore is pointing out that school leaders are not extraneous to or independent of the position that they hold. The conditions school leaders find themselves in and the choices they face are not someone else's fault. As part of the campus or district, school leaders have helped to create the conditions that are present. Thus, accepting responsibility for leadership decisions means more than simply following policy or past practice. Responsibility is accepting the freedom to choose between competing interests to promote educational equity, social justice, and meeting the needs of all stakeholders.

It is certainly appropriate, and healthy, not to internalize or agonize over all conflict generated by the daily interactions and demands of campus and district leadership. It is vitally important to respond in a healthy way to the conflict generated by school leadership. Seemingly interminable conflict makes it quite easy for school leaders to become disenchanted, cynical, and resentful. However, a firm knowledge of legal and ethical principles and healthy reflection provide a framework for meeting possibly the biggest challenge of educational leadership. This challenge is "to remain optimistic in the face of adversity" (Rebore, 2001, p. 272).

Summary

School leaders are expected to advocate for the success of all students, effectively communicate with stakeholders, and forge consensus when faced with issues of competing interests. This chapter illustrates how an understanding of law and ethics can serve as a guide in finding the sometimes difficult equilibrium necessary for meeting the needs of all stakeholders.

CONNECTING STANDARDS TO PRACTICE

1. Review the opening case study "So Many Detentions, So Little Time." This text has presented several ways to examine or audit campus culture for relative cooperativeness, fairness, and equality. As a class or group project, select one and describe how Charleston Jones could use the tool to examine the culture of Jefferson Middle School.

2. Assume the role of Sharon Grey in her meeting with Charleston Jones. What plan of action would you present to Charleston? What ISLLC standards are addressed in this case and in your plan?

3. Review the five examples of conflicting demands presented in this chapter. As a group or class project, give another example to illustrate each concept.

4. As a class or group project, identify values of competing interests other than those presented as samples in this text that school leaders face. Use the knowledge, skills, and dispositions gleaned from this text to present a two- or three-paragraph essay to the class.

5. Interview a principal or superintendent in your district. Ask her or him to briefly describe a recently encountered conflict. Prepare a brief summary (two or three paragraphs). Outline the conflicts inherent in the scenario.

APPENDIX

Amendments to the Constitution of the United States of America

Articles in addition to, and amendment of, the Constitution of the United States of America, proposed by Congress, and ratified by the several states, pursuant to the Fifth Article of the original Constitution. The first 10 amendments collectively are commonly known as the **Bill of Rights.**

AMENDMENT I: FREEDOM OF RELIGION, PRESS, EXPRESSION. RATIFIED 12/15/1791.

Congress shall make no law respecting an establishment of religion, or prohibiting the free exercise thereof; or abridging the freedom of speech, or of the press; or the right of the people peaceably to assemble, and to petition the Government for a redress of grievances.

AMENDMENT II: RIGHT TO BEAR ARMS. RATIFIED 12/15/1791.

A well regulated Militia, being necessary to the security of a free State, the right of the people to keep and bear Arms, shall not be infringed.

AMENDMENT III: QUARTERING OF SOLDIERS. RATIFIED 12/15/1791.

No Soldier shall, in time of peace be quartered in any house, without the consent of the Owner, nor in time of war, but in a manner to be prescribed by law.

AMENDMENT IV: SEARCH AND SEIZURE. RATIFIED 12/15/1791.

The right of the people to be secure in their persons, houses, papers, and effects, against unreasonable searches and seizures, shall not be violated, and no Warrants shall issue, but upon probable cause, supported by Oath or affirmation, and particularly describing the place to be searched, and the persons or things to be seized.

AMENDMENT V: TRIAL AND PUNISHMENT, COMPENSATION FOR TAKINGS. RATIFIED 12/15/1791.

No person shall be held to answer for a capital, or otherwise infamous crime, unless on a presentment or indictment of a Grand Jury, except in cases arising in the land or naval forces, or in the Militia, when in actual service in time of War or public danger;

Source: Amendments to the Constitution of the United States of America. Retrieved from http://caselaw. lp.findlaw.com/data/constitution/amendments.html

nor shall any person be subject for the same offense to be twice put in jeopardy of life or limb; nor shall be compelled in any criminal case to be a witness against himself, nor be deprived of life, liberty, or property, without due process of law; nor shall private property be taken for public use, without just compensation.

AMENDMENT VI: RIGHT TO SPEEDY TRIAL, CONFRONTATION OF WITNESSES. RATIFIED 12/15/1791.

In all criminal prosecutions, the accused shall enjoy the right to a speedy and public trial, by an impartial jury of the State and district wherein the crime shall have been committed, which district shall have been previously ascertained by law, and to be informed of the nature and cause of the accusation; to be confronted with the witnesses against him; to have compulsory process for obtaining witnesses in his favor, and to have the Assistance of Counsel for his defence.

AMENDMENT VII: TRIAL BY JURY IN CIVIL CASES. RATIFIED 12/15/1791.

In Suits at common law, where the value in controversy shall exceed twenty dollars, the right of trial by jury shall be preserved, and no fact tried by a jury, shall be otherwise re-examined in any Court of the United States, than according to the rules of the common law.

AMENDMENT VIII: CRUEL AND UNUSUAL PUNISHMENT. RATIFIED 12/15/1791.

Excessive bail shall not be required, nor excessive fines imposed, nor cruel and unusual punishments inflicted.

AMENDMENT IX: CONSTRUCTION OF CONSTITUTION. RATIFIED 12/15/1791.

The enumeration in the Constitution, of certain rights, shall not be construed to deny or disparage others retained by the people.

AMENDMENT X: POWERS OF THE STATES AND PEOPLE. RATIFIED 12/15/1791.

The powers not delegated to the United States by the Constitution, nor prohibited by it to the States, are reserved to the States respectively, or to the people.

AMENDMENT XI: JUDICIAL LIMITS. RATIFIED 2/7/1795.

The Judicial power of the United States shall not be construed to extend to any suit in law or equity, commenced or prosecuted against one of the United States by Citizens of another State, or by Citizens or Subjects of any Foreign State.

AMENDMENT XII: CHOOSING THE PRESIDENT, VICE-PRESIDENT. RATIFIED 6/15/1804.

The Electors shall meet in their respective states, and vote by ballot for President and Vice-President, one of whom, at least, shall not be an inhabitant of the same state with themselves; they shall name in their ballots the person voted for as President, and in distinct ballots the person voted for as Vice-President, and they shall make distinct lists of all persons voted for as President, and of all persons voted for as Vice-President and of the number of votes for each, which lists they shall sign and certify, and transmit sealed to the seat of the government of the United States, directed to the President of the Senate;

The President of the Senate shall, in the presence of the Senate and House of Representatives, open all the certificates and the votes shall then be counted;

The person having the greatest Number of votes for President, shall be the President, if such number be a majority of the whole number of Electors appointed; and if no person have such majority, then from the persons having the highest numbers not exceeding three on the list of those voted for as President, the House of Representatives shall choose immediately, by ballot, the President. But in choosing the President, the votes shall be taken by states, the representation from each state having one vote; a quorum for this purpose shall consist of a member or members from two-thirds of the states, and a majority of all the states shall be necessary to a choice. And if the House of Representatives shall not choose a President whenever the right of choice shall devolve upon them, before the fourth day of March next following, then the Vice-President shall act as President, as in the case of the death or other constitutional disability of the President.

The person having the greatest number of votes as Vice-President, shall be the Vice-President, if such number be a majority of the whole number of Electors appointed, and if no person have a majority, then from the two highest numbers on the list, the Senate shall choose the Vice-President; a quorum for the purpose shall consist of two-thirds of the whole number of Senators, and a majority of the whole number shall be necessary to a choice. But no person constitutionally ineligible to the office of President shall be eligible to that of Vice-President of the United States.

AMENDMENT XIII: SLAVERY ABOLISHED. RATIFIED 12/6/1865.

1. Neither slavery nor involuntary servitude, except as a punishment for crime whereof the party shall have been duly convicted, shall exist within the United States, or any place subject to their jurisdiction.
2. Congress shall have power to enforce this article by appropriate legislation.

AMENDMENT XIV: CITIZENSHIP RIGHTS. RATIFIED 7/9/1868.

1. All persons born or naturalized in the United States, and subject to the jurisdiction thereof, are citizens of the United States and of the State wherein they reside. No State shall make or enforce any law which shall abridge the privileges

or immunities of citizens of the United States; nor shall any State deprive any person of life, liberty, or property, without due process of law; nor deny to any person within its jurisdiction the equal protection of the laws.

2. Representatives shall be apportioned among the several States according to their respective numbers, counting the whole number of persons in each State, excluding Indians not taxed. But when the right to vote at any election for the choice of electors for President and Vice-President of the United States, Representatives in Congress, the Executive and Judicial officers of a State, or the members of the Legislature thereof, is denied to any of the male inhabitants of such State, being twenty-one years of age, and citizens of the United States, or in any way abridged, except for participation in rebellion, or other crime, the basis of representation therein shall be reduced in the proportion which the number of such male citizens shall bear to the whole number of male citizens twenty-one years of age in such State.

3. No person shall be a Senator or Representative in Congress, or elector of President and Vice-President, or hold any office, civil or military, under the United States, or under any State, who, having previously taken an oath, as a member of Congress, or as an officer of the United States, or as a member of any State legislature, or as an executive or judicial officer of any State, to support the Constitution of the United States, shall have engaged in insurrection or rebellion against the same, or given aid or comfort to the enemies thereof. But Congress may by a vote of two-thirds of each House, remove such disability.

4. The validity of the public debt of the United States, authorized by law, including debts incurred for payment of pensions and bounties for services in suppressing insurrection or rebellion, shall not be questioned. But neither the United States nor any State shall assume or pay any debt or obligation incurred in aid of insurrection or rebellion against the United States, or any claim for the loss or emancipation of any slave; but all such debts, obligations and claims shall be held illegal and void.

5. The Congress shall have power to enforce, by appropriate legislation, the provisions of this article.

AMENDMENT XV: RACE NO BAR TO VOTE.
RATIFIED 2/3/1870.

1. The right of citizens of the United States to vote shall not be denied or abridged by the United States or by any State on account of race, color, or previous condition of servitude.
2. The Congress shall have power to enforce this article by appropriate legislation.

AMENDMENT XVI: INCOME TAXES AUTHORIZED.
RATIFIED 2/3/1913.

The Congress shall have power to lay and collect taxes on incomes, from whatever source derived, without apportionment among the several States, and without regard to any census or enumeration.

AMENDMENT XVII: SENATORS ELECTED BY POPULAR VOTE. RATIFIED 4/8/1913.

The Senate of the United States shall be composed of two Senators from each State, elected by the people thereof, for six years; and each Senator shall have one vote. The electors in each State shall have the qualifications requisite for electors of the most numerous branch of the State legislatures.

When vacancies happen in the representation of any State in the Senate, the executive authority of such State shall issue writs of election to fill such vacancies: Provided, that the legislature of any State may empower the executive thereof to make temporary appointments until the people fill the vacancies by election as the legislature may direct.

This amendment shall not be so construed as to affect the election or term of any Senator chosen before it becomes valid as part of the Constitution.

AMENDMENT XVIII: LIQUOR ABOLISHED. RATIFIED 1/16/1919. REPEALED BY AMENDMENT XXI, 12/5/1933.

1. After one year from the ratification of this article the manufacture, sale, or transportation of intoxicating liquors within, the importation thereof into, or the exportation thereof from the United States and all territory subject to the jurisdiction thereof for beverage purposes is hereby prohibited.
2. The Congress and the several States shall have concurrent power to enforce this article by appropriate legislation.
3. This article shall be inoperative unless it shall have been ratified as an amendment to the Constitution by the legislatures of the several States, as provided in the Constitution, within seven years from the date of the submission hereof to the States by the Congress.

AMENDMENT XIX: WOMEN'S SUFFRAGE. RATIFIED 8/18/1920.

The right of citizens of the United States to vote shall not be denied or abridged by the United States or by any State on account of sex.

Congress shall have power to enforce this article by appropriate legislation.

AMENDMENT XX: PRESIDENTIAL, CONGRESSIONAL TERMS. RATIFIED 1/23/1933.

1. The terms of the President and Vice President shall end at noon on the 20th day of January, and the terms of Senators and Representatives at noon on the 3rd day of January, of the years in which such terms would have ended if this article had not been ratified; and the terms of their successors shall then begin.
2. The Congress shall assemble at least once in every year, and such meeting shall begin at noon on the 3rd day of January, unless they shall by law appoint a different day.

3. If, at the time fixed for the beginning of the term of the President, the President elect shall have died, the Vice President elect shall become President. If a President shall not have been chosen before the time fixed for the beginning of his term, or if the President elect shall have failed to qualify, then the Vice President elect shall act as President until a President shall have qualified; and the Congress may by law provide for the case wherein neither a President elect nor a Vice President elect shall have qualified, declaring who shall then act as President, or the manner in which one who is to act shall be selected, and such person shall act accordingly until a President or Vice President shall have qualified.

4. The Congress may by law provide for the case of the death of any of the persons from whom the House of Representatives may choose a President whenever the right of choice shall have devolved upon them, and for the case of the death of any of the persons from whom the Senate may choose a Vice President whenever the right of choice shall have devolved upon them.

5. Sections 1 and 2 shall take effect on the 15th day of October following the ratification of this article.

6. This article shall be inoperative unless it shall have been ratified as an amendment to the Constitution by the legislatures of three-fourths of the several States within seven years from the date of its submission.

AMENDMENT XXI: AMENDMENT XVIII REPEALED. RATIFIED 12/5/1933.

1. The eighteenth article of amendment to the Constitution of the United States is hereby repealed.

2. The transportation or importation into any State, Territory, or possession of the United States for delivery or use therein of intoxicating liquors, in violation of the laws thereof, is hereby prohibited.

3. The article shall be inoperative unless it shall have been ratified as an amendment to the Constitution by conventions in the several States, as provided in the Constitution, within seven years from the date of the submission hereof to the States by the Congress.

AMENDMENT XXII: PRESIDENTIAL TERM LIMITS. RATIFIED 2/27/1951.

1. No person shall be elected to the office of the President more than twice, and no person who has held the office of President, or acted as President, for more than two years of a term to which some other person was elected President shall be elected to the office of the President more than once. But this Article shall not apply to any person holding the office of President, when this Article was proposed by the Congress, and shall not prevent any person who may be holding the office of President, or acting as President, during the term within which this Article becomes operative from holding the office of President or acting as President during the remainder of such term.

2. This article shall be inoperative unless it shall have been ratified as an amendment to the Constitution by the legislatures of three-fourths of the several States within seven years from the date of its submission to the States by the Congress.

AMENDMENT XXIII: PRESIDENTIAL VOTE FOR DISTRICT OF COLUMBIA. RATIFIED 3/29/1961.

1. The District constituting the seat of Government of the United States shall appoint in such manner as the Congress may direct: A number of electors of President and Vice President equal to the whole number of Senators and Representatives in Congress to which the District would be entitled if it were a State, but in no event more than the least populous State; they shall be in addition to those appointed by the States, but they shall be considered, for the purposes of the election of President and Vice President, to be electors appointed by a State; and they shall meet in the District and perform such duties as provided by the twelfth article of amendment.
2. The Congress shall have power to enforce this article by appropriate legislation.

AMENDMENT XXIV: POLL TAX BARRED. RATIFIED 1/23/1964.

1. The right of citizens of the United States to vote in any primary or other election for President or Vice President, for electors for President or Vice President, or for Senator or Representative in Congress, shall not be denied or abridged by the United States or any State by reason of failure to pay any poll tax or other tax.
2. The Congress shall have power to enforce this article by appropriate legislation.

AMENDMENT XXV: PRESIDENTIAL DISABILITY AND SUCCESSION. RATIFIED 2/10/1967.

1. In case of the removal of the President from office or of his death or resignation, the Vice President shall become President.
2. Whenever there is a vacancy in the office of the Vice President, the President shall nominate a Vice President who shall take office upon confirmation by a majority vote of both Houses of Congress.
3. Whenever the President transmits to the President pro tempore of the Senate and the Speaker of the House of Representatives his written declaration that he is unable to discharge the powers and duties of his office, and until he transmits to them a written declaration to the contrary, such powers and duties shall be discharged by the Vice President as Acting President.
4. Whenever the Vice President and a majority of either the principal officers of the executive departments or of such other body as Congress may by law provide, transmit to the President pro tempore of the Senate and the Speaker of the House of Representatives their written declaration that the President is unable to discharge the powers and duties of his office, the Vice President shall immediately assume the powers and duties of the office as Acting President.

Thereafter, when the President transmits to the President pro tempore of the Senate and the Speaker of the House of Representatives his written declaration that no inability exists, he shall resume the powers and duties of his office unless the Vice President and a majority of either the principal officers of the executive department or of such other body as Congress may by law provide, transmit within four days to the President pro tempore of the Senate and the Speaker of the House of Representatives their written declaration that the President is unable to discharge the powers and duties of his office. Thereupon Congress shall decide the issue, assembling within forty-eight hours for that purpose if not in session. If the Congress, within twenty-one days after receipt of the latter written declaration, or, if Congress is not in session, within twenty-one days after Congress is required to assemble, determines by two thirds vote of both Houses that the President is unable to discharge the powers and duties of his office, the Vice President shall continue to discharge the same as Acting President; otherwise, the President shall resume the powers and duties of his office.

AMENDMENT XXVI: VOTING AGE SET TO 18 YEARS. RATIFIED 7/1/1971.

1. The right of citizens of the United States, who are eighteen years of age or older, to vote shall not be denied or abridged by the United States or by any State on account of age.
2. The Congress shall have power to enforce this article by appropriate legislation.

AMENDMENT XXVII: CONGRESSIONAL PAY INCREASES. RATIFIED 5/7/1992.

No law, varying the compensation for the services of the Senators and Representatives, shall take effect, until an election of Representatives shall have intervened.

GLOSSARY

Academic freedom: A teacher's right to speak freely about political or ideological issues in the classroom without fear of reprisal. Academic freedom is severely restricted for K–12 employees.

Adverse employment decision: An action by a school district that negatively affects an employee's status, such as termination of a contract, demotion, suspension, denial of a promotion, or transfer to a less desirable location or position.

Affirmative action: Deliberate efforts on the part of a school district to eliminate effects of past discrimination and create systems and hiring processes to prevent future discrimination (Garner, 2006).

Assumption of risk: The concept that one who voluntarily and knowingly takes on a risk of injury or damage cannot then sue for negligence because of an injury or loss sustained by participating in the activity. For example, an inherent risk of injury is part of competitive sports (especially football). Consequently, if students claim that they did not know that they could be injured by participating in an inherently dangerous activity, they usually cannot prevail. In most jurisdictions this concept has been replaced by contributory or comparative negligence (Garner, 2006).

Behavioral intervention plan (BIP): A set of strategies, interventions, and supports the school will provide for a student with a disability. IDEIA 04 requires a BIP for any student whose behavior "impedes" their learning or the learning of others.

Bona fide occupational qualification (BFOQ): A condition or requirement that is reasonably necessary as a condition of a particular job. All BFOQs should be included in the job description.

Breach of duty: In tort law, the failure to exercise the amount of care a "reasonably prudent" teacher, principal, superintendent, or other such person would exercise in a similar situation.

Bullying: Bullying includes being made fun of; being the subject of rumors; being threatened with harm; being pushed, shoved, tripped, or spit on; being pressured into doing things one did not want to do; being excluded from activities on purpose; and having property destroyed on purpose.

Cause-in-fact: The "but for" cause. The cause without which the event could not have occurred (Garner, 2006).

Child find: Child find requires state educational agencies (SEAs) and local education agencies (LEAs) to initiate procedures to locate qualified children with a disability who are not being served and notify parents of available services.

Collective bargaining: The right of school district employees to band together to collectively bargain with the school district. The right to collectively bargain as well as the scope of bargaining is defined by state law.

Common (case) law: Evolves from various court decisions that interpret or apply constitutional law, statutory law, or regulations to a particular set of circumstances. The concept of judge-made law developed from the English legal system premise that all legal problems cannot and should not be covered by a law or statute.

Comparative negligence: The principle of tort liability that allows for a reduction in recovery proportional to the plaintiff's degree of fault in the damages.

Constitutional law: The body of law deriving from the U.S. Constitution dealing primarily with governmental powers, civil rights, and civil liberties (Garner, 2006).

Continuing contracts: A type of contract issued by a school district that bestows a property right to continuing employment in the district until the teacher voluntarily leaves the district, dies, or retires. The terms and requirements of continuing contracts are defined by state law. Continuing contracts can be terminated only by good cause set forth by state law. Terminating a continuing contract requires considerable documentation of deficiencies. The burden of proof shifts from the teacher to the school district to demonstrate a good and valid reason for the decision.

Contributory negligence: Occurs when a person's (teacher, student, parent, etc.) own negligent actions results in an injury or loss.

Corporal punishment: Applying physical force usually with a paddle, hand, or other instrument to intentionally inflict pain as a disciplinary measure. Not legal in every state.

Culture: The shared patterns of behavior and thinking that determine and perpetuate the normative interactions in a school or district.

Cyberbullying: Sending or posting harmful or cruel text or images using the Internet or cell phones.

Dating violence: Violence that occurs between two people in a close relationship.

De facto segregation: Occurs without the direct intent of a state or school board, but because of housing patterns that naturally create enclaves of children of the same color or race (Garner, 2006).

De jure segregation: An illegal state or school board policy that intends to separate children by race, color or national origin that results in a dual school system (Garner, 2006).

Defamation: A false written or oral statement that damages the reputation of another (Garner, 2006). As a public figure (superintendents are always public figures; principals are public figures in some states), it is often difficult for school leaders to win a defamation suit.

Defendant: The person or organization (school board, for example) being sued. Listed second in court proceedings.

Deliberate indifference: Failure on the part of school officials to take reasonable action once they knew or should have known of student-on-student victimization or allegations of employee misconduct or harassment. Also applies to harassment based on race, color, national origin, sex, or disability.

Directory information: FERPA permits schools to designate certain information such as names, addresses, degrees and honors received, participation in officially recognized activities and sports, and dates of attendance that may be released without specific written permission of the parents or eligible student. School districts must provide a yearly notice to parents and eligible students of any information that will be designated for release by the school without written permission from the parent or eligible student.

Discourse ethics: A communications model proposed by the contemporary German philosopher Jürgen Habermas designed to promote active communication, seeking the perspectives of others, and rational argumentation in reaching a decision.

Disparate impact: One of two basic types of discrimination defined by Title VII. Disparate impact occurs when school district policy or practice has a disproportional impact on members of a protected class.

Disparate treatment: One of two basic types of discrimination defined by Title VII. Disparate treatment occurs when a school district intentionally deals with persons (employees, applicants for employment, or students) differently because of their race, sex, national origin, age, or disability. Disparate treatment is very difficult to demonstrate.

Due process: The minimum requirements of notice and a hearing required by the Fifth and Fourteenth Amendments.

Duty of care: The legal obligation owed or due to another that needs to be satisfied. Educators stand *in loco parentis* (in place of the parent). Consequently, educators have nearly the same duty of care as parents. The parameters of these duties depend on several factors, including the age of the student (the younger the child, the greater the duty of care) and the circumstances involved (the greater the inherent risk, the greater the duty of care).

En banc: With all judges present and participating in a decision (Garner, 2006).

English language learners: Students attending school in the United States or other English-speaking countries whose native language is not English.

Equal Access Act: Federal law that requires secondary schools that allow noncurriculum clubs to meet during the school day or use school facilities after school hours (creating a limited open forum) to allow participation in constitutionally protected prayer and religious expression on an equal basis. The Equal Access Act has been applied in ways not envisioned by Congress. For example, the EAA has been used to require Gay–Straight Alliance (GSA) and other sexual minority support groups equal access to school facilities.

Equal Employment Opportunity Commission (EEOC): Federal agency created by the Civil Rights Act of 1964 to enforce the statutory requirements of the law to end discrimination in employment. The EEOC receives, investigates, and attempts to mediate disputes between teachers, students, parents, and school districts. When school districts are found in violation of one of the statutory requirements or regulations, the commission seeks voluntary compliance with directives to remediate past wrongs. Failure by the school district to comply may result in referral to the U.S. Department of Justice.

Equal protection: The requirement that the government (schools in this case) treat similarly situated persons similarly. An equal protection claim requires the showing that school officials did not abide by their own policies or that the person was treated differently from other similarly situated persons. For example, if school administrators or teachers enforce rules against harassment for heterosexual students, but fail to enforce the same rules for LGBT students, then an equal protection violation may have occurred.

Equality of opportunity: Based on Principle Two of John Rawls's concept of justice as fairness, where all participants have equal access to the best basket of goods and services available to all. Requires not only that opportunities be open in the formal sense, but that all members have a fair chance to attain and benefit from these opportunities.

Establishment Clause: The first clause of the First Amendment to the Constitution that requires governmental (school district) neutrality and prohibits governmental advancement of religion.

Ethics: The theoretical study and consideration of how school leaders ought to act.

Federalism: The system of government in the United States, characterized by several sovereign governments functioning independently of one another.

FERPA: The Family Educational Rights and Privacy Act protects student academic and personal information.

Foreseeability: Whether or not harm to students or others was a predictable result of the conduct or lack of conduct in question.

Forum: A place or vehicle of communication. Speech rights can be determined by the nature of the forum. Courts have identified nonpublic fora, limited open fora, and open fora. The speech rights of students (as well as community groups) and access to facilities are determined by the type of forum established by the school.

Free and appropriate public education (FAPE): The basic floor of opportunity provided by IDEIA. Consists of access to individualized specialized instruction and related services designed to provide an educational benefit to the handicapped child. A FAPE is defined by the answers to two questions: (1) Has the LEA complied with the procedures and requirements of the act, and (2) is the IEP reasonably calculated to enable the child to receive educational benefits? A free and appropriate public education must meet both prongs of the definition.

Free Exercise Clause: The second clause of the First Amendment that prohibits governmental interference with religion.

Functional behavioral assessment (FBA): Information about the student that describes problem behaviors, identifies possible causes and effects, and develops ideas for teaching alternatives. Functional behavioral assessments are required by IDEIA when a child's behavior interferes with his or her learning or when the child has first been removed from his or her current placement for more than 10 school days in a school year, or when commencing a removal that constitutes a change in placement.

Hearing: A formal adversarial process under IDEIA (2004) in which an impartial hearing officer listens to evidence presented by both sides. Different from mediation in that there is usually a winner and a loser and blame is often attached to the losing party.

IEP team: The group of individuals responsible for developing and writing the IEP.

Ill-structured problems: Situations with no easy or clear-cut solutions. Ill-structured problems present leaders with a dilemma.

Immorality: A Missouri court of appeals defined immorality as "contemplated behavior sufficiently contrary to justice, honesty, modesty or good morals, or involving baseness, vileness or depravity so as to support the inference that the teacher understands the conduct to be wrong" (*Youngman v. Doerhoff*, 1994). Basically, immorality is anything the school board says it is, as long as the behavior can be connected to a fitness to teach.

Incompetence: Inability to perform the duties to which a teacher has been assigned. Deficiencies in lesson planning, instructional methodology, and classroom management are common areas for charges of incompetence. Requires considerable documentation, especially if the teacher has a history of good evaluations from previous administrators.

Individualized Education Program (IEP): Outlines the provisions of an appropriate education for children with disabilities.

Insubordination: The willful and deliberate defiance of reasonable school rules or school district policy, or refusal to follow the reasonable directions of a person in a supervisory position. Insubordination is grounds for dismissal of continuing contract teachers in virtually every state. The easiest remediable charge to document and demonstrate.

ISLLC standards: The six standards developed by the Council of Chief State School Officers. Designed to provide a conceptual framework for practicing leaders as well as school leader preparation program design.

Just cause: A catch-all phrase in some state statutes that gives broad latitude to school boards to dismiss continuing-contract teachers. Like immorality, just cause can be whatever the school board says it is, as long as the behavior can be linked to the teacher's fitness to teach.

Least restrictive environment (LRE): Inclusion, to the maximum extent appropriate, of a student with a disability in the general curriculum with students who do not have a disability.

Legal brief: A summary of the elements of a court opinion into a usable document (usually one page) for further study and referral.

Liability waivers: Roughly analogous to a contract, a liability waiver is an express assumption of risk. These documents are sometimes called *hold harmless, consent, indemnity,* and various other labels. School districts typically require liability waivers for activities such as field trips signed by a minor child's parent or guardian. These documents generally provide the parent or guardian the opportunity to assume some of the risk inherent in the activity. Although considerable debate surrounds how much protection these documents provide educators, it remains good practice to continue to use them.

Liberty interest: A fundamental right protected by the due process clauses of state and federal government.

Lifeworld: Composed of culture, community, and person. Combines with the campus or district systemsworld to create a normative culture of thinking and behaving.

Manifestation determination: The manifestation determination is a review and assessment by the IEP team of the relationship between the behavior and the child's disability. This relationship is determined by two questions: (1) Is the behavior in question caused by, or does it have a direct and substantial relationship to, the child's disability? (2) Is the conduct in question a direct result of a failure to implement the IEP? If the IEP team and parents determine that the answer to either question 1 or 2 is yes, *the conduct is a manifestation of the child's disability.*

Matters of public concern: School-related issues that affect the general welfare of stakeholders such as

allocation of resources, concerns about discrimination, or presently dangerous campus facilities. Matters of public concern are protected speech, as long as the speech does not interfere with good order and efficiency. Matters of personal concern are issues that may be important to one teacher or a small group of stakeholders, such as the assignment of a particular student or rules regarding hallway supervision.

Mediation: (1) As part of the discourse ethics model, mediation is viewed as participants striving to reach understanding. (2) Under IDEIA, mediation occurs when an impartial third party assists the parents and school district in reaching a mutually acceptable agreement.

Middle-tier (intermediate) scrutiny: A midlevel of review in cases involving a quasisuspect class (such as gender). The classification must be related to the achievement of an *important* governmental objective (Garner, 2006).

***Mt. Healthy* retaliation test:** The *Mt. Healthy* retaliation test considers whether or not the protected speech in question was a motivating factor in an adverse employment decision, or if the decision would have been reached for other legitimate reasons. For example, in *Mt. Healthy v. Doyle* (1968), the school board cited both Doyle's protected speech and his questionable professional decisions as reasons for his termination. The U.S. Supreme Court upheld Doyle's termination primarily because of a preponderance of the evidence that the board would, or could, have reached the same conclusions without considering the protected speech. This ruling not only has been beneficial to employees, but also has allowed school districts to claim the "*Mt. Healthy* defense." The *Mt. Healthy* defense is simply stated as, "We would have taken the action anyway."

Negligence: The failure to provide the standard of care that a similarly situated reasonably prudent person would exercise.

Nexus principle: (1) Demonstrating a relationship between a teacher's behavior and the teacher's professional responsibilities and teaching effectiveness or fitness to teach. Most courts consider intent, foreseeability, and knowledge in determining nexus. (2) Demonstrating a relationship between a student's off-campus behavior or speech and substantial disruption in the school. Student off-campus speech is protected by the First Amendment, except when the speech is a true threat or results in substantial disruption at school. Because a basic constitutional right is involved, most courts set a fairly high standard of review.

Office for Civil Rights: A department within the U.S. Department of Education that handles discriminatory complaints based on race, color, sex, or national origin.

Performance appraisals: Evaluation of teacher performance, usually defined by state law. Formative appraisals are used to gather and collect information about a teacher's job duties. The summative appraisal consists of a summarization and conclusions from formative appraisals. The summative appraisal is the document used to justify employment decisions.

Plaintiff: The person (or organization) bringing suit. Listed first in court proceedings.

Positive behavioral support (PBS): A process that helps students with behavioral problems to succeed in school by analyzing negative behavior triggers and the use of positive reinforcement to effect change.

Principle of proportionality: Jeremy Bentham's thoughts on the purpose of government included considerable attention to the authority of the government to punish individuals. To this end, he developed several guidelines concerning the legitimacy of punishment and the proportion between punishments and offenses.

Private right of action: The ability to bring suit and seek remediation when a school district violates a statute. However, the statute must generally outline the right. For example, the U.S. Supreme Court has found that FERPA does not contain an individual right to enforcement. Consequently, only the federal government could punish a school district for violating FERPA by withholding federal funds.

Probable cause: A reasonable ground to suspect that a person has broken a law or is committing a crime. Probable cause requires more than a suspicion but less evidence than would justify a conviction (Garner, 2006). Generally required when school resource officers are acting as law enforcement agents and not agents of the school.

Probationary contract: A contract typically issued by a school district to a beginning teacher or a teacher new to the district. Probationary contracts are for one school year and may be terminated for any good reason (but never a bad reason) at the end of the school year. Termination requires only that the school district follow state notification laws. The burden of proof is on the teacher to demonstrate that the district terminated the contract for a bad or discriminatory reason.

Procedural due process: The protection afforded students, teachers, or other school employees. Includes the rule, policy or legal violation, a chance to deny the allegation or tell his or her side of the story, and an explanation of the evidence against him or her.

Procedural safeguards: In special education law, the requirements necessary to ensure a cooperative process that assures that children with disabilities benefit from school and that the school is providing the appropriate services and placements. Parents must receive written notice of procedural safeguards once per year. A copy of procedural safeguards must also be provided on initial referral or parental request for evaluation, on the filing of a complaint, and on request of the parent. The notice must contain the legal rights of parents and the obligations of the school district in plain, easy-to-understand language. The notice should be in the parental native language if possible.

Property interest: Something that is due a person by legal right or moral claim (Garner, 2006).

Proximate causation: In tort law, the relative foreseeability by a similarly situated reasonably prudent educator of the potential for harm or injury.

Qualified immunity: Immunity from liability when the conduct does not violate clearly established law or policy.

Rational basis: The lowest form of review in an equal protection claim. Courts will uphold a law or policy that bears a *reasonable relationship* to the attainment of a legitimate governmental interest (Garner, 2006).

Reasonable cause: The legality of a school search of a student or teacher should depend on the *reasonableness under the circumstances* of the search. *Reasonable under the circumstances* can be defined as follows: (1) The search should be justified at inception; (2) the search should be reasonably related in scope to the reason for the search; (3) the search should be reasonably related to the objective of the search; and (4) the search should not be excessively intrusive in light of the age and sex of the student or the nature of the infraction.

Reasonable suspicion drug testing: Student or employee drug testing (urinalysis or breathalyzer) based on the reasonable suspicion that the person has violated district policy regarding alcohol/drug use. For example, an odor of alcohol or marijuana, a reliable tip, or erratic behavior may justify the suspicion that the person has violated district policy.

Regulations: Sometimes called an administrative rule. Regulations are statements issued by a governing body (such as a state board of education or the U.S. Department of Education) that interprets and explains how a law passed by the legislative body is to be enacted.

Remediation plan: A document that outlines specific observable areas in need of improvement. A remediation plan is always required for continuing-contract teachers and is a good idea for probationary teachers before recommendations for the termination of the contract.

Risk management: The process of managing and reducing the inherent liability of teachers, administrators, and school boards by purchasing insurance protection, regulating student and employee behavior, and periodically inspecting and responsibly maintaining facilities.

Safety-sensitive position: The test for *safety-sensitive* involves two questions: (1) Are the duties performed by the employee so fraught with risks of injury to others that even a momentary lapse of attention may have disastrous consequences, and (2) does a clear nexus exist between the nature of the employee's duty and the risk of injury (*Skinner v. Railway Labor Executives Assn.*, 1989)? For example, employment in a safety-sensitive position substantially lowers the bar for determining the legality of suspicionless drug testing. *Safety-sensitive* basically means that the potential for harm of illicit drug or alcohol use is great enough to justify a compelling state interest in suspicionless testing.

School culture: The normative written and unwritten rules that define and perpetuate how students, teachers, and administrators interact with one another.

School resource officers: A law enforcement officer assigned on a permanent or semipermanent basis to a school or district.

Sexting: Generally refers to teens taking sexually explicit photos of themselves or others in their peer group and transmitting those photos by text messaging to their peers.

Sexual harassment: Unwelcome or unwanted conduct of a sexual nature. Title IX protects students from sexual harassment.

Shocks the conscience: The standard used by most federal courts to determine whether or not a student's substantive due process right has been violated in cases of injury or harm because of the acts of school employees. This is a very high standard defined differently by various circuit courts. For example, the

10th Circuit Court defines the substantive due process inquiry to be "whether the force applied caused injury so severe, was so disproportional to the need presented, and was so inspired by malice or sadism . . . that it amounted to a brutal and inhumane abuse of official power literally shocking to the conscience."

Slander: Defamation that is spoken is slander.

Social capital: Social capital (or *fraternity*) can be defined as the "ability to perceive other members of one's society as brothers and sisters, to have a sense of responsibility for them, and to feel that in difficult times one can turn to them for help" (Fowler, 2009, p. 114).

Social justice: The values of equality and fraternity. Furman and Gruenewald (2004) view social justice as a *critical-humanistic* role for school leaders. The critical-humanistic role is one that (1) assumes that schools are inherently value laden, (2) engages in an analysis of school structure for inequalities that result from unequal power relationships, and (3) works to overcome these inequalities. This view assumes that school leaders should play an activist role in confronting and changing schools to more adequately address inequalities.

Sovereign immunity: A government's immunity from being sued in its own courts (Garner, 2006). For example, the state of Ohio cannot sue itself unless an action is taken to allow this to happen. The federal government has waived most of its sovereign immunity; however, most states have not.

Standing: The right of a person or party (e.g., a school board) to make a legal claim or ask a court to enforce a duty or right. To have standing in federal court, a person or party must demonstrate that the action (or lack of action) caused an injury or deprived the person of a right (such as a public education) and that the right or interest is actually protected by a law or constitutional guarantee.

Stare decisis: To "stand by decisions made." The doctrine of following the precedent of previous decisions made by a court.

State boards of education: Policy-making bodies that function immediately below the state legislature.

Statutory immunity: State law that grants immunity from suit to individuals (teachers, counselors, principals, etc.). The immunity granted by state law varies widely by state.

Statutory law: A statute is a law passed by a legislative body. Statutory law derives from the written law.

Strict scrutiny: A standard of review in equal protection analysis that requires the state (or school district) to establish a *compelling* interest that justifies and necessitates different treatment for members of a protected class such as race (Garner, 2006). This is the highest standard of review.

Student victimization: A catch-all phrase including bullying, cyberbullying, sexual harassment, and so forth.

Substantive due process: Considers the basic fairness of a decision. Usually involves notice, the legitimacy of the rule, the rationality of the punishment in light of the offense, and whether the rule or policy is applied equally and fairly.

Supplemental (related) services: Related services including transportation and other supportive services such as speech–language pathology and audiology services, counseling services, and medical services required for a child with a disability to benefit from special education.

Systemsworld: The policies, rules, and regulations used to establish and enforce normative behavior in a school or district. Combines with the school lifeworld to create a culture that is unique to every campus and district.

Threat assessment: A commonsense analysis of facts and evidence to determine the true danger presented by a student for either verbal or written threats or weapon possession. Threat assessment in this text is based on the 2004 final report by the U.S. Secret Service/Department of Education analysis of school shooters, available free of charge from the U.S. Department of Education.

Title IX (Title IX of the Educational Amendments of 1972): Federal law that prohibits sex discrimination and harassment in educational settings that receive federal funds (Garner, 2006). Title IX applies to students.

Title VII: Federal law that prohibits employment discrimination and workplace harassment based on race, color, national origin or sex, religion, or pregnancy. Also prohibits retaliation for reporting illegal harassment or discrimination (Garner, 2006).

Tort: A civil wrong for which a remedy may be obtained, usually in the form of damages (Garner, 2006).

Union: Any time teachers or other groups negotiate collectively with a school district, the employee group is essentially functioning as a union.

Unitary status: Standard used by courts to continue or dissolve desegregation orders. Requires that the school district be desegregated to the extent practical.

Urinalysis: The process of collecting urine samples from students or employees with the intent to deter illegal drug use.

Useful strategic knowledge: A combination of knowledge with an understanding of how to apply the knowledge in the appropriate manner. Synonymous with *higher-order thinking skills.*

Utilitarianism: Ethical concept present by Jeremy Bentham and his student J. S. Mill. Utilitarianism views the purpose of all action (policy, etc.) as promoting the "greatest happiness" and diminishing pain. Bentham coined the term *utility* to describe this concept. For this text, utility is presented as "the greater good." That is, the purpose of all policy should be to promote the greater good of all stakeholders.

Viewpoint discrimination: Allowing one protected view to be expressed while not allowing other viewpoints equal access or equal rights to the same vehicles of expression. Courts generally take a very dim view of viewpoint discrimination in schools.

Voucher: A payment made by the government (state) to a parent or institution on a parent's behalf to be used for a child's education expenses.

Well-ordered school: A school culture based on Principle One of Rawls's concept of justice as fairness characterized by a fair system of social cooperation established by public justification.

Writ of certiorari (writ): A writ is a court's written order. Certiorari is a writ issued by an appellate court directing a lower court to forward the record for review (Garner, 2006).

Zero reject: Zero reject is a rule against exclusion of special education students regardless of the nature or degree of their disabilities. IDEIA 04 expands the concept of zero reject further to include children who are homeless or wards of the state.

Zero tolerance: School district policy that requires mandatory predetermined consequences or punishment for specific offenses regardless of the circumstances. Often used in conjunction with the Gun-Free Schools Act, weapons, and illegal drug possession on school property. Zero tolerance has come under intense criticism over the past few years, but remains common in most school district policies.

REFERENCES

A. B. v. State, 863N. E. 2d 1212 (Ind Ct. App. 2007).

A. G. v. Sayreville Board of Education, 2003 WL 21404111 (3d Cir. 2003).

Abbott, P. (2002). Sain v. Cedar Rapids Community School District: Providing special protection for student-athletes? *Brigham Young University Education and Law Journal, 2,* 291–312.

Abington School District v. Schempp, 374 U.S. 203 (1963).

Addington, L., Ruddy, S., Miller, A., Defoe, J., & Chandler, K. (2002). *Are America's schools safe? Students speak out: 1999.* School Crime Supplement (NCES 2002-331). Project Officer K. Chandler. Washington, DC: U.S. Department of Education, National Center for Educational Statistics.

Adler v. Duval County School Board, 206 F.3d 1071 (11th Cir. 2000).

Administrative Office of the U.S. Courts. (2003). *Understanding the federal court system.* Retrieved from www.utd.uscourts.gov/forms/ufc03.pdf.

Agostini v. Felton, 521 U.S. 203 (1997).

Aguilar v. Felton, 473 U.S. 402 (1985).

Alexander v. Holmes County Board of Education, 396 U.S. 19 (1969).

Alexander, K., & Alexander, M. D. (2012). *American public school law* (8th ed.). Belmont, CA: Wadsworth.

Almontaser v. New York City Department of Education, 519 F.3d 505 (2nd Cir. 2008).

American Civil Liberties Union (ACLU). (2004). *Settlement fact sheet: Flores v. Morgan Hill Unified School District.* Retrieved from www.aclu.org.

American Educational Research Association (2011, February). Code of ethics. *Educational Researcher, 40*(3), 145–156.

Anderson v. Milbank School District 25-4, 2000 DSD 49; 2000 U.S. Dist. LEXIS 19418 (2000).

Arizona Christian School Tuition Organization v. Winn, 563 U.S. _____ (2011).

Armenta, T., & Lane, K. E. (2010). Tennessee to Texas: Tracing the evolution controversy in public education. *The Clearing House, 83*(3), 76–79.

Association of Mexican-American Educators v. State of California, 231 F.3d 572 (9th Cir., 2000).

B. W. A. v. Farmington R-7 School District, 554 F. 3d 734 (8th Cir., 2009).

Barber v. Dearborn Public Schools, 286 F. Supp.2d 847 (E.D. Michigan, 2003).

Barr v. Lafon, 538 f.3d 554 (6th Cir. 2008).

Beall v. London City School District, No. 2:04-cv-290 (S.D. Ohio, E. D., 2006).

Begley, P. T. (2001). In pursuit of authentic school leadership practices. *International Journal of Leadership in Education, 4*(4), 353–366.

Begley, P. (2004, September–October). *Professional valuation processes: Balancing personal motivations and ethical leadership actions.* Keynote address presented at the 9th annual Values and Leadership Conference, Christ Church, Barbados.

Begley, P. T. (2006). Self-knowledge, capacity, and sensitivity: Prerequisites to authentic leadership by school principals. *Journal of Educational Administration, 44*(6), 570–589.

Bentham, J. (1970). In J. H. Burns & H. L. A. Hart (Eds.), *An introduction to the principles of morals and legislation.* New York, NY: Oxford University Press. (Original work published 1780)

Bethel School District No. 403 v. Fraser, 478 U.S. 675 (1986).

Beussink v. Woodland R-IV School District, 30 F. Supp.2d 1175 (E.D. Mo. 1998).

Bivens v. Albuquerque Public Schools, 899 F. Supp. 556 (D.N.M. 1995).

Blau v. Fort Thomas Public School Dist, 401, F. 3d 381 (6th Cir. 2005).

Board of Education of Central Community United School District 301 v. Scionti, unpublished case (Ill. App Ct. 2000).

Board of Education of Hendrick Hudson Central School District v. Rowley, 458 U.S. 176 (1982).

Board of Education of Independent School District No. 92 of Pottawatomie v. Earls, 536 U.S. 822 (2002).

Board of Education of Rogers, Arkansas v. McCluskey, 458 U.S. 966 (1982).

Board of Education v. Mergens, 496 U.S. 226 (1990).

Board of Education v. Pico, 457 U.S. 853 (1982).

Bochenek, M., & Brown, A. W. (2001). *Hatred in the hallways: Violence and discrimination against lesbian, gay, bisexual, and transgender students in U.S. schools* (2001). New York, NY: Human Rights Watch.

Borger v. Bisciglia, 888 F. Supp. 97 (E.D. Wis., 1995).

Boring v. Buncombe County Board of Education, 136 F.3d 364 (4th Cir., 1998).

Boroff v. Van Wert City Board of Education, 220 F.3d 465 (6th Cir. 2000).

Boucher v. School Board of the School District of Greenfield, 134 F.3d 821 (7th Cir., 1998).

Boyd County High School Gay Straight Alliance v. Board of Education of Boyd County, KY, 258 F. Supp.2d 667 (E.D. KY, 2003).

Boyle, J., & Weishaar, M. (2001). *Special education law with cases.* Boston: Allyn & Bacon.

Bradford, C. (2001). What's the big IDEA? *Principal Leadership, 1*(8), 73–74.

Brady, K. P. (2008). "Big brother" is watching, but can he hear, too? Legal issues surrounding video camera surveillance and electronic eavesdropping in public schools. *ELA Notes, 43*(2), 4–7.

Brady, K. P. (2010). Student-created fake online profiles using social networking websites: Protected online speech parodies or defamation? *ELA Notes, 45*(2), 4–7.

Brannum v. Overton County School Board, 516 F.3d 489 (6th Cir. 2008).

Brentwood Academy v. TSSAA, 531 U.S. 288 (2001).

Bridgman v. New Trier High School District, 128 F.3d 1146 (7th Cir., 1997).

Brookhart v. Illinois, 697 F. 2d 179 (7th Cir., 1983).

Broussard v. School Board of City of Norfolk, 801 F. Supp. 1526 (E.D. Va. 1992).

Brown v. Board of Education (Brown II), 349 U.S. 294 (1955).

Brown v. Board of Education of Topeka et al. (Brown I), 347 U.S. 483 (1954).

Brown v. Gilmore, 278 F.3d 265 (4th Cir. 2001, cert denied).

Burlington Industries, Inc. v. Ellerth, 524 US 742 (1998).

Butler v. Rio Rancho Public School Board, 341 F.3d 1197 (10th Cir., 2003).

C. B. & T. P. v. Driscoll 82 F.3d 383 (11th Cir., 1996).

C. H. v. Oliva, 990 F. Supp. 341 (D. N. J. 1997).

C. N., et al. v. Wolf, et al. Case No SACO 05-860 JVS (C.D. Cal., 2006).

Camreta v. Greene, No. 09-1454 (U.S. Supreme Court, 2011).

Canady v. Bossier Parish School Board, 240 F.3d 437 (5th Cir. 2001).

Cantor, D., Crosse, S., Hagen, C. A., Mason, M. J., Siler, A. J., & von Glatz, A. (2001). *A closer look at drug and violence prevention efforts in American schools: Report on the study on school violence and prevention.* Washington, DC: U.S. Government Printing Office.

Carlson, C. N. (2003). Invisible victims: Holding the educational system liable for teen dating violence at school. *Harvard Women's Law Journal, 26,* 351–393.

Casey v. West Las Vegas Independent School District, 473 F.3d 1323 (10th Cir. 2007).

Castaneda v. Pickard, 648 F. 2d 989 (5th Cir. 1981).

Castorina v. Madison County School Board, 246 F.3d 536 (6th Cir. 2001).

Caudillo v. Lubbock, 311 F. Supp. 2d 550 (N. D. TX, Lubbock Division, 2004).

Cedar Rapids Community School District v. Garret F. 526 U.S. 66 (1999).

Centers for Disease Control and Prevention. (2008). *Teen dating violence: Fact sheet*. Retrieved from www.cdc.gov/injury.

Chalifoux v. New Cancy Independent School District, 976 F. Supp 659 (S.D. Texas, 1997).

Chambers v. Babbitt, 145 F. Supp.2d 1068 (Minnesota, 2001).

Chaplinsky v. New Hampshire, 315 U.S. 568 (1942).

Child Evangelism Fellowship of Maryland, Incorporated v. Montgomery County Public Schools 373 F.3d 589 (4th Cir 2004). Cole v. Oroville Union Free School District, 228 F.3d 1092 (9th Cir. 2000).

City of Indianapolis v. Edmond, 531 U.S. 32 (2000).

City of Ontario v. Quon, 130 S. Ct. 2619 (2010).

Clark v. Bibb County Board of Education, 174 F. Supp. 2d 1369 (M.D. Ga. 2001).

Clifford Eugene Davis Jr., et al. v. East Baton Rouge Parish School Board, unpublished case (Middle District Court of Louisiana, 2003).

Cockrel v. Shelby County School District, 270 F.3d 1036 (6th Cir., 2001).

Cohen v. California, 403 U.S. 15 (1971).

Colasanti, M. (2008a, March). *School uniform and dress codes: State policy*. Retrieved from www.ecs.org.

Colasanti, M. (2008b, January) *State collective bargaining policies for teachers*. Retrieved from www.ecs.org.

Cole v. Oroville Union Free School District, 228 F.3d 1092 (9th Cir. 2000).

Coles v. Cleveland Board of Education, 171 F.3d 369 (6th Cir. 1999).

Colgan, C. (2004). The ethical choice. *American School Board Journal, 191*(5), 12–16.

Colin v. Orange Unified School District, 83 F. Supp.2d 1135 (C.D. Cal. 2000).

Colquitt v. Rich Township High School District, WL 476734 (Ill App. Dist. 1998).

Communities for Equity v. Michigan High School Athletic Association, 178 F. Supp.2d 805 (W.D. Michigan, 2001).

Compton, C., & Nance, B. (2002). *Building leadership capacity through professional conversation*. Paper presented at the ASCD Annual Conference, San Antonio, TX.

Conn, K. (2002). *The Internet and the law: What educators need to know*. Alexandria, VA: ACSD.

Conn, K. (2010). Cyberbullying and other student technology misuses in K–12 American schools: The legal landmines. *Widener Law Review, 16*, 89–100.

Conn, K., & Brady, K. P. (2008). MySpace and its relatives: The cyberbullying dilemma. *ELA Notes, 42*(4), 4–7.

Connick v. Myers, 461 U.S. 138 (1983).

Copland, M. (2000). Problem-based learning and prospective principals' problem-framing ability. *Educational Administration Quarterly, 36*(4), 585–607.

Council of Chief State School Officers. (2008). *Interstate School Leaders Licensure Consortium (ISLLC) standards for school leaders*. Washington, DC: Author.

Counts v. Cedarville School District, 295 F.Supp.2d 996 (W.D. Ark. 2003).

Covington County v. G. W., 767 So 187 (Miss., 2000).

Cranston, N., Ehrich, L., & Kimber, M. (2003). The "right" decision? Towards an understanding of ethical dilemmas for school leaders. *Westminster Studies in Education, 26*(2), 135–147.

Crist v. Alpine Union School District, LEXIS 8699 (Cal. App. 4 Dist. Unpub. 2005).

Croft v. Perry, 562 F.3d 735 (5th Cir. 2009).

Croft v. Perry, 624 F.3d 157 (5th Cir. 2010).

Dadich v. Syosset High School, 717 N.Y.S. 2d 634 (N.Y. App. Div., 2000).

Daggett, L. (2002, November). *FERPA update 2002: The two new Supreme Court FERPA cases and post-9/11 Congressional balancing of student privacy and safety interests*. Paper presented at the 48th Annual Education Law Conference, New Orleans, LA.

Daly, K. (2001). Balancing act: Teachers' classroom speech and the First Amendment. *Journal of Law and Education, 30*(1), 1–62.

Darden, E. (2002, November). *Flame on: The fight over vouchers will be a war within the states.* Paper presented at the 48th Annual Education Law Association Conference, New Orleans, LA.

Davis v. Monroe County Board of Education, 526 U.S. 629 (1999).

Dear Colleague. (2010, October 26). Office for Civil Rights. Retrieved from www.ocr.gov.

Dear Colleague. (2011, April 4). Office for Civil Rights. Retrieved from www.ocr.gov.

Dear Colleague. (2011, May 6). *Office for Civil Rights.* Retrieved from www.ocr.gov.

Debra P. v. Turlington 644 F.2d 397 (5th Cir., 1981).

Debra P. v. Turlington 730 F.2d 1405 (11th Cir., 1984).

Defoe v. Spiva, No 09-6080 (6th Cir. 2010).

DeMitchell, T., Fossey, R., & Cobb, C. (2000). Dress codes in the public schools: Principals, policies, and precepts. *Journal of Law and Education, 29*(1), 31–49.

Demmitt, A. D., Russo, C., & Hunley, S. (2003). Children with attention deficit hyperactivity disorder, Ritalin, and the law: Recommendations for practice. *Education Law Association, 38*(3), 14–18.

Desert Palace, Inc. v. Costa, 539 U.S. 90 (2003).

DesRoches v. Caprio, 156 F.3d 571 (4th Cir., 1998).

Devine, J., & Cohen, J. (2007). *Making your school safe: Strategies to protect children and promote learning.* New York, NY: Teachers College Press.

Dieterich, C. N., Vaillani, C. S., & Bennett, P. T. (2003). Functional behavioral assessments: Beyond student behavior [Electronic version]. *Journal of Law & Education, 34*(375).

DiLoreto v. Downey Unified School District 196 F.3d 969 (9th Cir. 1999).

District Attorney for the Northern District v. School Committee of Wayland, 455 Mass. 561 (2009).

Doe v. Gonzaga Univ., 24 P.3d 390 (Wash. 2001).

Doe v. Little Rock School District, 380 F.3d 349 (8th Cir., 2004).

Doe v. Perry Community School Dist., 316 F. Supp. 2d 809 (S. D. Iowa, 2004).

Doe v. Porter, 370 F.3d 558 (6th Cir. 2004).

Doe v. Pulaski County Special School District, 263 F.3d 833 (8th Cir. 2002).

Doe v. School Administrative District No. 19, 66 F. Supp.2d (D.Me 1999).

Doe v. School Board of Ouachita Parish, 274 F.3d 289 (5th Cir. 2001).

Doe v. Tangipahoa Parish School Board, 4/631 F. Supp. 2d 823 (D. La 2009).

Doe v. Tangipahoa Parish School Board, 473 F. 3d 188 (5th Cir. 2006).

Doe v. Tangipahoa Parish School Board, Docket No. 03-2870 (E.D. LA, 2005).

Doe v. Yunits and Brockton Sch. Comm., No. 2000-J-638 (Mass. App. 2000).

Doninger v. Niehoff, 527 F.3d 41 (2d Cir. 2008).

Doninger v. Niehoff (Doninger II), No. 09-1452-cv (2nd Cir. 2011)

Donovan v. Punxsutawney, 336 F.3d 211 (3rd Cir. 2003).

Downs v. Los Angeles Unified School District, 228 F.3d 1003 (9th Cir., 2000).

Draker v. Schreiber, 271 SW 3d 318 (Tex: Court of Appeals, 4th Dist. 2008).

Dydell v. Taylor, 332 S.W.3d 848 (2011).

Earls v. Board of Education, Tecumseh Public School District, 115 F. Supp.2d 1281 (W.D. Okla. 2000).

Earls v. Board of Education of Tecumseh Public School District, 242 F.3d 1264 (10th Cir., 2001).

East High School Prism Club v. Seidel, 95 F. Supp.2d 1239 (C. D. Utah, 2000).

Education Commission of the States (1998). *State-level policies regarding corporal punishment in public schools.* Retrieved from www.ecs.org.

Education Commission of the States (2000, July). *School prayer, moment of silence, other policies concerning religion.* Retrieved from www. ecs.org.

Education Commission of the States (2002, December). *Vouchers, tax credits and tax deductions.* Policy brief. Retrieved from www.ecs.org.

Education Commission of the States (2005). *State boards/chiefs/agencies.* Retrieved from www.ecs.org.

Education Commission of the States (n.d.). *Recent state policies/activities: School safety-bullying prevention/conflict resolution.* Retrieved from www.ecs.org.

Edwards v. Aguillard, 482 U.S. 578 (1987).

Emmett v. Kent School District No. 415, 92 F. Supp.2d 1088, W.D. Washington, Seattle Division (2000).

Engel v. Vitale, 370 U.S. 421 (1962).

Epperson v. Arkansas, 393 U.S. 97 (1968).

Equal Employment Opportunity Commission (1999). *Policy guidance on current issues of sexual harassment.* Retrieved from www.eeoc.gov.

Equal Employment Opportunity Commission (2002). *Guidelines on discrimination because of sex.* Retrieved from www.eeoc.gov.

Equal Employment Opportunity Commission (2005a). *Race/color discrimination.* Retrieved from www.eeoc.gov.

Equal Employment Opportunity Commission (2005b). *Employment discrimination based on religion, ethnicity, or country of origin.* Retrieved from www.eeoc.gov.

Etheredge v. District of Columbia, 635 A.2d 908 (D.C. 1993).

Fales v. Garst, No. 99–2272 (8th Cir., January 2, 2001).

Farrin v. Maine, 165 F. Supp.2d 37 (D. Maine, 2001).

Fein, R., Vossekuil, B., Pollack, W., Borum, R., Modzeleski, W., & Reddy, M. (2004). *Threat assessments in schools: A guide to managing threatening situations and to creating safe school climates.* Washington, DC: U.S. Department of Education.

Feinberg, T., & Robey, N. (2008). Cyberbullying. *Principal Leadership, 9*(1), 10–14.

Fetter-Harrott, A. S. (2010). Between a *Marsh* and a *Lemon*: Reconciling the standard governing Establishment Clause challenges to school board prayer.

Fewless v. Board of Education of Wayland Schools, 208 F. Supp.2d 806 (W.D. Mich. 2002).

Fischer, A. (1999). "Immoral conduct": A fair standard for teachers? *Journal of Law and Education, 28*(3), 477–483.

Fleming v. Jefferson County School District R-1, 298 F.3d 918 U.S. App LEXIS 12779 (10th Cir. 2002).

Florence County School District Four v. Carter, 510 U.S. 7 (1993).

Flores v. Morgan Hill, 324 F. 3d 1130 (9th Cir. 2003).

Foley v. Special School District of St. Louis County, 153 F.3d 863 (8th Cir., 1998).

Fowler v. Board of Education of Lincoln County Kentucky, 819 F.2d 657 (6th Cir., 1987).

Fowler, F. (2009). *Policy studies for educational leaders: An introduction* (3rd ed). Boston, MA: Pearson/Allyn & Bacon.

Franklin v. Gwinnett Cty. Pub. Sch., 503 U.S. 60 (1992).

Freeman v. Pitts, 503 U.S. 467 (1992).

Freiler v. Tangipahoa Parish Board of Educ., 185 F.3d 337 (5th Cir. 1999).

Frey, D. (2010, September). *State teacher tenure/continuing contract laws.* Retrieved from www.ecs.org.

Fricke v. Lynch, 491 F. Supp. 381 (RI, 1980).

Fuhr v. School District of City of Hazel Park, 131 F. Supp.2d 947 (E.D. Mich. 2001).

Fullan, M. (2003). *The moral imperative of school leadership.* Thousand Oaks, CA: Corwin Press.

Fuller v. Decatur Public Schools, 78 F. Supp.2d 812 (C.D. Ill., 2000).

Fulmer, J. R. (2002). Dismissing the "immoral" teacher for conduct outside the workplace—do current laws protect the interests of both school authorities and teachers? *Journal of Law and Education, 31*(3), 271–289.

Furman, G. (2003). Moral leadership and the ethic of community. *Values and Ethics in Educational Administration, 2*(1), 1–8.

Furman, G. C., & Gruenewald, D. A. (2004). Expanding the landscape of social justice: A critical ecological analysis. *Educational Administration Quarterly, 40*(1), 47–76.

Gabrielle M. v. Park Forest-Chicago Heights, 315 F.3d 817 (6th Cir., 2002).

Garcetti v. Ceballos, 547 US 410 (2006).

Garcia v. Miera, 817 F.2d 650 (10th Cir., 1987).

Garner, B. A. (Ed.). (2006). *Black's law dictionary* (3rd pocket edition.). St. Paul, MN: West.

Gathwright v. Lincoln Insurance Co., 688 S.W.2d 931 (1985).

Gebser v. Lago Vista Independent School, 542 U.S. 274 (1998).

Gernetzke v. Kenosha Unified School District, 274 F.3d 464 (7th Cir. 2001).

Giuttari, T. R. (1970). *The American law of sovereign immunity. An analysis of legal interpretations.* New York, NY: Praeger.

Givhan v. Western Line Consolidated School District, 439 U.S. 410 (1979).

Glover v. Williamsburg Local School District Board of Education, 20 F. Supp.2d 1160 (S.D. Ohio, 1998).

Golden v. Anders, 324 F.3d 650 (8th Cir., 2003).

Gollnick, D. M., & Chinn, P. C. (2004). *Multicultural education in a pluralistic society* (6th ed). Upper Saddle River, NJ: Merrill/Prentice Hall.

Gonzaga University v. Doe, 534 U.S. 426 (2002).

Good News Club v. Milford Central Sch., 121 S. Ct. 2093 (2001).

Gordon, R., Piana, L., & Keleher, T. (2000). *Facing the consequences: An examination of racial discrimination in U.S. public schools.* Retrieved from www.arc.org/erase/index.html.

Goss v. Lopez, 419 U.S. 565 (1975).

Gottlieb v. Laurel Highlands School District, WL 1433182 (3rd Cir. 2001).

Graca, T. J., & Stader, D. L. (2007). Student speech and the Internet: A legal analysis. *NASSP Bulletin, 91*(2), 121–129.

Gratz v. Bollinger, 123 S. Ct. 2411 (2003).

Green v. County School Board of New Kent County, 391 U.S. 430 (1968).

Greene v. Camreta, 06-35333 (9th Cir., 2009).

Greenfield, W. D., Jr. (2004). Moral leadership in schools. *Journal of Educational Administration, 42*(2), 174–196.

Griggs v. Duke Power Co., 401 U.S. 424 (1971).

Gruenke v. Seip, 225 F.3d 290 (3rd Cir., 2000).

Grutter v. Bollinger, 123 S. Ct. 2325 (2003).

Guidance on constitutionally protected prayer in public elementary and secondary schools (2003, February). Retrieved from www.ed.gov/inits/religion and schools/prayerguidance.html.

Habermas, J. (1987). *The theory of communicative action: Vol. 2. Lifeworld and system: A critique of functionalist reason* (T. McCarthy, Trans.). Boston: Beacon Press. (Original work published 1981).

Habermas, J. (1990). *Moral consciousness and communicative action* (C. Lenhardt & S. W. Nicholsen, Trans.). Cambridge, MA: MIT Press. (Original work published 1983).

Habermas, J. (2001). *Between facts and norms: Contributions to a discourse theory of law and democracy* (W. Rehg, Trans.). Cambridge, MA: MIT Press. (Original work published 1992).

Hackett v. Fulton County School District, 238 F. Supp.2d 1330 (N.D. Ga. 2002).

Hageman v. Goshen County School District, No. 10-0009 (Wyo., 2011).

Harper v. Poway United School District, 455 F3d 1052 (9th Cir. 2006).

Harrah Independent School District v. Martin, 440 U.S. 194 (1979).

Harris v. Pontotoc County School District, No. 10-60392 (5th Cir., 2011).

Harris v. Robinson, 273 F.3d 927 (10th Cir., 2001).

Hawkins v. Sarasota County School Board, 322 F.3d 1279 (11th Cir., 2002).

Haynes, C. (2003). *Graduation prayers a tricky issue, but consider this approach.* Retrieved from www. firstamendmentcenter.org/commentary.

Haynes, C. C., & Thomas, O. (2001). *Finding common ground: A guide to religious liberty in public schools.* Retrieved from www. freedomforum.org.

Hazelwood School District v. Kuhlmeier, 484 U.S. 260 (1988).

Hearn v. The Board of Public Education, 191 F.3d 1329 (11th Cir., 1999).

Henderson v. Walled Lake Consolidated School District, 469 F. 3d 479 (6th Cir. 2006).

Henkle v. Gregory, 150 F. Supp. 2d 1067 (Nev. Dist. 2001).

Hills v. Scottsdale Unified School District No. 48, 329 F.3d 1044 (9th Cir. 2003).

Hilyerd, W. (2004). Using the law library: A guide for educators—Part I: Untangling the legal system. *Journal of Law and Education, 33*(2), 213–274.

Horton v. Goose Creek Independent School District, 690 F.2d 470 (5th Cir., 1982), cert. denied.

Howard, P. (2004). The least restrictive environment: How to tell? *Journal of Law & Education, 33*(2), 167–180.

Hudson, D. L., Jr. (2002). *Balancing act: Public employees and free speech.* Publication #02-F04. Retrieved from www.freedomforum.org.

Human Rights Watch. (2008). *A violent education: Corporal punishment of children in U.S. public schools.* New York, NY: Author.

Hyman, R. T. (2006). *Death threats by students. The law and its implications.* Dayton, OH: Education Law Association.

Illinois v. Gates, 462 U.S. 213 (1983).

In re D. E. M., 727 A. 2d 570 (PA Super 59, 1999).

In re Roberts, 563 S. E. 2d 37 (N.C. App. 2002).

In the Matter of J. D. B., 190A09 (Fla Supreme Court, 2009).

Ingraham v. Wright, 430 U.S. 651 (1977).

Interstate School Leaders Licensure Consortium (1996). *Standards for school leaders.* Washington, DC: Council of Chief State School Officers.

Irving Independent School District v. Tatro, 468 U.S. 883 (1984).

J. B. D. v. North Carolina, No. 09-1121 (U.S. Sup. Court, 2011).

J. C. ex rel. R. C. v. Beverly Hills Unified School District, 711 F. Supp.2d 1094 (C. D. Cal., 2010).

J. S. v. Bethlehem Area School District, 807 A.2d 847 (Pa. 2002).

Jabr v. Rapides Parish School Board, 171 F. Supp.2d 653 (E.D. La, 2001).

Jaynes v. Newport News, 13 Fed. Appx. 166 (4th Cir., 2001).

Jeglin v. San Jacinto Unified School District, 827 F. Supp. 1459 (C.D. Cal. 1993).

Johnson, D., & Thurlow, M. (2003). *A national study on graduation requirements and diploma options for youth with disabilities* (Technical Report 36). Minneapolis, MN: University of Minnesota, National Center on Educational Outcomes. Retrieved from http://education.umn. edu/NCEO/OnlinePubs/Technical36.htm.

Johnson, O. A. (1999). *Ethics: Selections from classical and contemporary writers* (8th ed). New York, NY: Harcourt Brace College.

Johnson v. Newburgh Enlarged School District, 239 F.3d 246 (2nd Cir., 2001).

Joines v. State, 591 S.E. 2d 454 (Court of Appeals of Ga., 2nd Div., 2003).

Jones v. Clear Creek Independent School District, 977 F.2d 963 (5th Cir. 1992).

Joy v. Penn-Harris-Madison School Corporation, 212 F.3d 1052 (7th Cir., 2000).

Kallio, B. R., & Geisel, R. T. (2010, November). *To speak or not to speak? Analyzing the expressive rights of public school employees in the wake of Garcetti.* Paper presented at the Education Law Association 2010 annual conference, Vancouver, B.C.

Katz v. United States, 389 U.S. 347 (1967).

Keefe v. Geankos, 418 F.2d 359 (1st Cir., 1969).

Kemerer, F. R., & Crain, J. A. (2010). *The documentation handbook: Appraisal, nonrenewal, termination* (4th ed., updated April 2010). Denton, TX: Texas School Administrators' Legal Digest (www.legaldigest.com).

Kennedy v. Seaford Union Free School District, 672 N.Y.S. 2d 407 (N.Y. App. Div., 1998).

Keyes v. School District No 1, Denver, Colorado, 413 U.S. 189 (1973).

Keyishian v. Board of Regents, 385 U.S. 589 (1967).

Killion v. Franklin Regional Board of School Directors, 136 F. Supp.2d 446 (W.D. Penn, 2001).

Kirkland v. Greene, D. C. Docket No. 01-01008-CV-C-W (N.D. Alabama, 2003).

Kitzmiller v. Dover Area School District, 400 F. Supp. 2d 707 (Dist. Court, MD PA, 2005).

Knox County Education Association v. Knox County Board of Education, 158 F.3d 361 (6th Cir., 1998).

Kosciw, J., & Diaz, E. (2006). *2005 national school climate survey*. New York, NY: Gay, Lesbian, and Straight Education Network.

Kowalski v. Berkeley County Schools, No. 10-1098 (4th Cir. 2011).

Krizek v. Cicero-Stickney Tp. High School D. 201, 713 F. Supp. 1131 (N.D. Ill., 1989).

Kyle P. Parker et al. v. Board of Education of the Town of Thomaston (1998). Supreme Court of Connecticut, 246 Con. 89; 717 A.2d 117; 1998 Conn. LEXIS 297.

Kyllo v. United States, 533 U.S. 27 (2001).

L.W. v. Toms River Regional Schools Board of Education, A-111-05. (New Jersey Supreme Court 189 N.J. 381, 915 A.2d 535 2007).

Lacks v. Ferguson Reorganized School District R-2, 147 F.3d 718 (8th Cir., 1998).

Lamb's Chapel v. Center Moriches Union Free School District, 508 U.S. 384 (1993).

Lambda Legal. (2001). *Summary of the policy changes adopted as a result of the settlement in Henkle v. Gregory*. New York, NY: Lambda Legal. Retrieved from www.lambdalegal.org.

Lassonde v. Pleasanton Unified School District, 320 F.3d 979 (9th Cir. 2003).

Lau v. Nichols, 414 U.S. 563 (1974).

LaVine v. Blaine School District, 257 F.3d 981 (9th Cir., 2001).

Layshock v. Hermitage School District, 593 F.3d 249 (3rd Cir. 2010).

Lee v. Weisman, 55 U.S. 577 (1992).

Lehto v. Board of Education of the Caesar Rodney School District, No. 07A-08-007 Del Superier Ct. (2008).

Leithwood, K., & Steinbach, R. (1992). Improving the problem-solving expertise of school administrators: Theory and practice. *Education and Urban Society, 24*(3), 317–345.

Leithwood, K., & Steinbach, R. (1995). *Expert problem solving: Evidence from school and district leaders*. Albany: State University of New York Press.

Lemon v. Kurtzman, 403 U.S. 602 (1971).

Lenhart, A. (2009). Teens and sexting: How and why minor teens are sending sexually suggestive nude or nearly nude images via text messaging. *Pew Internet & American Life Project*. Retrieved from www.pewinternet.org/Reports/2009/TeenSexting.

Lewis Center School District, 42 IDER 247 (SEA IA 2005).

Lewis v. City of Chicago, Illinois, No. 08-974 S. Ct. (2010).

Linke v. Northwestern School Corp, 734 N. E, 2d 972 (Ind. 2002).

Little Rock School Dist. v. Pulaski County Special School District No. 1., 237 F. Supp.2d 988 (E.D. Ark. 2003).

Littlefield v. Forney Independent School District, 108 F. Supp.2d 681 (N.D. Tex. 2000).

Loudermill v. Cleveland Board of Education, 470 U.S. 532 (1985).

Lovell v. Poway Unified School District, 90 F. d 367 (9th Cir., 1996).

Lynch v. Donnelly, 465 U.S. 668 (1984).

M. L. et al. v. Federal Way School District, Docket Number 02-35547 (9th Cir., 2003).

Mahaffey v. Aldrich, 236 F. Supp.2d 779 (E.D. Michigan, Southern Division, 2002).

Manning v. The School Board, 244 F.3d 927 (11th Cir., 2001).

Mardis v. Hannibal Public School District, 684 F. Supp.2d 1114 (E. D. Mo 2010).

Marsh v. Chambers, 463 U.S. 783 (1983).

Mawdsley, R. (1998). The principal and religious activity. *NASSP Bulletin, 82*(599), 10–17.

Mawdsley, R., & Permuth, S. (2003). Nondisclosure provisions in school district settlement agreements. *ELA Notes, 38*(2), 8–9, 18–19.

Mawdsley, R., & Russo, C. (2004). Religious holiday celebrations in public schools: What is permissible and what is prohibited? *ELA Notes, 39*(3), 3–5, 9.

McCormick v. The School District of Mamaroneck and the School District of Pelham, 370 F.3d 275 (2nd Cir., 2004).

McIntire v. Bethel School District, 804 F. Supp. 1415 (W.D. Okla. 1992).

McLaughlin v. Pulaski County Special School District, 296 F. Supp.2d 960 (E.D. AR, W.D., 2003).

McQueen v. Beecher Community Schools, 433 F. 3d 460 (6th Cir. 2006).

Melzer v. Board of Education of the City School District of the City of New York, 336 F.3d 185 (2nd Cir., 2003).

Meredith v. Jefferson County Board of Education, 548 U.S. 938 (2006).

MetLife. (2003). *Metlife Survey of the American teacher: An examination of school leadership.* Retrieved from www.metlife.com.

Meyer, E., & Stader, D. L. (2009). Queer youth and the culture war: From the classroom to the courtroom. *Journal of LGBT Youth, 6*(2), 135–154.

Mill, J. S. (1998). *Utilitarianism* (R. Crisp, Ed.). New York, NY: Oxford.

Miller v. Mitchell, 598 F.3d 139 (2010).

Miller v. Skumanick, 605 f. Supp. 2d 634 (M. D. Pa. 2009).

Milliken v. Bradley (Milliken I), 418 U.S. 717 (1974).

Milliken v. Bradley (Milliken II), 433 U.S. 267 (1977).

Missouri v. Jenkins, 495 U.S. 33 (1990).

Mitchell v. Helms, 530 U.S. 793 (2000).

Morrison v. Board of Education, 461 P.2d 375 (Cal. 1969).

Morse v. Frederick, 551 U.S. 393 (2007).

Mota v. University of Texas Houston Health Science Center, 261 F.3d 512 (5th Cir., 2001).

Mt. Healthy City School District Board of Education v. Doyle, 429 U.S. 274 (1977).

Myers v. Loudon County Pub. Schs., 418 F.3d 395 (4th Cir. 2005).

NAACP, Jacksonville Branch v. Duval County School, unpublished opinion (11th Cir., 2001).

Nabozny v. Podlesny, 92 F.3d 446 (7th Cir., 1996).

National Center for Missing Children (2009). *Policy statement on sexting.* Retrieved from www. missingkids.com.

National Conference of State Legislatures. (2010). *Legislation related to "sexting."* Retrieved from www.ncsl.org/?tabid=19696.

National Forum on Education Statistics. (2006). *Forum guide to the privacy of student information: A resource for schools* (NFES 2006–805). U.S. Department of Education. Washington, DC: National Center for Education Statistics. Retrieved from www.edpubs.org.

National School Boards Association's Council of School Attorneys (2003). Off-campus misbehavior: Are your hands tied? *Principal Leadership, 4*(1), 72–76.

Nelson v. Heyne, 491 F.2d 352 (7th Cir., 1974).

New Jersey v. Best, No. A-0891-07T4 (Superior Court N.J., Appellate Division, 2008).

New Jersey v. T. L. O., 469 U.S. 325 (1985).

Newman, M. L., Holden, G. W., & Delville, Y. (2005). Isolation and the stress of being bullied. *Journal of Adolescence, 28,* 343–357.

Newton v. Slye, 116 F. Supp.2d 677 (W.D. Va., 2000).

Nichols v. DeStefano, 70 P.3d 505 (Colo. App. 4th Div., 2002).

Nicol v. Auburn-Washburn USD 437, 232 F. Supp.2d 1107 (D. KS, 2002).

Nidiffer, P. (2010). Tinkering with restrictions on educator speech: Can school boards restrict what educators say on social networking sites? *University of Dayton Law Review, 36*(1), 116–142.

Normore, A. (2004). Ethics and values in leadership preparation programs: Finding the North Star in the dust storm. *Values and Ethics in Educational Administration, 2*(2), 1–8.

Nuxoll v. Indian Prairie School District #204, No. 10-2455, 10-3635(7th Cir., 2011).

O'Connor v. Ortega, 480 U.S. 709 (1987).

Office for Civil Rights. (2000). *Annual report to Congress.* Retrieved from www.ed.gov.

Office for Civil Rights. (n.d.). *Protecting students with disabilities: Frequently asked questions about Section 504 and the education of children with disabilities.* Retrieved from www.ocr.gov.

Oklahoma City Schools v. Dowell, 498 U.S. 237 (1991).

Ollier v. Sweetwater Union High School District, 604 F. Supp. 2d 1264 (S.D. Cal. 2009).

Oncale v. Sundowner Offshore Services, 523 U.S. 75 (1998).

Orfield, G., Frankenberg, E., & Lee, C. (2003). The resurgence of school segregation. *Educational Leadership, 60*(4), 16–20.

Owasso Independent School District v. Falvo, 534 U.S. 426 (2002).

P. H. v. The School District of Kansas City, Missouri. 265 F3d 653 (8th Cir., 2001).

Parents Involved in Community Schools v. Seattle School District No. 1, 551 U.S. 701 (2007).

Payne, A. A., Gottfredson, D. C., & Gottfredson, G. D. (2003). Schools as communities: The relationships among communal school organization, student bonding, and school disorder. *Criminology, 41*(3), 749–777.

Peterson, R. L., Larson, J., & Skiba, R. (2001). School violence prevention: Current status and policy recommendations. *Law & Policy, 23*(3), 345–371.

Pickering v. Board of Education of Township High School District 205, 391 U.S. 563 (1968).

Pierce v. St. Urain Valley School District, 981 P.2d 600 (Colo. 1999).

Pierce v. Sullivan, U.S. App. LEXIS 16520 (2nd Cir. 2004).

Plessy v. Ferguson, 163 U.S. 537 (1896).

Plyler v. Doe, 457 U.S. 202 (1982).

Pope v. East Brunswick Board of Education, 12 F.3d 1244 U.S. App LEXIS 3354 (3rd Cir. 1993).

Price Waterhouse v. Hopkins, 490 U.S. 228 (1998).

Public Agenda Foundation (2004, May 11). *Teaching interrupted survey.* Retrieved from Lexis Nexis database.

R. O. v. Ithaca City School District, No. 09-1651 (2nd Cir., 2011).

R. D. S. v. State of Tennessee, No. II-CRO4274 (Tenn. Ct. App. 2008).

R. V. A. v. City of St. Paul, Minn., 505 U.S. 377 (1992).

Ratner v. Loudoun County Public Schools, 16 Fed. Appx. 140; 2001 U.S. App. LEXIS 16941 (4th Cir., 2001).

Rawls, J. (2001). In E. Kelly (Ed.), *Justice as fairness: A restatement.* Cambridge, MA: Belknap Press of Harvard University Press.

Ray v. Antioch Unified School District, 107 F. Supp. 2d 1165 (N.D. Cal. 2000).

Ream v. Centennial School District, 765 A. 2d 1195 (Penn. Commonwealth, 2001).

Rebore, R. (2001). *The ethics of educational leadership.* Columbus, OH: Merrill/Prentice Hall.

Rebore, R. (2011). *Human resources administration in education: A management approach* (9th ed). Boston: Pearson.

Rebore, R. W. (2003). *A human relations approach to the practice of educational leadership.* Boston, MA: Pearson Education.

Rene v. Reed, 751 N. E.2d 736 (Ind. App., 2001).

Reno v. American Civil Liberties Union, 521 U.S. 844 (1997).

Requa v. Kent School District, 492 F. Supp. 2d 1272 (W. D. Washington, 2007).

Restatement (second) of torts. (1974). Philadelphia: American Law Institute.

Rhodes v. Guarricino, 54 Supp.2d 186 (S.D.N.Y. 1999).

Ricci v. DeStefano, 129 S. Ct. 2658 (2009).

Riddick v. School Board of Norfolk 784 F.2d 521 (4th Cir., 1986).

Robers, S., Zhang, J., & Truman, J. (2010). *Indicators of school crime and safety:* 2010 (NCES 2011-002/NCJ 230812). Washington, DC: National Center for Education Statistics, U.S. Department of Education, and Bureau of Justice Statistics, Office of Justice Programs, U.S. Department of Justice.

Roberts v. Houston Independent School District, 788 S. W. 2d 107 (Tex. Ct. App. 1990).

Roberts v. Madigan, 921 F.2d 1047 (1990).

Roberts, N. (November, 2003). *A teacher's constitutional right to be free from unreasonable searches and seizures in the school workplace: What standard should be applied?* Paper presented at the 48th Annual Education Law Association Conference, Savannah, GA.

Roderick Jackson v. Birmingham Board of Education, 73 U.S. L.W. 4233 (2005).

Romer v. Evans, 517 U.S. 620 (1996).

Ross, J. (2011, March 30) *Parents blame school for son's suicide*. Retrieved from www.courthousenews.com.

Rossow, L. F., & Tate, J. O. (2003). *The law of teacher evaluation* (2nd ed.). Dayton, OH: Education Law Association.

Roy, L. (2001). Corporal punishment in American public schools and the rights of the child. *Journal of Law and Education, 30*(3), 554–563.

Safford Unified School District #1 v. April Redding, 557 U.S. ___ (2009).

Santa Fe Independent School District v. Doe, 530 U.S. 290 (2000).

Saucier v. Katz, 533 U.S. 194 (2001).

Schaffer v. Weast, 126 S. Ct. 528 (2005).

Schaller, L. E. (2000). *The evolution of the American public high school: From prep school to prison to new partnerships*. Nashville, TN: Abingdon Press.

Schenck v. United States, 249 U.S. 47 (1919).

Schlemmer v. Buffalo R. & P. R. Co., 205 U.S. 1 (1907).

School Community of Burlington v. Department of Education of Massachusetts, 471 U.S. 359 (1996).

Scott v. School Board of Alachua County, 324 F.3d 1249 (11th Cir., 2003).

Seal v. Morgan, 229 F.3d 567 (6th Cir., 2000).

Sechler & Saxe v. State Coll. Area Sch. Dist., 121 F. Supp.2d 439 (M.D. Pennsylvania, 2000).

Secretary's Commission on Opportunities in Athletics. (2002). *Questions and answers*. Retrieved from www.ed.gov.

Sergiovanni, T. (2000). *The lifeworld of leadership: Creating culture, community, and personal meaning in our schools*. San Francisco, CA: Jossey-Bass.

Sergiovanni, T. J. (1992). *Moral leadership: Getting to the heart of school improvement*. San Francisco, CA: Jossey-Bass.

Settle v. Dickson County School Board, 53 F.3d 152 (6th Cir. 1995).

Settlegoode v. Portland Public Schools, 362 F.3d 1118 (9th Cir., 2004).

Shade v. City of Farmington, 309 F.3d 1054 (8th Cir., 2002).

Shanklin v. Fitzgerald, 397 F.3d 596 (8th Cir., 2005).

Sharp v. Lindsey, 285 F.3d 479 (6th Cir., 2002).

Sherman v. Cmty. Consol. Sch. Dist. 21, 980 F.2d 437 (7th Cir.1992).

Shore v. P. S., U.S. App. LEXIS 17740 (3rd Cir., 2004).

Shrum ex rel. Kelly v. Kluck, 249 F.3d. 773 (8th Cir., 2001).

Singleton v. Board of Education USD 500, 894 F. Supp. 386 (D. Dan. 1995).

Skarin v. Woodbine Community School District, 204 F. Supp.2d 1195 (S.D. Iowa, 2002).

Skinner v. Railway Labor Executives Association, 489 U.S. 602 (1989).

Snyder v. Millersville University, No. 07-1660 (Dist. Court, ED Pennsylvania, 2008).

Soper v. Hoben, 195 F.3d 845 (6th Cir., 1999).

South Gibson School Board v. Sellman, 768 NE2d 437 (Indiana, 2002).

Spanierman v. Hughes, 576 f. Supp. 2d 292 (D. Connecticut, 2008).

Sperry, D. (1999). *Working in a legal & regulatory environment: A handbook for school leaders*. Larchmont, NY: Eye on Education.

Stader, D. (2000). Preempting threats with a sound school policy. *NASSP Bulletin, 84*(617), 68–72.

Stader, D. (2001a). Responding to student threats: Legal and procedural guidelines for high school principals. *Clearing House, 74*(4), 221–224.

Stader, D. (2001b). *Student searches, urinalysis and drug dogs*. Paper presented at the Annual Weir Law Institute, Laramie, WY. (ERIC Reproduction Service No. EA031375.)

Stader, D. (2003). Student searches: Policy guidelines for secondary principals. *The Clearing House, 76*(2), 66–70.

Stader, D. L. (2011). *A leaders guide for safe schools*. Norwood, MA: Christopher-Gordon Publishers.

Stader, D., Armenta, T., & Hill, M. (2002, November). *Education and religion in Louisiana*. Paper presented at the 48th Annual Education Law Association Conference, New Orleans, LA.

Stader, D. L., & Francis, D. (2003). Knocking on the schoolhouse gate. *The Clearing House, 26*(3), 116–119.

Stader, D. L., Greicar, M. B., Stevens, D. W., & Dowdy, R. (2010). Drugs, strip searches, and educator liability: Implications of Safford v. Redding. *The Clearing House, 83*(3), 109–113.

State of Florida v. J. A., 679 So. 2d 316 (Fla. App., 1996).

State v. Canal, Jr., 773 N.W.2d 528 (2009).

Staub v. Proctor Hospital, 130 U.S. 2089 (2010).

Stephenson v. Davenport Community School District, 110 F.3d 1303 (8th Cir., 1997).

Stone v. Graham, 449 U.S. 39 (1980).

Straights and Gays for Equity v. Osseo Area Schools (Civ. No. 05-21000 (JNE/FLN), Mn 2006).

Strike, K., Haller, E., & Soltis, J. (1998). *The ethics of school administration* (2nd ed.). New York, NY: Teachers College Press.

Student Alpha ID Number Guiza v. The School Board of Volusia County, Florida, 1993 Fla. App. LEXIS 2234 (Court of Appeal of Florida, 5th District).

Students filmed in locker room win case. (2007, July 30). *USA Today*. Retrieved from http://usatoday.com.

Swann v. Charlotte-Mecklenberg Board of Education, 402 U.S. 1 (1971).

Synder v. Blue Mountain School District, No. 08-4138 (3rd Cir., 2011).

Sypniewski v. Warren Hills Regional Board of Education, 307 F.3d 243 (3rd Cir., 2002).

T. K. v. New York City Dep't of Educ., No. 10-752 (E.D. N.Y. Apr. 26, 2011).

Tasby v. Moses, 265 F. Supp.2d 757 (N.D. Tex, 2003).

Taylor, K. (2002). Questioning students about violations of the law: Do you have the answers? *Principal Leadership, 2*(7), 74–77.

Terry v. Ohio, 389 U.S. 804 (1967).

The National Center for Missing & Exploited Children. (2009, September 21). *Policy statement on sexting*. Retrieved from www.missingkids.com.

Theno v. Tonganoxie Unified School Dist. No. 464, 377 F. Supp. 3d 952 (D. Kan. 2005).

Thomas v. Board of Education, 607 F. 3d 1043 (2nd Cir. 1979).

Theodore v. Delaware Valley School District, 836 A.2d 76 (Pa. 2003).

Thompson v. Mt. Diablo Unified School District, Court of Appeal of California, First Appellate District, Division Two (2003 Unpub. 8366).

Tinker v. Des Moines School District, 393 U.S. 503 (1969).

Todd v. Rush County Schools, 133 F.3d 984 (7th Cir., 1997). Cert. denied.

Todd, M. A., DiJohn, J. L., & Aldridge, S. L. (2008). *Employee use, misuse, and abuse of social network sites.* Retrieved from www.nsba.org.

Trinidad School District No. 1 v. Lopez, 963 P.2d 1095 (Colorado Supreme Court 1998).

Tristan Kipp v. Lorain Board of Education, Ohio App Lexis 1579 (2000).

Trotter, A. (2003). Arkansas district settles lawsuit with gay student. *Education Week, 22*(43), 4, 1/9p.

Tuma v. Dade County Public Schools, 989 F. Supp. 1471 (S. D. Fla. 1998).

Turnbull, H. III, Wilcox, B., Turnbull, A., Sailor, W., & Wickham, D. (2001). IDEA, positive behavioral supports and school safety [Electronic version]. *Journal of Law & Education, 30*(445).

United States General Accounting Office (USGAO) (2003, September). *Numbers of formal disputes are generally low and states are using mediation and other strategies to resolve conflicts.* GAO-03-897, a report to the Ranking Minority Member, Committee on Health, Education, Labor and Pensions, U.S. Senate. Retrieved from www.gao.gov.

United States General Accounting Office. (2010, December). *Selected cases of public and private schools that hired or retained individuals with histories of sexual misconduct.* Retrieved from www.gao.gov.

United States v. American Library Association, 539 U.S. 194, 2003.

U.S. Department of Education, Office of Safe and Drug-Free Schools. (2010). *Report on the implementation of the Gun-Free Schools Act in the states and outlying areas for school years 2005–06 and 2006–07,* Washington, DC: Author.

U.S. Government Accounting Office (GAO) (2010, December). *Selected cases of public and private schools that hired or retained individuals with histories of sexual misconduct.* GA-11-200. Retrieved from www.gao.gov.

Vance v. Spencer County Public School District, 231 F.3d 253 (6th Cir., 2000).

Vargas-Harrison v. Racine Unified School District, 272 F.3d 964 (7th Cir., 2001).

Vernonia School Dist. 47J v. Acton, 515 U.S. 646 (1995).

Virginia v. Black, 538 U.S. 343 (2003).

Waldman, S. (2008). *Founding faith: Providence, politics, and the birth of religious freedom in America.* New York, NY: Random House.

Wallace v. Jaffree, 472 U.S. 38 (1985).

Warnock v. Archer, 443 F.3d 954 (8th Cir. 2006).

Warren v. Reading School District, 278 F.3d 163 (3rd Cir., 2002).

Wastler, S. (2010). The harm in "sexting"? Analyzing the constitutionality of child pornography statues that prohibit the voluntary production, possession, and dissemination of sexually explicit images by teenagers. *Harvard Journal of Law & Gender, 33,* 688–702.

Watkins v. Millennium School District, 290 F. Supp.2d 890 (S.D. Ohio, 2003).

Watts v. U.S. 394 U.S. 705 (1969).

Wax v. Horne, No 4D02-2832 (Fla. App. 4th Dist., 2003).

West v. Derby Unified School District No. 260, 206 F.3d 1358 (10th Cir., 2000).

West Virginia Board of Education v. Barnette, 319 U.S. 624 (1943).

Westfield High School L. I. F. E. Club v. City of Westfield (Westfield), 249 F.Supp.2d 98 (District of Mass, 2003).

White County High School Peers in Diverse Education v. White County School District, Civil Action No. 2:06-CV-29-WCO N. D. Georgia, Gainesville Division (2006).

Williams v. Dallas Independent School District, 480 F.3d 689 (5th Cir 2010).

Willis v. Anderson Community School Corporation, 158 F.3d 415 (7th Cir., 1998).

Wise v. Pea Ridge School District, 855 F.2d 560 (8th Cir., 1988).

Wisniewski v. Board of Education of the Weedsport Central School District, 5:02-CV-14o3 (N. D. NY, 2006).

Wood v. Strickland, 420 U.S. 308 (1975).

Woodard v. Los Fresnos ISD, 732 F.2d 1243 (5th Cir., 1984).

Wooten v. Pleasant Hope R-VI School District, No. 01-1181WM (8th Cir., 2001).

Wygant v. Jackson Board of Education, 476 U.S. 267 (1986).

York v. Wahkiakum School District No 200, 178 P.3d 995 (2008).

Young v. Board of Education of the City of Chicago (338 Ill. App. 3d 522, 2003).

Youngman v. Doerhoff, 890 S. W. 2d 330 (Mo. Court of Appeals, 1994).

Zelman v. Simmons-Harris, 536 U.S. 639 (2002).

Zirkel, P. (2003). Disciplining students for off-campus misconduct: Ten tips. *ELA Notes: Education Law into Practice, 38*(2), 12–13.

NAME INDEX

SUBJECT INDEX